Gallica

Volume 44

THE LOGIC OF IDOLATRY IN SEVENTEENTH-CENTURY FRENCH LITERATURE

Gallica

ISSN 1749-091X

Founding Editor: Sarah Kay

Series Editors: Simon Gaunt and Peggy McCracken

Gallica aims to provide a forum for the best current work in medieval and early modern French studies. Literary studies are particularly welcome and preference is given to works written in English, although publication in French is not excluded.

Proposals or queries should be sent in the first instance to the editor, or to the publisher, at the addresses given below; all submissions receive prompt and informed consideration.

Professor Simon Gaunt (simon.gaunt@kcl.ac.uk)
Professor Peggy McCracken (peggymcc@umich.edu)

The Editorial Director, Gallica, Boydell & Brewer Ltd., PO Box 9, Woodbridge, Suffolk IP12 3DF, UK

Previously published volumes in this series are listed at the end of this volume.

THE LOGIC OF IDOLATRY IN SEVENTEENTH-CENTURY FRENCH LITERATURE

ELLEN McCLURE

D. S. BREWER

© Ellen McClure 2020

All Rights Reserved. Except as permitted under current legislation no part of this work may be photocopied, stored in a retrieval system, published, performed in public, adapted, broadcast, transmitted, recorded or reproduced in any form or by any means, without the prior permission of the copyright owner

The right of Ellen McClure to be identified as the author of this work has been asserted in accordance with sections 77 and 78 of the Copyright, Designs and Patents Act 1988

First published 2020
D. S. Brewer, Cambridge

ISBN 978-1-84384-550-8

D. S. Brewer is an imprint of Boydell & Brewer Ltd
PO Box 9, Woodbridge, Suffolk IP12 3DF, UK
and of Boydell & Brewer Inc.
668 Mt Hope Avenue, Rochester, NY 14620–2731, USA
website: www.boydellandbrewer.com

A CIP catalogue record for this book is available
from the British Library

The publisher has no responsibility for the continued existence or accuracy of URLs for external or third-party internet websites referred to in this book, and does not guarantee that any content on such websites is, or will remain, accurate or appropriate

This publication is printed on acid-free paper

Contents

Notes on Translations   vi

Introduction: The Logic of Idolatry and the Question of Creation   1

1   Idolatry and Instability in Honoré d'Urfé's *L'Astrée*   27

2   Descartes' *Meditations* as a Solution to Idolatry   74

3   Idolatry and the Questioning of Mastery in La Fontaine's *Fables*   114

4   Idolatry and the Love of the Creature in Sévigné's Letters   144

5   Theatrical Idolatry in Molière and Racine   182

Conclusion: The End(s) of Idolatry   211

Acknowledgments   223

Bibliography   225

Index   233

Notes on Translations

I have used the French versions of texts, even those that originally appeared in Latin, such as Calvin's *Institution* and Descartes' *Meditations*, in order to better constellate the discursive field of idolatry such as it existed in French. Unless otherwise indicated, all translations into English are mine. Although I have left the original spelling and capitalization in the French sources I use, I have modernized spelling and capitalization in my translations into English.

Introduction:
The Logic of Idolatry and the Question of Creation

"Il paraît qu'il n'y a eu aucun peuple sur la terre qui ait pris le nom d'idolâtre." (It appears that there has never been a people on earth that has claimed the name of idolater.) With these words, Voltaire transformed a term that had only recently been the source of bitter religious and civil division into an empty insult.[1] Indeed, in the lines that follow, Voltaire illustrates that the term was used, quite simply, to denigrate religions other than one's own, asking of the "pagans,"

> De quel œil voyaient-ils donc les statues de leurs fausses divinités dans les temples? Du même œil, s'il est permis de s'exprimer ainsi, que les catholiques voient les images, objets de leur vénération. L'erreur n'était pas d'adorer un morceau de bois ou de marbre, mais d'adorer une fausse divinité représentée par ce bois et ce marbre.[2]

> How do they then view the statues of false divinities in temples? The same way, if I may express myself thus, that Catholics see images which are the objects of their veneration. The error was not in adoring a piece of wood or marble, but rather a false divinity represented by this wood and marble.

Voltaire's equation of "pagan" worship with Catholic religious practices is, as his "s'il est permis de s'exprimer ainsi" indicates, meant to provoke. But it is also meant to turn the reader's attention away from the central question posed by idolatry: that of the status of the material supports – the wood or marble – of religious practice, and, by extension, that of the precise relationship between heaven and earth. By dismissing the question of materiality and jumping straight to the issue of the legitimacy of that which is represented by the wood or marble, Voltaire is able to conclude that idolatry is, and always

---

[1] Voltaire, *Dictionnaire philosophique* (Paris: Flammarion, 1964), article 'idole, idolâtre, idolâtrie', pp. 224–36, here, p. 225.
[2] *Dictionnaire*, p. 225.

has been, a cover for bigotry, for preferring one's own objects of worship to those of others.

Unsurprisingly, given the place of the Enlightenment in the unfolding of Western thought, Voltaire's dismissal of idolatry closely resembles our own. From the vantage point of a culture that celebrates materiality while viewing the subordination of that materiality to the otherworldly with deep suspicion, idolatry appears as an atavistic, regrettable concept, one that is best confined to the bloodshed and polemics that characterized the sixteenth-century religious wars and that was mercifully overcome, beginning in the period that Voltaire himself called the *siècle de Louis le Grand*. Indeed, the Taliban's 2001 destruction of the giant Buddhist statues of Bamyan, not to mention their iconoclastic campaign throughout the Middle East, appear horrifyingly foreign to the society that acclaimed the spring 2018 exhibit at the Metropolitan Museum of Art on "Fashion and the Catholic Imagination."[3] What, then, could idolatry possibly teach us today?

Scholars have, in fact, begun to address this question, spurred on in part by the rapidity with which idolatry transitioned from cultural centrality to alien strangeness. A variety of outstanding studies and reassessments of idolatry have begun to appear, and this volume contributes to that conversation all while taking it in new directions.[4] By arguing that what I call "the logic of idolatry" permeated the cultural imagination of seventeenth-century France, persisting long after the civil wars of the sixteenth century and well beyond the polemics that Catholics and Protestants continued to exchange, I trace the influence of this strange and complex concept beyond the problems addressed by art history or even religious history. Indeed, in the unique context of early modern France, where the coexistence of Catholics and Protestants was at least nominally protected by the 1598 Edict of Nantes, the discourse surrounding idolatry was fueled not only by the period's revival of Augustinianism, prominent both in Calvinism and also in Jansenism, but further inflamed by the contributions of the French Jesuit Louis Richeome, who untethered idolatry from its close association with images (and Catholics) and extended it

---

[3] For a provocative argument that the two worlds are more alike than different, see Kathryn Lofton, *Consuming Religion* (Chicago: University of Chicago Press, 2017).

[4] See Jonathan Sheehan's special issue of the *Journal of the History of Ideas* (67.4, October 2006) as well as Zorach and Cole, eds., *The Idol in the Age of Art: Objects, Devotions, and the Early Modern World* (New York: Routledge, 2009), Ellenbogen and Tugendhaft, eds., *Idol Anxiety* (Stanford: Stanford University Press, 2011), Marie-José Mondzain, *Image, Icône, Economie: Les sources byzantines de l'imaginaire contemporain* (Paris: Seuil, 1996), and the exhibit and accompanying volume *Iconoclash: Beyond the Image Wars in Science, Religion, and Art* by Bruno Latour (Cambridge, MA: MIT Press, 2002), as well as the scholarly work by Olivier Christin and Ralph Dekoninck on early modern images and iconoclasm.

to any attempt to elevate human creation.⁵ Richeome's intervention therefore heralded the beginning of a century during which nearly every major writer and thinker – Catholic, Protestant, or even skeptical of Christianity – engaged with the variety of complex questions that idolatry raised, questions that were rendered even more urgent by cultural shifts that rival our own in their depth and rapidity.⁶

Part of the lingering discomfort surrounding the concept of idolatry lies in the extreme emotional pull surrounding it. As Voltaire implicitly recognized, accusing someone of "idolatry" was an effective means of unleashing a litany of defensive polemics grounded in the deep-seated and very real fear of what "idolatry" had come to represent. Tertullian's description, in the third century, of idolatry as the root of all crimes merely elaborated upon the vehement condemnation of it in the Bible, from the ten commandments to the Book of Wisdom.⁷ Despite Martin Luther's attempt to mitigate the force of iconoclasm by characterizing images as *adiaphora*, or indifferent to worship, Reformation leaders and their followers moved idolatry to the center of their objections to Catholic worship in language that evoked the mortal peril perceived in the elevation of created (and seductive) objects over the Creator. For Luther's contemporary Andreas Karlstadt, Catholic image worshippers were "impious whores";⁸ over a century later, this visceral disgust remained just as potent, as evidenced in the memoirs of Charlotte-Amélie de la Trémoille, the daughter of one of the most prominent noblemen in France who had himself (along with her brother) converted from Protestantism to Catholicism. In an anecdote from her childhood, she seeks to express the deep-seated nature of her instinctual aversion to Catholic practice, noting that she used to play with two "petites camarades papistes" who gave her

---

⁵ For an astute overview of the early modern French religious climate, including the uneasy but lengthy cohabitation of Protestants and Catholics, see Joseph Bergin, *The Politics of Religion in Early Modern France* (New Haven: Yale University Press, 2014).

⁶ Jan Assmann notes, following an evocation of Eric Santner's distinction between globalism and universalism, that "concern over such questions as monotheism, violence, and intolerance has much to do with the process of globalization and the conflicting universalisms of our time" (*Of God and Gods: Egypt, Israel, and the Rise of Monotheism* (Madison: University of Wisconsin Press, 2008), p. 57).

⁷ "all sins are found in idolatry and idolatry in all sins." Tertullian, *De Idolatria*, trans. J. H. Waszink and J. C.M. Van Winden (New York: Brill, 1987), p. 25.

⁸ "You say: I do not venerate the images of saints for their own sake but for the sake of what they represent. Ah, you impious whore, do you think God does not know your heart more profoundly and better than you? If God did not know that someone could so easily make an idol for which he feels nothing, then God would have allowed us to venerate images in names other than his own." Andreas Karlstadt, 'On the Removal of Images', in *A Reformation Debate: Three Treatises in Translation*, trans. Bryan D. Mangrum and Giuseppe Scavizzi (Ottawa: Dovehouse Editions, 1991), pp. 19–39, here p. 35.

images and told her to pray before them, which she does with a child's taste for pretty ceremonies and mystery. She continues:

> Je tombai dans le péché, sans raisonner ni sans penser que cela fût plus ou moins conforme à la volonté de Dieu. Après avoir donc exercé cette terrible idolâtrie quelques quinze jours environ, ne pouvant m'en souvenir au juste, je jouois un jour avec mes poupées & comme je voulois laver un petit verre que j'aimois extrêmement, à cause de sa jolie forme, sans y faire d'effort, ni sans le heurter, un morceau me tomba dans la main, & comme Dieu m'a toujours témoigné sa bonté particulière, il me la montra aussi icy, car je puis dire que ce petit malheur fut en moy le regard de Jésus-Christ vers saint Pierre ou le chant du coq ... Je jettay mes images dans le feu, je demandai pardon à Dieu de fort bon coeur & je puis bien dire que j'ay une vraie repentance de ma faute, & que je la reconnus par la grâce de Dieu aussi fortement que si j'avois eu vingt ans: ce qui m'en a encore mieux fait juger, c'est que, depuis cela, je n'ay jamais eu une pensée de doute sur le sujet de ma religion & que j'ay abominé le papisme, ce qui a assez paru à la mort de Madame ma grand'mère & au temps du changement de religion de feu mon père. Admirez sur cela, mon cher fils, la foiblesse de notre chair.[9]

> I fell into sin, without thinking about whether it was or was not in line with God's wishes. After having practiced this terrible idolatry for around two weeks – I can't remember exactly how long – I was playing with my dolls and, wanting to wash a small glass that I loved because of its pretty form, without trying or without banging it against something, a piece of it fell into my hand, and just as God has always shown me his special goodness, he did so here, for I can say that this small misfortune was for me the look that Jesus gave Saint Peter or the cry of the rooster... I threw my images in the fire, I wholeheartedly asked God for forgiveness, and I can say that I truly repented my fault, and that I recognized the grace of God as if I were 20 years old, and the proof of that is that ever since then, I have never had an ounce of doubt concerning my religion, and I abominated papism, as was evident when my grandmother died and when my late father converted.

Charlotte's initial and unwitting attraction to the Catholic girls' images is the vehicle for her discovery of the ultimate truth of Protestantism, a certainty that alienated her completely from her father and younger brother (who had converted with him).[10] Her disgust for Catholicism, still clear in her memory

---

[9] Edouard de Barthélemy, ed., *Mémoires de Charlotte-Amélie de la Trémoille 1652–1719, comtesse d'Altenbourg* (Geneva: J-G. Fick, 1876), pp. 32–3.

[10] It should be noted that Charlotte's father converted to Catholicism in part to escape

so many years later, centers on her conviction that the disordered alignment of heaven and earth, expressed through the dangerous seductiveness of a glass that cannot be seen through or used as a vessel but instead becomes an object of admiration in its own right, represents a mortal danger to her soul. Such language reflects the visceral horror that Frank Lestringant has identified as characterizing Protestant attitudes towards Catholic practice, especially around the question (not unrelated to that of idolatry) of the Eucharist, and which is often downplayed by historical accounts of the Reformation that seek its source in economic or political discontent.[11] Such disgust was perhaps uniquely persistent in France, where, unlike in other European countries that demanded religious conformity, Protestants and Catholics coexisted uneasily side by side under the fragile yet official sanction of the Edict of Nantes, issued in 1598 and at least nominally in force until its revocation in 1685.

This book argues that the forceful (and, as we shall see, slippery) concept of idolatry exerted a deep pull on the intellectual and cultural life of seventeenth-century France. Indeed, it would not be inappropriate to characterize idolatry as the "dark matter" of the period; almost invisible to the twenty-first century Western reader, it in fact lends a curious spin to the works of the time. Reading these works through the lens of idolatry, therefore, can shed new light on questions that have continued to vex scholars. Why have attempts to explain d'Urfé's pastoral masterpiece in terms of Neoplatonism remained frustratingly incomplete? What does Descartes' insistence on the existence of a God who created everything have to do with his efforts to minimize the role of human imagination in the discovery of truth? Why is Phèdre so

---

a similar doubt brought on by the new religions. As he states in his manuscript *Motifs de la Conversion de Feu Monseigneur le Prince de Tarente, Ecrits par luy-même vers l'Année 1671*, "j'ay outre cela esté fortement persuadé que la soumission que lon rend a l'Eglise est une grand consolation a un Chretien et qu'au contraire l'Independance des nouvelles sectes cause bien du trouble et du desordre dans les ames et particulierement a l'heure de la mort dans laquelle nous avons continuellement devant les yeux tout ce qui nous peut donner le plus d'inquietude et de douleur." (p. 272, r/v) (besides that, I am also strongly persuaded that the submission that one renders to the Church is a great consolation to a Christian and that on the contrary the Independence of the new sects causes much trouble and disorder in souls and particularly at the hour of death when we have before us everything that can cause us the most worry and pain.) Susan E. Schreiner examines the role that uncertainty played in the Reformation in her *Are You Alone Wise? The Search for Certainty in the Early Modern Era* (New York: Oxford University Press, 2011).

[11] Frank Lestringant, *Une Sainte horreur ou le voyage en Eucharistie* (Paris: Presses Universitaires de France, 1996). See also Bernard Dompnier, *Le Vénin de l'hérésie: image du protestantisme et combat catholique au XVIIe siècle* (Paris: Le Centurion, 1985). For an account of the limitations of academic history with regard to religious themes, see Dipesh Chakrabarty, *Provincializing Europe: Postcolonial Thought and Historical Difference* (Princeton: Princeton University Press, 2007).

terribly undone by her attraction to her stepson? My assertion that well-known figures such as Honoré d'Urfé, René Descartes, Jean de La Fontaine, the marquise de Sévigné, Molière, and Racine were deeply conversant with the logic of idolatry may seem surprising or provocative. The neoclassical seventeenth century, *siècle de Louis le Grand*, continues to be regarded as the foundation of the French cultural canon, characterized by works seen to transcend their Christian, monarchical context to become the cornerstone of the republican, secular educational system.[12] Consequently, while excellent studies of explicitly religious texts from the period exist and continue to be done, there has been no "religious turn" in early modern French studies to rival recent developments in English studies, wherein religious categories and frameworks are brought to bear on ostensibly non-religious literary or philosophical texts.[13]

Bringing idolatry into the ongoing scholarly conversation regarding these works therefore also serves to complicate the narrative of progressive secularization that led to the emergence not only of art, literature, philosophy, and religion as separate spheres, but also of the autonomous, creative individual human author.[14] The story of that emergence has been told, and told well, but by perceiving the ways in which the works considered here, and the French seventeenth century more generally, engaged with the logic of idolatry, we can appreciate how they used this logic to contemplate alternative models of human agency and artistic creation that have largely gone unnoticed. Such models not only serve to complicate what Ayesha Ramachandran has characterized as "a renewed celebration of *homo faber*" in this period; they also can point the way

---

[12] For accounts of the relationship between the seventeenth-century literary canon and French national identity forged through the school system, see the work of Ralph Albanese, including *La Fontaine à l'école républicaine: du poète universel au classique scolaire* (Charlottesville: Rookwood Press, 2003). See also the play *L'Entretien entre M. Descartes avec M. Pascal le jeune*, by Jean-Claude Brisville (1992), in which Descartes is portrayed as the jovial, rational counterpart to Pascal's feverish religious fervor.

[13] This development in English studies was described by Ken Jackson and Arthur F. Marotti in their article 'The Turn to Religion in Early Modern English Studies', *Criticism* 46.1 (2004), pp. 167–90. Recent work in early modern French studies has begun to change this. See, most notably, Andrea Frisch, *Forgetting Differences: Tragedy, Historiography, and the French Wars of Religion* (Edinburgh: University of Edinburg Press, 2015), which traces the profound effects of the French religious wars into seventeenth-century French theater.

[14] For accounts of this emergence, see the following landmark studies: A. J. Minnis, *Medieval Theory of Authorship: Scholastic Literary Attitudes in the Later Middle Ages* (London: Scolar Press, 1984), David Quint, *Origin and Originality in Renaissance Literature: Versions of the Source* (New Haven: Yale University Press, 1983), and Alain Viala, *Naissance de l'écrivain: sociologie de la littérature à l'âge classique* (Paris: Editions de Minuit, 1986).

to reimaginings of the relationship between humanity and the world that are urgently needed in today's social, political, environmental, and even religious context.[15]

Idolatry: An Overview

Idolatry is as old as monotheism; the close association between the two is evident in what has come to be called the second commandment, articulated first in Exodus 20:4 and then in Deuteronomy 5:8:

> You shall not make for yourself a graven image, or any likeness of anything that is in heaven above, or that is in the earth beneath, or that is in the water under the earth; you shall not bow down to them or serve them; for I the Lord your God am a jealous God, visiting the iniquity of the fathers upon the children to the third and the fourth generation of those who hate me, but showing steadfast love to thousands of those who love me and keep my commandments.[16]

This is the wordiest of the commandments, and the most complex, and its slippery ambiguity combined with the severity of the direct threat that it contains fueled the debates throughout Church history that culminated in the Reformation.[17] The commandment is commonly seen to condemn the worship of statues and images, an interpretation reinforced by the episode, severely punished by God, of the golden calf that follows Moses' descent from the mountain.[18] Yet even this stricture almost immediately proved complicated.

---

[15] See Ayesha Ramachandran's excellent *The Worldmakers: Global Imagining in Early Modern Europe* (Chicago: University of Chicago Press, 2015), p. 10. In a recent essay, Victoria Kahn heralds a similar triumph of humanly authored work out of the demise of what she terms "poetic theology": "Instead of mediating divine truth, poetic theology became a vehicle of attending to poetic form. Instead, that is, of referring to a transcendent signified, poetic theology tipped on its axis and became the name of a human capacity. In the process, allegory as human invention supplanted allegory as a description of the cosmos or as the revelation of truth in history. In time, allegory became another name for the reader's construction of meaning, as well as a sign of the autonomous literary artifact." 'Allegory, Poetic Theology, and Enlightenment Aesthetics', in *The Insistence of Art: Aesthetic Philosophy after Early Modernity*, ed. Paul A. Kottman (New York: Fordham University Press, 2017), pp. 31–54, here, p. 37.

[16] Biblical quotes are taken from *The New Oxford Annotated Bible*, ed. Herbert G. May and Bruce M. Metzger (New York: Oxford University Press, 1977).

[17] For an excellent overview of the complexities inherent in idolatry, see Moshe Halbertal and Avishai Margalit's *Idolatry* (Cambridge, MA: Harvard University Press, 1992).

[18] For an overview of increased attention to the golden calf episode in the early modern period, see Jonathan Sheehan, 'Sacred and Profane: Idolatry, Antiquarianism and the

Those seeking to justify the use of images in religious worship pointed to other biblical episodes, such as the carefully described cherubim decorating the ark of the covenant (Exodus 25:18–22) or the bronze serpent erected by Moses on God's command (Numbers 21:8–9), where God seems to express a deep appreciation for the power of images as such, and does not hesitate to use them to inspire his followers. The relationship between God and visibility would, of course, grow even more blurred when read through God's self-manifestation in the Incarnation. In other words, as Counter-Reformation Catholics would point out in their polemics, condemning any and all physical, non-verbal manifestations of God was tantamount to denying the full divinity of Christ; it also could entail a failure to properly acknowledge, and admire, the created nature of the world.[19]

Running through these examples and arguments is a debate concerning whether images are, as Gregory the Great argued during an outbreak of iconoclastic fervor in the seventh century, merely words for the illiterate, or whether images possess a seductive power that the abstraction of the verbal lacks.[20] The particular power of images – to inspire, to evoke, to transmit, to heal – was acknowledged by the Council of Trent in the sixteenth century, convened to counter Protestant objections to the faith practiced by Catholics. The Council singled out images for special regulation, laying out the proper placement of and attitude towards images, and recommending, among other things, that "figures shall not be painted or adorned with a beauty exciting to lust" (Session 25, second decree). In the same session, the Council also attempted to settle the longstanding and sticky question of what, exactly, is meant by the biblical prohibition of bowing down or serving images. As early

---

Polemics of Distinction in the Seventeenth Century', *Past & Present* 192 (August 2006), pp. 38–46. On the close link between monotheism and idolatry, see Assmann's *Of God and Gods*).

[19] For a beautiful account of the ambiguous status of the material world in medieval Christianity, see Carolyn Walker Bynum, *Christian Materiality: An Essay on Religion in Late Medieval Europe* (New York: Zone Books, 2011). Frédéric Cousinié's *Le Peintre chrétien: Théories de l'image religieuse dans la France au XVIIe siècle* (Paris: L'Harmattan, 2000) traces the ways in which Counter-Reformation Catholics came to emphasize the divinity of the created world as a means of defending themselves against charges of idolatry.

[20] In his letter to Serenus, the bishop of Marseille, in 600, Gregory stated that "For to adore a picture is one thing, but to learn through the story of a picture what is to be adored is another. For what writing presents to readers, this a picture presents to the unlearned who behold, since in it even the ignorant see what they ought to follow; in it the illiterate read. Hence, and chiefly to the nations, a picture is instead of reading." In Gregory the Great, Book XI, Letter 13, translated by James Barmby. From *Nicene and Post-Nicene Fathers*, second series, vol. 13, ed. Philip Schaff and Henry Wace (Buffalo, NY: Christian Literature Publishing Co., 1898).

as the fourth century, following the Council of Nicaea, Basil of Caesarea articulated the influential formula that attention paid to the image is not paid to the image as such, but rather "passes to the prototype," thereby according the image a semi-transparency that protected it, ideally, from obscuring a referent that would otherwise remain inaccessible.[21] Thomas Aquinas later contributed to the discourse surrounding the appropriate attitude towards images by building on the distinction, first established by Jerome and Augustine, between *dulia*, the worship reserved for and accorded to God, and *latria*, a lesser form of respect to be afforded "excellent creatures."[22] Aquinas's formulation, which would be marshalled by early modern Catholics in the face of Protestant critiques, served to justify not only the use of images in worship, but also the practices surrounding saints, relics, and even the Virgin Mary. Insofar as the distinction between *dulia* and *latria* was outwardly invisible and instead depended entirely on the faith accorded the worshipper's own interpretation of his attitudes, however, Protestants greeted it with skepticism and often outright derision.

While depictions of Catholic abuses and excess were fundamental to the Reformation, John Calvin's objections to the use of images, relics, and saints in religious worship were particularly vehement. For Calvin, the two-way communication between heaven and earth described by Catholics in terms of gradations such as *dulia* and *latria* represented a degradation of divine majesty and, consequently, an unacceptable compromise of the incommensurability of God and humanity. The eleventh chapter of the 1561 French edition of his *Institution de la religion chrétienne* declares this opposition plainly in its title, "Qu'il n'est licite d'attribuer à Dieu aucune figure visible, et que tous ceux qui se dressent des images se révoltent du vray Dieu" ("That it is illicit to attribute any visible figure to God, and that all of those who set up images are revolting against the true God"). Here, Calvin argues that images are much more than misguided, but ultimately harmless, human attempts to communicate with the divine. Rather, insofar as their existence undermines the only tangible and intermediary form used by God to enter into contact with humanity – Jesus Christ – images actually insult the majesty and self-sufficiency of God.[23] Moreover, as Calvin goes on to

---

21 See Basil of Caesarea, *De Spiritu Sancto*, 18: 45, in *Nicene and Post-Nicene Fathers*, second series, vol. 8.

22 The question of adoration, and the distinction between *dulia* and *latria*, arises in the *Summa Theologica*, II II, 84, 1.

23 "il nous faut tenir ceste maxime: toutefois et quantes qu'on représente Dieu en image, que sa gloire est faussement et meshamment corrompue." *Institution de la religion chrestienne* (Paris: Vrin, 1957), vol. I, p. 120. (we must hold to this maxim: each and every time God is represented by an image, his glory is falsely and meanly corrupted).

remind the reader, images and relics are closely associated with mortality; the Book of Wisdom notes that idolatry began with a father's desire to preserve the memory of his dead son. Fabricating images of the divine, or locating the divine in images that already exist, is a heretical attribution to God of qualities that belong to fallen humanity, a criminal attempt to contain and understand God's ineffable and ultimately incomprehensible majesty: "Il reste donc qu'on ne peinde et qu'on ne taille sinon les choses qu'on voit à l'oeil. Par ainsi que la majesté de Dieu, qui est trop haute pour la veue humaine, ne soit point corrompue par fantosmes, qui n'ont nulle convenance avec elle."[24] ("One only paints and sculpts what one sees with the eye. Therefore, the majesty of God, which is too great for human sight, should not be corrupted by phantoms that have no relationship with it.") Calvin's arguments in the *Institution* take direct aim at nearly all of the arguments articulated by the Church Fathers that Catholics marshalled in defense of their practices. The "nulle convenance" in the citation above contradicts John of Damascus's reassurance that honor paid to the image passes to the prototype, something that Calvin regards as impossible, given the complete lack of similarity between the two. Calvin also undercuts Gregory the Great's idea that images are merely a more practical way than text to instruct the ignorant by citing Scripture and the prophets to illustrate that all efforts to understand God through visual representation are doomed.[25] Finally, early in the twelfth chapter, entitled "Comment Dieu se sépare d'avec les idoles, afin d'estre entièrement servi luy seul" ("How God separates himself from idols in order to be worshipped entirely by himself"), Calvin questions the distinction between *dulia* and *latria*, asserting that the difference between them is illusory, and rests upon a dubious distinction between honor and servitude.[26]

---

[24] *Institution*, I, p. 135.
[25] "De fait, aux passages que j'ay allégué, ce poinct est couché comme résolu: comme ainsi soit qu'il n'y ait qu'un seul vray Dieu, lequel les Juifs adoroyent, que toutes figures qu'on fait pour représenter Dieu sont fausses et perverses, et que tous ceux qui pensent cognoistre Dieu par ce moyen sont malheureusement deceuz." (*Institution*, I, p. 126). (In fact, in the passages that I have cited, this point is treated as resolved: since there is only one true God, whom the Jews adored, every figure that has been made to represent God is false and perverse, and those who think they know God through these means are sadly mistaken.)
[26] "Certes, comme nous avons dit, Dulie emporte servitude, Latrie honneur. Or nul ne doute que servir ne soit beaucoup plus qu'honnorer, car il nous seroit souvent dur et fascheux de servir à ceux que nous ne refusons pas d'honnorer." (*Institution*, I, p. 142). (Certainly, as we have said, Dulia implies servitude and Latria honor. That said, no one doubts that to serve is more important than to honor, since it would often be difficult and impractical to serve those whom we do not refuse to honor).

Idolatry and the Question of Creation

In insisting upon the ultimate incommensurability of God and humanity, Calvin points beyond the more commonly argued points regarding images (as opposed to text) and their worship to gesture towards the question of creation, a question central to modernity but that has been neglected in studies of idolatry. In his objection to the distinction between *dulia* and *latria*, Calvin relates the story of Cornelius the centurion, who kneels before Saint Peter, who in turn refuses this gesture of worship. The lesson that Calvin draws from this episode is that human language is itself ill-equipped to distinguish between creature and creator; we slide into idolatry merely by speaking: "Et pourquoy, sinon d'autant que les hommes ne sauront jamais si bien discerner en leur langage l'honneur de Dieu d'avec celuy des créatures, qu'en adorant les créatures par dévotion ils ne ravissent de faict à Dieu ce qui luy est propre, pour le faire commun à qui il n'appartient pas?"[27] ("And why, if not because men will never be able to discern through language the honor due to God from that due to creatures, do they not, in worshipping creatures through devotion, in fact take away from God that which is his in order to give it to what it does not belong to?") Significantly, the violation that occurs here occurs not through images, but through language; the seemingly crucial distinction between words and images is rendered moot. The sinfulness of humanity is instead located in our nearly inevitable tendency to forget our status as dependent creatures, a forgetting which then implicitly compromises God's sole possession of the power to create by misattributing this power to ourselves.

Calvin's emphasis on the incommensurability between Creator and creature owes much to Augustine. Augustine's clearest articulation of this distinction occurs in his treatise *On the Trinity*, where he warns against interpreting the similarity between God and humanity (made, after all, in God's image and likeness) as in any way implying an overcoming of the vast dissimilarity between the two, even in the afterlife:

> Accordingly, since there is now so great an unlikeness in this enigma both to God and to the Son of God, in which, however, some likeness has been found, we must also confess that even when "we shall be like to him," when "we shall see him just as he is" (certainly he who spoke thus was undoubtedly aware of the unlikeness that now exists), not even then shall we be equal to that nature, for a nature that is made is always less than He who made it.[28]

---

[27] *Institution*, I, p. 143.
[28] Augustine, *The Trinity*, trans. Stephen McKenna (Washington, DC: Catholic

The human tendency to forget, minimize, or ignore this distinction is identified as the root of all sinfulness, the "sacrilegious error of attributing to the Trinity that which does not belong to the Creator, but rather to the creature, or is imagined by mere empty thought."[29] Augustine's desire to establish and maintain the essential difference between Creator and creature gives rise to his articulation of the proper attitude to be maintained towards the created world, expressed in the key distinction, articulated in the *De Doctrina Christiana*, between use (*uti*) and enjoyment (*frui*). Enjoyment is to be reserved for the divine source of the created world; material, terrestrial, and man-made words, objects, and institutions should properly be viewed as instruments leading towards, and reminders of, their divine creator. Sinfulness arises when humans fall into a quasi-bestial literalism, allowing themselves to be seduced by objects which they mistakenly believe to exist in and of themselves and thereby forgetting that the world (and the humans inhabiting it) are created, and therefore dependent.[30] Augustine's interpretation of idolatry, then, extends beyond a suspicion of images as such to encompass any incorrect interpretation of signs which ultimately have only one legitimate referent:

> For what the Apostle says concerning idols and the sacrifices that are made in their honor should be understood concerning all imaginary signs which lead to the cult of idols or to the worship of a creature or its parts as God, or pertain to the concern for remedies and other observations which are not as it were publicly and divinely constituted for the love of God and of our neighbor but rather debauch the hearts of the wretched through their love for temporal things.[31]

In other words, the proper way to live in the world is to bear in mind, always, its created nature, its quasi-transparent status as an expression of God's goodness and power. To fail to do so, to become seduced by the beauty of the world or the ingenuity of our own fantasies, is to fall prey to idolatry, to voluntarily turn away from the divine source of all that is and to commit the "sacrilegious error of attributing to the Trinity that which does not belong to the Creator,

---

University Press, 1963), pp. 490–1.

[29] *Trinity*, p. 271.

[30] "Nor can anything more appropriately be called the death of the soul than that condition in which the thing which distinguishes us from beasts, which is the understanding, is subjected to the flesh in the pursuit of the letter. He who follows the letter takes figurative expressions as though they were literal and does not refer the things signified to anything else." *On Christian Doctrine*, trans. D. W. Robertson, Jr. (New York: Liberal Arts Press, 1958), p. 84.

[31] *On Christian Doctrine*, p. 59.

but rather to the creature, or is imagined by mere empty thought."[32] This expanded definition of idolatry places human authorship under suspicion, a suspicion that Augustine extends to his own activities in the closing lines of *On the Trinity*, which consist of a prayer asking God to deliver Augustine "from the multitude of words with which I am inwardly afflicted in my soul" before concluding with the following entreaty: "O Lord, the One God, God the Trinity, whatever I have said in these books as coming from You, may they acknowledge who are Yours; but if anything as coming from myself, may You and they who are Yours forgive me."[33] Augustine's efforts to legitimize his own authorial production by placing his words in service to the divine mirror his suspicion of natural philosophers, whom he accused of wanting "to attribute to themselves what they saw."[34]

Augustine's ideal of self-effacement, and the concomitant ideal of a quasi-effacement of the materiality of the world, guaranteed, in a way, that humanity could always potentially be found guilty of idolatry, and that constant vigilance was needed to avoid falling into this most terrible of sins. And indeed, the ensuing centuries were characterized by complex responses to the dilemma posed by, as Caroline Walker Bynum puts it in the title of her excellent study of the subject, "Christian materiality." If Walker Bynum examines the issues surrounding "miraculous matter," which was "simultaneously – hence paradoxically – the changeable stuff of not-God and the locus of a God revealed,"[35] Hans Belting traces the horizon of Christian art to the ideal of the *acheiropoeton*, or the legendary image spontaneously generated by the holiness of the incarnated Christ, one of the most famous examples of which was the *Veronica*, or *vera icona*, said to be generated when Christ wiped his face with a cloth given to him by Saint Veronica.[36] As in Augustine, the impossible ideal here is one in which humanity is the observer and admirer of divine creation; the absence of human creative activity, of the artistry that almost inevitably gives rise to idolatry, guarantees that the divine presence

[32] *Trinity*, p. 271.
[33] *Trinity*, pp. 524–5. Lisa Freinkel explores Augustine's vexed relation to authorship, suggesting, against critics like Robbins and Vance, that Augustine conceives of himself, first and foremost, not as an author but as a reader. See *Reading Shakespeare's Will: The Theology of Figure from Augustine to the Sonnets* (New York: Columbia University Press, 2002), p. 32.
[34] For a useful survey of the link between idolatry and theories of creation in early philosophy and Christian thought, see Isaac Miller, 'Idolatry and the Polemics of World-Formation from Philo to Augustine', *The Journal of Religious History* 28.2 (June 2004), pp. 126–45, here, p. 145.
[35] Caroline Walker Bynum, *Christian Materiality*, p. 35.
[36] Hans Belting, *Likeness and Presence: A History of the Image Before the Era of Art*, trans. Edmund Jephcott (Chicago: University of Chicago Press, 1994).

in creation will remain intact and unmuddied. This ideal, of course, was impossible to sustain, if indeed it was ever possible to realize. In his masterful study, A. J. Minnis carefully traces both the prohibitions surrounding human authorship in medieval biblical commentary and, paradoxically, the ways in which the attribution of ultimate authorship to God provided space for a complex theory of authorial role and literary form to emerge.[37] The hard-won, fragile equilibrium between divine and human modes of authorship that Minnis describes came under increased pressure during the Renaissance, a period whose name has become shorthand for the triumphant emergence of human flourishing and creativity. Hans Belting ties the aestheticization of art, the emergence of art as an end in itself and an expression of the individual artist, to Alberti's 1435 textbook on painting, which abandoned the idea of the image as an emanation or irruption of the sacred endowed with its own reality: "Now the image was, in the first place, made subject to the general laws of nature, including optics, and so was assigned wholly to the realm of sense perception. Now the same laws were to apply to the image as to the natural perception of the outside world... In addition, the new image was handed over to artists, who were expected to create it from their 'fantasy'."[38] Georgio Vasari's *Lives of the Artists*, published in 1550, demonstrated the extent to which the association of art works with their human creators had intensified during the Renaissance. As Thierry Lenain points out, Vasari's adoption of religious categories and vocabulary to describe the artistic process led to the sacralization of secular art, whereby the art work became a "relique auctoriale," thereby ushering in the reversal of divine and profane that had been so feared.[39]

Innovations in Idolatry: the Polemics of Louis Richeome (1544–1625)

Viewing the intellectual and cultural life of this period through the lens of idolatry serves to emphasize the extent to which the triumph of human autonomy and authorship in what we have come to recognize as individual artistic expression was still an open question which elicited a variety of responses. We have already seen how Calvin, more than the other Reformers, placed the threat of idolatry at the center of a theology heavily indebted to Augustine, for whom the topic was central. The Counter-Reformation response to Calvin's attack on idolatry was largely defensive; the Council of Trent's defense of the

---

[37] A. J. Minnis, *Medieval Theory of Authorship: Scholastic Literary Attitudes in the Later Middle Ages* (London: Scolar Press, 1984).

[38] *Likeness and Presence*, p. 471.

[39] Thierry Lenain, 'Les images-personnes et la religion de l'authenticité', in *L'Idole dans l'imaginaire occidental*, pp. 303–24, here p. 310.

use of religious images is unoriginal and tepid. Catholic theologians reiterated the well-worn arguments of John of Damascus, Basil of Caesarea, Gregory the Great, and Thomas Aquinas even as Protestants seized on the impossibility of reconciling these ultimately incompatible defenses of the image. And, as Emile Mâle notes, the Jesuit response to Protestant criticisms of the image was to double down defiantly on images and luxury.[40] As Frédéric Cousinié remarks in his valuable overview of early modern French conflicts over the religious use of images, the resulting interchange was less a conversation than a *dialogue de sourds*, with each side repeatedly and predictably marshalling the same examples (the brazen serpent, the golden calf): "La lecture de cette production littéraire confirme qu'en général, au moins pour la première moitié du XVIIe siècle, il s'agissait moins de contribuer à une réflexion nouvelle ou plus approfondie sur l'image, que d'éviter absolument de laisser une attaque sans réponse." (Reading this literary production confirms that in general, at least for the first half of the seventeenth century, these arguments were less about contributing a new or deeper reflection on the image than about avoiding, by any means possible, leaving an attack without a response.)[41]

This predictability was broken by the interventions of the French Jesuit Louis Richeome. In his influential *Tableaux sacrez des figures mystiques du tres-auguste sacrifice et sacrement de l'Eucharistie*, published in 1601 and dedicated to the French queen, Richeome sought to formulate a new Catholic theory of images. Richeome opens this beautiful work, where the richness of the prose vies with the sumptuousness of the illustrations, by establishing three kinds of images: those, such as palm trees or cherubim, that are visually self-evident and have no need of a verbal supplement; those, such as histories or "fictions verbales," that are given to the ear; and finally, those things or actions that symbolically represent spiritual mysteries, such as circumcision representing baptism or manna representing the Eucharist. By categorizing "images" in this fashion, Richeome follows Augustine and Calvin in blurring the distinction between word and picture.[42] Yet he does so not with the

---

[40] "La Papauté affirma ce que l'hérésie niait. Les Jésuites répondaient aux protestants en multipliant dans leurs églises les fresques, les tableaux, les statues, le lapis-lazuli, le bronze et l'or ..." (The papacy affired that which heresy denied. The Jesuits responded to the Protestants by multipying in their churches frescoes, paintings, statues, lapis lazuli, bronze, and gold ...). Emile Mâle, *L'Art religieux après le Concile de Trente* (Paris: Armand Colin, 1932), p. 22.
[41] Frédéric Cousinié, *Le peintre chrétien: Théories de l'image religieuse dans la France du XVIIe siècle* (Paris: L'Harmattan, 2000), p. 28.
[42] Discussing the *Tableaux sacrez*, Ralph Dekoninck notes that "c'est de l'apport conjoint de l'écrit et de l'image, de l'union de leurs qualities respectives, que dépend la plus large réception du message spirituel, mais aussi la plus sûre, puisque l'écrit ou la parole peuvent contrebalancer les excès ou pallier les déficiences de l'image, et, inversement,

intent of casting a shadow on all figures that are not explicitly generated or authorized by the divine, but rather with the completely opposite goal of celebrating representation in its dizzying proliferation and beauty, seeing in human artistry a symbolic homage to the divine Creator.[43]

While the unapologetic lushness of the *Tableaux sacrez* constituted an indirect provocation, Richeome took direct aim at the Reformers in his biting polemic *L'Idolatrie huguenote figurée au patron de la vieille payenne*, published in 1608 and dedicated to Henri IV, the French king who had himself converted from Protestantism. In this work that has remained in the shadow of the more glorious *Tableaux sacrez* – in fact, Henri Bremond, who bemoans Richeome's lack of originality, fails to mention either this polemical work or its sequel – Richeome dares to upend the now-familiar, near-automatic conversation between Catholics and Protestants around idolatry by maintaining that the Protestants are, in fact, the true idolaters. After decades of Catholic defensiveness, such an accusation had real shock value; as Richeome declares in the dedication to Henri IV that opens the treatise, his goal in writing it is that the Reformers "entendront, Dieu aydant, qu'ils ont tort, & que ce sont eux mesmes, qui tiennent, & enseignent l'Idolatrie, pensans estre le troupeau mignon du Seigneur" (will understand, God willing, that they are wrong, and that it is they who hold and teach Idolatry while thinking of themselves as the favored flock of the Lord).[44] As Richeome recognizes, in order to make this accusation, he would need to redefine idolatry, expanding it beyond its traditional association with the images that Protestants deplored

---

celle-ci peut donner accès à un mode de connaissance plus élevé car plus intuitif … Il n'y a donc pas lieu de se préoccuper de la hiérarchie de ces deux modes de représentation, par les mots et par les images, puisqu'ils se trouvent tous deux dépassés par le troisième type de figure, qui est 'figure de signification'." (it is upon the conjoined contributions of the written word and the image, from the union of their respective qualities, that the widest, and also most certain, reception of the spiritual message depends, since the written or spoken word can counterbalance the excesses or remedy the deficits of the image, and, inversely, the image can give rise to a mode of knowledge that is higher because it is more intuitive … There is therefore no reason to become preoccupied with the hierarchy of these two modes of representation, word or image, since they find themselves surpassed by the third type of figure, which is the "figure of signification".) *Ad Imaginem*, pp. 75–6.

[43] In the same year that Richeome published the *Tableaux sacrez* (1601), another extraordinary and richly illustrated Jesuit defense of images was published: Jan David's *Veridicus Christianus*, which posits images, properly conceived, as essential to faith. For more on the *Veridicus*, see Walter Melion, 'The Jesuit Engagement with the Status and Functions of the Visual Image', in *Jesuit Image Theory*, ed. Wieste De Boer, Karl A. E. Enenkel, and Walter Melion (Leiden: Brill, 2016), pp. 1–49.

[44] Louis Richeome, *L'Idolatrie huguenote figurée au patron de la vieille payenne, Divisée en huit livres & dediée au Roy tres chrestien de France & de Navarre Henri IIII* (Lyon: Pierre Rigaud, 1608), n.p.

and even destroyed. He announces the broad lines of this redefinition in the "Lettre à Messieurs de la Religion Prétendue Réformée" that follows the royal dedication and precedes the text. Instead of following a faith initiated and sustained by God and upheld by Catholic tradition, Protestants, Richeome maintains, have elevated human opinion and the "fantaisie flottante des hommes" (floating fantasy of men), thereby losing any contact with divinely sanctioned authority and truth.[45]

In other words, Richeome strikes back at the Reformers by emphasizing the aspect of idolatry that touches on invention, and downplaying the relationship between idolatry and images. Building on the distinction elaborated in the *Tableaux Sacrez* between material and spiritual images, Richeome invents the concept of "spiritual idolatry," which occurs whenever humans collapse the distinction between Creator and creature, elevating their own opinion or invention to the status of divinity, and worshipping it accordingly. After noting that this redefinition allows for the categorization of Turks and Jews as idolaters, since they worship the inventions of Mohammed and the Kabbalists, respectively, Richeome offers this summary:

> Mais sur toutes Idolatries, qui regnent dedans l'ame, celle qu'on appelle Heresie en l'escole Chrestienne, merite d'estre censée Idolatrie, prenant le mot d'Idolatrie en son large, avec les saincts Peres, & non si precisement que les Docteurs scholastiques: Car elle s'usurpe malignement, & superbement sur toutes erreurs le droict & le voile de divinité, & suppose ce qu'elle a forgé, comme chose divine, & saincte, & le faict honorer en titre de religion, qui est l'essence, & la vive couleur, qui forme l'Idolatrie.[46]

> But among all of the Idolatries that rule over the soul, that which we call Heresy in Christian schools deserved to be called Idolatry, taking the word "Idolatry" in the broad sense of the Church fathers rather than the precise sense of the Scholastics: For it usurps from all other errors the rights and veil of divinity, and supposes that what it has forged is a divine and holy thing, asking that it be honored as a religion, and that is the essence and living color of what forms Idolatry.

---

[45] "Et si vostre Eglise, selon leur foy, peut encor errer en corps, comme tous les membres d'icelle, & si elle est posee sur le sable, & fantaisie flottante des hommes, ne voyez vous pas, qu'elle n'est point l'Eglise de Dieu, laquelle est fondee sur le roc, qui se mocque des flots du mensonge, & de l'Enfer?" n.p. (And if your Church, according to their faith, can wander in its body like its members, and if it is placed upon the sand and floating fantasy of men, do you not see that it is not the Church of God, which is founded upon rock and which has no care for the floating of lies and hell?)

[46] *Idolatrie huguenote*, p. 25.

By rather ingeniously seizing upon the more capacious definition of idolatry espoused by Tertullian, Augustine, and Calvin, Richeome levels the charge of idolatry – still an unspeakably grave sin – at the Reformers themselves, whom he views as unmoored both from Catholic tradition and, paradoxically, from the Scripture that they claim to follow. Worse yet, Protestants could be described as *more* guilty of idolatry than the pagans themselves, since they have willingly turned away from revealed truth:

> Le Payen Idolatre transfere la gloire de Dieu, qu'il ignore, aux Idoles, & Dieux estrangers, laissant le Createur, & adorant le creature, faisant un faux Dieu, & ne tenant compte du vray ... l'Heresie va bien plus avant, car d'un costé cognoissant Dieu, & le confessant, elle le mesprise en effect, & se faisant adorer à sa place, luy ravit son honneur par une trahison d'autant plus damnable, qu'il est certain, que c'est moindre mal de n'avoir point cogneu la voye de verité, que de l'avoir quitté.[47]

> The Idolatrous Pagan transfers the glory of God, of which he is unaware, to Idols, and foreign Gods, abandoning the Creator and adoring the creature, making a false God and forgetting the true one ... Heresy goes farther, for on the one hand knowing and recognizing God, it insults him, and by asking that it be adored in his place steals honor from him through a betrayal that is even more damnable since it is clear that it is better to never have known the way of truth than to have known it and left it.

The remaining 700 pages of Richeome's treatise are devoted, first, to demonstrating that Protestantism bears all of the marks of heresy – among which are lying, pride, cruelty, and corruption, and all of which denote the substitution of human "opinion" for divine truth – and finally, to drawing scrupulous parallels between Protestantism and pagan religion, god by god. Richeome seizes upon inconsistencies in the Reformers' writings in order to demonstrate the free-floating nature of their theology; he uses Protestant doubts concerning the Trinity to allege that their inability to conceive of a triune god demonstrates their inveterate allegiance to polytheism. Throughout all of these rather enthusiastic "proofs," Richeome remains focused on the central issue of authorship and creation. On the one hand, he reproaches his Protestant adversaries for having lost sight of the divine author and putting themselves in God's place:

> vostre Foy donc, voire selon vostre confession, n'a aucun appuy, sinon l'authorité de Calvin, de Beze, & d'autres expositeurs de la Bible, que vous

---

[47] *Idolatrie huguenote*, p. 39.

> croyez comme à des hommes subjects à erreur: vostre Foy donc est humaine, fondée sur l'authorité des hommes, sur vostre jugement, & presomption, & non sur l'authorité Divine.[48]
>
> Your faith then, according to your own admission, is based on nothing other than the authority of Calvin, Beza, and other expositors of the Bible, whom you believe as men subject to error: your faith, then, is human, founded on the authority of men, upon your judgment and presumption, and not upon divine authority.

On the other hand, he condemns Calvin for what he sees as an overemphasis on divine authorship. In the section of the treatise devoted to drawing parallels between the Protestant God and Jupiter, Richeome alleges that Calvin makes God the author of human sinfulness, since he holds (again, accordingly to Richeome) that human will after the Fall is nonexistent. In so doing, he reduces humanity to the status of beasts, trapped by their senses in the realm of the material. This Goldilocks-like logic, wherein Richeome accuses the Protestants of inappropriately elevating the creative powers of humanity against those of God before reproaching them for viewing humans as incapable of any authorship whatsoever, even that of sin, is confounding, and makes sense only if we view these positions against the equilibrium advocated for in the *Tableaux sacrez*, wherein the miracle of divine creation spreads throughout the universe, reflected in subsequent events and creatures like light striking a prism. Without this anchoring in Catholic faith and tradition, the Protestants, Richeome is convinced, sway wildly to and fro, unable to agree on, or even to see, humanity's proper place in the created universe.[49]

In the end, and unsurprisingly, Richeome's attack did not result in a Protestant admission of heretical error. Indeed, Jean Bansilion, a Protestant minister from Aigues-Mortes in the south of France, took it upon himself to respond to Richeome point by point, pagan god by pagan god, in an almost equally massive treatise entitled *L'Idolatrie papistique opposée à l'idolatrie huguenote de Louys Richeome, Provincial des Jesuites*, published in Geneva within a year of the *Idolatrie huguenote*. Bansilion's counter-argument followed the predictable tack of opposing Protestantism, which followed divinely inspired Scripture, to Catholicism, which followed an institution composed of "hommes fautifs." Richeome counter-attacked the following year, with the *Panthéon huguenot découvert et ruiné contre l'aucteur de*

---

[48] *Idolatrie huguenote*, p. 414.

[49] For an overview of how the Reformation destabilized notions of divine and human creation, see Kathryn Tanner, *God and Creation in Christian Theology: Tyranny or Empowerment?* (New York: Basil Blackwell, 1998), especially pp. 2–3.

l'Idolatrie papistique ministre de Vauvert, cy devant d'Aigues Mortes. In this response to Bansilion's response, Richeome emphasizes the fundamental difference between Protestants and Catholics regarding human will, alleging that the Calvinist refusal of free will amounts to a failure to recognize humanity as the true image of God on earth, separate from other creatures. He also challenges Bansilion's defense of Calvin's doctrine of authorship, wherein all good works are, properly speaking, the work of God. Noting that evil deeds earn their perpetrators a place in hell and questioning why good deeds cannot lead to heaven, Richeome asserts that authorship can, in fact, be attributed to humans:

> Je dis ... qu'encore que [les bonnes oeuvres] viennent de Dieu, qui par sa grace nous donne le vouloir, & puissance de les faire, neantmoins elles sont nostres veritablement. Je prouve mon assertion par les exemples des autres choses: Tout le bien que nous avons, vient de Dieu, le corps & l'ame, & les vertus, & tout; & toutes-fois nous disons, sans mentir que le corps, & l'ame, & les vertus sont nostres; les enfans que le pere engendre, sont dons de Dieu, & neantmoins sont oeuvres du pere: les biens, les richesses, & autres commodites sont presens de la bonté divine, & toutes fois celles d'Abraham, de Job, voire encore des Egyptiens, & de tous les autres mondains, estoyent à eux. Les arbres, & autres creatures produisent, par vertu divine, niera on pour cela que ce ne soyent leurs fruicts?[50]

> I say that although all good acts come from God, who through his grace gives us the will and power to do them, nevertheless they are truly ours. I prove my assertion with examples of other things: All of the good that we have comes from God – the body, the soul, the virtues, and everything else, and nevertheless we say, without lying, that the body and soul and virtues are ours; the children that fathers sire are gifts from God and nevertheless the works of the father: the goods, riches, and other commodities are gifts of divine bounty and nevertheless those of Abraham, Job, and even the Egyptians and other worldly souls, were theirs. Trees and other creatures produce through divine virtue, but would one deny for all that that these are not their fruits?

Richeome's proof of his assertion through examples "of other things," with its embrace of the created world and the multiple manifestations of divine presence and power, stands in stark contrast to Calvin's attempt to hew

---

[50] Louis Richeome, *Le Panthéon huguenot découvert et ruiné contre l'aucteur de l'Idolatrie papistique ministre de Vauvert, cy devant d'Aigues Mortes* (Lyon: Pierre Rigaud, 1610), pp. 152–3.

closely to Scripture and to keep the categories of creator and creature separate. The elasticity of Richeome's rhetoric allows theological room for human initiative, especially since humans themselves defy strict categorization. Take, for example, Richeome's argument against restricting creation to the divinity alone:

> Mais, dit-il [Bansilion], selon l'opinion des grands Theologiens, Dieu ne peut pas communiquer à la creature, la puissance de créer une chose: Premierement, je respons qu'il y en a d'autres qui tiennent qu'il se peut servir d'une creature, comme d'un instrument, pour en créer une autre. Secondement, je dis qu'il y a grande difference entre créer, & meriter: car la creation se faict de rien, & requiert une puissance infinie; meriter se faict de quelque chose avec la grace de Dieu, & c'est assez que telle action soit assistée de Dieu.[51]

> But, he says, according to the opinion of great Theologians, God cannot communicate to the creature the power to create a thing: Firstly, I respond that there are others who say that he can indeed use a creature as an instrument to create another creature. Secondly, I say that there is a great difference between creating and deserving: for creation is done from nothing, and requires infinite power; deserving is done by something through the grace of God, and it is enough that such an action is assisted by God.

Richeome's arguments and objections, as well as the Protestant response to them, reveal more than the lengths to which both Catholics and Protestants went to defend themselves against the grievous sin of idolatry. They also demonstrate the way in which, at least in France, the bitter polemics surrounding idolatry exceeded arguments over religious images and the proper attitude towards them, to instead encompass the increasingly fraught question of whether humans possessed the capacity for creation or whether such a capacity should be reserved for the divine. Richeome's stigmatization of Protestantism as the illegitimate elevation of baseless human "opinion" and his concomitant celebration of a human ingenuity rooted in the divine constitute the neglected counterpoint to the celebrations of *homo faber* to which Ramachandran refers. As we will see in the chapters that follow, the emergence of unfettered human authorship – and the abandonment of a creationist worldview that this emergence was seen to imply – were both anticipated and deeply feared. A world unanchored by a creative divinity could be a world threatened with a potentially crippling loss of legitimacy;

---

[51] *Panthéon huguenot*, p. 195.

it could also be a place of possibilities unthreatened by the jealous mastery set forth as an ideal in Christian monotheism.[52] It could be a world bereft of the meaning conferred by providence; it could also be a place open to the surprises conferred by chance encounters or the indifference of fortune.

Idolatry in Seventeenth-Century France

All of these possibilities were explored with wit, imagination, and style throughout the French seventeenth century. For behind the apparent symmetry and celebrated mastery of a period dominated by the reign of Louis XIV was a culture characterized by bold explorations of alternative ways of thinking about the relationship between the divine, the terrestrial, and the human. The intensity of efforts to properly convey the increasing instability of that relationship has been well documented in art-historical studies of the period. Louis Marin's examination of the Jansenist artist Philippe de Champaigne's efforts to establish a style that would simultaneously assert and erase the visual – to paradoxically condemn idolatry through the image – echoes the important work of Koerner and Mochizuki on the effects of the Reformation on visual art.[53] Similarly, Dalia Judovitz's recent work on the neglected seventeenth-century French artist Georges de la Tour examines "the enigma of the visible" in his art, noting in the opening pages how his *oeuvre*, "in the privilege accorded to its symbolic efficacy as an instrument of faith instead of a focus on its visual and material character" reflects a new understanding of sacred painting.[54] Her careful examinations of his paintings demonstrate his acute awareness that at any moment the viewer (not to mention the subjects of the paintings themselves) may fall into a fatal forgetting of the ultimate source and destination of the visual and into the seduction of idolatry. Typically, however, when ostensibly secular or neoclassical work is studied, the religious lens falls away, even when it could enrich the authors' studies substantially. Marin's earlier work on Poussin and Caravaggio, despite its focus on what could be characterized as the transitive (Poussin) vs. disturbingly intransitive

---

[52] For an overview of the ways in which questions of legitimacy and divine creation shaped the emergence of modernity in the scientific context, see Stephen Gaukroger, *The Emergence of a Scientific Culture: Science and the Shaping of Modernity 1210–1685* (New York: Oxford University Press, 2006).

[53] See Louis Marin, *Philippe de Champaigne ou la présence cachée* (Paris: Editions Hazan, 1995), as well as Joseph Leo Koerner's landmark *The Reformation of the Image* (Chicago: University of Chicago Press, 2004) and Mia M. Mochizuki, *The Netherlandish Image after Iconoclasm 1566–1672: Material Religion in the Dutch Golden Age* (Burlington, VT: Ashgate, 2008).

[54] Dalia Judovitz, *Georges de la Tour and the Enigma of the Visible* (New York: Fordham University Press, 2018), p. 5.

(Caravaggio) aspects of visual art, fails to mention the larger religious context of such conflicts, just as Jacqueline Lichtenstein's excellent account of the *querelle du coloris* that split the French art world in the latter half of the century neatly raises the political and philosophical implications of the *querelle* but remains silent about the ways in which it continues longstanding, religiously rooted, conflicts over the potential seduction of the representation of flesh rather than story.[55]

As I have already noted, this reluctance to consider the religious origins of conflicts surrounding artistic production and representation is even more striking in studies of seventeenth-century French literature. This neglect is in part because of that corpus's central position in the French cultural canon, but it can also be attributed to the longstanding perception, particularly acute in French studies, that religion is the enemy of complexity and of critical thought. As I hope to have shown, the concept of idolatry, with its slippery ambiguity, its profound implications simultaneously for authorship and artistic representation, and its terrifying implications for the fate of the human soul, demonstrates that religion can be a source of dynamism and even the vehicle for rethinking fundamental assumptions about the place of humanity in the world.[56] In the pages that follow, I demonstrate how attention to the heretofore neglected presence of idolatry in some of the most well-known seventeenth-century French texts enables us to reassess how these works interrogate authorship and artistry in a rapidly changing world.

I begin with a reconsideration of Honoré d'Urfé's pastoral masterpiece, *L'Astrée*. Arguing that d'Urfé, once a prominent figure in the Catholic Ligue that opposed the accession of the Protestant Henri IV to the French throne, was acutely aware of the representational crisis at the heart of religious tensions in France, I call into question the work's status as a Neoplatonic celebration of the transformative power of love. Rather, I demonstrate that concern with idolatry and its attendant issues of representation and authorship suffuse the work, from the author's dedications to the French kings Henri IV and Louis

---

[55] See Louis Marin, *Détruire la peinture* (Paris: Galilée, 1977), and Jacqueline Lichtenstein, *La Couleur éloquente: rhétorique et peinture à l'âge classique* (Paris: Flammarion, 1989).

[56] Michael Moriarty, an acute observer of seventeenth-century French intellectual culture to whose work this study is indebted, has noted both the prevalence and richness of the concept of idolatry in the period, especially (but not exclusively) in writers and thinkers strongly influenced by Jansenism. Yet, although he touches on the theme in Racine's *Britannicus* and also in La Fontaine, his analysis is mainly centered on overtly religious thinkers and moralists even as it eloquently demonstrates the importance of idolatry to "some rich and subtle analysis of the illusory conceptions and images with which we burden our selves, our lives, and our personal and social relationships." 'Image and Idol', *Seventeenth-Century French Studies* 25 (2003), pp. 1–20, here, p. 20.

XIII to the decision to disguise Celadon as a priestess. The result is less a newfound harmony between heaven and earth than an acknowledgment of the persistent inability to join the two spheres neatly, an inability that arguably accounts for the text's length, inventiveness, and lack of obvious closure.

If d'Urfé seems both to luxuriate in and to lament the disjunction between the terrestrial and the divine, Descartes, in his quest to provide an indisputable point of stability to anchor human knowledge, seeks to do away with the category of idolatry altogether. In the second chapter, I suggest that Descartes' effort to solve the divisive (and distracting) problem of idolatry explains the presence, in the *Méditations métaphysiques*, of two arguments that have puzzled philosophers: first, that images are peripheral, and even deleterious, to the human search for truth, and second, that creation is the sole purview of God. Descartes' contemporaries were less than convinced, and I show how the objections to the *Méditations* demonstrate the persistence of the fundamental issues preventing the easy dismissal or resolution of idolatry.

Jean de la Fontaine also challenged the assumptions fundamental to idolatry, but from a completely different direction that rested in large part on his wholesale dismissal of Cartesian philosophy as it was popularly understood. In three separate fables, La Fontaine takes subtle aim at the three aspects of the biblical prohibition of idolatry: images, worship, and creation. La Fontaine's deep familiarity with the discourse of idolatry leads him away from Descartes' placement of a creative divinity at the stable center of the universe and instead towards a radical questioning of the ideals of authority and mastery inherent in monotheism itself. La Fontaine's example shows how the discourse of idolatry could be deployed in a way that opens up the possibility of a human coexistence no longer governed by jealousy and fear, a possibility beautifully exemplified by the fables themselves.

If La Fontaine sought to expose the ridiculousness of subordinating the deliciousness of the material world to the intangibility of abstract salvation, the marquise de Sévigné remained haunted by the threat of idolatry throughout her life as a mother to her adored daughter, the comtesse de Grignan. Indeed, near the beginning of their lengthy separation, the prominent Jansenist Arnauld d'Andilly, a longtime family friend, reproaches her absorption in the loss of her daughter in precisely those terms, sternly but lovingly calling her a "jolie païenne." Thereafter, the threat of idolatry hovers over the correspondence; like d'Urfé, Sévigné both relishes and regrets her ability to lose herself in the world and, more specifically, her at times defiant care for her daughter. Unlike d'Urfé, however, Sévigné is able to find a way to hold the terrestrial and the divine in a tenuous harmony through her increasingly enthusiastic espousal of the concept of providence.

In the final chapter, I examine the close confluence, already recognized in the third century by Tertullian, between theater and idolatry before considering two radically different theatrical treatments of the topic. In his early play, *Sganarelle ou le cocu imaginaire*, Molière playfully suggests that the entangling of the languages of religion and love is responsible for the impossibility of pleasure. I then move to consider one of the most iconic works of seventeenth-century France, Racine's *Phèdre*. In my reading, I show how the energy and torment surrounding idolatry throughout the seventeenth century render the gravity of the title character's crime legible, and how the play as a whole dramatizes the unbalanced and newly complicated communication between humanity and the divine.

In choosing the works that I examine in this book, I have deliberately chosen texts at the heart of the French cultural canon. By arguing that these works are deeply engaged with the discourse of idolatry, I am not seeking to reduce them to commentaries on longstanding, and sometimes tedious, religious polemics. Rather, I hope to show how religion and literature enrich and enliven each other as they struggle to accommodate the seduction of the specific with the legitimizing abstraction of the beyond. Indeed, it is through this struggle that what we now recognize as the literary emerges, as that which exposes any neat accommodation of the human with the divine as ultimately impossible.[57]

In the closing pages of the book, I point beyond literature to demonstrate how a deep-seated awareness of the logic of idolatry persisted in France until late in the seventeenth century. Here, I analyze the *Mercure Galant*'s depiction of the visit of Siamese ambassadors to the court of France in 1686 by placing it against the texts submitted by the *Mercure Galant*'s readers a year earlier to celebrate Louis XIV's revocation of the Edict of Nantes, thereby prohibiting Protestants from remaining in France without changing their religion. By juxtaposing these two seemingly unrelated events, I demonstrate that, while the Siamese visit could be (and has been) read on its own terms as a disturbing indulgence in idolatry, the Revocation served to inoculate the French monarch against such suspicions, legitimizing an unprecedented celebration of the royal person through statues and spectacle. My association of the Siamese visit with

---

[57] The close examination of the treatment of idolatry in literature can allow us to track the emergence of the literary as described by Hélène Merlin-Kajman in her *L'Animal ensorcellé: traumatismes, littérature, transitionnalité* (Paris: Ithaque, 2016), which she concludes with the following: "La littérature entre en effet dans les choses sacrées pour perturber leur stabilité, puisqu'elle comprend l'investigation du familier, du mortel, de l'aléa, puisqu'elle est devenir, mouvement, toutes choses contradictoires avec la permanence du sacré. Aussitôt qu'elle entre dans les *sacra*, la littérature y entre pour être profanée" (p. 421). (Literature enters into sacred things to perturb their stability, since it comprehends the investigation into the familiar, the mortal, the random, since it is becoming, movement, all things which contradict the permanence of the sacred. As soon as it enters into the *sacra*, literature enters into it to become profaned.)

continuing religious divisions also serves to further refute the narrative that characterizes seventeenth-century France as somehow immune to, or safely beyond, the polemics that nearly tore the country apart a century earlier.

Indeed, the variety and scope of the works considered here demonstrate that the logic of idolatry suffused seventeenth-century literature and culture. It provided the framework for thinking through the dizzying possibilities of a world unmoored from its divine origins, and for thinking about the dangers, and pleasures, of getting lost in the strangeness of terrestrial beauty. Our current queasiness regarding religion, and especially creationism, has rendered idolatry nearly invisible, and the strong emotions that it excited nearly incomprehensible. My hope is that the work presented here will serve to illuminate heretofore neglected aspects of these beautifully complex texts, shedding light on how they can help us to think of human agency and artistic beauty in new ways.

1

Idolatry and Instability in Honoré d'Urfé's *L'Astrée*

"Des bergères d'Urfé chacun est idolâtre."[1]
(Everyone is idolatrous of d'Urfé's Shepherdesses.)

The Eye and the Ear

"Je ne represente rien à l'oeil: mais à l'oüye seulement, qui n'est pas un sens qui touche si vivement l'ame"[2] (I represent nothing for the eye, but only for the ear, which is a sense that touches the soul less intensely). Honoré d'Urfé's declaration, placed at the end of the preface to the first volume of his sprawling novel, is meant to justify his idealized depiction of shepherds and shepherdesses, who have little in common with actual villagers forced to tend sheep to make a living. His distinction between the eye and the ear, between the visual and the verbal, follows his observation that if pastoral theater can represent its characters with golden staffs and refined manners, he may certainly do the same in a novel, with fewer strains to credibility, since his characters are not seen, but heard. Interestingly, this observation occurs immediately following d'Urfé's explanation of why he chose a real place – Forez and the banks of the Lignon – as his novel's setting. From the outset, then, *L'Astrée* is characterized by representational instability. Idealized shepherdesses converse in a realistic setting, their adventures recounted by an author keenly aware of the stakes involved in the materiality of sight, sound, and the soul.

The argument of whether sight or sound is a more efficient means of touching the human soul is not new. In her footnote to this passage in her new edition of *L'Astrée*, Delphine Denis notes that d'Urfé's allusion to a hierarchy between the senses comes from Aristotelian sources, and thereby contradicts Celadon's espousal, at the end of the second volume, of the

---

[1] Jean de La Fontaine, 'A Monseigneur l'Evèque de Soissons', in *Oeuvres complètes*, ed. Pierre Clarac (Paris: Gallimard, 1958), vol. 2, p. 649.
[2] Honoré d'Urfé, *L'Astrée*, première partie, ed. Delphine Denis (Paris: Honoré Champion, 2011), p. 114, emphasis mine. All quotes from the first volume of the novel come from this edition.

Neoplatonist view – which he claims to have heard from a druid whom he met years ago – that all of the senses, along with reason, equally equip humans to appreciate and experience true beauty. Denis's efforts to locate the foundations of d'Urfé's aesthetic theories in ancient philosophical texts recently discovered and interpreted in the Italian Renaissance are characteristic of much of the scholarship surrounding *L'Astrée* and its well-read, curious author. While Antoine Adam located the "origin of the sentimental theories" in *L'Astrée* in an Aristotelianism transmitted through Averroes and his Italian Renaissance commentators, with whom d'Urfé was undoubtedly familiar, other scholars have emphasized d'Urfé's espousal of Neoplatonism, expressed through an appreciation of the materiality of the world as a vehicle towards a divine ideal.[3] As Jacques Ehrmann states in the first lines of his subtle study of the novel,

> La beauté devient une sorte d'entité abstraite (entraînant par là même vers l'abstraction la femme qui la *porte*) vers laquelle tout l'être de l'amant tend, pour s'y confondre. La femme n'est plus alors que l'agent d'une volonté qui va au-delà d'elle. La femme est dépassée par sa propre beauté. Elle n'est plus que l'instrument d'une révélation, qu'une étape sur le chemin de cette révélation, de ce salut qu'est la beauté.[4]

> Beauty becomes a kind of abstract entity (entailing through this the abstraction of the woman that bears it) towards which the entire being of the lover leans, in order to merge with it. The woman is no longer the agent of a will that surpasses her. The woman is surpassed by her own beauty. She becomes merely an instrument of revelation, a stage on the path to this revelation, to this salvation which is beauty.

More recent critics have begun to conclude, however, that it would be inaccurate to attribute the novel's complex unfolding to a single philosophical apparatus. We have already seen Delphine Denis's demonstration that d'Urfé's Aristotelianism is at odds with the Neoplatonism of his male lead character. Likewise, Jean-Brice Rolland suggests that Neoplatonism is not the *telos* of the novel, but marks the point of departure of a sustained interrogation of its terms, noting pointedly that "ce passage de l'universel au particulier

---

[3] Antoine Adam, 'La Théorie mystique de l'amour dans *L'Astrée* et ses sources italiennes', *Revue d'histoire de la philosophie et d'histoire générale de la civilisation* 4 (1936), pp. 193–206.

[4] Jacques Ehrmann, *Un paradis désespéré: L'amour et l'illusion dans* L'Astrée (New Haven: Yale University Press, 1963), p. 10.

s'avère éminemment problématique"[5] (this passage from the universal to the particular is, in fact, eminently problematic). For Clifton Cherpack, the seductive possibility that *L'Astrée* was meant to be an illustration of Neoplatonist philosophy has hidden the novel's indebtedness to the model of Greek romance.[6]

This tracking of sources and influences to literary and philosophical models, however, has largely elided the possibility that d'Urfé's fraught depiction of representation in his novel might owe something to the religious debates that had only recently threatened to fracture the French polity irrevocably. And d'Urfé, who had been imprisoned because of his activities on behalf of the Catholic Ligue opposed to the Protestant Henri de Navarre's accession to the French throne, was more intimately familiar with these debates than most; indeed, critics involved in tracing d'Urfé's sources through the books in his library have overlooked that alongside humanistic classics such as Castelvetro's commentary on Aristotle stood the complete works of Gregory of Nazianzus, a crucial figure in the establishment of Trinitarian orthodoxy in the fourth century and whose oration roundly condemned idolatry.[7] Moreover, d'Urfé's *Epistres morales*, written during his imprisonment and often cited as evidence of his evolving taste in, and exposure to, philosophy and aesthetics, is also run through with sharp references to the religious divisions splitting the French kingdom. This text is haunted by the death of d'Urfé's protector and employer, the young duke of Nemours, who on his deathbed exhorts his friend "de ne vous esloigner jamais de l'Eglise Catholique"[8] (to never stray from the Catholic Church). And although the duke's remark, upon learning of the pope's acceptance of Henri IV's conversion to Catholicism, that "Tant mieux; nous vivrons en un repos honorable"[9] (So much the better; we will live in an honorable peace/repose) can and has been read as evidence of a progressive privileging of political unity over religious identity, it is also the case that elsewhere the duke is unrepentant, citing his refusal of his enemies' conditions for peace as proof that religion, rather than ambition, guided his choices in life, or exclaiming, after it is suggested that a Huguenot doctor may be able to treat him, that "Les huguenots ... sont ennemis du Dieu que je sers. Recourre

---

[5] Jean-Brice Rolland, '*L'Astrée*, Roman néoplatonicien ou roman du néoplatonisme?' in *Lire L'Astrée*, ed. Delphine Denis (Paris: Presses de l'Université Paris-Sorbonne, 2008), pp. 165–75, here p. 168.

[6] Clifton Cherpack, 'Form and Ideas in *L'Astrée*', *Studies in Philology* 69.3 (June 1972), pp. 320–33.

[7] See Gilles Banderier, 'La Bibliothèque d'Honoré d'Urfé: Notes complémentaires', *Bibliothèque d'Humanisme et Renaissance*, 68.2 (2006), pp. 321–32.

[8] Honoré d'Urfé, *Epistres morales* (Lyon: Jean Laudret, 1627), p. 90.

[9] *Epistres*, p. 229.

à eux pour luy sauver un serviteur, n'est-ce pas offenser sa puissance?"[10] (The Huguenots ... are enemies of the God that I serve. If I go to them to save His servant, does this not offend His might?)

In other words, d'Urfé's opening reference to the idea that sight touches the soul more deeply than sound is not just a self-deprecating aside requesting that the reader not take what follows too seriously; nor is it solely an invitation to consider the conflicts between Aristotelianism and Platonism that characterize the text as well as the thought of the time. In the context of sixteenth-century religious polemics, the assertion that sight is a more efficient way of touching the soul than sound can be read as an allusion to Catholicism's unapologetic use of images. Indeed, by ostensibly placing sight over sound, d'Urfé eschews the more moderate doctrine first articulated by Gregory the Great through which images and words are, in fact, interchangeable, moving instead to the celebration of the image that would characterize Jesuit texts such as Richeome's *Tableaux sacrez*, published just one year after the apparition of *L'Astrée*'s first volume.

That said, d'Urfé's declaration of the superiority of sight over sound occurs in a context that seeks to *defend* his own work as a novel, not a play – in other words, as a work whose access to the visual is mitigated through text. Moreover, d'Urfé's sly introduction of a third sense through his remark that sound "n'est pas un sens qui *touche* si vivement l'âme" (is not a sense that *touches* the soul as intensely) complicates the equation by inviting the reader to consider both sight *and* sound as inferior to the physicality of contact, all while raising the thorny question of whether the immaterial soul can be touched. In other words, this brief yet resonant remark announces the novel about to unfold not by positing a settled re-hierarchization of the senses, but by pointing to the ultimate impossibility of fixing the issue of the precise relation between the physical and the spiritual, the soul and the body, once and for all. The result is an interplay between word and image, neither of which is complete in and of itself, that Dalia Judovitz has identified as a baroque, emblematic aesthetic that apprehends the world "not as image, but as changing semblance."[11]

This is all the more the case insofar as D'Urfé's own categorical claim that his novel is less damaging than theater, since it is less in thrall to the visual, serves to draw an almost comic attention to the predominance of the visual in the novel's first pages, and indeed, the entire first book. Not only are the human inhabitants of Forez introduced with the phrase "Or sur les bords

---

[10] *Epistres*, p. 221, then p. 95.
[11] Dalia Judovitz, 'Emblematic Legacies: Hieroglyphs of Desire in *L'Astrée*', in *EMF 1: Word and Image*, ed. David Lee Rubin (Charlottesville: Rookwood Press, 1994), pp. 31–54, here, p. 49.

de ces delectables rivieres on a veu de tout temps quantité de Bergers ..."[12] (On the banks of these delectable streams many Shepherds have always been seen); the pages that follow are awash with references to looking, noticing, watching, and seeing.[13] The opening encounter between Astrée and Celadon begins when the shepherdess's dog notices Celadon and runs towards him; the ensuing glances, perceptions, and emotionally motivated blindnesses result in Astrée's demand that Celadon never again appear before her eyes: "garde toy bien de te faire jamais voir à moy que je ne te le commande"[14] (beware of appearing before my eyes unless I order you to do so). This request causes Celadon to throw himself into the Lignon; considered dead by those who witnessed his fall before losing sight of him, he washes up on shore, where he is noticed by Galathée, Silvie, and Léonide, whose lengthy contemplation of his broken, bloated, and unconscious body is conveyed by a bravura display of ekphrastic prose that can be characterized only with great difficulty as representing nothing to the eye. The emblematic, provocative *renvoi* between text and image only intensifies as the novel progresses from the paintings depicting the gods that Celadon sees when he first awakens to the pictorial depiction of Gallic history that decorates Adamas's palace.[15] D'Urfé's insistent return to the fascination of the visual, as well as its unique pitfalls, demonstrates his keen awareness of the interdependency of word and image, and marks less an effort to represent "rien à l'oeil" than to cast great doubt on the ultimate efficacy of any effort to scrub the seductiveness of the visual from language.

---

[12] Honoré d'Urfé, *L'Astrée. Première Partie*, ed. Delphine Denis (Paris: Honoré Champion, 2011), p. 119.

[13] See Jean-Marc Ghitt, 'Le Forez comme foyer poétique dans *L'Astrée*', in *Audace et modernité*, pp. 225–33, who argues that "Ce 'on a veu' désigne non pas la vue mais la vision ... Le Forez est un foyer poétique dans le sens où de lui émane une vision pastorale que le poète discerne et traduit en mots pour la communiquer à d'autres que lui" (This "one has seen" designates not seeing but the vision. The Forez is a poetic realm in the sense that from it comes a pastoral vision that the poet discerns and translates into words to communicate to others than himself) (pp. 228–9). Eglal Henein also notes the theme of vision in the opening sentences, adding "Alors que les aventures qui reposent sur les erreurs de la vue foisonnent dans le roman, les yeux, les corps des personnages, les costumes, transmettent des informations fiables. Ce paradoxe signifie qu'un rébus peut se cacher derrière toute image" (While adventures that turn on errors of vision abound in the novel, the eyes, the bodies of the characters, the costumes all transmit reliable information. This paradox signifies that a rebus may hide behind every image). (*Protée romancier: Les déguisements dans* L'Astrée *d'Honoré d'Urfé* (Paris: Nizet, 1996), p. 62).

[14] *Astrée* I, p. 125.

[15] For an extensive and subtle reading of the various paintings in *L'Astrée*, see Eglal Henein's *Protée romancier*, especially pp. 109–44. It is worth noting that Henein opens this chapter on "iconologie" with an epigraph taken from Richeome's *Tableaux sacrez*.

Moreover, d'Urfé's proclamation that he represents only for the ear is particularly curious coming from an author whose work repeatedly engages with the materiality of the written word. Throughout the novel, letters are lost and found, tablets are erased and corrected, and names and messages are inscribed upon and placed inside trees. That d'Urfé would occlude the materiality of his own text, which was certainly not meant to be read aloud, and whose thousands of pages indisputably constitute a very visible object, should cause us to examine closely the author's engagement with the ostensibly simple opposition between visual and verbal representation. His apparent desire to sublimate his text into audible speech rather than written signs would seem to convey a faith in the ability of art to connect with the transcendent without entrapping the reader in the seductive amber of the representational instrument used. This is the ideal pursued by Protestants and Catholics with equal fervor, and at least one astute reader of *L'Astrée* believes that d'Urfé largely succeeds. Eglal Henein concludes her brief examination of religious themes in the novel by noting that the author, newly converted to the cause of Henri IV and a religiously inclusive French state, "imagine une religion nouvelle en écrivant une sorte de précoce *Traité de la tolérance*. Il accole, comme les poètes, des divinités. Il prétend, comme les peintres, représenter l'au-delà à travers un objet d'art"[16] (imagines a new religion while writing a precocious *Treaty on Tolerance*. He frequents, like poets, divinities. He claims, like painters, to represent the beyond through a work of art). Henein's easy equivalence between poetry and painting mirrors Richeome's redefinition of the image as something encompassing both word and image, just with varying degrees of abstraction. It holds out the possibility that word and image, incomplete in themselves, can, when combined, gesture towards the completeness of the divine, and thereby elevate humanity.

Yet this irenic vision of wholeness, while undeniably attractive as an ideal, is repeatedly problematized in d'Urfé's novel. As Laurence A. Gregorio notes, "as is eminently clear in the text's action, stability in love remains an impossible dream" in part because "the guarantee of an *a priori* metaphysical truth remains in a state of uncertainty."[17] While Gregorio makes this perceptive remark in the context of an article examining the novel's debates on love, I would like to argue that an examination of d'Urfé's sustained and sophisticated engagement with the question of idolatry – an engagement almost completely neglected by scholars of *L'Astrée* – can serve to shed further light on this fundamental instability all while linking the work to its larger cultural context and thereby considerably altering our interpretation of what the work was trying to do.

[16] *Protée*, p. 57.
[17] 'Implications of the Love Debate in *L'Astrée*', *French Review* 56, no. 1 (October 1982), pp. 31–9, here p. 38.

Astrée's Commandment

Hinted at in the first of the novel's prefaces, the representational conflict at the heart of the confessional divide splitting France resonates throughout the narrative that follows. The conflict between Astrée and Celadon that leads the latter to throw himself into the Lignon, thereby beginning the long series of events that constitute the novel, has its roots in Astrée's jealousy after Celadon, following Astrée's orders, pretends to be in love with the shepherdess Aminthe. Given Celadon's explicit deification of his lover – he explains his strange conduct in a letter to his brother by asking, "Que si ceste vie te semble estrange, ressouviens-toy, que les miracles sont les oeuvres ordinaires des Dieux, & que veux-tu que ma Déesse cause en moy que des miracles?"[18] (If this life seems strange to you, remember that miracles are the ordinary works of the gods, and therefore what would my goddess cause in me other than miracles?) – the reader is invited to hear in her outrage at the possibility that Celadon may convincingly enact love for another an echo of the God of the first commandment forbidding his people from worshipping any other deity. In fact, as Celadon's brother Lycidas reminds Astrée, Celadon reacted to her "commandment" with horror, asking that she instead demand that he sacrifice his own life:

> Mon astre, vous dit-il, (je me ressouviendray toute ma vie des mesmes paroles) ce n'est point pour refuser: mais pour ne pouvoir observer ce commandement, que je me jette à vos pieds, & vous supplie que pour tirer preuve de ce que vous pouvez sur moy, vous me commandiez de mourir, & non point de servir comme que ce soit autre qu'Astrée.[19]

> My star, he said to you (I will always remember these words exactly), it is not in order to refuse you, but because I cannot observe this commandment, that I throw myself at your feet and beg you that, in order to see the power you have over me, you command me to die rather than serve anyone else other than Astrée.

And indeed, as Celadon suspected and as the biblical parallel implies, his obedience leads, quite literally, to disaster, as Astrée is a self-proclaimed jealous god(dess); as she admits to Celadon in a letter,

> je suis soupçonneuse, je suis jalouse, je suis difficile à gagner, & facile à perdre; & puis aisée à offenser, & tres mal-aisée à rappaiser; la moindre doute

---

[18] *Astrée* I, p. 139.
[19] *Astrée* I, pp. 135–6.

est en moy une asseurance; il faut que mes volontés soient des destinées, mes opinions des raisons, & mes commandemens des loix inviolables.[20]

I am suspicious, I am jealous, I am hard to win and easy to lose, as well as easy to offend and very difficult to appease; the slightest doubt is in me a certitude; I require that my will be destiny, my opinions reasons, and my commandments inviolable laws.

The parallels that d'Urfé draws between the demands of Judeo-Christian monotheism and those of an earthly mistress announce, at the outset of the novel, the significant difficulties inherent in viewing romantic love as a precursor of, or conduit to, knowledge of the divine. Combined with his calculated turning away from Ficinian Neoplatonism in the preface, d'Urfé's demonstration of the tragic consequences of assigning divine attributes to one's beloved is less an implicit argument for the need to espouse the Christian faith than a careful examination of whether the two kinds of love – divine and human – can coexist at all.

Tircis, Hylas, and the threat of idolatry

Astrée's announcement of her wish to be obeyed combines with her demand that Celadon pretend to worship another shepherdess to constitute a strange parody of the Judeo-Christian deity, one that follows rather closely the unfolding of the ten commandments. For just as the prohibition of the making of graven images unfolds inevitably and imperceptibly out of the first commandment, so much so that the demand that no other gods be worshipped moves, depending on the tradition followed, in and out of the space between the first two commandments, the idea and threat of idolatry is present in coiled potentiality in both Celadon's worship of Astrée's beauty and Astrée's proclamation of her jealousy. Significantly, this threat becomes manifest in the first incursion of outsiders into the previously paradisiacal world inhabited by Celadon, Astrée, and their friends, which occurs when the Forezian shepherds and shepherdesses, still absorbed in grief over Celadon's presumed demise, unintentionally happen upon ("de fortune") a young shepherd lying in the grass accompanied by two shepherdesses, one holding his head in her lap and the other playing a harp. The crying shepherd, Tircis, is reciting verses that mourn the death of his lover, Cleon. The curious Forezian shepherds and shepherdesses stop to listen, at which point they hear another voice approaching: "A peine estoit party Lycidas qu'ils ouyrent d'assez loin une

---

[20] *Astrée* I, p. 206.

autre voix, qui sembloit s'approcher d'eux, & la voulant escouter, ils furent empeschez par la Bergere qui tenoit la teste du Berger dans son giron ..."[21] (Lycidas had hardly left when they heard, far off, another voice, which seemed to approach them, and wanting to listen to it, they were kept from doing so by the Shepherdess who held the head of the Shepherd in her lap). The interrupting shepherdess is Laonice, who upbraids Tircis for preferring a dead woman to herself. This preference for someone who can do nothing for him, she exclaims, is not love, but idolatry:

> jusques à quand as tu ordonné que je sois dédaignée pour une chose qui n'est plus? & que pour une morte je sois privée de ce qui luy est inutile? Regarde Tyrcis, regarde Idolatre des morts, & ennemy des vivans, quelle est la perfection de mon amitié, & apprends quelquesfois, apprens à aymer les personnes qui vivent, & non pas celles qui sont mortes ...[22]

> until when did you order that I be disdained for something that is no longer? and for a dead woman I should be deprived of what is useless to her? Look, Tyrcis, look, idolater of the dead and enemy of the living, at how perfect my friendship is, and learn from time to time to love those who are living and not those who are dead ...

Laonice's accusation of idolatry could easily be dismissed as the ravings of a spurned lover whose blinding jealousy is repeatedly confirmed and enacted in the pages that follow. Yet it is reinforced by the identity of the singing shepherd, whose approaching voice eventually becomes so strong that it drowns out the arguing Tircis and Laonice. This voice belongs to Hylas, who arrives singing the virtues of inconstancy, which protects lovers from one-sided affection by enabling them to look elsewhere. Indeed, he notes, "Le trop fidele opiniastre/ Qui déceu de sa loyauté,/ Aime une cruelle beauté:/ Ne semble-t'il point l'idolastre,/ Qui de quelque idole impuissant/ Jamais le secours ne ressent?"[23] (The stubborn and too faithful person/ Who, disappointed in her loyalty/ Loves a cruel beauty/ Does he not resemble an idolater/ Who from some powerless idol/ Never receives any aid?) Although Hylas is not speaking of Tircis, whom he has not yet met, his use of the word "idolastre" to describe the stubborn victim of unrequited love in his song combines with Laonice's accusation to bring the problem of idolatry to the forefront of this scene. For when Laonice calls Tircis an idolater, she does so out of anger that *she* is not the goddess whom Tircis worships. Hylas, on the other hand, espouses an

---

[21] *Astrée* I, p. 145.
[22] *Astrée* I, pp. 145–6.
[23] *Astrée* I, p. 147.

entirely different representational system, one that casts serious doubt on the entire project of attempting to align human and divine love; as the final verse of his song proclaims, "Moy qui veux fuir ces sottises,/ Qui ne donnent que de l'ennuy,/ Sage par le mal-heur d'autruy,/ J'use tousjours de mes franchises:/ Et ne puis estre mécontant,/ Que l'on m'en appelle inconstant"[24] (I who flee these trifles/ which only cause trouble/ wise through the misfortune of others/ I always use my liberties/ and cannot be unhappy/ when others call me inconstant). Hylas's use of the term idolatry therefore invites the reader to consider the ways in which Tircis's extremely strange situation – the result, we later learn, of the deceptions he practiced to win the heart of Cleon as well as Cleon's tragic death in the plague – is not a singular aberration, but rather the logical extension of a certain way of envisioning, imagining, and practicing love, which almost all of the shepherds and shepherdesses in the novel share.

Tircis's idolatry consists mainly in his persistent service to his lover Cleon, who represents, in a sense, the extreme extension of the indifferent lover in Hylas's song, insofar as she is not herself cruel, but has fallen to cruel death. In other words, Tircis's love for Cleon is, by definition, unrequited; it is a love that can do nothing for him in this world. It is *impuissant*, and therefore fulfills the definition of idolatry as the term is used by Hylas. But Tircis can also be said to be an idolater insofar as, like Celadon with Astrée, he worships Cleon as a goddess, attributing to her the authorship of his actions (he renames her eyes "auteurs de douces entreprises") and crediting her with keeping him alive: "Non, vous ne mourez pas,/ mais c'est plustost moy-mesme,/ Puis que vivant je fus de vous seule animé"[25] (No you do not die/ instead, it is I who die/ since living, I was animated only by you). Such attribution of causality, immortality, and the ability to give life to the (obviously) mortal Cleon rather than to the gods whose powers those are is theologically problematic, even in the pre- or proto-Christian world of the novel. Cleon claims to fear the gods, but his divinization of Cleon serves only to obscure them. Just before Hylas arrives, Tircis utters a wish that is troubling in its effort to place religion in the service of his amorous devotion, rather than the other way around: "Ah! que je voye plustost le Ciel pleuvoir des foudres sur mon chef, que jamais j'offense ny mon serment ny ma chere Cleon"[26] (Ah! I would rather have the heavens rain lightning upon my head than betray my vow or my dear Cleon).

Tircis's hyperbolic idealization of his Cleon resonates with Celadon's divinization of Astrée to cast in doubt the desirability of a model of love that inappropriately elevates the love object to an extent that it obscures the actual

---

[24] *Astrée* I, p. 149.
[25] *Astrée* I, p. 144.
[26] *Astrée* I, p. 146.

gods. This similarity, however, also serves to highlight the major difference between the two situations: Cleon, unlike Astrée, is dead. The appearance of the word "idolatry" in conjunction with the unfathomable pain occasioned in the living by grief for one who has departed too soon recalls the way in which the biblical Book of Wisdom recounts the emergence of this gravest of sins. In Wisdom, the slippery slope towards idolatry begins with a father undone by his son's "untimely" and "sudden" death. As he seeks to pay tribute to his son, his efforts at remembrance slide into worship: "and he now honored as a god what was once a dead human being" (14: 15). This idealization, understandable in the context of the father's grief, leads directly to the establishment, and even political legitimization, of idolatry among humanity. The father's worship of his son's image is passed on to his descendants, and in turn is sanctioned by royal decree. This passage of idolatry into law leads to the creation of images of monarchs who cannot be present in the far reaches of their kingdoms. Finally, the work and ambition of the craftsmen who make these images is such that the artist himself becomes worshipped as a god before, finally, the statues are worshipped in turn: "And this became a hidden trap for mankind, because men, in bondage to misfortune or to royal authority, bestowed on objects of stone or wood the name that ought not to be shared" (14: 21). The result of this inappropriate worship is a social calamity that Wisdom describes as "a raging riot of blood and murder, theft and deceit, corruption, faithlessness, tumult, perjury, confusion over what is good, forgetfulness of favors, pollution of souls, sex perversion, disorder in marriage, adultery, and debauchery." For, as the text continues, "the worship of idols not to be named is the beginning and cause and end of every evil" (14: 26–27).

Granted, Tircis does not make or carry an image of Cleon; rather, he invokes her presence and memory through verse and song. In depicting Tircis as an idolater without an image, d'Urfé may well be arguing that idolatry may be perpetrated just as easily through language as through the visual arts. The intent, not the medium, constitutes the sin. Leaving the lack of an image aside, the striking similarity between Tircis and the biblical father points to the danger that his idolatrous obsession represents. As the first non-Forezian whom the friends of Astrée and Celadon meet, he is not unlike the carrier of a fatal disease, whose presence causes the theologically problematic nature of romantic love to emerge. And indeed, from this point forward, the language and logic of idolatry are frequently used to describe the shepherds' love for their shepherdesses. As we learn in the fourth book, in which Astrée recounts the history of her relationship with Celadon, soon after meeting Celadon at a ball, Astrée had tried to avoid his advances by referencing the hatred that separated their fathers. Celadon's reply directly references the divine prohibition of idolatry, both in Exodus and in Deuteronomy, before brushing it aside:

> J'ay bien oüy dire, repliqua Celadon, que 'les Dieux punissent les erreurs des peres sur les enfants': mais entre les hommes cela n'a jamais esté accoustumé: ce n'est pas qu'il ne doive estre permis à vostre beauté qui est divine, d'user des mesmes privileges des Dieux: mais si cela est, vous devez aussi comme eux le pardon quand on le vous demande.[27]

> I have heard, replied Celadon, that "the gods punish the errors of the fathers on their children": but between men that has never been the custom; not to say that it should not be permitted that your beauty, which is divine, should enjoy the same privileges as the gods, but if that is the case, you must show forgiveness when it is requested.

Celadon's strategy here is curious, and not merely because he transposes the foundation of Judeo-Christian law into a pagan context by pluralizing the "gods." His quotation of biblical language is, in fact, diverted from its original meaning; given the context of the conversation, it is legitimate to read the reference to the sins of the fathers as a nod to the long-running conflict that separates his father from Astrée's. What follows, however, demonstrates Celadon's awareness, however muted, of the quote's original context. After noting that this punishment across generations does not apply to conflicts between humans, he goes on to allude to the divinity of Astrée's beauty, which nonetheless is not, itself, a god, before concluding by stating that if, perchance, her beauty does allow her to participate in the privileges of divinity, she should, like the gods, pardon those who pray for forgiveness. In other words, Celadon's statement makes a hash out of the biblical prohibition of idolatry. The confused syntax and theology could be attributed to the as yet undeveloped state of Christianity among the Forezians; it can also, quite plausibly, given the way that the novel begins, be attributed to Celadon's problematic tendency to idealize his lover, regarding her as a goddess and treating her demands as inviolable commandments. A third possibility, however, that does not undercut the other two, is that d'Urfé is gently mocking the entire discourse of idolatry that so dominated the intellectual life of religiously minded Frenchmen during the end of the sixteenth century and the beginning of the seventeenth. This possibility would seem to be borne out by another of Celadon's references to idolatry, uttered in a song he composes as a reaction to a letter that Astrée's father had forged, and in which "Astrée" states her intention to submit to an arranged marriage rather than pursue her relationship with Celadon: "Vous m'avez dédaigné, parjure,/ Pour un que vous n'aviez point veu,/ Par ce qu'il eut par aventure,/ Plus de bien que je n'ay pas eu:/ Infidelle, osez-vous encor/

---

[27] *Astrée* I, p. 262.

Sacrifier à ce veau d'or?"[28] (You have disdained me, perjurer/ For someone you have never seen/ Because he happened to have/ More wealth than me/ Unfaithful one, do you still dare/ Sacrifice to this golden calf?). Once again, the parallel between human and divine love is drawn, but in such a hyperbolic fashion that the distance between heaven and earth is not held in respectful, hierarchical allegory but rather humorously, and incongruously, collapsed.

The Sources of Idolatry

Further investigation of d'Urfé's invocations of idolatry in the novel supports the idea that the novelist is invested in exploring the genesis and ideological implications of what has long been considered the most serious of sins, the font from which all sin springs. Astrée's history of her relationship with Celadon, which she recounts in the fourth book of the first volume, also contains the story of how Lycidas and Phillis met and fell in love. Lycidas, like his brother, is swept away by the beauty of Phillis, and, again like Celadon, expresses his passion in a manner that directly evokes the threat of idolatry that attaches almost immediately to earthly love. Raising his eyes to heaven, he exclaims:

> O Dieux! si vous estes en colere contre moy, parce que j'adore avec plus de devotion l'oeuvre de vos mains que vous mesmes; pourquoy n'avez-vous compassion de l'erreur que vous me faites faire? que si vous n'aviez agreable que Phillis fust adorée, ou vous deviez mettre moins de perfections en elle, ou en moy moins de connoissance de ses perfections: car n'est-ce profaner une chose de tant de merite, que de luy offrir moins d'affection?[29]

> O Gods! If you are angry with me because I adore the work of your hands more than you yourselves, why do you not have compassion for the error into which you have led me? If you are not happy that Phillis be adored, you should have either put fewer perfections in her, or less awareness of these perfections in me: for does it not profane something of such merit to give it less affection?

Adoring the work of the gods more than the gods themselves is precisely the definition of idolatry offered by the Bible (in the Book of Wisdom and elsewhere), by Augustine, and, later, by Calvin, for whom the confusion of creator and creature constituted a fundamental, and grave, heresy. Here, however, Lycidas objects to the severity of this prohibition; like his brother, he pleads for pardon. He points out that the gods should have pity on him, since

---

[28] *Astrée* I, p. 296.
[29] *Astrée* I, p. 277.

they made Phillis so irresistibly perfect, and ends by asking whether loving her less would not, in fact, be the greater crime, insofar as it would dishonor the gods who made her so beautiful. Certainly, calling the beloved's beauty "divine" is a time-honored literary tradition, verging on cliché. As I have already noted, scholars of *L'Astrée* have seized upon such language to call attention to the author's attraction to Ficinian Neoplatonism, in which earthly beauty is an essential step and conduit from the terrestrial to the divine – a theory that would not be in fundamental conflict with the theories of the image set forth by Counter-Reformation Jesuits like Richeome.[30] Yet by deliberately invoking the biblical prohibitions of idolatry in the stories of Celadon, Lycidas, and Tircis, d'Urfé points towards the ways in which Neoplatonism and Christian orthodoxy rub against each other. Idolatry represents nothing less than the myriad ways in which the lover can become distracted from, or even forgetful of, the divine; it thereby undercuts, and menaces, any kind of smooth transition from earth to heaven and back again.

This issue is rendered even more acute by d'Urfé's choice of historical setting – fifth-century Gaul, at the crossroads of paganism and Christianity. By referencing the prohibition of idolatry while invoking the divine through the plural "dieux," Lycidas and Celadon raise doubts over whether idolatry and paganism are, as the polemicists of the sixteenth and seventeenth centuries held, synonymous. Their consciousness of the dangers of idolatry seems to mark them as sensitive to, if not yet fully aware of, Judeo-Christian truth. However, they seem to remain unaware or unsuspecting of monotheism itself, instead attributing the powers of creation and punishment to a confused collective.[31] This issue will resurface during Adamas's attempt to deliver a

---

[30] The authors of the introduction to the new edition of the first volume of *L'Astrée* point to the way in which d'Urfé departs from strict adherence to Ficino's philosophy: "Mais il convient de nuancer et de relativiser l'influence de cette première source [Ficino] en observant qu'Honoré d'Urfé reconnaît la dignité et l'autonomie de l'amour profane sans s'empresser de le dissoudre dans l'*amor Dei* dont il serait comme la préfiguration. Peut-être doit-il un peu à cet égard au *Traité de l'amour humain* de Flaminio e Nobili, et plus largement aux trattatistes mondains dont les considérations tendent à desserrer les liens du platonisme et la mystique" (But it is appropriate to shade and relativize the influence of this first source (Ficino) by observing that Honoré d'Urfé recognizes the dignity and autonomy of profane love without wanting to dissolve it in the divine love that it would prefigure. Perhaps he owes something in this matter to Flaminio e Nobili's *Treatise on human love*, and more broadly to the worldly treatise-writers whose thought tends to untie the binds of Platonism and mysticism) (p. 55). I would argue that d'Urfé's repeated references to idolatry mark an awareness of the ways in which the issues raised in recent religious polemics in France force a re-thinking of the validity and applicability of Ficino's philosophy as well.

[31] For a wonderful exploration of the implications of the shift from polytheism to monotheism in Western literature, see Tobias Gregory, *From Many Gods to One: Divine*

proper religious education to Celadon in the second volume of the novel, and to which I will return. For the moment, however, it is worth considering the way in which d'Urfé's separation of monotheism and idolatry points to a more general uncertainty, pervading the first two volumes of the novel, regarding the nature and very existence of the gods.

Silvandre and the Ambiguity of Religion

The Bible closely associates the threat of idolatry with the affirmation of monotheism; after all, the second commandment, prohibiting the making and worship of graven images, stems directly from God's proclamation of his identity and his demand that no other gods be worshipped. To the early seventeenth-century French reader even dimly aware of the theological controversies that had threatened to tear the country apart, the discourses held by Celadon and Lycidas, combining biblical condemnations of idolatry with references to the "dieux," would have seemed exceedingly strange, and possibly nonsensical. Idolatry is a threat that afflicts those who refuse to acknowledge the identity of the one true God, to the exclusion of all others; yet for Celadon, Lycidas, and Tircis, the symptom and the cause are reversed. Knowledge of the divine does not temper or inform their passion for their beloved. Instead, the violence of their passion leads them to add their mistresses to the pantheon of gods, even while asking those gods for forgiveness. This reversal of cause and effect, wherein romantic love engenders consciousness of the threat of divine punishment rather than the other way around, serves to call attention to the highly ambiguous nature of religion in the first two volumes of *L'Astrée*. Guilt over, and punishment for, idolatry makes sense only in the context of a singular God who has created all that exists. Insofar as the first two volumes of the novel repeatedly call this existence into question, they point out the ideological freight, borne of insecurity and fear, that attaches to the charge of idolatry.

The first appearance of religious ritual in the novel does nothing to reassure the reader that the novel's characters are under the care of a loving deity who intervenes in the world to protect his creation. This is not to say that the novel does not explore the need to believe in such a deity. The nymphs' discovery of the half-drowned Celadon on the shores of the Lignon is welcomed by the nymph Galathée as the fulfillment of a prophecy informing her that she will marry the man she meets at that time, at that place, or else become the unhappiest person on earth. In the following book, however, we learn that this "prophecy" was cynically staged by Climanthe for the benefit of his friend

Action in Renaissance Epic (Chicago: University of Chicago Press, 2006).

Polemas, who was meant to be the man she would meet by the river. Galathée is completely taken in by Climanthe's deception; the prophecy is revealed as false only through a chain of coincidences that themselves seem unbelievable. The nymph Leonide, traveling through Forez on her way to Feurs to find Adamas, sleeps in, and therefore must break her journey at Ponsins, where she finds a place to spend the night. It so happens that the narrowness of the house where she stays had obliged the hospitable owner to partition the space so as to have more rooms. She wakes up before dawn, and, not wanting to leave for her destination without daylight, stays in her bed, which is placed against the partition separating her from a room in which, by chance ("par hazard"), one of the occupants raises his voice. Leonide realizes the voices belong to Polemas and Climanthe, and listens to their conversation, which just happens to turn precisely on the false oracle delivered by Climanthe to Galathée. D'Urfé's emphasis on chance in the startling series of events that lead Leonide to discover the truth about Climanthe's trickery is striking. At no point does he attribute, or invite the reader to attribute, these coincidences to the hand or favor of a divinity, even though if ever there were a situation that invited such a conclusion, this would be it. Instead, he lets the randomness of the fortuitous combination of Leonide's sleep habits, the narrowness of the house, the occupants of the next room, and the subject of their conversation quietly subsist, thereby drawing a subtle yet jarring comparison between Leonide's credibility-straining situation, which she, the narrator, and reader attribute to chance, and Galathée's eagerness to believe that the gods are intimately involved with her life.

By introducing the topic of divine intervention in human affairs not through the devotion of Adamas but instead through the deception of Climanthe and the gullibility of Galathée, d'Urfé places all claims of divine foreknowledge and favor in the novel under suspicion, even when they are not as manifestly deceptive as those of the false druid. And none of the growing group of pastoral friends makes such bold claims to divine access as the mysterious shepherd Silvandre. In the seventh book of the first volume, he proclaims that although, according to appearances, man should be at the bottom of the hierarchy of creatures, given that other animals are faster and stronger, "quand on considere que les Dieux ont fait tous ces animaux pour servir à l'homme, & l'homme pour servir aux Dieux, il faut avoüer que les Dieux l'ont jugé estre d'avantage"[32] (when one considers that the gods made all of the animals to serve man, & man to serve the gods, one must admit that the gods gave humans an advantage). In this self-assured statement, the reality of the gods' existence is not only confirmed, but set against our intuitive

---

[32] *Astrée* I, p. 409.

sense of everyday experience.[33] Moreover, the gods are identified as authors of creation endowed with a specific intent, which is deemed accessible to humanity (and which happens to set humanity in the center of the world). Yet these words are addressed to Leonide, who, along with the reader, has had the experience of discovering the ease with which divine intent can be invented by its ostensible interpreter; in addition, Silvandre makes this statement in the context of his efforts to impress the shepherdess Diane, whose mother was renowned for her piety.

Significantly, Silvandre's declaration of knowledge of divine reality and purpose occurs in the seventh book of the novel's first volume – the same book in which Tircis and Laonice fill out their story. The reader learns that Tircis and Laonice were drawn to Forez by an oracle that instructed them to go to the shores of the Lignon and tell their story to the first shepherd who asks what troubles them. This shepherd, the oracle notes, should be obeyed, "car le Ciel l'élit pour vous juger"[34] (for the Heavens have elected him to judge you). This is a strange sort of oracle. Not only is its language of a crystalline clarity, devoid of the ambiguities that traditionally characterize messages from the divine; it also refrains from alluding to what the shepherds' judgment will be. In other words, the oracle contents itself with directing Tircis and Laonice to a specific location. We have no indication that the gods are invested or involved in the outcome of the story they tell this shepherd.[35] It so happens that the curious shepherd of the oracle is none other than Silvandre, who listens to the Parisians' stories, as well as the summations of their Forezian representatives, and renders the judgment that Laonice should stop pursuing Tircis, who continues, rightfully, to be devoted to Cleon's soul, even though her body has died.[36] Yet just as significant as Silvandre's verdict are the words

---

[33] In this manner, Silvandre's reasoning is representative of what Michael Moriarty has called the "age of suspicion," wherein the evidence provided by the body or appearances is viewed as misleading, if not dangerous. (Michael Moriarty, *Early Modern French Thought: The Age of Suspicion* (New York: Oxford University Press, 2003).

[34] *Astrée* I, p. 434.

[35] For an exhaustive treatment of oracles, signs, and dreams in *L'Astrée*, see Eglal Henein, *La Fontaine de la vérité d'amour* (Paris: Klincksieck, 1999), pp. 71–110. Henein notes the curious status of oracles in the work, which seeks to preserve human liberty along with a sense of divine providence: "Jamais l'oracle n'inspire une expérience mystique du lien avec l'ineffable" (An oracle never inspires the experience of a mystical link to the ineffable) (p. 109).

[36] In a touch that reinforces the association between the two characters that was first drawn in the novel's opening book, Laonice is represented during summations by Hylas, who accuses Tircis of impiety and ingratitude. The association between the two continues well into the novel's second volume, where Hylas asks Tircis "Comment ... que pour bien aymer, il faut idolatrer une morte comme vous?" (How is it ... that to love well, one should idolize a dead person such as yourself?) (Honoré d'Urfé, *L'Astrée. Deuxième partie*, ed.

he utters to legitimize his decision: "car telle est la volonté du Dieu qui parle en moy"[37] (for this is the will of the God that speaks through me). While there are many such trials in the novel, this is the only instance in which the judge overtly references the divine source of his or her authority. Granted, often the novel's other judges possess a status – that of nymph or druid, in the cases of Leonide and Adamas – that implicitly conveys the authority needed to act in this capacity. The other human who renders judgment, Diane, merely alludes, in the case of Silvandre and Phillis, to the "pouvoir qui en cet endroict nous a esté donné"[38] (power that was given to us in this place), and later, in the case of Delphire and Dorisée, to "nous, à qui la charge en a esté commise par la voix de l'Oracle"[39] (us, to whom the charge has been conferred by the voice of the Oracle). Silvandre's confident claim that the will of a god speaks through his voice goes beyond the meaning of the original oracle, which told Tircis and Laonice only that the shepherd they meet in Lignon would serve as their judge; the judgment itself is left to Silvandre, just as in the other cases it is left to Laonice, Adamas, and Diane.

Silvandre recounts his own history in the following book of the volume, and this history begins to explain his particularly intense relationship with oracles and the divine. Having been torn from his family of origin during a war and adopted by a Swiss father who sent him to the university in Marseille, Silvandre is tormented by ignorance of his origins. A friend of his points out that the good fortune that Silvandre has enjoyed since his abduction must be proof of the special care that the heavens ("le Ciel") take of him, and recommends that he consult an oracle. This oracle tells him that he will find out who he is only once he dies: "Jamais tu ne sçauras celuy dont tu és né/ Que Sylvandre ne meure, & à telle fortune/ Tu fus par les destins au berceau destiné"[40] (You will never know your father/ Until Sylvandre dies, and to this fortune/ You were destined from the cradle). Silvandre's response to this disquieting news is to stop worrying about his past: "je me resolus de ne m'en enquerir jamais, puis qu'il estoit impossible que je le sceusse sans mourir, & vesquis par apres avec beaucoup plus de repos d'esprit, m'en remettant à la conduitte du Ciel …"[41] (I resolved to never ask, since it was impossible to know without dying, and lived thereafter with much more tranquility, giving

---

Delphine Denis (Paris: Honoré Champion, 2016, p. 262)).

[37] *Astrée* I, p. 442.

[38] Honoré d'Urfé, *L'Astrée*, vol. 3, ed. Hugues Vagannay (Geneva: Slatkine Reprints, 1966), p. 520.

[39] Honoré d'Urfé, *L'Astrée*, vol. 4, ed. Hugues Vagannay (Geneva: Slatkine Reprints, 1966), p. 348.

[40] *Astrée* I, p. 455.

[41] *Astrée* I, p. 455.

myself up to the gods). Silvandre's recipe for peace of mind – to relinquish curiosity and allow providence to guide one's path – is proffered not as advice that everyone would do well to follow, but as a solution engendered by the singular particularities of his own life as well as the strange words of the oracle. Silvandre's certitude that the heavens not only exist, but also take special care of him, can be read not as infallible proof of the reality of the divine but as a symptom of his uncertain origin and orphanhood; in the gods, he finds the benevolent father(s) that he is lacking on earth.

D'Urfé encourages this skeptical, utilitarian reading of Silvandre's religiosity. He notes, in several instances, Silvandre's discomfort with an uncertainty that seems to remind him of the "continuel supplice" (continual torture) occasioned in his youth by his ignorance of his origins. At the beginning of the novel's second volume, Silvandre is alarmed by the love he feels for Diane, since the violence of his passion has led to the loss of his self-mastery: "il connoissoit bien qu'il avoit fait un changement fort desavantageux, se souvenant de quel heur il estoit accompagné, lors que maistre absolu de ses pensées il disposoit tout seul de sa vie & de ses desseins"[42] (he knew that he had made an unfortunate change, remembering what luck accompanied him while, absolute master of his thoughts, he alone disposed of his life and his intentions). Neither reason nor force can free Silvandre from love's shackles. The ensuing loss of control leads him, as before, to resign himself to providence, concluding that "c'est en vain que l'homme s'efforce contre les ordonnances du Ciel, & que celuy est le plus avisé qui sçait mieux y ployer & conformer sa volonté"[43] (it is in vain that man struggles against the orders of the Heavens, and that he is most astute who knows best how to conform his will to them). Love is thereby transformed from a threatening, all-consuming chaos into a reassuring sign of a divine plan, yet once again the specificity of Silvandre's circumstances and character should lead us to regard this transformation less as proof of d'Urfé's attraction to Neoplatonism than as evidence of d'Urfé's awareness that the attempt to align earthly love with divine intent is, especially in the age of idolatry, far from simple or smooth. Indeed, d'Urfé suggests, the gods may well be an invention of humans seeking to fend off or contain the unbearable loss of autonomy brought about by love. Silvandre's resolution to surrender himself to the will of the gods is complicated by the inscrutability of their intentions. Utterly at a loss as to how to proceed, Silvandre encourages himself: "Faisons, disoit-il, en se respondant, ce que le Ciel veut que nous fassions"[44] (Do, he said, responding to himself, what the Heavens want us to do). In a move that recalls Lycidas's unapologetic turn towards idolatry, he

---

[42] *Astrée* II, p. 35. All further quotes from this volume will be taken from this edition.
[43] *Astrée* II, p. 35.
[44] *Astrée* II, p. 36.

decides to see a sign of divine intent in Diane's beauty: "Pourquoy peut-on juger que les dieux l'ayent faicte si belle, sinon pour estre aymée de ceux qui la verront?"[45] (Why do we think that the gods made her so beautiful, if not to be loved by those who see her?) Yet a residual awareness that this solution may be more complicated than it first appears leads him to consult Echo, who lives in the rocks near the spot on the banks of the Lignon where, "de fortune," Silvandre finds himself. In the ingeniously crafted stanzas that follow, the rock sends back to Silvandre the last syllable of his verse, seeming to answer his queries; for example, to his question "Où vont les cris que je vais émouvant?" (Where do the cries that I movingly utter go?) Echo replies "Au vent" (to the wind).[46] Echo's answers determine Silvandre's next question, as he carries on a conversation, essentially, with himself. The narrator's commentary on this scene is significant, insofar as it underscores the human propensity to believe in gods and in divine design when in love:

> Encore que le berger n'ignorast point que c'estoit luy-mesme qui se respondoit, et que l'air frappé par sa voix rencontrant les concavitez de la roche, estoit repoussé à ses oreilles, si ne laissoit-il de ressentir une grande consolation des bonnes responces qu'il avoit receues, luy semblant que rien n'estant conduit par le hazard, mais tout par une tres-sage providence, ces paroles que le rocher luy avoit renvoyées aux oreilles n'avoient esté prononcées par luy à dessein, mais par une secrette intelligence du demon qui l'aymoit, et qui les luy avoit mises dans la bouche. Et en cette opinion il suivoit la coustume de ceux qui ayment, qui d'ordinaire se flattent en ce qu'ils desirent, et trouvent des apparences d'espoir où il n'y a poinct d'apparence de raison.[47]

> Although the shepherd knew that he was answering himself, and that the air struck by his voice, meeting the concavities of the rock, came back to him, he was nonetheless greatly consoled by the good answers he received. Since it seemed to him that nothing was done by chance, but instead by a very wise providence, the words that the rocks sent back to his ears were not deliberately pronounced by him, but rather by the secret intelligence of the demon who loved him, and who had put them in his mouth. And in this opinion he followed the custom of those who love, who ordinarily flatter themselves in their desires and find the appearance of hope there where the appearance of reason is absent.

---

[45] *Astrée* II, p. 36.
[46] For an account of the sources of this scene, especially in the *Pastor fido*, see Stéphane Macé, 'La Double italianité de *L'Astrée*: pour une approche des formes poétiques', in *Lire L'Astrée*, pp. 65–76, here 71–2.
[47] *Astrée* II, pp. 39–40.

The narrator's refusal to participate in Silvandre's illusion, to suggest that the events of the novel are driven by something other than the "hazard" and "fortune" which governed Leonide's overhearing of Polemas's plot and which guided Silvandre's steps towards the echoing rock clears a space in the novel for religion to be regarded not as revealed, universal truth, but as a construct that responds to a human need for stability.[48] As Celadon exclaims in response to Galathée's suggestion that "fidelité" and "constance" are just words invented to curb the natural liberty of the soul,

> y a t'il quelque chose plus honteuse que de n'observer pas ce qui est promis? y a t'il rien de plus leger, qu'un esprit qui va comme l'abeille, volant d'une fleur à l'autre, attirée d'une nouvelle douceur? Madame, si la fidelité se pert, quel fondement puis-je faire en votre amitié?[49]
>
> is there anything more shameful than to fail to observe that which is promised? is there anything more flighty than a soul that imitates a bee, flying from flower to flower, attracted by new sweetness? Madame, if loyalty is lost, what foundation can I find in your friendship?

Celadon's own propensity to accord divine attributes to his beloved and to view his relationship with Astrée in religious terms can therefore be read, just like Silvandre's eagerness to discern divine design at work in his own life, as a consequence of his fear of the foundationlessness that often accompanies romantic love.[50] Indeed, Celadon's exclamation to Galathée is echoed in the stanzas to love sung by Silvandre in the novel's second volume, which

---

[48] D'Urfé's care to show Silvandre's terror alongside his self-assurance complicates efforts to read Silvandre as a committed Neoplatonist, or, as Twyla Meding calls him in an otherwise superb reading of the Hylas–Silvandre dynamic that points out its relevance for the contrast d'Urfé draws between the written and the oral, "the consummate champion of amatory constancy." See Twyla Meding, 'Pastoral Palimpsest: Writing the Laws of Love in *L'Astrée*', *Renaissance Quarterly* 52, no. 4 (Winter 1993), pp. 1087–117, here p. 1102.

[49] *Astrée* I, p. 631.

[50] D'Urfé's use of "fortune" and "hazard" as alternatives to the divine design that Silvandre wishes for serves to set forth two competing explanations for the events in the novel, all while obscuring his own agency as author. This interpretation runs against that of Jacques Ehrmann, for whom "Fatalité, hasard, fortune sont des données qui paraissent suspectes à force d'être imposées au lecteur. La valeur attribuée à ces concepts est beaucoup trop imprécise, flottante pour qu'on puisse les considérer autrement que comme une sorte de "bain métaphysique" dans lequel les personnages seraient indifféremment plongés." (Fatality, chance, fortune are givens that seem suspect insofar as they are imposed upon the reader. The value attributed to these concepts is far too imprecise and floating for them to be considered as anything other than a "metaphysical bath" in which the characters are arbitrarily plunged.) *Un paradis désespéré*, p. 35.

begin with a hopeful invocation of faith as a rampart against the stormlike disruptions caused by the insecurity that love produces:

> Amour, grand Artisan, a fait un autre Monde:
> La terre, c'est ma foy, qui n'a nul mouvement,
> Et comme l'Univers sur la terre se fonde,
> Ma foy de ce beau Monde est le seur fondement.[51]

> Love, great Artisan, has made another World:
> Earth is my faith, which does not move,
> And since the Universe is grounded on the earth,
> My faith is the sure foundation of this beautiful World.

The thirst of Celadon, Silvandre, and Tircis for a reassuring and smooth link between their troubling passion and the sense and stability of the transcendent is further highlighted, of course, by the disturbances caused by the presence of Hylas. The reader and the Forezian shepherds made his acquaintance in the very first chapter of the novel, when, significantly, he appeared not through his visually accessible physical presence but through his disembodied voice. Hylas is heard before he is seen, and this curious introduction, and contract with Tircis – who is presented to the reader in a tableau lying on the grass and surrounded by two shepherdesses – echoes d'Urfé's own claim in the preface to represent nothing to the eye, but "à l'oüye seulement". From the outset, then, Hylas is designated more as a possible spokesperson for the author than either Silvandre or Celadon, the two characters who are often invoked as such, and his presence in the novel and difference from the other characters is weighted with significance.[52]

---

[51] *Astrée* II, p. 380.

[52] See Eglal Henein, *La Fontaine*, p. 33, where she identifies Silvandre and Celadon as "les deux *alter ego* du romancier." The question of whether Hylas represents a viable philosophical alternative to Silvandre's Neoplatonism or Adamas's proto-Christianity remains open to debate. The introduction to the new Champion edition of the novel's first volume asks if Hylas is the expression "d'un matérialisme hédoniste pleinement réfléchi, constituant une alternative à la philosophie dont nous avons tracé les contours?" (of a fully conscious hedonistic materialism that would constitute an alternative to the philosophy whose contours we have drawn?) before responding "C'est possible, mais à la condition d'observer que le jeu polémique est en l'occurrence très inégal. Si le roman d'Honoré d'Urfé accepte la contradiction, il l'intègre dans un univers de normes et de biens hiérarchisé" (It's possible, but on the condition of observing that the polemical game is actually very unequal. If d'Urfé's novel accepts contradiction, it also integrates it into a universe of hierarchized norms and goods) (pp. 56–7). Similarly, Laurence A. Gregorio notes that "Hylas is never seen by his peers as mounting a real challenge to their status quo." ('Implications of the Love Debate in *L'Astrée*', p. 32).

For if Celadon and Silvandre are forever in search of a "seur fondement," Hylas persistently questions not only whether foundations are necessary, but whether they even exist. His repeated praise of inconstancy, often accompanied by a gentle mocking of those faithful lovers, like Silvandre and Tircis, who seem only to cry and complain, can certainly be read as the self-interested ode to pleasure of an "irrepressible harlequin."[53] Yet in reversing the positive and negative valences surrounding loyalty and *inconstance*, Hylas threatens to turn the world on its head, or, at the very least, to undermine the grounds upon which that world is built. At one point in the novel, Silvandre and Leonide overhear Hylas (whose presence, once again, is manifested through sound rather than sight) singing a *vilanelle* in praise of the movement that characterizes his existence, and whose theme is "La belle qui m'arrestera/ Beaucoup plus d'honneur en aura" (The beauty capable of stopping me/ Will receive great honor). Leonide smiles and remarks to Silvandre that Hylas's honesty is refreshing, insofar as he does not dissimulate his imperfections, but celebrates them in song. Silvandre's response manifests his consciousness of the challenge, the reversal of social order and values, that Hylas represents: "C'est parce ... qu'il ne croit pas que ce soit vice, & qu'il en fait gloire"[54] (It is because he does not believe that it is a vice that he celebrates it).

It is quite tempting to say that Hylas's praise of movement and inconstancy reaches beyond his approach to romantic love and into the realms, so comfortably inhabited by Silvandre, of philosophy and theology. Yet such a statement would mitigate the radicality of the challenge represented by his character, insofar as Hylas places in question the very possibility of a "beyond."[55] Love conveys pleasure; it is not a sign of divine harmony or the noble origins of the human soul. It does not *mean* anything. Accordingly, Hylas argues that those who love the same person even after she has lost her beauty are the ones who should bear the stigma of inconstancy:

> Si aimer le contraire de ce que l'on a aimé est inconstance, & si la laideur est le contraire de la beauté, il n'y a point de doute que celuy conclut fort bien, qui soustient celuy estre inconstant, qui ayant aimé un beau visage, continuë de l'aimer quand il est laid.

---

[53] Gregorio, 'Implications', p. 31.

[54] *Astrée* I, p. 417.

[55] This reading is at odds with that of Louise Horowitz, who notes the importance of Hylas while viewing him as representative of something other than himself, instead of calling into question the very foundations of representation: "[Hylas] is really not a corrective to the code of absolute fidelity, but rather an alternative. Hylas is simply 'other.' As the essence of infidelity, he incarnates other values, other systems, and thereby reflects other textual traditions." *Honoré d'Urfé* (Boston: Twayne Publishers, 1984), p. 85.

> If loving the opposite of what one has loved is inconstancy, and if ugliness is the contrary of beauty, there is no doubt that he who concludes that continuing to love someone who was once beautiful but has become ugly constitutes inconstancy is correct.

Indeed, he continues, "Ceste consideration m'a fait croire, que pour n'estre inconstant, il faut aimer tousjours & en tous lieux la beauté, & que lors qu'elle se separe de quelque subjet, on s'en doit de mesme separer d'amitié, de peur de n'aimer le contraire de ceste beauté"[56] (This consideration made me believe that in order to avoid inconstancy, one must love beauty wherever one finds it, and that once it is separated from its subject, one must separate one's friendship from that person for fear that one might love the contrary of that beauty). As he himself recognizes, this reasoning is precisely the opposite of what the "vulgaire opinion" holds to be true. His unrepentant materialism calls upon those who listen to him to furnish *proof* that physical beauty is merely a signpost to something more significant, rather than something that should be enjoyed for itself. In response to this call for proof, Silvandre can offer only rhetoric, as when he points out to Hylas, using Phillis as an example, that "le corps n'est pas partie, mais instrument de l'aimé"[57] (the body is not a part of, but rather the instrument of the beloved). Hylas's response is predictably jocular, but also significant in light of the idolatry debates over the status to be accorded to the material vehicle of representation, whether statue, painting, relic, or even word: "S'il est vray que le corps ne soit que l'instrument dont se sert Phillis, je vous donne Phillis, & laissez-moy le reste, & nous verrons qui sera plus content de vous ou de moy"[58] (If it is true that the body is only the instrument that Phillis uses, I'll give you Phillis, and you can leave me the rest, and we'll see who of the two of us is happiest). Hylas follows this gleeful rejection of the signified in favor of the deliciousness of the signifier, as it were, by the suggestion that sleep would be an appropriate way to finish the discussion, once again calling attention to the needs of the physical body. Everyone obeys, and retires for the night, yet significantly, and in keeping with his tortuous attempts to reconcile love and religious devotion in his own life, Silvandre, the text notes, "ne peut clorre l'oeil de long temps apres"[59] (could not close his eyes for a long while afterwards).

The stakes of the conflict between Hylas and Silvandre become even clearer later in the ninth book of the second volume. Silvandre is increasingly frustrated with Hylas's embrace of the impermanence that he finds so troubling, as well

---

[56] *Astrée* II, pp. 180–1.
[57] *Astrée* II, p. 341.
[58] *Astrée* II, p. 341.
[59] *Astrée* II, p. 342.

as his persistent questioning of whether the transcendence to which Silvandre repeatedly refers, and upon which he relies, is more than a rhetorical trick along the lines of the ruse performed by Polemas and Climanthe. As Hylas himself proclaims at the outset of the debate that sets him, once again, against Silvandre, "quant à moy je sçay bien que l'experience est plus certaine que les paroles. Or Silvandre n'a que des paroles pour preuver ce qu'il dit, & moy j'ay les effects & l'experience si familiere, que je n'en veux point chercher de plus esloignée qu'en moy-mesme"[60] (as for me I well know that experience is more certain than words. Yet Silvandre only has words to prove what he says, and I have such familiar experience and effects that I don't want to look any farther than myself). Silvandre's irritation with Hylas's insistence on immanence and on proof is rooted in his consciousness that the shepherd's skepticism threatens to bring down the entire structure that links heaven and earth while holding them apart, and that thereby provides a foundation for his own identity and existence. While the heated debate between the two characters that follows Leonide's judgment of the conflict between Doris, Palemon, and Adraste (a judgment that results in Adraste's descent into madness, and with which Hylas disagrees) begins as, once again, a conflict over the true nature of love, it quickly takes on theological significance, at least for Silvandre. Buffeted by Hylas's increasingly impertinent challenges and provocations regarding desire, possession, and love, Silvandre is moved to point out that his opinions are inconsistent with the love of God; in other words, Hylas's pronouncements are those of an atheist:

> Ne dis donc plus Hylas, que mon amour estant un desir ne peut estre parfait sans la possession, & ne m'oppose plus pour m'accuser d'arrogance qu'il faut qu'il y ayt de la proportion entre Diane et moy, car si tu nies que l'homme doive aymer Dieu, je t'accorderay ce que tu dis; mais si tu avoues que c'est un des premiers commandemens qu'il nous faict, je te demanderay Berger, quelle plus grande disproportion y a-t'il entre Diane & moy, que celle qui est entre le grand Thautates, & Hylas?[61]

> Do not say any longer, Hylas, that my love, being a desire, cannot be perfect without possession, and do not oppose me any longer to accuse me of arrogance that there should be a proportion between Diane and myself, for if you deny that man must love God, I will accord you that, but if you admit that it is one of the first commandments that he gave, I ask you, Shepherd, what greater disproportion is there between myself and Diane than that which is between the great Thautates and Hylas?

[60] *Astrée* II, pp. 481–2.
[61] *Astrée* II, p. 486.

Hylas responds to this challenge to his religious beliefs by ignoring it, focusing instead, in keeping with his previous statement, on his personal experience. Silvandre responds in turn by defending his statement that one can love only what one knows, and moves on to note that "l'une des premieres Ordonnances d'Amour c'est QUE L'AMANT CROYE TOUTES CHOSES TRES PARFAITES EN LA PERSONNE AIMÉE"[62] (one of the first commandments in love is that THE LOVER BELIEVE THAT ALL THINGS IN THE PERSON LOVED ARE PERFECT). From here, it is a short step to the conclusion that those who love, and love well, not only receive an access to the transcendent that is denied to others, but are themselves transformed into godlike creatures who are exempted from the vicissitudes of existence and the changing nature of the flesh:

> Et contente-toy pour ce coup de sçavoir que le bien dont Amour recompense les fideles amants, est celuy-là mesme qu'il peut donner aux Dieux, & à ces hommes qui s'eslevant par dessus la nature des hommes, se rendent presque Dieux. Car les autres plaisirs dont tu fais tant de compte, ne sont que ceux qu'un amour bastard donne aux animaux sans raison, & à ces hommes qui s'abbaissant par dessous la nature des hommes, se rendent presque animaux privez de raison.[63]

> And content yourself with knowing, for now, that the good with which love recompenses faithful lovers is the same that it gives to the gods, and to those men who raise themselves above human nature, making themselves nearly godlike. For those other pleasures which you esteem so much are only those of a bastard love that is given to animals deprived of reason, and to those men who lower themselves beneath human nature, making themselves similar to dumb beasts.

Silvandre's statement reflects his inability to accept the human condition on its own terms. It must be an instrument, a signifier rather than a signified, that either pulls one upwards, towards the divine, or downwards towards an animality that he qualifies, in the exclamation that follows, as monstrous: "Et c'est en ce monstre, ô Hylas, que tu degeneres, quand tu aimes autrement que tu ne dois"[64] (And it is into this monster, o Hylas, that you degenerate, when you love in a way that you should not). On the contrary, Silvandre notes, his own love is "quelque chose de si parfaict que rien n'y peut estre adjousté ni

---

[62] *Astrée* II, p. 488.
[63] *Astrée* II, p. 489.
[64] *Astrée* II, p. 489.

diminué sans faire offence à la raison"[65] (something so perfect that nothing can be added or taken away from it without offending reason).

This last proclamation, once again based less on anything that can be proven through experience than on the stigmatization of Hylas's approach to life and love, causes Hylas to lose patience, and he cuts Silvandre off: "Jusques à quand en fin Silvandre abuseras-tu de la patience de ceux qui t'escoutent? Jusques à quand nous rempliras-tu les aureilles de tes vanitez & de tes imaginations? Et jusques à quand esperes tu que je puisse souffrir l'impertinence de tes paroles?"[66] (Until when, Silvandre, will you abuse the patience of those who listen to you? Until when will you fill our ears with your vanities and imaginations? And until when do you hope that I can suffer the impertinence of your words?) The assembled troop of shepherds, taken aback at the violence of Hylas's "voix," considers him for a moment before dissolving into laughter, and Leonide puts an end to the conversation, but not before Hylas, still "à moitié en colere" (half angry), marks his profound opposition to the perfection claimed and pursued by Silvandre by reminding her that "il faut comment que ce soit que nous tenions tousjours quelque chose de l'imperfection de nostre nature"[67] (we must somehow hold something of the imperfection of our nature).

The radically different views of Silvandre and Hylas serve as endpoints of a spectrum that is not just philosophical, but also theological. Silvandre professes, at length, a belief in divine providence that is necessary to give shape to the chaos that threatens human attempts to construct meaning and identity. Hylas, on the other hand, embraces impermanence, contenting himself with the imperfect, embodied nature of existence and seeing no reason why humans should exempt themselves from the mutability that characterizes the rest of creation. On the contrary; they should learn, like him, to take pleasure in it. Both characters' positions are extreme, and unlikely to be adopted wholesale by the others. Silvandre's faith in the divine, and his conviction that love is part of the divine plan, is too closely linked to the peculiarities of his own life and education to be a viable model for anyone other than himself; Hylas's materialist skepticism, while effective at undermining Silvandre's claims to godlike perfection, is too unstable to form a ground for anything other than laughter. Yet both positions share an important characteristic: they rule out the possibility of idolatry. For Silvandre, as we have seen, love and the beloved are purely instrumental, a conduit towards the perfect and superior reality of the divine. While he recognizes that idolatry might be a danger for others, as long as he places his

---

[65] *Astrée* II, p. 490.
[66] *Astrée* II, p. 490.
[67] *Astrée* II, p. 490.

passion in service of a higher good, or being, he is safe from such charges; as he declares to Phillis in the third volume,

> Et quand vous me dites que cette Diane est telle que les yeux ne doivent la regarder que pour l'*idolatrer*, pourquoy ne dites-vous *adorer*? puis que s'il y a quelque chose en terre qui pour ses perfections merite les autels et les sacrifices, je croy que c'est cette Diane que je n'idolatre pas comme vous, mais que j'adore pour la vraye Diane en terre, qui esclaire dans la ciel, et qui commande dans les enfers.[68]

> And when you tell me that this Diane is such that eyes cannot look at her without *idolizing* her, why do you not say *adoring*? since if there is something on earth whose perfections deserve altars and sacrifices, I believe that it is this Diane which I do not idolize like you, but whom I adore as the true Diane on earth, who shines in the sky and who commands in the hells.

On the contrary, for Hylas, people and objects are simply what they are, and should be appreciated as such. They are neither signposts towards divine perfection nor warnings of a slippage towards animality. Loving creatures for their own sake does not pose any particular difficulty. Towards the end of the second volume, Hylas begins flirting with Alexis, who is actually Celadon disguised as a female druid. Silvandre reproaches him in terms that mark his own consciousness that attention paid to the instruments of the divine is not just inappropriate, but dangerous: "Mais, Hylas, comment ne craignez-vous l'ire de Teutates, ayant la hardiesse de vous addresser à une personne qui luy est consacrée?" (But Hylas, how do you not fear the rage of Teutates, daring to address yourself to a person who is consecrated to him?) Hylas's response demonstrates a fundamentally different understanding of the relationship between Creator and creature: "Ignorant, respondit Hylas, les Dieux ne nous deffendent pas de les aymer eux-mesmes, et comment seroient-ils courroussez si nous aymons ce qui est à eux?" (Ignorant, Hylas responded, the gods do not forbid us from loving them, so how would they be angry if we love what is theirs?)[69]

Idolatry and the Temple de l'Amitié

The differing approaches of Silvandre and Hylas not only to love, but to meaning and the appropriate relationship between the divine and the human, are nowhere as clearly on display as during the shepherds' and shepherdesses'

---

[68] *Astrée* III, p. 507.
[69] *Astrée* II, p. 573.

visit to the Temple de l'Amitié, which takes place in the second volume's fifth book. The friends stumble upon the curious structure while following Silvandre along a narrow path through the woods. The trees that form the temple block the way; Silvandre, the narrator notes, "estoit fasché d'avoir perdu le chemin"[70] (was annoyed to have lost the way). Upon closer examination, Silvandre discovers that the trees are not a natural occurrence, but constitute a temple erected by someone who has also placed verses at the entrance which warn, "Loin, bien loin, profanes esprits:/ Qui n'est d'un sainct Amour espris,/ En ce lieu sainct ne fasse entrée:/ Voicy le bois où chaque jour,/ Un coeur qui ne vit que d'Amour/ Adore la déesse Astrée"[71] (Far, far away, profane souls/ who are not possessed by a saintly love/ In this holy place do not enter:/ Here is the forest where every day/ A heart that only lives for love/ Adores the goddess Astrée).

The friends, astonished, enter the temple, with the exception of Hylas, who stays behind. His reasons for doing so underscore both his humility and his skepticism that divine intention can ever be truly understood. Responding to Phillis's taunt that he is afraid that he does not have enough love to enter the temple, he notes, "Quand à moy, j'en ay bien tres-grande quantité à ma façon, mais que sçai je si elle est comme l'entend celui qui a escrit ces vers? J'ay tousjours oüy dire qu'il ne se faut point joüer avec les Dieux"[72] (As for me, I have many loves in my fashion, but how should I know if they are what the person who wrote these lines meant? I have always heard that one should not trifle with the gods). This skepticism places him, once again, at odds with Silvandre, who, we may recall, is given to the conviction that not only is divine will accessible but, on occasion, it manifests itself through him. Indeed, Silvandre's response to the verses is to kneel to the earth and lift his eyes to the sky, exclaiming,

> O grande Deité! qui es adorée en ce lieu, voicy j'entre en ton sainct Boccage, tres-asseuré que je ne contreviens point à ta volonté, sçachant que mon Amour est si sainct et si pur que tu auras agreable de recevoir les voeux & supplications d'une ame qui aime si bien que la mienne.[73]

> O great Divinity! who is adored in this place, here I am entering in your holy glade, quite sure that I do not violate your will, knowing that my love is so holy and so pure that you will gladly receive the vows and supplications of a soul that loves so well as mine.

---

[70] *Astrée* II, p. 236.
[71] *Astrée* II, p. 237.
[72] *Astrée* II, p. 238.
[73] *Astrée* II, pp. 238–9.

Hylas issues yet another challenge to Silvandre's hyperbolic piety by altering the Twelve Tables of the Laws of Love, then offering to follow them if Silvandre promises to do the same.[74] Silvandre, of course, promises, but is taken aback when the laws advocate inconstancy and pleasure rather than loyalty and submission. Hylas's ruse is eventually discovered by Diane, who notices that the letters on the tablets have been altered, and Hylas subsequently restores the original text – not by erasing his alterations, but by crossing them out and writing the initial words in the margins, a process that permanently alters the tablets by monumentalizing their instability. As Twyla Meding notes, "Hylas challenges the status of inscribed text as authoritative transmission of accepted rules: his facile gesture of palimpsest converts the Laws' generalized dictates into a mere 'cas particulier de la représentation,' dismantling their anonymous, authoritative foundation as 'anciens statuts d'amour'."[75]

And yet the Laws are not completely anonymous. Before presenting his alterations to the group, Hylas performs a ceremony that has escaped the attention of commentators, despite the prominence of the episode of alteration in *Astrée* scholarship.[76] As Phillis, having performed a "profonde reverence," hands him the altered tablets, Hylas removes his hat, kneels to the ground, and proclaims,

> Je reçois ces sacrées ordonnances, comme venant d'un Dieu, & aportées par ma Déesse, protestant de nouveau, & jurant aux grands Dieux devant ce boccage sacré, & prenant ceste trouppe pour tesmoin, que toute ma vie je les observeray aussi religieusement que si Hesus, Teutates, Taramis Dieu me les avoient données visiblement.[77]

> I receive these holy orders as coming from a God and brought by my Goddess, protesting anew, and swearing to the great Gods in front of this holy glade, and taking this troop as my witness, that all of my life I will observe them as religiously as if Hesus, Teutates, Taramis God had visibly given them to me.

---

[74] For a beautiful reading of this scene and its implications, see Twyla Meding's 'Pastoral Palimpsest', especially pp. 1101–8.

[75] 'Pastoral Palimpsest', pp. 1106–7.

[76] Leaving out this ceremony allows, as we have seen, Meding to qualify the Laws as "anonymous"; it also leads Kathleen Wine to characterize Hylas's transgression of altering the tablets as "a sideshow that allows Celadon's to pass unnoticed." *Forgotten Virgo: Humanism and Absolutism in Honoré d'Urfé's* L'Astrée (Genève: Libraire Droz, 2000), p. 162. Similarly, Horowitz's overlooking of the ceremony leads her to conclude that "both sets of laws are firmly literary" (p. 95).

[77] *Astrée* II, p. 270.

Hylas's carefully placed qualifiers – a "comme" and a "si" – ensure that his statement stops just short of outright blasphemy. Yet once again, the Ten Commandments continue to haunt the text, as Hylas compares himself to Moses by invoking a visible transmission of the tablets from a god to himself. More significantly, however, Hylas's suggestion that the tablets are divinely authored just after he himself has altered them mocks Silvandre's propensity to attribute events to a providential divinity all while calling to mind the ruse of Polemas and Climanthe. By changing the tablets, Hylas strikes at the very foundation of authority and belief, raising the possibility that all communication between the divine and the human is a fiction. The radical implications of Hylas's false piety are underlined by the former *ligueur* d'Urfé by the phrase "protestant de nouveau"; while it ostensibly describes Hylas's discursive intervention, this is the first time that the word "protestant" is used in the work, and the only time that it is combined with the "de nouveau" evoking not merely novelty, but the illegitimacy of human invention as opposed to divine creation.

Hylas's quasi-blasphemous questioning of the authenticity of artifacts – like the tablets – purported to issue from the divine is particularly pertinent in the Temple de l'Amitié. The characters, like the reader, do not know the circumstances of the temple's construction; they do know, from their examination of the poems and paintings that decorate it, that this place, repeatedly qualified as "sainct," is devoted to the goddess Astrée, even though the portrait on the altar clearly depicts a shepherdess who is not, in fact, a deity. The Temple is, quite simply, a monument to idolatry. It displays, repeatedly and in various forms, precisely the problematic idealization that led to Celadon's attempted suicide. A poem that Astrée discovers on the altar after viewing her own portrait is entitled "Privé de mon vray bien, ce bien faux me soulage," whose last verse, referring to the "beaux traits" of the beloved, declares "Je les adore donc, non pas comme un' image,/ Mais comme Dieux tres-grands,/ Car par effet j'apprends/ Que privé du vray bien ce bien faux me soulage"[78] (I adore them then, not as an image,/ But as very great Gods/ For from their effect I learn/ That deprived of the true good, this false good calms me). Ostensibly a sweet, if slightly hyperbolic, love poem, this text in fact openly flaunts the prohibition of idolatry, first by defiantly noting that the "bien faux" comforts the poet deprived of the "vray bien," and then by proclaiming adoration of aspects of the representation *not* as parts of an image signifying something beyond itself, but as themselves "Dieux tres-grands." Likewise, the poem unrolled by Diane notes of the beloved eyes that not only do they have the power to confer life or death, but they are, themselves, gods by way

---

[78] *Astrée* II, p. 253.

of a solar metaphor: "Et ces soleils aussi, ne sont-ce pas des Dieux?/ Les aimer comme humains, c'est donc erreur extrême ..."[79] (And these suns, are they not gods? To love them as human is thus an extreme error). In the poem that Phillis unrolls, the sin of idolatry is no longer implicit, but rather proudly declared: "Qui ne l'admireroit! & qui n'aimeroit mieux,/ Errer en l'adorant plein d'Amour et de crainte:/ Et rendre courroucez contre soy tous les Dieux,/ Que n'idolatrer point une si belle Sainte?"[80] (Who would not admire her! and who would not prefer/ Erring by adoring her full of love and fear/ and making the gods angry/ than to not idolize such a beautiful saint?) Although the verses that follow immediately back off of this declaration, reminding the reader and the poet that "en effet elle est peinte"[81] (in fact, she is a painted image), the specter of unapologetic adoration of the beloved not, as Silvandre would have it, as a vehicle that moves the lover away from self-regard and towards the divine, but on her own extremely seductive terms, has been released. Indeed, the last text that the visitors encounter before leaving the temple and discovering the tablets altered by Hylas is an "oraison" dedicated to Astrée, who is characterized and addressed as a "grande et toute-puissante Déesse"[82] (a great and all-powerful goddess).

The flagrant idolatry on exhibit in the Temple is, perhaps, precisely what provokes Hylas's turn, "protestant de nouveau," towards heresy and even blasphemy. Yet it appears even more astonishing once the story of the Temple's origin and construction is recounted in the second volume's eighth book, three books after it is first discovered and described. Here, we learn that Adamas devised the Temple precisely as a way for Celadon to *escape* the threat of idolatry by placing his love for Astrée in its proper perspective. Adamas's lessons in religious orthodoxy begin immediately after he first sees the lovelorn shepherd, who has been foraging for food and sleeping on moss, and who is consequently wasting away. Alarmed, Adamas reminds Celadon that his life is not his to dispose of; rather, it belongs to Taramis, the god who endowed humanity with reason:

> Tout ce qui est sous l'estenduë du Ciel est à luy, & nous n'en sommes que les gardiens ... Encores qu'il nous ait remis sous nostre volonté, si ne sommes nous pas nostres, & faut que nous attendions un rude chastiment, si nous avons disposé de nous mesmes autrement que nous n'avons deu.[83]

---

[79] *Astrée* II, p. 254.
[80] *Astrée* II, p. 255.
[81] *Astrée* II, p. 256.
[82] *Astrée* II, p. 262.
[83] *Astrée* II, p. 402.

Everything that is under the Heavens belongs to him, and we are only the guardians of it ... Even though he placed the world under our will, we do not belong to ourselves, and must expect to be severely punished if we spend our time on what we are not supposed to.

Celadon's response notes with sadness that all traces of reason that Taramis may have placed in him have been obliterated by love: "l'usage de la parole m'est permis pour respondre au grand Dieu Taramis & à tout ce que vous m'opposez, il suffit que je vous die seulement ce mot, J'AYME"[84] (the use of language is allowed to me to respond to the great god Taramis and everything that you have said against me; it is enough for me to say to you this word alone: I LOVE). As a result, Celadon himself is no longer a creation of the gods, son of Alcippe and Amarillis and friend of Adamas, "mais seulement une vaine idole que le Ciel conserve encores parmy ces bois pour marque que Celadon sceut aymer"[85] (but only a vain idol that the heavens keep in these woods to mark the fact that Celadon knew how to love). Before the Temple is constructed, then, romantic love and the realm of the divine are set in opposition to one another, in no small part because Adamas associates the gods not with love, but with reason.[86] Celadon's survival depends upon bringing romantic love and theology in line with one another; otherwise, Celadon, mistaking his beloved for a goddess and thereby losing his connection with Taramis, to whom he truly belongs, will continue to waste away.

Yet although Celadon's life is certainly important, and indeed, it is central to the novel, what is ultimately at stake is much larger. Celadon's situation has, as he and Adamas recognize, forced a confrontation between the God of reason (and creation) and the God of love, between Christianity and paganism. In the terms set forth by Celadon and Adamas at the outset of this book, the Neoplatonist solution, offered by a Silvandre who is terrified of losing his way, is unavailable. Celadon is almost literally consumed with desire for his deified beloved, and Adamas, in a reflection of the controversies surrounding idolatry that dominated the years of the novel's composition, must find a way to put this enthrallment to a higher use, to convince Celadon that the sublimely beautiful Astrée should not be adored on her own terms, but as an instrument of devotion to something higher.

Adamas therefore allows Celadon to set aside part of the sacred grove to Astrée, but he frames this decision in terms of the accommodation afforded

---

[84] *Astrée* II, p. 403.
[85] *Astrée* II, p. 403.
[86] Laurence A. Gregorio provides an excellent analysis of the difference between the theories of love of Silvandre and Adamas, including Adamas's association of God and reason, in his 'Implications of the Love Debate', especially pp. 34–6.

the pagan Romans, who were allowed to worship their gods alongside the God of the druids. He also redefines Astrée as a way of gently nudging Celadon out of melancholia and towards a more recognizable faith. Astrée will no longer be considered, heretically and problematically, as a goddess in her own right, but rather as the creation of Taramis. Attention paid to her, like that paid to a religious image, will therefore flow forth to her divine origin and prototype. As Adamas explains,

> & parce que la coustume est passée en fin en loy, il vous sera permis, Celadon, de dedier une partie de ce Boccage, non pas comme à une premiere divinité, mais comme à un tres parfait ouvrage de ceste divinité, à vostre belle Astrée; ce que nostre Dieu ne trouvera point plus mauvais que les Temples dediez par ces estrangers à la Déesse Fortune, à la Déesse Maladie, ou à la Déesse Crainte: principalement si vostre ouvrage luy estant directement consacré, vous n'adorez pas sur leurs Gazons ceste Déesse Astrée, mais luy en eslevant d'autres à costé de leurs chesnes, vous adressez vos voeux à ceste belle, comme à l'oeuvre le plus parfait qui soit sorty de ses mains.[87]

> and because custom finally became law, you will be allowed, Celadon, to dedicate a part of this grove not to a first divinity, but to the perfect work of that divinity, to your beautiful Astrée; and our God will not object to this any more than he does to temples dedicated by these foreigners to the goddess Fortune, the goddess Illness, or the goddess Fear: primarily since if your work was directly consecrated to him, you would not adore on these lawns this goddess Astrée, but by erecting others next to their oaks, you address your vows to this beauty, as the most perfect work that has ever emerged from his hands.

Adamas's explanation of why an altar dedicated to Astrée would not diminish the honor paid to God but would, in fact, augment it would have been completely familiar to the seventeenth-century reader. Like the Catholic defenders of images in worship, Adamas reminds Celadon of God's identity as author and creator of the universe, and in so doing relocates agency from the created world, where Celadon had mistakenly placed it, to the divine. Celadon's confusion over the proper identity and role of God stems in part from his failure to understand monotheism; after all, he has no problem identifying Astrée as a goddess. Adamas's response to Celadon's confusion – when the druid invokes Teutates, Hesus, Belenus, and Taramis but says "notre Dieu," Celadon exclaims, "Comment, mon pere, vous en nommez quatre, &

---

[87] *Astrée* II, p. 409.

vous ne dites que nostre Dieu? Il faudroit dire nos Dieux"[88] (How is it, father, that you name four, but only say our God? you should say our gods) – is a direct echo of the fourth-century response, articulated at the first Council of Nicaea, to the Arian objection that worship of the Father, Son, and Holy Spirit represents a drift back to polytheism. Like those assembled at Nicaea a century earlier, Adamas struggles to articulate a relationship that, as he himself recognizes, "n'est pas le moindre de nos misteres"[89] (is not the least of our mysteries). Yet Adamas is a druid, not a Catholic, and as such he is spared from having to formulate the complicated notion of *homoousios*, which was used at Nicaea to explain that Christ, although the son of God, was formed from the same substance, and was therefore not a God in his own right. For Adamas, the profusion of divine names stems instead from "l'ignorance du peuple grossier"[90] (the ignorance of the vulgar populace), which led them to domesticate the supreme goodness and omnipotence of the one God by giving different aspects of it different names, which were eventually themselves thought of as gods.

The conversation does not stop there, however; Celadon goes on to ask Adamas why, if there is only one God, Tautates, does one see temples dedicated to others? Adamas tells him that this practice, too, represents a drift away from the original purity of the Druidic religion, which allowed neither manmade temples nor images:

> par nos loix il nous est deffendu de faire image de Dieu, parce que l'image n'estant que la representation de quelque chose, & estant necessaire qu'il y ayt quelque proportion, entre la chose representée & celle qui represente, nostre grand Dryus ne jugeant pas qu'il y eust rien entre les hommes qui en peust avoir avec Dieu nous deffendit tres expressément d'en faire, non plus que des Temples, luy semblant que c'estoit une grande ignorance de penser de pouvoir enclorre l'immense deïté dans des murailles, & une tres-grande outre cuidance de luy pouvoir faire une maison digne d'elle.[91]

> in our laws it is forbidden to make an image of God, since images are only the representation of something, and since it is necessary that there be some proportion between the thing represented and what represents it, our great Dryus judging that there is nothing among men that can be proportionate with God forbade us expressly from making any, including temples, since it seemed to him that it was great ignorance to think that one could enclose the

---

[88] *Astrée* II, p. 410.
[89] *Astrée* II, p. 410.
[90] *Astrée* II, p. 414.
[91] *Astrée* II, pp. 418–19.

immense deity within walls, and a great recklessness to make him a house worthy of him.

While the druid's explanation of monotheism recalls the Catholic position first articulated at Nicaea, his explanation of the aniconism of the Gauls' religion before the advent of the idolatrous Romans echoes the history expounded by Reformers like Calvin, who viewed images as an illegitimate, late addition to Christianity that compromised the immense distance between humanity and the divine.

On the question of images, therefore, the druid Adamas achieves a compromise between what would become the intractable, irreconcilable Catholic and Protestant positions in d'Urfé's France. He is able to achieve this in part because, as a druid, he remains technically outside of Christianity. But he also advocates an accomodation and a syncretism that ensures the peaceful coexistence of Romans and Gauls. When Celadon asks Adamas what he should do when he enters temples in which there are statues devoted to Jupiter, Mars, Pallas, and Venus, Adamas does not advise him to destroy the images or to refuse to enter the temples. Rather, he should simply view these images as symbols of the various attributes of the single God Teutates, and pay respect to them accordingly. Once again, a practice of worship that seemed to threaten the true religion is transformed into a means of honoring it even more: "Par ce moyen les adorant comme je dis, vous refererez tout à nostre grand Teutates ..."[92] (By these means, adoring them as I say, you will refer everything to our great Teutates).

However, there is one major problem with the utopic irenism advocated and practiced by Adamas: it doesn't work. As we have already seen, the poems that Celadon places in the Temple are starkly and unapologetically idolatrous.[93] Worse yet, perhaps, is the fact that none of the shepherds and shepherdesses who read them seems to find them problematic. Adamas himself repeatedly recognizes that the theology he espouses is mysterious and ultimately out of reach; these abstractions are easily, and almost immediately, eclipsed by the physicality of Astrée's beauty and the passion of romantic love. Indeed, one night Celadon happens upon ("de fortune") Astrée sleeping, with the rest of the shepherds and shepherdesses, near the temple. He contemplates "la blancheur

---

[92] *Astrée* II, p. 423.

[93] Kathleen Wine notes the curious disjuncture between Celadon's poetry and Adamas's lessons: "Each of the three poems, playing on the distinction between Astrée and her portrait, affirms Celadon's obdurate idolatry in ways that seem designed to reverse the druid's teachings." *Forgotten Virgo*, p. 181. Wine also points to the source of this backsliding in Adamas's accommodation of Celadon's passion: "pedagogical devices may end up transforming the discourse of the pedagogues" (p. 183).

de sa gorge," her hair, her arm: "O quelle veuë fut celle-cy pour Celadon!"[94] (the whiteness of her breast/ O what a sight this was for Celadon!) At first unsure how to proceed, Celadon decides to stay and watch her sleep, and his decision is nominally cloaked in religious legitimacy, insofar as he professes, at least initially, to worship Love through Astrée, rather than Astrée herself: "Prenons donc Amour pour guide, & sous sa conduitte, allons le adorer en elle, comme au lieu où il est en sa plus grande gloire"[95] (Take love as a guide, and under her guidance, adore her in it, as the place where it is in its greatest glory). Careful attention to Celadon's prayer, however, reveals that Adamas's attempt at religious education has been largely unsuccessful. Celadon identifies Love not as the origin or creator of Astrée, but as residing in her. As place, rather than instrument, Astrée is vulnerable, once again, to becoming the object of idolatrous worship. As Celadon composes a prayer that he addresses to the sleeping shepherdess on his knees and, so as not to wake her, in a low voice, this is, in fact, what occurs. The prayer begins, "Grande et puissante Déesse, puis que les Dieux ne font pas mieux paroistre leur divinité en punissant qu'en pardonnant, voicy je me jette à genoux"[96] (Great and powerful goddess, since the gods best make their divinity appear in punishing rather than in pardoning, here I throw myself on my knees). Any notion of Astrée as an exemplar of the glory of the one God, creator of the universe, is completely lost; Celadon's passion is as physically grounded and all-consuming as ever.

The experiment of the Temple has failed. Configuring romantic love so that it leads to recognition and worship of the divine runs the risk of an almost inevitable fall into idolatry, which is not felt to be an unpardonable sin, but rather a delicious pleasure. In the contest between the proto-Christian creator Teutates and the pseudo-Lucretian god of Love, Love wins. Yet d'Urfé does not let matters rest there. If it is impossible to work from the material delights of the world to the abstract sublimity of the Creator, perhaps it is possible to infuse romantic love with religious legitimacy by working from the other direction, from, as it were, the top down. D'Urfé finds an ingenious way to conduct this experiment: he disguises Celadon as the daughter of Adamas.

Alexis and the Reality of the Divine

Recent scholarship, informed by excellent critical work on the fluidity of gender identity, has made much of Celadon's transformation into the female Alexis, and justifiably so. Celadon's adopted gender allows him to enjoy an unprecedented level of intimacy with Astrée all while raising questions about

[94] *Astrée* II, p. 427.
[95] *Astrée* II, pp. 428–9.
[96] *Astrée* II, p. 429.

his "true" identity. But what has gone relatively unnoticed is the religious aspect of Celadon's transformation. As Alexis, he is not only a woman; he is also a druidess-in-training, someone who has ostensibly devoted her life to the service of God. The transformation of Celadon into the druidess Alexis is initiated by Adamas, who is responding to the impasse in which Celadon finds himself, having promised Astrée to never show his face to her again. As Adamas notes, it is a promise whose fulfillment is impossible to verify; as long as Celadon hides himself from Astrée, she has no idea that he is alive, and, therefore, that he is obeying his promise. Communication between the goddess and her worshipper has been completely cut off, and the religion of love has become a deathlike stasis.

Faced with this conundrum, Adamas recognizes that "violents remedes" are useless, and even counter-productive. He therefore tries not to eliminate the dangerous energies that traverse the novel, but to redirect them. First, in an echo of Astrée's ill-fated request, he makes Celadon promise to do something for him: "vous ne me devez point refuser, puis que c'est pour mon contentement"[97] (you should not refuse me, since it is for my happiness). He then proceeds to explain that he has a daughter whose absence pains him. In terms that echo the origin of idolatry as recounted in the Book of Wisdom, he identifies Celadon as the image of his absent daughter, and admits that the affection that he has for Alexis has been transferred, in part, to the young shepherd:

> il faut que je confesse que mon amitié s'augmenta beaucoup par la veuë que j'eus de vostre visage: car d'abord il me sembla de voir ma chere fille, tant vous avez de l'air l'un de l'autre. Cela est cause que je vous conjure par tout ce qui a plus de puissance sur vous, d'avoir agreable que je vienne quelquefois interrompre vostre solitude pour me donner cette satisfaction de voir en vostre visage un pourtraict vivant de ce que j'ayme le plus au monde.[98]

> I must confess that my friendship became even greater when I saw your face: for I at first seemed to see my dear daughter, since you resemble each other so much. This is why I beg you by everything that has power over you, to agree that I come from time to time to interrupt your solitude to give myself the satisfaction of seeing in your face the living portrait of that which I love the most in the world.

Kathleen Wine has noted that the admiration that Adamas shows at the end of the chapter towards Celadon's portrait of Astrée marks his own vulnerability

---

[97] *Astrée* II, p. 405.
[98] *Astrée* II, p. 405.

to the sin that his teachings are meant to fend off: "It is not the disciple who assimilates the teachings of the master, but the master who falls into the profane errors of his pupil."[99] But the passage above, where Adamas designates Celadon as the living portrait of what he loves most in the world, demonstrates that Adamas's affection for his daughter, like that of Tircis for Cleon or of the biblical father for his dead son, creates a desire for presence that is the very opposite of the hopeless absence that governs the relations, pre-Alexis, between Celadon and Astrée.

In making the living Celadon the focus of this desire, however, d'Urfé has found a way to point out the dangers of the kinds of representation that give rise to idolatry in a particularly ingenious and poignant way. Emphasis on the differences between Celadon and Alexis would shatter the pleasant illusion of a living link between father and daughter all while creating space for a reconciliation between Celadon (as Celadon) and Astrée. Yet completely subsuming Celadon under the appearance and name of Alexis, as happens in the text, renders the shepherd invisible, and thereby precludes any possible fulfillment of material desire or romantic love. In short, Celadon's situation from this point forward poses the question of what it would feel like to *be* a religious painting or relic. Caught between visibility and invisibility, Celadon-Alexis is at once an idol whose materiality constantly threatens to subvert his promise to the divine Astrée and a figuration of the faraway druidess whose life is dedicated to the chaste pursuit of divine transcendence. The impossibility of this position is not minimized, but rather emphasized, and exploited for maximum dramatic effect. The third volume of the novel dawns, literally, with Celadon greeting the first rays of the day and putting on his new clothes: "en prenant les habits d'Alexis, elle laissa le nom de Celadon pour celuy de la fille d'Adamas"[100] (by taking the clothes of Alexis, she left the name of Celadon for that of the daughter of Adamas). The transformation, however, can never be complete, despite the shift to the feminine pronoun: "Mais le coeur de Celadon, qui sous ces habits empruntez, ne laissoit de luy demeurer dans l'estomach, n'eust jamais consenty à ce change, non pas mesme quand la mort l'eust voulu ravir du lieu où il estoit"[101] (But the heart of Celadon, under these borrowed clothes, still stayed in his stomach, and would never have consented to this change, not even if death had wanted to take him away from the place where he was).

The repercussions and implications of Celadon's appearance as Alexis have been the subject of impressive and subtle scholarly commentary, much of which seizes upon the theme of disguise as a useful lens through which to

---

[99] *Forgotten Virgo*, p. 183.
[100] *Astrée* III, p. 14.
[101] *Astrée* III, p. 14.

view the novel as a whole. Largely escaping critical attention, however, has been the way in which the transformation from shepherd to druidess marks a significant shift in the novel's theological grounding. As Alexis, Celadon is asked to embody instrumentality and service. If Celadon's romantic passion for Astrée endangered his ties to his parents and his religion, Alexis's status as "fille d'Adamas" and as a chaste potential druidess denotes a self-effacement that precludes the very possibility of romantic entanglement. Yet this self-effacement is possible only if the reality and identity of the gods, and their role in the novel's universe, have been secured. This was certainly not the case in the novel's first two volumes, where signs of divine intervention in the affairs of humans and even druids could almost invariably be viewed as compensatory fictions crafted in response to earthly insecurities and passions. Even Adamas's attempt to establish religious orthodoxy to counter the devastating impact of Celadon's passion is, as we have seen, surprisingly fragile and short lived.

All of this changes in the third volume, the first volume published under Louis XIII, in 1619. D'Urfé's written dedication calls attention to the king's name, shared by his beatified thirteenth-century ancestor: "celuy (le nom) de Louys ne pouvant estre escrit, que l'on n'y lise aussi cette sacrée parole de Louys"[102] (the name of Louis cannot be written without also reading in it the sacred word of Louis). This overlay of names establishes a framework of precedent and legitimacy that ensures the return of peace and justice, and that the king's assassinated father, the former Protestant Henri le Grand, lacked. The dedication to Henri IV that opens the 1612 edition of the novel's first volume tellingly presents the king as the true author of *L'Astrée*. Certainly, d'Urfé ascribes this authorship to the peace which the monarch has brought to the kingdom and without which the work would have been impossible, but the author's longtime sympathy to the Catholic Ligue and the common tactic of delegitimizing the Reformers by ascribing to them an unseemly thirst for authorship serve to mitigate the novelist's ostensible praise. Indeed, d'Urfé slyly notes that the title of "Sire," signifying "Dieu," that is accorded to Henri is due not to any special favor accorded by the Christian God, but rather to the French adoption of the practices of the pagan Persians and Ancients. God's benevolence towards the French king is expressed through a subjunctive that conveys that it is not yet proven, but something to be wished for: "Et Dieu vous remplisse d'autant de contentements & de gloires, que par vostre bonté vous obligez les peuples qui sont à vous, de vous benir, aimer, & servir"[103] (And may God fill you with as many contentments and glories

---

[102] *Astrée* III, p. 3.
[103] *Astrée* I, p. 107.

than by your goodness you oblige the people who are yours to bless you, love you, and serve you). By contrast, the dedication to Louis XIII, fortified by the symmetry established by the king's name, presents the monarch not as an author but as the instrument of a God "qui a tousjours maintenu la couronne que vous portez avec de particuliers soins"[104] (who has always maintained the crown which you wear with his explicit care). Consequently, the novel itself no longer appears as a created work whose legitimacy remains to be established, but as one of the very supports of the king's glory; as d'Urfé notes, Dieu "augmentera le nombre de ses graces en V. M., tant que ceste Astrée sera en vostre ame et en vos desseins, et tant que l'espée que vous aurez au costé ne sera employée que pour la maintenir, on ne tranchera que par ses mains"[105] (will augment the number of his graces in Your Majesty as long as this Astrée will be in your soul and your intentions, and as long as the sword which you wear will only be used to maintain her, one will only slice with her hands). Braced by the force of precedent and example, we have passed from the uncertainty of the subjunctive to the firmness of the future.

This shift in tone inaugurates a broader shift in the novel that has not escaped the critical attention of *Astrée* scholars. Eglal Henein notes that "c'est dans la troisième partie seulement, en 1619, que le culte forézien ressemble de près au christianisme"[106] (it is only in the third part, published in 1619, that the Forezian cult closely resembles Christianity). Elsewhere, she documents another shift between the first two volumes of the novel and the third, this time concerning the status of visual art: "Tout le long du roman, la métaphore de la peinture décrit ceux qui s'arrêtent aux apparences pour juger un acte ou une femme; ils ne savent pas percer le secret de l'image. Dans la troisième partie, la peinture devient dangereuse"[107] (all through the novel, the metaphor of painting describes those who stop at appearances to judge an act or a woman; they do not know how to penetrate the secret of the image. In the third part, painting becomes dangerous). In her own study of *L'Astrée*, Kathleen Wine locates the emergence of the ideal of negligence, which would later develop into that of the *honnête homme*, in the third volume, whose prefaces and stories highlight and bring into focus the self-effacement of the shepherds and of the author himself.[108]

In fact, all of the aspects of this shift identified by Henein and Wine – the Christianity, the status of paintings, and the self-effacement of the author and his shepherds – grow out of the same phenomenon that gives rise to the new

---

[104] *Astrée* III, p. 4.
[105] *Astrée* III, p. 4.
[106] *Protée*, p. 54.
[107] *Protée*, p. 143.
[108] *Forgotten Virgo*, pp. 220–4.

day whose dawning is depicted in the volume's opening pages, where Celadon appears as Alexis, and the new age in history augured by the coronation of a king whose name recalls that of his saintly ancestor. That phenomenon is a fundamental change in the depiction of God, who is no longer an entity whose doubtful existence is postulated by characters seeking to advance their own interests or assuage their own pain, but who is now instead identified, by nearly all of the novel's characters, as the benevolent creator of the universe in relation to whom shepherds, druids, and nymphs alike stand in awe and submissive dependence.

Indeed, the opening of the third volume stands in stark contrast to the paradigmatic scene described in the second volume, immediately after the shepherds' and shepherdesses' fortuitous visit to the Temple de l'Amitié. Seeking to lead his friends out of the forest, Silvandre steps on a plant, "l'herbe du fourvoyement" that allegedly induces confusion: "tant y a que Silvandre suivy de cette honneste trouppe, ne peust de toute la nuit retrouver le chemin, quoy qu'avec mille tours & détours il allast presque par tout le bois"[109] (so much that Silvandre, followed by this good troop, could not find the path throughout the night, even though with a thousand turns and detours he covered almost the entire forest). The darkness that surrounds the shepherds combines with their disorientation to echo, once again, the terrifying anxiety that often besets the mysterious Silvandre and that gives rise to his overconfidence in a benevolent providence. With no light to guide them and no stable knowledge of the forest's topography, the friends decide, after wandering aimlessly for a while, to sit down and wait for the moon to rise.

Significantly, this scene takes place in the middle of the second volume, at the end of the fifth book, the heart of the narrative forest which d'Urfé presents to the reader. At the outset of the third volume, dedicated to France's new and undoubtedly legitimate monarch, light is provided by the rising sun and the dawning of a new day. Confusion has, of course, not been eliminated from the text, but Celadon's appearance in the disguise of a druidess displaces that confusion from the metaphysical to the interpersonal. The devotion of Alexis and the legitimacy of her vocation are never called into question. In the second volume's forest scene, the first remedy against the complete absence of light and direction was for the friends to hold on to each other's clothing: "& en fin [Silvandre] s'enfonça tellement, que pour se suivre ils estoient contraints de se tenir par les habillements"[110] (and finally Silvandre got so lost that to follow each other they had to hold each other by their clothes). In the third and fourth volumes, the clarity afforded by a providential deity,

---

[109] *Astrée* II, p. 276.
[110] *Astrée* II, p. 276.

identified repeatedly by nearly all the characters as the author of the universe, enables the various adventures in clothing and re-clothing that characterize the friends' interactions.

Indeed, soon after Celadon's awakening, d'Urfé presents the reader with a debate between Hylas and Tircis, the two characters whose appearance in the first volume inaugurated the incursion of the outside world into Forez and set the parameters not just for the novel's events, but for its aesthetic. This time, however, the subject is not idolatry, the inappropriate attribution of divinity to created beings or objects. Rather, the debate turns on the question of divine authorship. Unaware that the druidess is actually a disguised Celadon, Hylas has turned his attentions from Phillis to Alexis, and attributes his change in affection to "le Ciel". The outraged Tircis exclaims that Hylas cannot possibly be attributing the authorship of his inconstancy to the gods, to which Hylas replies that the gods are no less the cause of his inconstancy than they are of the tears that Tircis continues to shed for the dead Cleon. Tircis's response attempts to carve out the spheres in which gods and humans can legitimately be said to be authors:

> Les choses qui ne dépendent pas de nous... et dont les causes nous sont incogneues, le respect que nous portons aux dieux, nous les fait ordinairement rapporter à leur puissance et volonté. Mais de celles dont nous cognoissons les causes, et qui sont en nous, ou que nous produisons, jamais nous n'en disons les dieux auteurs, et mesmes quand elles sont mauvaises, comme l'inconstance, car ce seroit un blaspheme.[111]

> Those things that do not depend upon us, and whose causes are unknown to us, we attribute to the gods' power and will out of respect for them. But for those things whose causes we know, and which are in us or which we produce, we never attribute authorship to the gods, even when they are bad, like inconstancy, for that would be blasphemy.

The sloppy theology that Tircis articulates in the first volume, where Cleon is both human lover and life-giving immortal goddess, is replaced here by a clear line between divine and human agency, a line policed by the concept of blasphemy. Hylas, as we have come to expect, pounces on this clarity by contesting the negative connotations that Tircis associates with inconstancy, but he does so in terms that reinforce the existence and role of the divine Author. Inconstancy, Hylas argues, cannot possibly be against divine will, "Car la beauté, n'est-ce pas une oeuvre de nostre grand Tautates? Et qu'est-

---

[111] *Astrée* III, pp. 38–9.

ce qui me fait changer que cette beauté?"¹¹² (For is not beauty a work of our great Tautates? and what makes me change other than that beauty?) Hylas's argument strongly resembles the objection voiced by Lycidas in the first volume, where he seeks to be absolved of idolatry precisely because the gods are responsible for Phillis's beauty; if they did not want him to worship her, they should have made her less beautiful. Yet this similarity merely underscores the ways in which Hylas's apparent impiety renders him uniquely immune to the charge of idolatry. Hylas's conviction that beauty itself provides the link between heaven and earth prevents him from viewing one person or one thing, including himself, as a symbol of or stand-in for divinity. The character of Hylas provides d'Urfé with the means for asking whether humanity has the stomach to embrace the uncertainty of constant change that appears to be the price of inoculation against the threat of idolatry.

This debate, which grows quite heated, over whether inconstancy should be read as a sign of human weakness (or, as Tircis pointedly puts it, a "nature dépravée"¹¹³) or of a joyful, carefree celebration of divine artistry can occur only when the framework provided by the gods' reality and benevolence, first alluded to in the volume's dedication to Louis XIII, is firmly in place. From here on in, at least in the parts of the novel that we can attribute with confidence to d'Urfé, it is as if the compass points are established, with true north found. Adamas takes a more central role, dispensing lectures on the history of Gaul and the Forezian religion and reassuring Celadon that "Ce Dieu que vous nommez m'a commandé de prendre soing de vous ... C'est luy qui fait par moy ce que vous voyez que je fais pour vostre salut, me l'ayant commandé par son Oracle. Ne doutez donc point que vous et moy n'en devions recevoir du contentement."¹¹⁴ (This God that you name ordered me to take care of you. It is he who accomplished through me what you see that I do for your salvation, having ordered me to do it through his oracle. Do not doubt that you and I will not receive some happiness from it). A similar absence of doubt now characterizes the ongoing adventures of Polemas and Climanthe; although Silvie and Leonide are briefly taken in by the ingenuity of Climanthe's trickery when they return to his false temple at the opening of the fourth volume, once their fear subsides, "lors qu'elles pouvoient parler, ce n'estoit que de la meschanceté de cet homme qui se servoit du manteau de piété avec tant d'impiété"¹¹⁵ (once they could speak, it was only about the evil intentions of this man who used the cover of piety with such impiety). Here, the word "impiety" functions like the "blasphemy" deployed by Tircis. Where

---

¹¹² *Astrée* III, p. 39.
¹¹³ *Astrée* III, p. 39.
¹¹⁴ *Astrée* III, p. 242.
¹¹⁵ *Astrée* IV, p. 24.

once Climanthe's false prophecies served to call into question all pretention to know the will of a god whose existence remained, in the end, uncertain, now, with the role and identity of the Gallic God secured, piety and impiety are clearly defined, and the villainy of the false druid and his friend Polemas is exposed.

Likewise, references to the heavens and to divine will occur with great frequency in the stories told by the characters introduced and developed in these volumes. The sympathetic Damon prefaces his adventures in the sixth book of the third volume by explaining that

> Je penserois avoir une grande occasion de me douloir de la fortune qui m'a si cruellement et si continuellement poursuivy depuis le jour de ma naissance, ou pour le moins, depuis que je me sçay cognoistre, si je ne considerois que ceux qui s'en plaignent sont plus cruels envers le grand Tautates qu'ils ne sont envers les hommes, puis que nous laissons bien à chacun la libre disposition de ce qui est sien, et nous ne voulons pas qu'ils puisse à son gré disposer de nous comme si toute l'univers, et tous les hommes, particulierement n'estoient pas siens, et faicts de ses mains.[116]

> I thought I had the opportunity to complain about the fortune that has so cruelly and continuously pursued me since my birth, or at least, since I know myself, if I considered that those who complain are more cruel to Tautates than they are towards men, since we leave everyone the free use of what is his, and we do not want him to dispose of us or as if the universe, and all humans, were not his, and made from his hands.

In noting how acknowledgment of divine authorship completely changes the emotional valence of his life and adventures, Damon provides a microcosm of the shift that occurs in the novel as a whole, as d'Urfé seeks to efface his own role in the work's production not just out of modesty or a precursor to *honnêteté*, but as a theologically informed position, a will to demonstrate that the structural foundation of the universe is, once again, sound.

Yet the continuing dilemma of Celadon serves to demonstrate that the transition to metaphysical certainty does not, and cannot, solve the question of how the divine and the terrestrial are linked. In the first two volumes, the overwhelming physicality, materiality, and sheer force of passionate love served to eclipse a god whose existence was tenuous and whose worship, insofar as it involved the sacrifice, or at least the subordination, of earthly pleasures, was resented. As a result, the threat of idolatry stalked all of the

---

[116] *Astrée* III, p. 302.

characters, including the druid Adamas, who ultimately sought to harness this energy by transforming Celadon into his druidess daughter. The resulting certitude regarding divine authorship and providence, and the legitimization of worship, settled many of the characters' moral issues and conferred new meaning to their stories and suffering.

Yet Celadon's disguise as Alexis leads to a different kind of impasse. Fulfillment of romantic passion between Celadon and Astrée is now impossible, not because Celadon is disguised as a woman, but because he is disguised as a druidess. In the first book of the fourth volume, Celadon asks Astrée to come get dressed near him, reminding her as well that she had promised to wear his clothes and "faire aujourd'huy le personnage de fille druide"[117] (impersonate today a girl-druid). Astrée obeys, but the sight of her undressing is almost more than he can take: "il n'y eut ny beauté du sein, ny presque de tout le reste du corps, qui ne fust permise à ses yeux qui, ravis de tant de perfections, desiroient que tout Celadon fust comme un autre Argus, couvert de divers yeux, pour mieux pouvoir contempler tant de parfaites raretez"[118] (he was able to take in the beauty of her breasts and all the rest of her body, so much that, ravished by such perfections, Celadon wished to become another Argus covered with eyes to better contemplate such rare perfections). However, Celadon's increasingly apparent physical desire is thwarted as Astrée, finally clothed in the druidess's robes, begins entertaining thoughts of devoting his own life "au service de Celuy que, par les loix naturelles, tous les humains sont obligez de servir"[119] (to the service of He who, by natural law, all humanity is obliged to serve). For if Tautates is indeed the benevolent creator of the universe, and if romantic love is, as we have seen, almost always a dangerous, even idolatrous, distraction from the worship due to him, becoming a druid or druidess becomes a perfectly logical course of action. Astrée's wish to enter the priesthood is adroitly thwarted by Celadon, who tells her that the first requirement is to love him/her as much as he/she loves Astrée. However, Celadon's disguise remains in place, and their passion remains unrequited.

D'Urfé died in 1625, before completing the fourth volume of the novel; this volume was completed by his secretary, Balthazar Baro, who also penned a fifth volume in which the characters' dilemmas and mysteries are resolved. Eglal Henein has argued forcefully and convincingly that the additions to *L'Astrée* betray the novel's underlying structure and philosophy. Calling the fourth volume "un mélange de laine et de polyester" (a mixture of wool and polyester) Henein laments the absence of an easily accessible

[117] *Astrée* IV, p. 38.
[118] *Astrée* IV, p. 38.
[119] *Astrée* IV, p. 40.

edition of what she calls the "true" fourth part, 900 pages that appeared in 1624, when the author was alive.[120] I have followed Henein in restricting my reading of *L'Astrée* to the first three volumes and the beginning of the fourth. Considering the novel without the tidy conclusions offered by Baro in the fifth volume serves, I believe, to underscore the significance, and the ultimate impossibility, of the questions that d'Urfé poses. Read in this fashion, *L'Astrée* is not a monument to Renaissance Neoplatonism, in which romantic love is securely placed in service to the divine. Rather, d'Urfé's work is an imaginative, inventive exploration of the same issues raised by the Catholic and Protestant polemicists whose often strident voices dominated the end of the sixteenth century and the beginning of the seventeenth. Seeking to square the circle of divine transcendence with the irresistible and seductive materiality of creation, d'Urfé instead demonstrates the fundamentally fractured nature of the world. Faced with, on the one hand, the incommensurability of the divine and the human, and, on the other, the pleasures of love, d'Urfé dares to ask whether idolatry is such a terrible sin after all.

---

[120] *Protée*, p. 14.

2

Descartes' *Meditations* as a Solution to Idolatry

"Quant à ceux qui nient d'avoir en eux l'idée de Dieu, et qui au lieu d'elle forgent quelque idole, etc., ceux-là, dis-je, nient le nom et accordent la chose."[1] (As to those who deny having in themselves the idea of God, and who instead of it forge some kind of idol, etc., those people, I say, deny the name and accord the thing.)

Descartes and Idolatry: Problem Solved?

In the letter addressed to the theologians at the Sorbonne that accompanied the publication of the Latin edition of the *Meditations on First Philosophy* in 1641, Descartes congratulates himself for having reached certainty regarding the existence of God and the incorporeal nature of the soul not through the theological tools of faith or revelation, but through the philosophical power of the human mind. Although the letter concludes with a humble request for helpful suggestions and corrections, it is clear that what Descartes is really seeking is official approval. If the Sorbonne can certify that his conclusions, having reached the highest summit of clarity and evidence humanly possible, have attained the status of "exactes démonstrations," Descartes declares, "je ne doute point ... que, si cela se fait, toutes les erreurs et fausses opinions soient bientôt effacées de l'esprit des hommes"[2] (I do not doubt that all the errors which have ever existed on these subjects would soon be eradicated from the minds of men[3]). Atheists would shed their "esprit de contradiction," and unbelievers throughout the world would be able to access the Christian religion through reason, rather than the circular logic of faith.[4] What go

---

[1] René Descartes, *Méditations métaphysiques* (Paris: Flammarion, 1993), p. 264. All citations in French will be from this edition, unless otherwise noted.
[2] *Méditations*, p. 39.
[3] Descartes, *Meditations on First Philosophy*, in *Philosophical Writings of Descartes*, vol. 2, ed., trans. John Cottingham, Robert Stoothoff, and Degald Murdoch (New York: Cambridge University Press, 1985), p. 6 (hereafter, *PW*). All English translations will come from this edition, unless otherwise noted.
[4] Descartes opens the letter by invoking this possibility, noting that "certainement il ne semble pas possible de pouvoir jamais persuader aux infidèles aucune religion, ni quasi

unmentioned by Descartes are the confessional divisions that had been tearing Europe apart for a century, divisions of which he, schooled by Jesuits and resident of the Dutch Republic, would have been keenly aware.

In this chapter, I argue that, despite this silence, the polemics surrounding the issue of idolatry provide a powerful, yet neglected, subtext to Descartes' insistence upon the immateriality of the human soul in the *Meditations* and throughout his responses to his contemporaries' objections. D'Urfé's *L'Astrée* amply, and at great length, demonstrated the risks involved in attempting to access the divine through the seductive materiality of the world before going on to acknowledge the difficulties inherent in appreciating the world on its own terms once the existence of a benevolent, transcendent, omnipotent creator God has been posited. Although the publics of the two works could not be more different – *L'Astrée* was widely read throughout the century, while Descartes originally published the *Meditations* in Latin to restrict their audience to those who had done the hard work of ridding themselves of prejudice – it is, I argue, possible to see Descartes' text as responding to the question that bedeviled the Reformers and Counter-Reformers and fascinated d'Urfé: how can the existence of God be established in a way that neither diminishes the divine nor elevates it beyond reach? In short, in terms that would make sense to those familiar with the logic of idolatry, can God be accessed without recourse either to images or to revelation? Descartes correctly saw that an affirmative answer to this question would radically change the European religious landscape and significantly reduce the "désordres que son doute produit" (disorders which come from their being doubted).⁵

Suggesting that Descartes' metaphysics might be influenced by the religious controversies of the time flies in the face of recent scholarship that goes to

---

même aucune vertu morale, si premièrement on ne leur prouve ces deux choses par raison naturelle," (certainly it does not seem possible to persuade infidels of any religion, or even of any moral virtue, if first one does not prove these two things through natural reason) going on to add that "Et quoiqu'il soit absolument vrai, qu'il faut croire qu'il y a un Dieu, parce qu'il est ainsi enseigné dans les Saintes Ecritures, et d'autre part qu'il faut croire les Saintes Ecritures, parce qu'elles viennent de Dieu; et cela parce que, la foi étant un don de Dieu, celui-là même qui donne la grâce pour faire croire les autres choses, la peut aussi donner pour nous faire croire qu'il existe: on ne saurait néanmoins proposer cela aux infidèles, qui pourraient s'imaginer que l'on commettrait en ceci la faute que les logiciens nomment un Cercle" (And even if it is absolutely true that one must believe that there is a God since it is taught in the Holy Scriptures, and if on the other hand, one must believe the Holy Scriptures because they come from God, and this because, faith being a gift from God, he who gives us the grace to believe in other things can also give it to us to make us believe he exists: one would nevertheless never propose this to infidels, who could imagine that one is committing in this the fault that logicians name a circle) (*Méditations*, pp. 35–6, translations mine).

5   *Méditations*, p. 40; *PW*, p. 6.

great lengths to explain away the appearance of God in Cartesian philosophy. As Desmond Clarke bluntly states in the introduction to his study of Descartes' theory of mind, "I read Descartes' discussion of theological and metaphysical issues as the engagement of a reluctant participant with the politically dominant ideologies of his time."[6] In this reading, Descartes constructs his metaphysics not, as he himself would state in the preface to his *Principes de la philosophie* (Latin: 1644; French: 1647), as the roots of the tree of human knowledge, but rather in order to provide theological cover for his physics. In the secularist context of contemporary philosophy, Descartes' assertion of the radical difference between the immaterial mind and the extended body – the difference that he alluded to in the letter to the theologians as one of the two great questions of metaphysics, along with the question of the existence of God – is uncoupled from the divine to become, as Clarke puts it, a "stop-gap measure, which indicates where an extremely ambitious Cartesian theory of the mind encounters apparently insurmountable obstacles."[7] In a similar vein, Deborah J. Brown's *Descartes and the Passionate Mind* quite understandably seeks traces of current breakthroughs in neuroscience and philosophy in Descartes' attempt to explain the interaction of mind and body in his treatise on the passions.[8] Yet this drive to prove that Descartes was, in her words, "a distinctively modern thinker" not only entails the neglect of works and passages where the philosopher asserts the importance of separating the mind from the body; it also leads to a certain underestimation of the complexity of the issues besetting Christianity during Descartes' time. Indeed, wishing to convey the intellectual sophistication of Princess Elizabeth, who famously challenged Descartes to better explain the interaction between mind and body, Brown approvingly notes that her concerns were more complex than "the bald one that exercises most philosophers today of how the immaterial and material per se could interact – hardly a pressing concern for Christians of the seventeenth century."[9] As I hope to have shown in the previous chapter, this concern – far from "bald" – was in fact central to the intellectual life of seventeenth-century France, where the label "Christian" papered over important ideological rifts on precisely this subject.

---

[6] Desmond M. Clarke, *Descartes's Theory of Mind* (Oxford: Clarendon Press, 2002), p. 7.

[7] Clarke, p. 10.

[8] "Quite understandably," since he is clearly not engaged in the history of philosophy per sc (and doesn't claim to be). For an overview of the difference between practicing philosophy and studying its history, as well as the benefits of the latter, see Daniel Garber, *Descartes Embodied: Reading Cartesian Philosophy through Cartesian Science* (New York: Cambridge University Press, 2001).

[9] Deborah J. Brown, *Descartes and the Passionate Mind* (New York: Cambridge University Press, 2006), p. 16.

In general, the scholarly divide over the importance of the divine (and therefore of the *Meditations* specifically) in Descartes' philosophy turns on the question of whether God is merely an extrapolation of human qualities or whether God is the entity from which all creaturely qualities, including existence, are derived. Put more simply, is the main focus of the *Meditations* God, or the human self?[10] If we decide that it is God, then Cartesian philosophy risks becoming a historical relic of minimal relevance to our own proudly secular times; if we decide that it is the human self, a large part of the text can be explained away as a relatively insincere effort to placate the religious authorities of the time. Descartes' own avowedly twofold purpose in writing the text – to prove, as he states in the letter to the faculty of theology in Paris, "qu'il y a un Dieu, et que l'âme humaine diffère d'avec le corps" (that God exists and that the mind is distinct from the body)[11] – contributes to the confusion, insofar as the relation between these questions, not to mention the hierarchy between them, remains unclear. It is my hope that by reading the *Meditations* against the context of seventeenth-century concerns over idolatry we can come to a better understanding of how Descartes viewed the human and the divine as profoundly interrelated.

In sharp contrast to Francis Bacon, who famously referenced idols in his effort to identify the sources of intellectual fallacies, Descartes avoids the term entirely in the text of the *Mediations* proper (though, as we shall see, the term and its cognates do make an appearance in the responses to the objections that were published with the *Meditations*). This avoidance can almost certainly be chalked up to the philosopher's desire to sidestep theological landmines by refraining from pronouncing himself on matters of faith. That said, the letter to the reader that accompanied the 1641 Latin edition contains a curious passage that indicates the extent to which Descartes viewed his work as a solution to the problems that idolatry posed:

> Je dirai seulement en général que tout ce que disent les athées pour combattre l'existence de Dieu, dépend toujours ou de ce que l'on feint dans Dieu des affections humaines, ou de ce qu'on attribue à nos esprits tant de force

---

[10] The different answers to this question are on display in *The Cambridge Companion to Descartes'* Meditations, ed. David Cunning (New York: Cambridge University Press, 2014), where an essay in which Olli Koistinen argues convincingly that our post-Kantian approach to the question of God's existence obscures what Descartes was doing is immediately followed by a chapter in which Deborah Brown asserts that the key questions of the *Meditations* are "What am I?" and "Who am I?" See Koistinen, 'The Fifth Meditation: Externality and True and Immutable Natures', pp. 223–39 and Deborah J. Brown, 'The Sixth Meditation: Descartes and the Embodied Self', in *The Cambridge Companion to Descartes'* Meditations, pp. 240–57.

[11] *Méditations*, p. 39; *PW*, p. 6.

et de sagesse que nous avons bien la présomption de vouloir déterminer et comprendre ce que Dieu peut et doit faire; de sorte que tout ce qu'ils disent ne nous donnera aucune difficulté, pourvu seulement que nous nous ressouvenions que nous devons considérer nos esprits comme des choses finies et limitées, et Dieu comme un être infini et incompréhensible.

I will only make the general point that all the objections commonly tossed around by atheists to attack the existence of God invariably depend either on attributing human feelings to God or on arrogantly supposing our own minds to be so powerful and wise that we can attempt to grasp and set limits to what God can or should perform. So, provided only that we remember that our minds must be regarded as finite, while God is infinite and beyond our comprehension, such objections will not cause us any difficulty.[12]

Here, Descartes professes that he is speaking not to idolaters, but to atheists, whose goal is to cast doubt on the very existence of God. Atheists are an attractive target insofar as both Catholics and Protestants could agree that atheism is a terrible thing, whereas the word "idolater" carried a polemical charge that would have inflamed at least half of Descartes' readership. Yet if we take a closer look at the passage above, we see that Descartes is not taking aim at those who deny the existence of God outright – what we would call atheists – but rather at those who inappropriately apply human attributes and emotions to the divine. In polemical literature, such misattribution would have immediately been identified as idolatrous. In avoiding that term, Descartes not only sidesteps a wasps' nest of theological contention; he also cleverly implies that idolatry and atheism are, in fact, one and the same. Reducing God to human dimensions is tantamount to eliminating the divine from the universe.

Freeing the Mind from Images

The challenge facing Descartes, then, is how to establish the existence of God using the limited and finite resources of humanity *without* thereby reducing the divine to a projection and amplification of human attributes. If we accept Descartes' statements in the letter to the theologians as well as in the preface to the reader that this is the goal of the *Meditations*, the reasons governing the text's order and method become clearer. In the first meditation, of course, Descartes uses skepticism to call into question the reliability of the senses; as he announces in the summary that precedes the text,

---

[12] *Méditations*, p. 43; *PW*, p. 8.

bien que l'utilité d'un doute si général ne paraisse pas d'abord, elle est toutefois en cela très grande, qu'il nous délivre de toutes sortes de préjugés, et nous prépare un chemin très facile pour accoutumer notre esprit à se détacher des sens, et enfin, en ce qu'il fait qu'il n'est pas possible que nous ne puissions plus avoir aucun doute, de ce que nous découvrirons après être véritable.

although the usefulness of such a general doubt does not immediately appear, it is in fact very great, since it delivers us from all sorts of prejudices and prepares an easy path to accustom our soul to detach itself from our senses, and finally, in that it makes it impossible that we shall have any doubt of what we discover afterwards to be true.[13]

Scholars have generally followed Descartes' own assertion, in his letter to Mersenne dated January 28, 1641, that this provisional wholesale rejection of the senses overturns centuries of Aristotelianism, which posited that the senses are the foundation of knowledge. Yet Descartes himself invites a larger interpretation of the views against which he is writing – not just Scholastic philosophy, but "toutes sortes de préjugés." This expansive phrase invites a reconsideration of what Descartes meant by "ce que nous découvrirons après être véritable," which Charles Larmore interprets not as God, but rather as mathematics, which founds a knowledge based on "order and measure."[14] While it is true that Descartes states, during the course of the first meditation, that the knowledge that two and three are five and that squares have four sides are truths so obvious that they can penetrate the dream state without distortion, he also immediately moves beyond these truths to wonder if they are only illusory, which they would be if God were a deceiver.[15] The state of mind that results from this contemplation recalls that of d'Urfé's shepherds lost in the forest. As Descartes' meditator considers the possibility that error has infiltrated everything that he has heretofore considered as true, he realizes, like the friends in *L'Astrée*, that the best solution is to stop wandering altogether: "il est nécessaire que j'arrête et suspende désormais mon jugement sur ces pensées, et que je ne leur donne pas plus de créance, que je ferais à des choses qui me paraîtraient évidemment fausses, si je désire trouver quelque

---

[13] *Méditations*, p. 49. Here, the English translation is mine, since it is not included in the *PW* edition.

[14] Charles Larmore, 'Descartes and Skepticism', in *The Blackwell Guide to Descartes' Meditations* (Malden, MA: Blackwell Publishing, 2006), pp. 17–29, here, p. 29.

[15] "il se peut faire qu'il ait voulu que je me trompe toutes les fois que je fais l'addition de deux et de trois, ou que je nombre les côtés d'un carré, ou que je juge de quelque chose encore plus facile, si l'on se peut imaginer rien de plus facile que cela" (*Méditations*, p. 65).

chose de constant et d'assuré dans les sciences" (So in future I must withhold my assent from these former beliefs just as carefully as I would from obvious falsehoods, if I want to discover any certainty [in the sciences]).[16] Yet as Descartes goes on to note, even this inaction is not enough. The custom of trusting one's senses, and the seductive power of the information they convey, is such that the meditator can be certain only that he will not be misled by preemptively misleading himself, and assuming that everything he knows is false and imaginary.

The use of the word "imaginary" here is significant.[17] As John D. Lyons has pointed out in a significant study, for Descartes, as for his contemporaries, "imaginary" did not mean "fictional," as it does today.[18] Rather, it referred to thoughts achieved by the intellect with the help of images, mental pictures that thereby derive their existence from the models provided by the senses, particularly vision. By pairing "imaginary" with "false," then, Descartes was not just emphasizing the lack of truth value in the meditator's thoughts. Rather, the conjunction "et" that appears in the French translation should be taken at face value. The meditator will provisionally treat all of his thoughts as false *and* as derived from or modeled upon images, and thereby unworthy of trust. Descartes, however, recognizes that this kind of skepticism, this resistance to the seduction and comfort of images and the senses, is almost impossible to maintain. If the systematic treatment of all thoughts as false and imaginary was necessary to prevent the "anciennes et ordinaires opinions"[19] from infiltrating the meditator's mind, maintaining radical skepticism is no less exhausting. The meditation ends not just with an acknowledgment that the meditator, left to his own devices, almost immediately begins to fall insensibly back into those "anciennes opinions/veteres opiniones," but that extraordinary courage and faith are needed to resist those comforting illusions. Like Silvandre, Descartes' meditator is haunted, and even terrified, by the possibility that no certainty can be found:

> j'appréhende de me réveiller de cet assoupissement, de peur que les veilles laborieuses qui succéderaient à la tranquillité de ce repos, au lieu de m'apporter quelque jour et quelque lumière dans la connaissance de la vérité, ne

---

[16] *Méditations*, p. 65; *PW*, p. 15.

[17] The passage in Latin reads "falsas imaginariasque esse fingam"; in French, "que toutes ces pensées sont fausses et imaginaires" (pp. 66–7).

[18] John D. Lyons, *Before Imagination: Embodied Thought from Montaigne to Rousseau* (Stanford: Stanford University Press, 2005). Indeed, Lyons credits Descartes with the crucial shift from the former, more literal uses of the word to something more abstract and less bound to images per se (p. xii).

[19] *Méditations*, p. 67.

fussent pas suffisantes pour éclaircir toutes les ténèbres des difficultés qui viennent d'être agitées.

I am afraid to awaken from this torpor, for fear that my peaceful sleep may be followed by hard labour when I wake, and that I shall have to toil not in the light, but amid the inextricable darkness of the problems I have now raised.[20]

Of course, the meditator soldiers on to the second meditation, where his search for something certain leads him to realize that even if everything around him is deceptive, he still exists. He moves on to consider *what* he is, and concludes that the only definition that he can reach with certainty is that he is a thing that thinks. Yet what does this really mean? Is it possible to separate the faculty of thinking from that of sensing and perceiving? Here, once again, the meditator is beset by doubt and by the seductive force of the sensory, which presents itself not only as autonomous, but as more *real* than abstract thought:

Mais je ne me puis empêcher de croire que les choses corporelles, dont les images se forment par ma pensée, et qui tombent sous les sens, ne soient plus distinctement connues que cette je ne sais quelle partie de moi-même qui ne tombe point sous l'imagination.

But it still appears – and I cannot stop thinking this – that the corporeal things of which images are formed in my thought, and which the senses investigate, are known with much more distinctness than this puzzling "I" which cannot be pictured in the imagination.[21]

Recognizing that his relatively untrained mind cannot sustain this onslaught without distraction, Descartes introduces the well-known ball of wax. As the meditator contemplates the wax, he realizes that the qualities that he believes inhere in it – its smell, its appearance, its color, its temperature – are all transformed as he brings it close to a flame. The wax remains, but what is it? Arriving at an answer involves recognizing that cognition can proceed independently of the senses, through the understanding. The meditator's fear that he will be completely lost without the senses is thereby revealed as groundless. Not only can he achieve knowledge without using his imagination; this knowledge is of a superior quality:

---

[20] *Méditations*, p. 69; *PW*, p. 15.
[21] *Méditations*, p. 83; *PW*, p. 20.

Mais ce qui est à remarquer, la perception [de cette cire], ou bien l'action par laquelle on l'aperçoit, n'est point une vision, ni un attouchement, ni une imagination, et ne l'a jamais été, quoiqu'il le semblât ainsi auparavant, mais seulement une inspection de l'esprit, laquelle peut être imparfaite et confuse, comme elle était auparavant, ou bien claire et distincte, comme elle est à présent, selon que mon attention se porte plus ou moins aux choses qui sont en elle, et dont elle est composée.

And yet, and here is the point, the perception I have of it [of this wax], or rather the act whereby it is perceived, is a case not of vision or touch or imagination – nor has it ever been, despite previous appearances – but of purely mental scrutiny; and this can be imperfect and confused, as it was before, or clear and distinct as it is now, depending on how carefully I concentrate on what the wax consists in.[22]

If, earlier, the meditator found himself periodically, and seemingly inevitably, overcome by the apparent power of images perceived through the senses, here, he is transformed into an agent. It is his attention, not any particular qualities of the thing perceived, that determines whether his knowledge of it is clear and distinct or confused.

That said, through the example of the ball of wax, Descartes seems to imply that knowledge achieved through the imagination or the senses is almost always "imperfect and confused." This makes sense, insofar as these aspects of the intellect proceed from our mind's embodiment and not from the intellect freed, by lengthy meditative effort, from the body's fetters.[23] Yet the example of the ball of wax does more than reassure the meditator of the existence of a "pure" mental faculty that is capable of operating without having recourse to the materiality of the world. It also strongly calls into question the usefulness and value of mimetic representation. The truth of the wax lies beyond the aspects of its appearance that serve only as dangerous distractions. The color, shape, temperature and size of an object have no more ability to designate that object than words, the product of a conventional agreement among people, have a natural resemblance to what they signify. And indeed, immediately following the example of the ball of

---

[22] *Méditations*, p. 87; *PW*, p. 21.

[23] Descartes notes the existence of this pure mind in a 1642 letter to Regius, which notes that angels in human bodies would still not have human sensations, and in a letter to Gibieuf which states that the faculties of imagination and sensation, while belonging to the soul, "only belong to the soul insofar as it is joined to the body." See Descartes, *Oeuvres*, 11 vols., ed. Charles Adam and Paul Tannery (Paris: Vrin, 1964) (hereafter AT), vol. III, p. 493 and p. 479, respectively.

wax, the meditator notes that the very process of using language subverts the abstract knowledge acquired with such effort: "Car encore que sans parler je considère tout cela en moi-même, les paroles toutefois m'arrêtent, et je suis presque trompé par les termes du langage ordinaire ..." (For although I am thinking about these matters within myself, silently and without speaking, nonetheless the actual words bring me up short, and I am almost tricked by ordinary ways of talking).[24] The mind seems to be programmed to jump to conclusions, and words, like images, at best only imperfectly grasp abstract truth, and at worst, mislead us completely. The meditator notes that when he looks out his window, he says that he sees men, when in fact all that he sees are coats and hats. It is a constant struggle to strip the world around us of its sensory qualities, but one that the meditator, in his quest for a firm foundation for knowledge, continues to pursue.

Although Descartes pointedly refrains from introducing God in this meditation, the theological implications of his rejection of images and suspicion of language would have begun to present themselves at this point to any religiously informed seventeenth-century reader. As Christia Mercer has pointed out, in choosing to name his work *Meditations*, Descartes inserted it into a tradition of Christian literature that stretched back to Augustine and had enjoyed renewed popularity through the writings of St. Ignatius of Loyola, the founder of the Jesuit order which educated Descartes.[25] Descartes' use of the term, however, is deliberately provocative, and even scandalous, and not just because, as Mercer points out, his text elides any mention of divine love, a traditional trope in the genre. Rather, the philosopher's stark opposition between "clear and distinct" and "confused and imperfect" flies in the face of the rhetorical fireworks deployed in the baroque masterpieces of the Counter-Reformation. These texts, meant to help the reader meditate upon the Church's mysteries, celebrated the richness of word and image, emphasizing the easy passage between the two. Take, for example, the following passage from the

---

[24] *Méditations*, p. 87; *PW*, p. 21.

[25] Mercer offers a helpful overview of the meditative tradition against which Descartes was writing, although her emphasis on the continuity and influence of Christian meditative writing ("Like Teresa, Descartes' meditator has to have an intellectual vision" (p. 37)) leads her to downplay Descartes' pointed rejection of previous meditative methods. See Christia Mercer, 'The Methodology of the *Meditations*: Tradition and Innovation', in *The Cambridge Companion to Descartes'* Meditations, pp. 23–47. For a recent example of the reluctance of scholars to view Descartes as criticizing the meditative tradition, even while exploiting it, see Huguette Courtès, 'Méditations métaphysiques et méditations chrétiennes', in *La Méditation au XVIIe siècle*, ed. Christian Belin (Paris: Honoré Champion, 2006), pp. 103–35, where she concludes that Descartes' reference to meditation techniques allows us to conclude that "la soumission de Descartes à l'Eglise va au-delà du simple respect et guide parfois son analyse" (p. 105).

preface to Louis Richeome's *Tableaux sacrez des figures mystiques du tres-auguste sacrifice et sacrement de l'Eucharistie* of 1601, where the author's prose demonstrates the fluidity it describes:

> s'il n'y a rien qui plus delecte, ne qui face plus suavement glisser une chose dans l'ame, que la peinture: ne qui plus profondement la grave en la memoire; ne qui plus efficacement pousse la volonté pour luy donner branle, & l'esmouvoir avec energie à aymer ou hair l'object bon ou mauvais qui luy aura esté propose, je ne vois pas en quelle maniere on puisse plus profitablement, vivement, & delicieusement enseigner les vertus, les fruicts, & les delices de ce divine & sacré mets du corps du Fils de Dieu, qu'avec les susdites expositions & avec l'air de ceste paincture triple, de pinceau, de parole, & de signification.[26]

> if there is nothing more delicious, nor which makes a thing slide more suavely into the soul, than painting, nor which engraves it more deeply in memory; nor which pushes the will more efficiently to set it in action and to move it with energy to love or hate the good or bad object which has been proposed to it; I do not know how one could more profitably, lively, and deliciously teach the virtues, fruits, and delights of this divine and holy meal of the body of Christ than with the abovementioned expositions and the air of this triple painting of brush, word, and signification.

Where Descartes spends a considerable amount of time and effort seeking to fend off the seductive and misleading power of the image on the soul, Richeome celebrates it, along with the soul's passivity. The meditator is encouraged to deploy all of his senses so as to better experience the union of himself with Christ and, therefore, with God. Layers of meaning – allegorical, tropological, anagogical – are set in place to reflect back and forth between each other, just as examples from the Old Testament melt into lessons from the New. Centuries of scholarship that have concentrated on Descartes as a key figure in philosophy, and therefore engaged primarily with Aristotle and his scholastic heirs, have obscured the extent to which the Frenchman was engaged in combatting the views of God that had become popular in his time. It may well be objected that Richeome and Descartes are addressing avowedly different publics, with vastly divergent purposes. As he himself notes, Richeome is interested in exciting the reader's soul towards the "vertus, fruits, & delices" of divine mystery; at no point does he promise access to divine truth. Nor does he need to – his reader is presumably already convinced

---

[26] Richeome, *Tableaux sacrez*, p. 7.

of God's existence. Descartes, on the other hand, is concerned here not with the feelings elicited by the divine, but, as he indicated in the first lines of his letter to the theologians, with proving the existence of God to pagans and atheists, those who do not believe. Indeed, as many scholars have pointed out, Descartes does not deny the usefulness of the imagination; it is a facet of the embodied mind that plays an important role in survival and even, as he notes in his treatise on the passions, cognition.[27]

However, Descartes' tone, both in the letter to the Paris theologians and in the preface to the reader, indicates that he considered that both the Catholic approach to attaining access to the divine through images or even through the created world and the Protestant approach to the divine through revelation and Scripture were not just inadequate for the conversion of unbelievers; they could actually contribute to a flawed idea of God, one dependent on human categories and constructions and therefore unable to provide a solid foundation for science. Descartes' painstaking demonstration that images and the imagination are not reliable guides to the truth, and that the human intellect is capable of grasping concepts that, in their clarity and distinctness, are *more* real and true than the confused knowledge accessed through the senses, is performed in service not, primarily, to a better understanding of the human self, but to a more accurate depiction of God.

And so, as the subtitle of the third meditation indicates ("De Dieu, qu'il existe/ De Deo, quod exista"), having discovered the non-figural, non-sensorial, non-material nature of the human mind, Descartes is ready to address the question of God's existence directly. Here, the meditator continues the work of uncoupling representations from what they ostensibly represent, noting that ideas, even of fictional objects or false conceptions, cannot be considered false if considered on their own, and the same can be said for desires. This is a deepening of the cogito, wherein thought itself is proof of the thinker's existence, *not* of the existence (or truth) of the object of thought; it is also an effort to replace the muddled way in which we usually conceive the world with the clear and distinct consciousness of our own thought as thought, rather than as representation:

> Or la principale erreur et la plus ordinaire qui s'y puisse rencontrer, consiste en ce que je juge que les idées qui sont en moi sont semblables ou conformes à des choses qui sont hors de moi; car certainement, si je considérais seulement les idées comme des certains modes ou façons de ma pensée,

[27] In addition to Deborah Brown's work, see Erec R. Koch, *The Aesthetic Body: Passion, Sensibility and Corporeality in Seventeenth-Century France* (Newark: University of Delaware Press, 2008) and John Cottingham, 'The Mind-Body Relation', in *The Blackwell Guide to Descartes' Meditations*, pp. 179–92.

sans les vouloir rapporter à quelque autre chose d'extérieur, à peine me pourraient-elles donner occasion de faillir.

And the chief and most common mistake which is to be found here consists in my judging that the ideas which are in me resemble, or conform to, things located outside me. Of course, if I considered just the ideas themselves simply as modes of my thought, without referring them to anything else, they could scarcely give me any material for error.[28]

Once again, these steps are necessary not to prove the ephemerality of the external world (which Descartes will bring back in the Sixth Meditation) or even the immateriality of the soul. They are meant to ensure that the God whose existence is about to be proven is not a projection of the human mind, but something whose very independence from human thought constitutes, somewhat paradoxically, the proof of its reality.[29] Yet this insistence on non-representationality raises a serious question: if the divine is irrevocably other, beyond the grasp of the human intellect or the projections of the imagination, how can we be certain of its reality? In order to answer this question, Descartes intensifies his examination of the source and the nature of human ideas, noting along the way that our ideas of other men, animals, and angels do not in any way imply the real existence of other men, animals, and angels, but could well be fictions composed by the ego, projections of the self.[30] At this stage, before the proof of God's reality, the world is an idolatrous nightmare, populated by creatures and entities that are nothing but the fantasies of a creative ego run amok. Animals, angels, hot, cold: "Et si ces idées sont vraies, néanmoins, parce qu'elles me font paraître si peu de réalité, que même je ne puis pas nettement discerner la chose représentée d'avec le non être, je ne vois point de raison pourquoi elles ne puisse être produites par moi-même, et que je n'en puisse être l'auteur" (If, on the other hand they are true, then since the reality which they represent is so extremely slight that I cannot even distinguish it from a non-thing, I do not see why they cannot originate from myself).

---

[28] *Méditations*, p. 99; *PW*, p. 26.
[29] This point is emphasized by Jean-Luc Marion in his outstanding survey of the implications of Descartes' original, somewhat scandalous, assertion that God created the eternal truths, *Sur la théologie blanche de Descartes* (Paris: Presses universitaires de France, 1981/2009).
[30] "Mais pour ce que regarde les idées qui me représentent d'autres hommes, ou des animaux, ou des anges, je conçois facilement qu'elles peuvent être formées par le mélange et la composition des autres idées que j'ai des choses corporelles et de Dieu, encore que hors de moi il n'y eût point d'autres hommes dans le monde, ni aucun animal, ni aucun ange" (p. 111).

Authorship, Creation, and the Divine

The only way out of this dizzying vortex of narcissistic projection, wherein the reality of objects, beings, and qualities is fundamentally uncertain, is to establish the existence of an entity who is the non-human, and indeed, super-human, source of creation: "Partant il ne reste que la seule idée de Dieu, dans laquelle il faut considérer s'il y a quelque chose qui n'ait pu venir de moi-même" (So there remains only the idea of God; and I must consider whether there is anything in the idea which could not have originated in myself).[31] And indeed, the more that the meditator contemplates the idea of "une substance infinie, éternelle, immuable, indépendante, toute connaissante, toute puissante, et par laquelle moi-même, et toutes les autres choses qui sont (s'il est vrai qu'il y en ait qui existent) ont été créées et produites" (a substance that is infinite, eternal, immutable, independent, supremely intelligent, supremely powerful, and which created both myself and everything else (if anything else there be) that exists),[32] the more he is convinced that this idea could not possibly have come from himself. While the qualities that Descartes attributes to the divine substance have come under sustained scholarly examination, the same cannot be said of Descartes' emphasis on God as *author*.[33] This, despite Descartes' clear view that God's creative activity is at least as important as, if not more so than, the identification and description of divine attributes. While Descartes does spend some time in the third meditation arguing why the positive qualities of the divinity cannot be merely projections of the finite human mind, he follows this exposition with a thought experiment in which the meditator examines whether his own existence can be attributed to something other than God. The alternatives are carefully considered before being dismissed: he could not be "l'auteur de mon être" (the author of himself)[34] because he would have given himself all of the perfections that he can conceive of, and would therefore be God. Moreover, the infinite divisibility of time into independent entities requires that he be able to sustain his existence from moment to moment, and, as Descartes notes, this ability is no different than the ability to produce and

---

[31] *Méditations*, p. 115; *PW*, p. 31.
[32] *Méditations*, p. 115; *PW*, p. 31.
[33] Two notable exceptions to this general reluctance to discuss what could be described as Descartes' creationism are Jean-Luc Marion, whose exploration of Descartes' insistence on the created nature of eternal truths I have already cited, and David Cunning, who notes that "Descartes takes the view (that God is the author of all reality) to an extreme. He thinks that God is not only the author of what is actual, but even the author of what is *possible*. That is in part to say – when God creates, He is not confronted with pre-existing possibilities from which to choose, but He is the author of possibility itself." 'The First Meditation: Divine Omnipotence, Necessary Truths, and the Possibility of Radical Deception', in *The Cambridge Companion to Descartes' Meditations*, pp. 68–87, here p. 70.
[34] *Méditations*, p. 121.

create something new. The meditator, aware that he lacks even the idea of how this ability would be possible, conceded that not only does God exist – God is "quelque être différent de moi" (some being distinct from myself),[35] and this essential difference, it is worth emphasizing, lies in the ability to create. While scholars have noted that, in a strict sense, Descartes maintains that only God is a true substance, it is at least as much the case, and arguably more relevant for his philosophical system, that only God can truly be called an author.[36]

The reality having been established, not merely of God's existence, but of the creative powers that serve to differentiate the divinity from humanity, the epistemological anguish that had beset the meditator gives way to the relief inherent in the realization that the human self is not, in fact, the author of the world, but instead is a part of creation, dependent upon the creator yet also uniquely endowed with consciousness of its own cloudy and limited possession of the attributes fully present in the divine and to which it aspires. The third meditation closes with an invitation to contemplate this divine perfection, noting that such contemplation affords the closest approximation to the boundless joy to be found in the afterlife, "[le] plus grand contentement que nous soyons capables de ressentir en cette vie" (the greatest joy of which we are capable in this life).[37]

It may be surprising to find a celebration of the created, dependent nature of the human, so very Augustinian in tone, in the philosopher who is credited with ushering in the ideal of the autonomous individual that grounds what we have come to call modernity.[38] However, I would argue that placing Descartes at the source of the modern self has been accomplished at least in part by overlooking the philosopher's vehement commitment to what we would today dismissively call "creationism."[39] For Descartes does not restrict his references

---

[35] *Méditations*, p. 125; *PW*, p. 34.
[36] See Jorge Secada, 'The Doctrine of Substance', in *The Blackwell Guide to Descartes' Meditations*, pp. 67–85.
[37] *Méditations*, p. 131; *PW*, p. 36.
[38] Here, it is worth recalling Henri Gouhier's important study, *Cartésianisme et augustinisme au XVIIe siècle* (Paris: Vrin, 1978).
[39] Charles Taylor's landmark study *The Sources of the Self: The Making of Modern Identity* (Cambridge, MA: Harvard University Press, 1989) emphasizes the discontinuity between Augustine and Descartes, stating, "The step from the imperfect self to a perfect God, so essentially Augustinian in its source, is in the process of mutating into something else. It is not carried out so as to make God appear at the very roots of the self, closer than my own eye. On the contrary, it is the sure *inference*, from powers that I can become quite certain of possessing, to their inescapable source. The Cartesian proof is no longer a search for an encounter with God within. It is no longer the way to an experience of everything in God. Rather what I now meet is myself: I achieve a clarity and a fullness of self-presence that was lacking before. But from what I find his reason bids me infer to a cause and transcendent guarantee, without which my now well-understood human powers

to divine authorship to the third meditation, but uses it throughout the rest of the text. He opens his consideration of the source of human error in the fourth meditation by noting that it cannot have come from God, asking "quel être nous imaginerons-nous avoir été produit par ce souverain Créateur de toutes choses, qui ne soit parfait et entièrement achevé en toutes ses parties?" (if this is so, how can anything produced by the supreme creator of all things not be complete and perfect in all respects?)[40] Likewise, he closes the fourth meditation by asserting that "toute conception claire et distincte est sans doute quelque chose de réel et de positif, et partant ne peut tirer son origine du néant, mais doit nécessairement avoir Dieu pour son auteur" (every clear and distinct perception is undoubtedly something real and positive, and hence cannot come from nothing, but must necessarily have God for its author).[41] Divine authorship of the clear, distinct, real, and positive is contrasted sharply with human attempts at invention, which can never be any more than the imagined products of fantasy, composed from parts of things that already exist. From the winged horse to chimeras, from the imagined men on the street to the great deceiver, Descartes provides examples of concepts and beings that are imaginary and illegitimate insofar as their existence is projected by a human mind not yet grounded in its divine origin. And as Jean-Luc Marion has shown, the seriousness with which Descartes took the attribution of ultimate authorship to God alone led him to postulate the surprising and original idea that the eternal truths of logic and mathematics are not consubstantial with the divinity, but created by it. In a letter to Mersenne dated April 15, 1630, he asserts that

> The mathematical truths which you call eternal have been laid down by God and depend on him entirely no less than the rest of his creatures. Indeed to say that these truths are independent of God is to talk of Him as if he were Jupiter or Saturn and to subject Him to the Styx and the Fates.[42]

Marion's thorough and beautiful exploration of the implications of this important statement, both in his *Questions cartésiennes* and his *Sur*

---

couldn't be as they are" (p. 177). This inaccessibility of God is the cost (and perhaps the goal) of Descartes' strong equivocity between the divine and the human, but by leaving out Descartes' emphasis on God's role as sole author of creation, Taylor further attenuates the ties between them. For one of the few explicit examinations of Descartes' commitment to divine creation, see Daniel Dennett, 'Descartes's Argument from Design', in *The Journal of Philosophy* 105.7 (July 2008), pp. 333–45.

[40] *Méditations*, p. 137; *PW*, p. 38.
[41] *Méditations*, p. 151; *PW*, p. 43.
[42] AT I, 145. This, and the other letters to Mersenne in 1630, form the foundation of Jean-Luc Marion's *Théologie blanche*.

la théologie blanche de Descartes, traces its emergence as a response to philosophers and scientists of the time, from Suarez to Galileo. But focusing on Descartes' choice of language in his letter to Mersenne allows us to discern the way in which Descartes thought of this statement not only as a rebuttal to developments in seventeenth-century science and philosophy, but also as an effort to transcend, once and for all, definitions of the divine that could plausibly be (and, in the heated atmosphere of the early seventeenth century, already were) characterized as idolatrous. In a move similar to the one he makes in the preface to the reader while discussing "atheists," here, Descartes notes that those who maintain that the eternal truths are not created by God are indistinguishable from pagans. Such remarks make clear that Descartes truly viewed his philosophically informed definition of the divinity – one in which the divine is incommensurable with the human and therefore qualified to serve as a foundation for knowledge – as an important corrective to the excesses and errors of both Catholicism and Protestantism, one that would be greeted with gratitude rather than, as was eventually the case, official condemnation.

Descartes' unprecedented emphasis on the creative power of God, a power that humans could not possibly share, combines with his suspicion of images to compose a treatise clearly meant to be idolatry-proof – indeed, as I have already mentioned, the word itself never occurs in the *Meditations* proper. However, his efforts to provide an irrefutable solution to nearly a century of religious contentiousness raise, with new urgency, the problem of the precise relation between the divine and the human, especially in light of the biblical assertion that God created man in his image. This phrase had been used for centuries as a (not unproblematic) support for viewing the Incarnation, the creation of humans, and the use of images in worship as points along a continuum or even allegorical reflections of each other.[43] Descartes' assertion that images can produce only confused and imperfect knowledge and are therefore inappropriate vehicles for apprehending the nature and existence of the divine threatens to subvert the centrality of Genesis 1: 27, placing the entire theological edifice that had been erected upon it in danger.[44] Descartes must

[43] For a fuller understanding of the place of Genesis 1:27 in Christian history and theology, see Robert Javelet, *Image et ressemblance au douzième siècle (De saint Anselme à Alain de Lille)*, 2 vols. (Paris: Editions Letouzey & Ané, 1967) and Ralph Dekoninck's excellent *Ad Imaginem: Statuts, fonctions et usages de l'image dans la littérature spirituelle jésuite du XVIIe siècle* (Genève: Droz, 2005).

[44] Although the inherent conflict between Cartesian philosophy and the Catholic doctrine of transubstantiation, a conflict which did not escape notice during the seventeenth century, has been the subject of scholarly attention, the same cannot be said of the relation between Descartes' wholesale suspicion of images and the theological doctrine of the Incarnation. For Cartesianism and the Eucharist, see Jean-Robert Armogathe, *Theologia cartesiana: L'explication physique de l'Eucharistie chez*

therefore find a way to describe the privileged relation between humanity and the divine in a way that avoids the blurriness of mimetic representationalism. He is aware of this issue; at the end of the third meditation, he notes that

> Et certes on ne doit pas trouve étrange que Dieu, en me créant, ait mis en moi cette idée pour être comme la marque de l'ouvrier empreinte sur son ouvrage; et il n'est pas aussi nécessaire que cette marque soit quelque chose de différent de ce même ouvrage. Mais de cela seul que Dieu m'a créé, il est fort croyable qu'il m'a en quelque façon produit à son image et semblance, et que je conçois cette ressemblance (dans laquelle l'idée de Dieu se trouve contenue) par la même faculté par laquelle je me conçois moi-même ...

> And indeed it is no surprise that God, in creating me, should have placed this idea in me to be, as it were, the mark of the craftsman stamped on his work – not that the mark need be anything distinct from the work itself. But the mere fact that God created me is a very strong basis for believing that I am somehow made in his image and likeness, and that I perceive that likeness, which includes the idea of God, by the same faculty which enables me to perceive myself.[45]

Descartes' emphasis on the creative power of God, which is here assumed to be both real and unique to the divinity, allows him to downplay the "image" aspect of the human. What God imprints upon the human is less a physical or visual image than an *idea*, which may or may not be different from that which it represents. That said, as Descartes adds, we may assume that there is, in fact and exceptionally, a similarity between the meditator and God for the simple reason that God created the meditator. Here, however, Descartes takes care to note that "similarity" and "image" do not, for all that, imply something that is accessible through the senses and that would thereby compromise the irreducibility of the divine to the human. Image quickly becomes, once again, "idea," and, just in case there is any confusion, Descartes specifies that we have access to this idea through the same faculty through which we have access to ourselves. This faculty, as Descartes proved in the first three meditations, is *not* the imagination, but rather the understanding, which, as we have seen through the example of the ball of wax, is perfectly capable, with sustained effort and attention, of conceiving ideas, even of physical objects, without relying upon images or sensory input.

Descartes et dom Desgabets (La Haye: Nijhoff, 1977) and Tad M. Schmaltz, *Radical Cartesianism: The French Reception of Descartes* (New York: Cambridge University Press, 2002).

[45] *Méditations*, p. 129; *PW*, p. 35.

In the fourth meditation, Descartes offers a more detailed explanation of the source of the similarity between the divine and the human. Once again, he eschews any reference to mimetic representation or to images, choosing instead to perform a thorough inventory of the human mind. Through the voice of the meditator, he notes that almost every aspect of the mind is a limited and small version of something that the meditator can imagine larger and more perfect in God. This is true of the "faculté de concevoir"; it is also true of the memory and the imagination: "En même façon, si j'examine la mémoire, ou l'imagination, ou quelqu'autre puissance, je n'en trouve aucune qui ne soit en moi très petite et bornée, et qui en Dieu ne soit immense et infinie" (Similarly, if I examine the faculties of memory or imagination, or any others, I discover that in my case each one of these faculties is weak and limited, while in the case of God it is immeasurable).[46] There is, however, one exception to these limitations of the human, and that is the will: "Il n'y a que la seule volonté, que j'expérimente en moi être si grande, que je ne conçois point l'idée d'aucune autre plus ample et plus étendue: en sorte que c'est elle principalement qui me fait connaître que je porte l'image et la ressemblance de Dieu" (It is only the will, or freedom of choice, which I experience within me to be so great that the idea of any greater faculty is beyond my grasp; so much so that it is above all in virtue of the will that I understand myself to bear in some way the image and likeness of God).[47] Descartes' language here and in the Latin (Sola est voluntas, sive arbitrii libertas, quam tantam in me experior, ut nullius majoris ideam apprehendam; adeo ut illa praecipue sit, ratione cujus imaginem quondam & similitudinem Dei me referre intelligo) is careful to avoid traditional representational formulations. The "image et ressemblance" to God that the human bears is never identified, or held out as something that the meditator can eventually behold. Moreover, as in the third meditation, the word "image" is not allowed to stand alone, but is immediately paired with the more abstract, less sensory "semblance" (in Latin, this word is the same, similitudo). Once again, Descartes is doing his best to avoid falling into the language characterizing the relationship between God and humanity whose legacy was a century of physical and verbal violence. The will is not something that can be visually represented; unlike the imagination, it functions without any reference to physicality or to visual form whatsoever. It is pure potentiality, pure force, and its independence from referentiality grants it an affinity with the "clear and distinct" that Descartes so values. It is through the qualities of the will that humans bear a resemblance to God, but given the immateriality of the will, this resemblance is characterized less through the

---

[46] *Méditations*, p. 141; *PW*, p. 40.
[47] *Méditations*, p. 141; *PW*, p. 40.

word "image," which conjures the "confused and imperfect" domain of visual representation, and more through the word "similitude."

Yet the word "similitude" poses a problem as well. It would seem to break down the absolute equivocity, the irreducible difference, between the divine and the human. Granted, some of this danger is mitigated by the fact that the will is characterized, first and foremost, by its independence. In other words, it is through the freedom and immateriality of the will that humans can be certain that they enjoy a privileged relationship with the divine. As Jean-Luc Marion points out, however, this configuration of similitude through independence simply cannot work as a means of establishing a divine foundation for knowledge.[48] We are left with a picture where humans float freely from their origin in God, and where this floating, rather than any representational or affective relationship, becomes a sign of the affinity between God and humanity. This affinity, established through a desire to preserve both God and the human mind from the dangers of the senses and from the confused nature of representational creep, is ultimately meaningless.

Objections

Like Honoré d'Urfé, Descartes fails to bridge the distance between heaven and earth without falling into the dangers and contradictions that were opened up by the collapse of scholastic theology, with its shades of gray and intricate distinctions. However, while d'Urfé luxuriated in the dilemmas generated by the imperfect fit between the material and the divine, Descartes remained convinced that he had discovered a way, accessible to anyone willing to do the hard work of meditation, to prove the existence of God and the distinction of the soul from the body through reason, or *entendement*, alone. Yet as Christopher Braider points out, not only was the content of the *Meditations* influenced by the contingencies of its publication, but from the very beginning, Descartes' solution to the problem of divine existence and the nature of the human soul was not universally adopted or admired.[49] Indeed, from the outset, the *Meditations* were accompanied by the objections of Descartes' contemporaries along with the philosopher's replies. These objections, many of which are made by theologians, testify stubbornly to the impossibility of supplanting theology with philosophy; Descartes' often impatient responses demonstrate his conviction that the objections stem most

---

[48] As Marion notes, "la volonté n'assure le rapport au fondement qu'en instaurant un rapport de deux fondements, d'autant plus indépendants qu'ils exercent la même prétention à l'indépendance." *Sur la théologie blanche de Descartes*, p. 411.

[49] See Christopher Braider, *The Matter of Mind: Reason and Experience in the Age of Descartes* (Toronto: University of Toronto Press, 2012), pp. 34–65.

often from a failure of radicalism, a refusal on the part of his interlocutors to abandon the old familiar (he would add confused and imperfect) categories used to speak about God and the soul. The objections and responses have enjoyed considerable scholarly attention; what I would like to focus on here is the ways in which they demonstrate the persistent sway that the logic of idolatry continues to exert, despite Descartes' best efforts, over definitions and discussions of divine creation and representation.

For what we see emerging in the objections is considerable skepticism regarding the efficacy of Descartes' firm separation of divine creation and human invention. The Dutch theologian Caterus asked whether ideas can really be said to be caused by something that exists, calling into question Descartes' method of proving God's reality: "Donc j'ai des idées, mais il n'y a point de causes de ces idées; tant s'en faut qu'il y en ait une plus grande que moi et infinie" (Hence, though I have ideas, there is no cause for these ideas, let alone some cause which is greater than I am, or which is infinite).[50] Moreover, in a rhetorical move that would be repeated throughout the seventeenth century, most notably by Pierre-Daniel Huet in his devastating *Censura philosophiae cartesianae* (1671), Caterus provides quotations from Thomas Aquinas, Suarez, and Pseudo-Dionysius to call into question the originality of Descartes' own arguments.[51] Such accusations of unacknowledged borrowing not only suggest that Descartes is needlessly reinventing a perfectly functional wheel with the same parts. They also reflect an issue raised by Descartes' own relentless focus on the key question of authorship in his text. On the one hand, the philosopher insists that the creative powers of the divine, just as much as the immensity, eternity, and goodness of divine nature, are the source of the incommensurability between the divine and the human. This argument, as we have already seen, was made most forcefully by Augustine, but was accompanied by an insistence on the resultant insufficiency of the human and necessity of revelation and grace. Descartes' assertion that the human will not only lacks nothing but is the most godlike aspect of humanity appears, in this context, to be unnecessarily arrogant, adding nothing to the understanding of God while seeming to clear the way for an unprecedented endorsement of human abilities, including Descartes' own. Descartes' somewhat naive insistence on the unprecedented nature of his discovery of a way to explain God and the soul without recourse to traditional theological categories can easily be read, especially when combined with his pronouncements on the

---

[50] *Méditations*, p. 217; *PW*, p. 67.

[51] On Huet, see Nicholas Jolley's 'The Reception of Descartes' Philosophy', in *The Cambridge Companion to Descartes* (New York: Cambridge University Press, 1992), pp. 393–423, although the essay is marred by its easy, even flippant, dismissal of theological objections to Descartes' positions.

will, as a disingenuous praise of his own creativity, despite his frequent (and sincere) efforts to emphasize that he is, in fact, inventing nothing.[52]

In his answer to Caterus, Descartes tries to establish more clearly the qualitative difference between the inventions of the human mind and the reality of God. He grants that his conclusion that God's existence follows naturally from the fact that we can conceive that existence clearly and distinctly is harder to follow than the idea that everything that we conceive clearly and distinctly is true. He attributes the difficulty of this conclusion to our habit of distinguishing essence and existence in all other matters, but adds that it is also due to our confusion regarding, in a word, truth and fiction:

> ne distinguant pas les choses qui appartiennent à la vraie et immuable essence de quelque chose, de celles qui ne lui sont attribuées que par la fiction de notre entendement, encore que nous apercevions assez clairement que l'existence appartient à l'essence de Dieu, nous ne concluons pas toutefois de là que Dieu existe, parce que nous ne savons pas si son essence est immuable et vraie ou si elle a seulement été inventée.

> we do not distinguish what belongs to the true and immutable essence of a thing from what is attributed to it merely by a fiction of the intellect. So, even if we observe clearly enough that existence belongs to the essence of God, we do not draw the conclusion that God exists, because we do not know whether his essence is immutable and true, or merely invented by us.[53]

The central question here, a question whose seriousness and difficulty Descartes fully recognizes, can be traced directly to the long controversies surrounding idolatry. If the reality of the divinity is to be established uniquely through the workings of the human mind, as Descartes suggests, what is to prevent us from inventing God, rather than discovering Him?

After demonstrating that, unlike other ideas, the idea of God refers to something that necessarily, rather than merely possibly, exists, Descartes proposes a test: ideas that proceed from the understanding can be divided by

---

[52] In *The Worldmakers*, Ayesha Ramachandran challenges Descartes' profession to make no claims to godlike creation by focusing on his unpublished treatise *Le Monde*, wherein she reads Descartes as "setting up a parallel between himself as a worldmaker and God's creative omnipotence," and thereby activating "an implicit analogy between poetic invention ('l'invention d'une fable') and the great miracle of Genesis I – both create worlds by making 'something' from 'nothing'." (p. 169). Ramachandran's reading serves to highlight the extent to which Descartes was quite familiar with the issues surrounding divine and human authorship, and likeness, but, as she herself recognizes, it runs counter to the positions he adopted in later texts such as the *Discourse on Method* and the *Meditations*.
[53] *Méditations*, p. 240; *PW*, p. 83.

that understanding in a "clear and distinct" operation, whereas "les choses que l'entendement ne peut pas ainsi diviser, n'ont point sans doute été faites ou composées par lui" (any ideas which the intellect cannot split up in this way were clearly not put together by the intellect).[54] The examples he gives to illustrate this point are a horse with wings, an existing lion, and a triangle in a square; in all of these cases, the parts can be easily separated, although he does note that the natures of the horse and lion are still unclear. He then proceeds to place this principle in service of his argument for the necessary existence of God, noting first that while bodies have no force that allows them to produce or conserve themselves, the same cannot be true of God, whose infinite power includes the positive ability to cause Himself and maintain His own existence. As Theo Verbeek has noted, this last assertion shocked Descartes' Orthodox Calvinist contemporaries: "According to [Orthodox Calvinists] causality was first and foremost the expression of the finitude of a being. To ask for the cause of an infinite being or of being as such is contradictory. As a result, Descartes' idea that all being, even that of God, ultimately depends on an efficient cause implied a radically new conception of being."[55] This is most certainly true, but I would also add that it reflects the weight that Descartes places on the concept of authorship, which carries most of the burden of the difference between the divine and the human in his stripped-down, rationalist philosophy. Indeed, Descartes continues to deploy the phrase "fictions de l'esprit/l'entendement" (fictions of the mind/of understanding) in his response to Caterus, driving home again, and again, and again the vast difference between the independent reality of God, a reality that grounds the entirety of human knowledge, and the floating fantasies of the human imagination.[56]

---

[54] *Méditations*, p. 241; *PW*, pp. 83–4.

[55] Theo Verbeek, *Descartes and the Dutch: Early Reactions to Cartesian Philosophy* (Carbondale: Southern Illinois University Press, 1994), p. 46.

[56] Beginning with his distinction between possible and necessary existence, Descartes invokes the "fictions de l'entendement" three times before the end of the paragraph – first to note that if possible existence is readily accorded to all things, "même à celles qui sont composées par les fictions de notre esprit," then it should certainly be accorded to God. Then, twice in the same sentence: "Car il est très manifeste, par la lumière naturelle, que ce qui peut exister par sa propre force, existe toujours; et ainsi nous connaîtrons que l'existence nécessaire est contenue dans l'idée d'un être souverainement puissant, non par aucune fiction de l'entendement, mais parce qu'il appartient à la vraie et immuable nature d'un tel être, d'exister; et nous connaîtrons aussi facilement qu'il est impossible que cet être souverainement puissant n'ait point en lui toutes les autres perfections qui sont contenues dans l'idée de Dieu, en sorte que, de leur propre nature, et sans aucune fiction de l'entendement, elles soient toutes jointes ensemble, et existent dans Dieu." (*Méditations*, p. 243) (For it is very clear, through natural light, that what can exist through its own force always exists; and therefore we know that necessary existence is contained in the idea of a sovereignly powerful being, not through any fiction of the understanding, but because it

Yet the question of divine and human authorship retains its centrality in the second objections, often attributed to Mersenne but more accurately authored by several theologians and philosophers, among them Jean-Baptiste Morin, and collected by Mersenne, and Descartes' response.[57] Indeed, Mersenne's opening, which refers to the "nouveaux géants du siècle, qui osent attaquer l'auteur de toutes choses" (new race of giants, who dare attack the author in all things),[58] immediately places the objections in relation to the need to protect and preserve divine authorship. In other words, the sharp division between human fantasy and divine reality, creative source of all that is, is accepted at face value, but as the first two questions demonstrate, this acceptance leads straight into difficulty. The objector endorses Descartes' terminology of "fiction de l'esprit," but pushes it farther, asking how one can be certain that the incorporality of thought is not itself a fiction of the mind. Likewise, it seems to the objector unclear that the divinity advanced in the meditations is also not merely another human construct; after invoking the examples of numbers and heat, he asks "Pourquoi pareillement ne pourrais-je pas ajouter à quelque degré d'être que j'aperçois être en moi, tel autre degré que ce soit, et, de tous les degrés capables d'être ajoutés, former l'idée d'un être parfait?" (In the same way, I can surely take a given degree of being, which I perceive within myself, and add on a further degree, and thus construct the idea of a perfect being from all the degrees which are capable of being added on).[59] In other words, the objector continues, the sovereign being of God might well be nothing less than an extrapolation of human qualities, based not only on one's own experiences or concepts, but even on books and culture. The lack of a conception of God among the native inhabitants of Canada and other "hommes sauvages" would seem to support this conclusion, or at least go a long way towards refuting the "clarity" of Descartes' proof.

In his response, Descartes acknowledges the piety of his interlocutors before reminding them that his decision to devote two entire meditations to skepticism can be attributed to the almost inevitable contamination of abstract thought by the senses. In fact, Descartes asserts, "nous n'avons eu jusques ici

---

belongs to the true and immutable nature of such a being to exist, and therefore we also easily know that it is impossible that this sovereignly powerful being does not have in itself all of the other perfections that are contained in the idea of God, in such a manner that, through their own nature and without any fiction of the understanding, they are joined together, and exist in God.) Translation mine.

[57] On the authorship of the second objections, see Daniel Garber, 'J-B. Morin and the Second Objections', in *Descartes and His Contemporaries: Meditations, Objections, and Replies*, ed. Roger Ariew and Marjorie Green (Chicago: University of Chicago Press, 1995) pp. 63–82.

[58] *Méditations*, p. 247. Translation mine.

[59] *Méditations*, p. 249; *PW*, p. 88.

aucune idée des choses qui appartiennent à l'esprit qui n'aient été très confuses et mêlées avec les idées des choses sensibles" (All our ideas of what belongs to the mind have up till now been very confused and mixed up with the ideas of things that can be perceived by the senses),[60] and therefore in order to examine whether abstract thought, or an idea of God that has not been compromised by human and sensory categories, is even possible, the meditator must exercise extreme and unrelenting vigilance over a long period of time.[61] He goes on to reiterate that the perfections to be found in God, and nowhere else, ensure that our idea of God is based on something that really exists, and is not a projection or fiction of our own minds. If humans could maintain this hard-won focus on divine perfections, we would all have true knowledge of the divinity; however, as Descartes notes, "ceux qui mêlent quelques autre idées avec celle-là composent par ce moyen un Dieu chimérique, en la nature duquel il y a des choses qui se contrarient" (But some people muddle things up by including other attributes, which leads them to speak in a contradictory way: they construct an imaginary idea of God).[62] It is therefore an error to call God a perfect corporeal being, insofar as bodies contain imperfections that contradict the perfection of divine nature. Eliding, no doubt wisely, the theological question of the Incarnation and Christ's godhead, Descartes goes on to answer the objector's question of whether our idea of an angel implies that angels really exist. Descartes' response – no, since our idea of an angel is nothing other than a composite of our ideas of God and man – provides a valuable illustration of his firm belief in the absolute equivocity of the divine and the human. We can be certain that God exists, he implies here, because the idea of God contains nothing human. This truth in turn allows us to infer that God created us, rather than the other way around, since any qualities we may have (with the exception of the will) are imperfect derivations of their divine source.

Tellingly, it is at this point that Descartes mentions idols explicitly for the first time: "Quant à ceux qui nient d'avoir en eux l'idée de Dieu, et qui au lieu d'elle forgent quelque idole, etc., ceux-là, dis-je, nient le nom et accordent la chose" (As for those who deny that they have the idea of God, but in its place form some image etc., although they reject the name, they concede the reality).[63] Descartes' judgment of idolaters flies in the face of the more

---

[60] *Méditations*, p. 257; *PW*, p. 94.
[61] "il est tel que ce n'est pas assez de l'avoir envisagé une fois, il le faut examiner souvent et le considérer longtemps, afin que l'habitude de confondre les choses intellectuelles avec les corporelles, qui s'est enracinée en nous pendant tout le cours de notre vie, puisse être effacée par une habitude contraire de les distinguer, acquise par l'exercice de quelques journées" (*Méditations*, p. 257).
[62] *Méditations*, p. 264; *PW*, p. 99.
[63] *Méditations*, p. 264; *PW*, p. 99.

common interpretation of idolatry, namely that those who worship idols are unbelievers. Descartes instead posits that since *everyone* has the innate idea of God, idolatry is a problem not of heresy, but of mislabeling. Idolatry does not and cannot threaten the innate idea of God that we all possess, insofar as the idea of God is of a completely different nature than the ideas that we generate ourselves: "Car certainement je ne pense pas que cette idée soit de même nature que les images des choses matérielles dépeintes en la fantaisie; mais, au contraire, je crois qu'elle ne peut être conçue que par le seul entendement" (I do not myself think that the idea is of the same kind as the images of material things which are pictured in the imagination; I maintain it is simply that which we perceive with the intellect).[64] Here, then, lies the true genius of Descartes' metaphysics; if we adopt his sharp distinction between the idea of God and the fantasies of humans, idolatry quite simply ceases to be a threat, insofar as material objects or physical representations are as irrelevant and inapplicable to the true idea of the divine as sloppy theology. The odd "etc." that follows the word "idol" in the passage above – an occurrence that is both unprecedented and unrepeated in Descartes' work – is an indication not, as one might suppose, of the strong ideological valence surrounding the term, but rather of an almost offhanded dismissal of the topic, a topic that had obsessed theologians on both sides of the Reformation for over a century.

Yet the persistence of the issues surrounding idolatry in the objections and responses testifies to the pull that the concept continues to exert on seventeenth-century thought. In the remainder of his response to the second objections, Descartes continues to insist upon the real distinction between divine creation and human invention. Thus, on the subject of whether infinity is a simple extension of finite numbers, Descartes objects that "cette puissance que j'ai de comprendre qu'il y a toujours quelque chose de plus à concevoir dans le plus grand des nombres que je ne puis jamais concevoir, ne me vient pas de moi-même, et que je l'ai reçue de quelque autre être qui est plus parfait que je ne suis" (but that I have the power of conceiving that there is a thinkable number which is larger than any number that I can ever think of, and hence that this power is something which I have received not from myself but from some other being which is more perfect than I am).[65] Indeed, the ability to create is a necessary consequence of divine perfection; as Descartes asks, "à quoi servirait l'infinie puissance de cet infini imaginaire, s'il ne pouvait jamais rien créer?" (what would the infinite power of this imaginary infinite amount to, if it could never create anything?).[66] In addition, during the axioms provided at the end of the response in an effort to satisfy the objector's request

---

[64] *Méditations*, p. 264; *PW*, p. 99.
[65] *Méditations*, p. 265; *PW*, p. 100.
[66] *Méditations*, p. 267; *PW*, p. 101.

for a geometric proof of God, Descartes provides the grounds for what would later become occasionalism, arguing that since moments of time have no relationship to each other, creating and conserving are essentially the same thing. The corollary of this demonstration, Descartes adds, is that God created "le ciel et la terre, et tout ce qui y est contenu, et outre cela, il peut faire toutes les choses que nous concevons clairement, en la manière que nous les concevons" (the heavens and the earth and everything in them. Moreover, he can bring about everything which we clearly perceive in a way exactly corresponding to our perception of it).[67] Implied in this corollary, of course, is the creation of eternal truths, to which Descartes had referred in his letters to Mersenne years earlier.

The third objections, written by a Thomas Hobbes who had yet to write his masterworks *De Cive* and *Leviathan*, are often viewed as disappointing, although Edwin Curley argues convincingly that Hobbes' assertion that the mind, if it is to possess the property of thought, must be corporeal is a reflection of the English philosopher's atheism, which he for obvious reasons cannot proclaim directly.[68] Yet if Hobbes' mocking of the *cogito* as either tremendously obvious or horribly inaccurate has attracted the attention of critics, the same cannot be said of the philosophers' sparring over the subject of divine creation. After noting that the very concept of an idea of God is blasphemous, since any idea or image of God gives us the impression of conceiving of that which is inconceivable, Hobbes moves on to note that not only does Descartes' idea of God fail to prove God's existence, it also fails to prove that God created the world. This line of questioning, which anticipates Spinoza, catches Descartes completely off guard, and indeed, he is stunned that the question even arises: "Enfin, ce qu'il ajoute ici de la création du monde, est tout à fait hors de propos; car j'ai trouvé que Dieu existe, avant que d'examiner s'il y avait un monde créé par lui, et de cela seul que Dieu, c'est-à-dire un être souverainement puissant, existe, il suit que, s'il y a un monde, il doit avoir été créé par lui" (Finally, what he adds here about the creation of the world is completely irrelevant, for I have found that God exists before examining if there was a world created by him, for the only reason that if God, that is to say, an all-powerful being exists, it follows that if there is a world, it must have been created by him).[69] For Descartes, the divide between

---

[67] *Méditations*, p. 293; *PW*, p. 119.

[68] Referring to Zarka's argument that Hobbes merely asserts the ultimate unknowability of God, Curley states, "I prefer a more radical interpretation: that Hobbes is an atheist, and that everything he says about God – that he exists, that he is unknowable, that he is a corporeal spirit – is a subterfuge, necessitated by the possibility of persecution." 'Hobbes versus Descartes', in *Descartes' Contemporaries*, 97–109, here p. 106.

[69] *Méditations*, p. 305. Translation mine (interestingly, the translators omit much of

a supreme, all-powerful being who can bring about its own existence and a created world which lacks any such power is absolute. It is worth noting that this frustrated answer to Hobbes clearly demonstrates Descartes' belief, at times called into question, that the world does, indeed, exist. It is not an illusory manifestation of the divine mind; rather, its very existence, its very solidity (proven in the sixth meditation) are proof that God exists, since only He could bring the world into being and maintain it.

Yet Hobbes insists on pressing the issue, noting that "il ne suffit pas, pour prouver la création, que nous puissions imaginer le monde créé" (But our ability to imagine the world to have been created is not a sufficient proof of the creation) before adding "C'est pourquoi, encore qu'on eût démontré qu'un être *infini, indépendant, tout-puissant, etc.*, existe, si ce n'est que quelqu'un pense qu'on infère fort bien, de ce que quelque chose existe, laquelle nous croyons avoir créé toutes les autres choses, que pour cela le monde a autrefois été créé par elle" (Hence, even if the existence of something infinite, independent, supremely powerful etc. had been demonstrated, it still would not follow that a creator exists. Unless anyone thinks that the following inference is correct: 'There exists a being whom we *believe* to have created all things; therefore, the world was *in fact* created by him at some stage').[70] Once again, Descartes' irritation is palpable. Where, he asks, would something have come from, if not from God? Moreover, positing things that can exist in the world without having been created by God would elevate these things to divine status by according them an independence and power that are God's alone.[71] Hobbes does not let the matter drop. In the following, eleventh objection, he reacts to Descartes' assertion in the *Meditations* that we would not have an idea of God if God did not exist by reiterating his previous points – first, that having an idea of God is blasphemous (one could easily say idolatrous), since "la Religion chrétienne nous oblige de croire que Dieu est inconcevable" (the Christian religion obliges us to believe that God is inconceivable), and second, that divine inconceivability means that we cannot demonstrate God's existence, and even less (beaucoup moins) the creation. At this point, Descartes gives up. After resignedly repeating that saying that God is conceivable does not mean that He is graspable, he sighs, "Au reste, j'ai déjà tant de fois expliqué

---

this passage).

[70] *Méditations* p. 311; *PW*, p. 132.

[71] "Mais d'autant que je me suis servi de l'idée de Dieu qui est en nous pour démontrer son existence, et que dans cette idée une puissance si immense est contenue, que nous concevons qu'il répugne (s'il est vrai que Dieu existe), que quelque autre chose que lui existe, si elle n'a été créée par lui, il suit clairement de ce que son existence a été démontrée, qu'il a été aussi démontré que tout ce monde, c'est-à-dire toutes les autres choses différentes de Dieu qui existent, ont été créées par lui." *Méditations*, p. 312.

comment nous avons en nous l'idée de Dieu, que je ne le puis encore ici répéter sans ennuyer les lecteurs" (As for how we can have an idea of God, I have gone over this *ad nauseam*).[72] The problem of divine creation, it seems, is not even worth mentioning.

Hobbes' insistence on the issue, however, illustrates the fracture at the heart of modernity. Hobbes is, in effect, taking God off the table by insisting that any conception of God is by definition blasphemous; his phrasing, that the Christian religion *obliges* us to believe that God is inconceivable, is a playful acknowledgment that the vociferous anti-idolatry of Christianity is, in the end, responsible for atheism. Without a functioning conception of the divinity, we are free to follow Lucretius in suggesting that the world may not, in fact, have been created at all. To suggest that it was is, by definition, to suggest an anthropomorphic (and thereby blasphemous) idea of the divine. We will see in the following chapter how La Fontaine levels this critique against Descartes with sustained efficacy and imaginative verve. Yet Hobbes' attacks on Descartes are somewhat unfair. As Descartes himself points out, he goes to great lengths to emphasize the equivocity, the unbridgeable *difference* between the divine and the human; as he notes in one of his responses to Hobbes, "il n'y a rien en Dieu de semblable aux choses extérieures, c'est-à-dire aux choses corporelles" (nothing in God resembles what is to be found in external, that is corporeal, things).[73] His emphasis on the non-mimetic relationship between ideas and their referents, or between sense impressions and the objects they describe, also serves this purpose. That said, Hobbes is certainly correct to note that Descartes' conception of divine creation is underexamined, merely inferred from the existence of objects other than God (knowledge of which, moreover, is suspended for much of the *Meditations*) and from its radical difference from human mental inventions, or "fictions de l'esprit." Indeed, Descartes' reference in the *Meditations* to the "marque de l'ouvrier" (mark of the fabricant) that God has imprinted on his creation demonstrates his own inability to describe divine creation in terms that avoid inviting comparisons with human authorship or making.

This phrase – the "marque de l'ouvrier" – plays a central role in the heated and prolonged debate between Descartes and his most vociferous and tenacious opponent. The Epicurean priest Pierre Gassendi's objections to the *Meditations* were so lengthy, thorough, and sustained that they were not included in the editions of the text. Rather, Descartes chose to include only his own responses to the objections; Gassendi responded to this slight by publishing, in 1644, a longer work that included not only his own original objections and Descartes'

---

[72] *Méditations*, pp. 312–3; *PW*, p. 133.
[73] *Méditations*, p. 311; *PW*, p. 132.

responses, but also a series of *instances* in which Gassendi further criticizes Descartes' responses, thereby granting himself, as it were, the last word. Gassendi's objections to the *Meditations* are quite similar to those of Hobbes, although they come from the opposite direction. If Hobbes' materialist atheism allowed him to attack the very possibility of divine creation, Gassendi's insistence on the inaccessibility of the central truths of Christianity through reason similarly led him to cast serious doubt on the validity of Descartes' arguments and even on their fundamental premises. For Gassendi, the idea that the human mind can successfully extricate itself from the materiality of the body and the specificity of lived experience is the height of philosophical arrogance, and he subjects Descartes' neat separation of idea and image to merciless critique. In his objections to the first two meditations, Gassendi asks Descartes whether, if the mind is completely independent of the body, fetuses possess reason and whether memory can operate without the physical traces of thoughts and sensations engraving themselves upon the brain. Yet Gassendi's attacks on the alleged incorporality of thought reach a crescendo during his objections to the third meditation, in which Descartes purports to prove the existence of God. Despite Descartes' repeated warnings that one can have clear and distinct ideas of something incomprehensible and ungraspable, like a chiliagon, Gassendi insists that having an idea of something is just as restrictive as forming an image of it. It is therefore impossible for humans to have any accurate idea of God; the gap between the divine and the human is simply too great: "Enfin qui donc peut-être considéré comme ayant de Dieu une idée juste, c'est-à-dire représentant Dieu tel qu'il est?"[74] (Who can be considered as having a correct idea of God, that is to say, as representing God as he is?) For Descartes, this line of argument merely demonstrates Gassendi's obstinate refusal to engage in the meditative discipline necessary to cleanse the mind of information conveyed by the senses and to think without images. As his derisive nickname for Gassendi, "Flesh," indicates, Descartes dismisses these objections as the confused ranting of a mind hopelessly trapped in the body. Indeed, he goes so far as to note that Gassendi's obstinate materialism disqualifies him as a reader of the *Meditations*: "Mais j'ai naguère protesté, ô Chair, que je n'avais point affaire avec ceux qui veulent user seulement de leur imagination, et non point de l'entendement"[75] (But I have already protested, Flesh, that I do not wish to deal with those who use only their imagination, rather than their understanding).

---

[74] Pierre Gassendi, *Disquisitio metaphysica seu, Dubitationes et instantiae adversus Renati Cartesii Metaphysicam et responsa. Recherches métaphysiques; ou, Doutes et instances contre la Métaphysique de R. Descartes et ses réponses*, ed., trans. Bernard Rochot (Paris: Vrin, 1962), p. 240 (hereafter, *DM*).
[75] *DM*, p. 240.

Such a counter-argument would work if Gassendi admitted any substantial difference between body and soul, imagination and intellect. However, Gassendi's refusal to entertain Descartes' dualism leads him to articulate an equivalency between ideas and images that we have seen, for example, in the work of Richeome, and that the Dutchman Revius would use against Descartes during the Leiden crisis later in the decade. For Gassendi, insofar as ideas and images are both signifiers, they are, for all intents and purposes, the same:

> quand vous dites que les Idées sont dans l'intellect, et que par elles l'Intellect connaît les choses dont elles sont les Idées, est-ce que dans l'Intellect il n'y a pas aussi des Images, et l'Intellect ne connaît-il pas par images? Qu'est-ce en effet d'autre que l'Idée d'une chose, sinon l'Image de cette chose même? L'Idée certes n'est pas une Idée si elle ne représente une chose, et l'Image n'est pas Image sinon en ce qu'elle représente une chose ... Dès lors quelle sera donc la différence entre l'imagination qui nous fait percevoir les choses par images et l'intellection qui nous fait percevoir les choses par images?[76]
>
> When you say that ideas are in the intellect, and through them the intellect knows the things that the ideas represent, does that mean that in the intellect there are no images, and the intellect cannot know through images? What is the idea of a thing if it does not represent the thing, and the image is not an image unless it represents something ... At that point, what would the difference be between the imagination which makes us perceive things by images and the intellect that makes us perceive things by images?

Insofar as this refusal to regard images and ideas as separate entities undercuts the entirety of Descartes' argument concerning the separability of the mind and the body, Descartes cannot engage with it seriously. Rather, he simply accuses Gassendi of readerly bad faith: "Quant à toute votre discussion présente sur les idées, elle n'a pas besoin de réponse, parce que vous restreignez arbitrairement le nom d'Idées aux seules images dépeintes en la fantaisie, tandis que moi je l'étends à tout ce que nous formons par la pensée"[77] (As for your present discussion concerning ideas, it does not require a response, since you arbitrarily restrict the name of ideas to images depicted in fantasy, whereas I mean by that name everything that we form in thought).

Yet Gassendi's objections are motivated by a deep desire to preserve the mystery of the divine against the incursions of Cartesian reason. Were he to admit Descartes' neat separation of body and mind, or his advocacy of the

---

[76] *DM*, p. 244.
[77] *DM*, p. 282.

clear and distinct, he would be rejecting the foundations of Christian theology along with centuries of tradition. Gassendi directly invokes his refusal to do so during the relentless challenge he mounts against Descartes' explanation of the necessity of divine creation – a topic which, as we have seen, is closely related to the question of dualism. Gassendi upbraids Descartes for smuggling the idea of divine creation into a world that he has (unnecessarily) destroyed through radical skepticism. Noting that Descartes says that he conceives of God "comme créateur de vous-même et de toutes les autres choses qui existent, s'il y en a" (as the creature of yourself and of all other things that exist, if there are any), Gassendi objects, "Mais comment le pouvez-vous, d'abord en ce qui vous concerne, si vous ne savez pas sur vous-même autre chose que le fait que vous pensez, que vous existez, que vous êtes une chose pensante? Est-ce que vous avez prouvé que vous êtes créé?"[78] (But how can you, in what concerns you, if you do not know anything about yourself other than that you think, that you exist, that you are a thinking thing? Have you proved that you were created?) Gassendi goes on to question whether Descartes can legitimately infer that our world is the only one that exists, or that there is only one, divine, creator of all that exists. There could be many worlds, or many creators. While Gassendi's line of reasoning resembles that of Hobbes, it comes from a very different place. Gassendi is demonstrating simultaneously that Descartes' skepticism does not go far enough, insofar as it does not subject human reason itself to ruthless critique, and that it goes too far, insofar as it scrutinizes aspects of the world that are best left unexamined. In other words, the mysteries of faith exist not just because humans have been too lazy or unintelligent to answer the questions behind them, but because the clumsy tool of human reason destroys the question in attempting to answer it. As Gassendi tells Descartes, "Il est fort croyable, dites-vous, que vous avez été fait à l'image et à la ressemblance de Dieu. Cela sans doute est croyable à la lumière de la foi religieuse: mais par la raison naturelle, comment cela pourrait-il se comprendre, à moins qu'on ne fasse Dieu pareil à un homme?"[79] (It is quite believable, you say, that you were made in the image and likeness of God. That is no doubt believable through the light of religion, but through natural reason, how can that be understood, unless you make God like a man?)

Descartes takes this last part of Gassendi's objection literally, as a further sign of his obtuseness, his obstinate refusal to understand the proper relation between Creator and creatures. To better illustrate what he means, Descartes uses the example of the famous Greek painter Apelles. He begins by noting that his reference in the *Meditations* to the "*marque de l'ouvrier*," which

[78] *DM*, p. 308.
[79] *DM*, pp. 360–1.

Gassendi seizes upon as evidence of Descartes' ultimate inability to speak of creation without using physical or material metaphors, should be understood in the sense that we can look at a painting by Apelles and immediately identify him as its artist.[80] "*Marque*" here refers, then, not to a physical mark that one can identify and locate, but to the "*artifice*" or style of Apelles. This slide from the physical, material language of "mark" to something much less tangible mirrors Descartes' persistent use of "likeness" alongside "image" to characterize what he maintains is a non-representational relationship between the human creature and the divine Creator.

Gassendi is having none of it. In his *instances* that respond to Descartes' own response, he continues to point out the ways in which this metaphor – this image of images – merely bolsters his own conviction that human efforts to understand God only cheapen his majesty. First, he notes that the artist's creation of an image comprises many stages, from the first sketches to the final fulgurance of color and detail, and therefore is a completely inappropriate way to think about divine creation, which is perfectly complete from the beginning. He then goes on to question the very legitimacy of Descartes' example by accusing him of dodging the real issue, which is "l'Idée ou l'image qui représente la chose telle qu'elle est"[81] (the Idea or the image which represents a thing as it is). Descartes, Gassendi states, seems to be saying that a bat (chauve-souris) painted by Apelles would therefore resemble the painter more than an egg resembles another egg. Gassendi grants that the Apelles example works if we are speaking of the loose, non-representational relation between Creator and creature that does indeed exist in the natural world, but holds that this metaphor is completely insufficient to explain the way in which humanity, in particular and unique among created things, bears the image and likeness of God: "de sorte que, la question portant non sur n'importe quelle créature, mais seulement sur l'esprit en tant que Dieu l'a créé à son image et à sa ressemblance, vous deviez aussi, en parlant d'Apelles, considérer non pas n'importe quel tableau, mais seulement celui qu'il aurait peint de façon à y faire voir sa propre image et ressemblance"[82] (such that, the question bearing not on any kind of creature, but only on the mind insofar as God created it in his image and likeness, you should also, in speaking of Apelles, consider not just any painting, but only

---

[80] Gassendi's objection to the phrase "marque de l'ouvrier" reads as follows: "Sur ce point, je suis sûr, ou je me trompe fort, que vous n'avez pas d'autre représentation imaginative que celle d'une figure imprimée dans une chose molle par un sceau, car tout ce que vous dites est en accord avec cette représentation imaginative-là; mais vous ne voulez pourtant pas l'avouer, ni même faire mention de ce décalque que vous avez dans l'esprit, de peur qu'on ne puisse trop facilement vous convaincre que vous concevez les choses de l'esprit sur le modèle des choses corporelles." (*DM*, p. 268).

[81] *DM*, p. 384.

[82] *DM*, p. 384.

that which he painted so he could see his own image and likeness). Gassendi is not denying the biblical assertion that God created humanity in His image and likeness. Rather, he is pointing out that Cartesian reason and, yes, material metaphor accomplish nothing more than the obliteration of religious mystery. They cannot account for the special relationship between the divine and the human that the Bible asserts. Gassendi never says so directly, but for a priest such as himself, this relation can be made manifest only through the Incarnation, a topic that Descartes (wisely) avoids altogether.

Here, once again, Descartes and Gassendi find themselves at a philosophical impasse. Yet while the sources of their profound disagreement are fascinating in themselves, if we place their debate over images, ideas, and divine creation in the context of ongoing polemics concerning idolatry, Descartes' decision to resort to the example of Apelles to explain the relation between the divine and the human is significant.[83] Along with the invocation of Praxiteles that opens the conversation between Gassendi and Descartes regarding the third meditation, it invites a comparison between divine creation and artistic production that, as we have seen, deeply concerns Gassendi. It is all the more curious given Descartes' concern, repeatedly expressed throughout his responses to all of the objections as well as in the *Meditations* themselves, to draw a firm line between the kind of creation that is unique to God and the chimerical, groundless inventions of human fantasy, those "fictions de l'esprit" to which he refers in his responses to the objections collected by Mersenne. It is indeed possible to argue that the Apelles example leaves this line intact. Descartes nowhere refers to the painter as the *inventor* of what he creates; Apelles does not represent nonexistent creatures pulled out of thin air. Rather, he paints the world around him, but in an accomplished style that, as we have seen, leads the spectator to immediately identify the work as his. In other words, it is not *what* he represents, but *how* he does it. God, on the other hand, is the ultimate cause of all that exists, not least because humans are incapable of creating something real out of nothing and sustaining it from moment to moment. As Descartes informs Gassendi,

> Et lorsque vous aimez mieux comparer la création de Dieu avec l'opération d'un architecte qu'avec la génération d'un père, vous le faites sans aucune raison; car, encore que ces trois manières d'agir soient totalement différentes, l'éloignement pourtant n'est pas si grand de la production naturelle à la divine que de l'artificielle à la même production divine.

---

[83] For an excellent exploration of the relation between Gassendi and Descartes, see Margaret J. Osler, *Divine Will and the Mechanical Philosophy: Gassendi and Descartes on Contingency and Necessity in the Created World* (New York: Cambridge University Press, 1994).

> You prefer to compare the creation of God to the labour of a workman rather than to parental procreation, but you have no reason to do so. Even if the three modes of action involved here are completely different in kind, nevertheless the analogy between natural procreation and divine creation is closer than that between artificial production and divine creation.[84]

The comparison with Apelles, then, is merely meant to adumbrate the connection between God and his creation, a connection that, once again, Descartes understands to be non-representational. It is not meant to illustrate the act of creation itself.

And yet. What happens in the passage above illustrates the persistent ambiguity of Descartes' discourse on creation, and explains why Gassendi and others persisted in believing that he was trying to smuggle a substantial likeness between humanity and divinity in through the back door. After establishing the absolute difference between the three types of creation he identifies – divine, natural, and artificial – he moves on to measure the distance between them, noting that natural production is closer to divine production than is artificial (that is, human and artistic) production. This placement of different modes of production along a spectrum, rather than in incommunicable spheres, mitigates the absolute incommensurability that Descartes seeks to preserve in the first part of the sentence. Moreover, the passage continues as follows:

> Mais ni vous ne trouverez point que j'ai dit qu'il y a autant de rapport entre Dieu et nous qu'il y en a entre un père et ses enfants; ni il n'est pas vrai aussi qu'il n'y a jamais aucun rapport entre l'ouvrier et son ouvrage, comme paraît lorsqu'un peintre fait un tableau qui lui ressemble.

> I did not say, however, that the resemblance between us and God is as close as that between children and parents. Again, it is not always true that there is no resemblance between the work of a craftsman and the craftsman himself, as is clear in the case of an artist who produces a painting that resembles himself.[85]

The rather tortured syntax here conveys Descartes' ongoing efforts to explain, in human terms and language, the relation between Creator and creature. Natural production is closer to divine creation than is artificial; yet, on the other hand, Descartes rejects any suggestion that the relation between God and humanity resembles that between a father and his son all while doing little to discourage the comparison, which he himself initiates, between God and an artist.

---

84 *Méditations*, p. 404; *PW*, p. 257.
85 *Méditations*, pp. 403–4; *PW*, p. 257.

The example of Apelles extends another example taken from ancient art that Descartes uses at the beginning of his responses to Gassendi's objections to the third meditation. Here, Descartes responds to Gassendi's assertion that all of our ideas come from outside of ourselves and are derived from already existing entities. The human mind therefore invents nothing, but rather assembles, divides, lengthens, etc., the primary sources offered to it by the world. By this logic, Descartes notes, "l'idée d'une chimère que l'esprit fait en composant, divisant, etc., n'est pas faite par lui, mais qu'elle vient de dehors ou qu'elle est étrangère" (the idea of chimeras, which the mind makes up by the process of putting together and separating etc., are not constructed by the mind but are adventitious).[86] For Descartes, this obliteration of human agency and authorship is absurd, and he uses the example of Praxiteles to illustrate his point:

> Mais vous pourriez aussi de la même façon prouver que Praxitèle n'a fait aucunes statues, d'autant qu'il n'a pas eu de lui le marbre sur lequel il les pût tailler; et l'on pourrait aussi dire que vous n'avez pas fait ces objections, parce que vous les avez composées de paroles que vous n'avez pas inventées, mais que vous avez empruntées d'autrui.

> By this argument you could prove that Praxiteles never made any statues on the grounds that he did not get from within himself the marble from which he sculpted them; or you could prove that you did not produce these objections on the grounds that you composed them out of words which you acquired from others rather than inventing them yourself.[87]

Against Gassendi, for whom non-divine authorship can be conceived only as recycling and reassembly, Descartes maintains that human authorship *is* possible. It is precisely the possibility of human authorship – the ability of humans to imagine chimeras, statues, winged horses, existing lions, a world in which nothing exists, a deceptive God – that renders the reality of divine creation so very necessary. Otherwise, humanity would be overrun with opinion, prejudice, and fantasy, with no foundation upon which to build knowledge of the world. It is only by ensuring a conception of the divine that is completely *other* from that of the human that science can begin. As Descartes states at the end of the fifth meditation:

> Et ainsi je reconnais très clairement que la certitude et la vérité de toute science dépend de la seule connaissance du vrai Dieu: en sorte qu'avant

---

[86] *Méditations*, p. 395; *PW*, p. 250.
[87] *Méditations*, p. 395; *PW*, p. 250.

que je le connusse, je ne pouvais savoir parfaitement aucune autre chose. Et à présent que je le connais, j'ai le moyen d'acquérir une science parfaite touchant une infinité de choses, non seulement de celles qui sont en lui, mais aussi de celles qui appartiennent à la nature corporelle, en tant qu'elle peut servir d'objet aux démonstrations des géomètres, lesquels n'ont point d'égard à son existence.

Thus I see plainly that the certainty and truth of all knowledge depends uniquely on my awareness of the true God, to such an extent that I was incapable of perfect knowledge about anything else until I became aware of him. And now it is possible for me to achieve full and certain knowledge of countless matters, both concerning God himself and also concerning things which belong to corporeal nature in so far as it can serve as the object of geometrical demonstrations which have no concern with whether that object exists.[88]

It therefore follows that atheists are incapable of science and, indeed, Descartes makes this point in his responses to the sixth objections:

Pour ce qui regarde la science d'un athée, il est aisé de montrer qu'il ne peut rien savoir avec certitude et assurance; car, comme j'ai déjà dit ci-devant, d'autant moins puissant sera celui qu'il reconnaîtra pour l'auteur de son être, d'autant plus aura-t-il occasion de douter si sa nature n'est point tellement imparfaite qu'il se trompe, même dans les choses qui lui semblent très évidentes; et jamais il ne pourra être délivré de ce doute, si, premièrement, il ne reconnaît qu'il a été créé par un vrai Dieu, principe de toute vérité, et qui ne peut être trompeur.

As for the kind of knowledge possessed by the atheist, it is easy to demonstrate that it is not immutable and certain. As I have stated previously, the less power the atheist attributes to the author of his being, the more reason he will have to suspect that his nature may be so imperfect as to allow him to be deceived even in matters which seem utterly evident to him. And he will never be able to be free of this doubt until he recognizes that he has been created by a true God who cannot be a deceiver.[89]

It could well be objected, however, that these two passages turn not on the difficult question of the legitimacy of human authorship, but rather on the possibility of human knowledge. Assurance that an existing God who shares

---

[88] *Méditations*, p. 171; *PW*, p. 49.
[89] *Méditations*, pp. 446–7; *PW*, p. 289.

no attributes with humanity created the world and its inhabitants renders science possible; it makes the world readable. Yet, as Elisabeth of Bohemia would object in the letters that she exchanged with the philosopher from 1643 to 1650, these examples do little to resolve the thorny issue of human initiative and invention. While Kim Sang Ong-Van-Cung has convincingly argued that Descartes' assertion, integral to his theory of divine creation, of God as a *causa sui* opens the path towards an unprecedented valorization of human creation, in Descartes' own work the possibility of legitimizing, and even imagining, human invention in a world authored by God remains murky.[90] His response to the rather inept objections articulated by the Jesuit Bourdin de-emphasizes his own role in the articulation of the *Meditations*, going so far as to suggest that his philosophy is not new at all:

> Je dis de plus, ce qui peut-être pourra sembler paradoxal, qu'il n'y a rien en toute cette philosophie, en tant que péripatéticienne et différente des autres, qui ne soit nouveau, et qu'au contraire il n'y a rien dans la mienne qui ne soit ancien: car pour ce qui est des principes, je ne reçois que ceux qui jusques ici ont été connus et admis généralement de tous les philosophes, et qui pour cela même sont les plus anciens de tous: et ce qu'ensuite j'en déduis paraît si manifestement, ainsi que je fais voir, être contenu et renfermé dans ces principes, qu'il paraît aussi en même temps que cela est très ancien, puisque c'est la nature même qui l'a imprimé dans nos esprits.

> I shall add something that may seem paradoxical. Everything in peripatetic philosophy, regarded as a distinctive school that is different from others, is quite new, whereas everything in my philosophy is old. For as far as principles are concerned, I only accept those which in the past have always been common ground among all philosophers without exception, and which are therefore the most ancient of all. Moreover, the conclusions I go on to deduce are already contained and implicit in these principles, and I show this so clearly as to make it apparent that they too are very ancient, in so far as they are naturally implanted in the human mind.[91]

Descartes' wording here recalls that used by Protestants and Catholics in their arguments over whose religion enjoyed the legitimacy of truth, but it also, in its declaration that "c'est la nature même qui l'a imprimé dans nos

---

[90] "Descartes invente cette manière de concevoir la création, et bien qu'il n'ait jamais admis que la créature puisse créer, sa philosophie constitue le point limite où une création humaine devient pensable." Kim Sang Ong-Van-Cung, *Descartes et l'ambivalence de la création* (Paris: Vrin, 2000), p. 18.
[91] *Méditations*, p. 530; *PW*, pp. 391–2.

esprits," (it is nature itself which impressed it upon our minds) sounds quite a bit like Gassendi's assertion that the human mind in fact creates nothing that can properly be called its own. We can begin to appreciate why the two examples that Descartes deploys against Gassendi are taken from ancient, pre-Christian art; by using Apelles and Praxiteles, Descartes manages to dodge the issue of the coexistence of a widely recognized doctrine of divine creation – something that emerged only well into Christian history – and human art.[92] For despite Descartes' philosophical and authorial modesty, both Hobbes and Gassendi picked up on the doors opened not just by his unprecedented assertion of God as *causa sui* but also by his description of the human will, in its unbounded and absolute freedom, as the locus of the similitude linking the human creature to its divine creator.

Descartes remained convinced that he had managed to solve the problems raised by the debates over idolatry. In a letter to the Jesuit Père Dinet that appeared in the second, 1642, edition of the *Meditations* that also included the objections of the Jesuit Bourdin and Descartes' rather acid responses, Descartes once again proudly claims to have solved the thorniest problems plaguing philosophy and religion:

> Enfin, il ne faut pas non plus appréhender qu'elles troublent la paix des écoles; mais tout au contraire, la guerre étant maintenant autant allumée entre les philosophes qu'elle le saurait être, il n'y a point de meilleur moyen pour établir la paix entre eux et pour réduire toutes les hérésies, qui renaissent tous les jours de leurs controverses, que de les obliger à recevoir des opinions qui soient vraies, telles que j'ai déjà prouvé que sont les miennes. Car leur claire perception *ôtera tout sujet de doute et de dispute*.

> Again, there is no need to fear that my opinions will disturb the peace of the Schools. On the contrary, philosophers already take sides against each other on so many controversies that they could hardly be more at war than they are now. Indeed, the best way of establishing peace between them, and curbing the heresies that spring up every day out of these debates, is to secure the acceptance of true opinions, such as I have proved mine to be. For the clear perception of these truths will *eliminate everything that could fuel doubt and controversy*.[93] [emphasis mine]

---

[92] Descartes' simultaneous embrace of and retreat from the valorization of human creation that his work enables adds another layer to Hans Belting's valuable account of the development of art as a human endeavor, a manifestation of human authorship in *Likeness and Presence*.

[93] *Méditations*, p. 530–1; *PW*, p. 392.

And yet. The ongoing theological difficulties surrounding the *Meditations* demonstrate that Descartes was overly optimistic. As Tad Schmaltz notes, seventeenth-century condemnations of the *Meditations* came from all sides, both during Descartes' lifetime and after his death.[94] As it turns out, the *Meditations* did, eventually, put an end to theological disputes, but only by opening avenues that allowed scholars and commentators to argue that although Descartes was undeniably convinced that he had proven both the existence of God and the immortality of the soul, religious questions were ultimately peripheral to the essence of his thought.

---

[94] "Already during his lifetime, Descartes had been condemned in both Utrecht and Leiden for proposing in the *Meditations* a sort of doubt that undermines both a traditional Aristotelian scholasticism that starts with trust in the senses and an orthodox Calvinism that starts with faith in the authority of scripture and the testimony of the Holy Spirit." Tad M. Schmaltz, 'Seventeenth-century Responses to the *Meditations*', in *The Blackwell Guide to Descartes's* Meditations, pp. 193–203, here, pp. 195–6. Schmaltz also reminds us that in 1676 a condemnation was issued in Leiden that accused Descartes of elevating the will; the Dutch Cartesians responded with an argument that was, in turn, condemned in a 1691 formulary issued in Paris that condemned Descartes for restricting human freedom (p. 201).

Idolatry and the Questioning of Mastery in La Fontaine's *Fables*

"Quand Prométhée voulut former l'homme, il prit la qualité dominante de chaque bête. De ces pièces si différentes il composa notre espèce, il fit cet ouvrage qu'on appelle le petit monde."[1] (When Prometheus wanted to make man, he took the dominant quality of every beast. From these very different pieces he composed our species, he made this work which we call the little world.)

Jean de La Fontaine offers this anecdote in the preface to the first volume of his *Fables*, ostensibly to explain why the information the fables convey about the properties and personalities of diverse animal species is useful to humanity; since we have been shaped from beasts, learning more about animals can help us to learn more about ourselves. Yet placed against seventeenth-century France's preoccupation not only with the divine creation of the world but also with the special standing of humans as images of God on earth, La Fontaine's rather nonchalant presentation of Prometheus fashioning man out of various animal parts is, like many of his fables, both mischievous and provocative. It serves to announce the central position that the question of creation, divine and artistic, occupies throughout the *Fables* by slyly suggesting that the poems' wisdom is only accessible to those who loosen their grip on the biblical creation story, with all that it implies concerning legitimacy and human uniqueness. Prometheus's activity is not the *ex nihilo* creation of the biblical divinity, and indeed, nowhere in this sentence is the verb "créer" used. Instead, Prometheus, a bit like La Fontaine himself, engages in a kind of *bricolage*, an assembly of diverse parts that forms a work, an *ouvrage*, whose identity as fabricated entity is contained in its name. And, La Fontaine goes on to note, the name is provisional and fabricated; what Prometheus fashions is not the World itself, but "ce qu'on appelle le petit monde," a much more humble entity.

---

[1] Jean de La Fontaine, *Préface*, in *Oeuvres complètes: Fables et contes*, ed. Jean-Pierre Collinet (Paris: Gallimard, 1991), pp. 8–9 (hereafter, *OC*). Quotations from the *Fables* will include line numbers from this edition in the text.

It might well be objected that La Fontaine's literary exploitation of pagan myth, here and elsewhere, is nothing more than a signal of his affection for the ancients and an announcement of his intent to distance himself from the messy theological disputes and concerns of his age. He is, after all, also the author of *Clymène*, a play which begins with a conference among the gods of Olympus, and the short novel *Les Amours de Psyché et de Cupidon*, a clever rewriting of the familiar tale placed in the seductive setting of the gardens of Versailles that appeared between the two volumes of his *Fables*. However, this neat separation of pagan and Christian, literary and theological, has already been problematized earlier in the *Préface*. A few paragraphs before the introduction of Prometheus, La Fontaine justifies the method of presenting wisdom through fables by noting that this method lies at the heart of Christianity:

> s'il m'est permis de mêler ce que nous avons de plus sacré parmi les erreurs du paganisme, nous voyons que la Vérité a parlé aux hommes par paraboles; et la parabole est-elle autre chose que l'apologue, c'est-à-dire un exemple fabuleux, et qui s'insinue avec d'autant plus de facilité et d'effet qu'il est plus commun et plus familier?[2]

> if I am allowed to mix what we hold most sacred among the errors of paganism, we can see that truth spoke to humans through parables, and is a parable anything other than an apologia, which is to say a fabulous example which insinuates itself with all the more ease and effect when it is more common and familiar?

With his apology for mixing "ce que nous avons de plus sacré" with the "erreurs du paganisme," La Fontaine calls attention to his awareness of the opposition between pagan and Christian, the sacred and the misguided, all while noting that literature, and more specifically, fables, serve to blur the line between, and even equate, the two. This vaguely scandalous mix of error and wisdom, of which La Fontaine demonstrates himself to be well aware, serves to prepare the reader for the unspoken comparison between Promethean fashioning and divine Creation that occurs only a few lines later.

In other words, far from occupying a literary space devoid of theological implications, La Fontaine highlights the uneasy juxtaposition of pagan and Christian, playing upon, and playing with, the seventeenth-century French reader's simultaneous attraction to and rejection of the benighted "other."[3]

---

[2] *OC*, p. 7.
[3] La Fontaine's slipperiness in this regard has led to difficulties in classifying him either as an "Ancien" or as a "Moderne" in the conflict which Larry Norman has described so brilliantly. Jean-Charles Darmon, in a footnote to his perceptive reading of *Clymène*,

He is always fully aware that his evocations of the council of Olympic gods or the curiosity of Psyché or the providence of Jupiter take place against an ever-present backdrop of Christian sensibility, and he gently uses pagan example to interrogate the coherence of the Christian faith. While this playful interrogation and unholy mix characterize most of La Fontaine's oeuvre, they are especially on display in his three idolatry fables, which are distributed between the two volumes that were published ten years apart from each other, in 1668 and 1678.

The Idolatry Fables

The first of these fables, *L'Homme et l'Idole de bois (The Man and the Wooden Idol)* (IV, 8), adapted from Aesop's *The Man Who Broke a Statue*, relates the story of a "certain pagan" who "chez lui gardait un Dieu de bois,/ De ces dieux qui sont sourds, bien qu'ayant des oreilles" (lines 1–2) (who kept at home a wooden God, one of those gods who are deaf, even though they have ears). Having sacrificed to this God for years without receiving any benefit, he loses his temper, strikes the statue, and finds that it is filled with gold. Outraged, the man upbraids the statue: "Quand je t'ai fait du bien,/ M'as-tu valu, dit-il, seulement une obole?/ Va, sors de mon logis: cherche d'autres autels" (lines 17–19) (When I treated you well, did you give me anything? Go, leave my house: go find other altars), before paraphrasing the *morale* that Aesop had placed at the end of his version of the story: "Tu ressembles aux naturels/ Malheureux, grossiers et stupides:/ On n'en peut rien tirer qu'avecque le bâton./ Plus je te remplissais, plus mes mains étaient vides:/ J'ai bien fait de changer de ton" (lines 20–24) (You resemble the uncultivated: unhappy, vulgar, and stupid. One can't get anything out of them

---

notes that "Ce Parnasse témoigne d'un malaise récurrent de la poétique de La Fontaine toute entière face au temps qui passe et face à sa propre modernité: un désir perpétuel de « nouveau » et de fraîcheur – par lequel La Fontaine plaît, et plaira tout particulièrement aux Modernes, qui, faisant au besoin la sourde oreille, comme Charles Perrault, en feront pour ainsi dire un moderne malgré lui; et, par ailleurs, de façon simultanée, un besoin de situer sa pratique d'écrivain, sa propre fragilité, dans l'espace littéraire familier aux Anciens, que la fiction du Parnasse servit si longtemps à ordonner et à revivifer dans la mémoire de ses devanciers." (This Parnassus expresses a recurrent malaise regarding the entire poetics of La Fontaine as it relates to the passage of time and its own modernity: a perpetual desire of "novelty" and freshness through which La Fontaine pleases, and particularly pleases the Moderns who, like Perrault, practicing deafness where need be, makes him a Modern despite himself while simultaneously feeling the need to situate his writing practice, his own fragility, in the literary space familiar to the Ancients, which the fiction of the Parnassus tried so long to revivify and order in the memory of its forerunners.) (*Philosophies de la fable: Poésie et pensée dans l'oeuvre de La Fontaine* (Paris: Hermann, 2011), p. 46, note 1).

without hitting them. The more I filled you, the more my hands were empty; I did well to change my tone).

As in the original, the fable's humor consists in the man's surprising reaction to the discovery of gold in the statue. Rather than expressing delight at the unexpected windfall, he persists in his personification of the statue, and the conclusion that he draws from the story is that, in the words of Aesop, one can get something from a bad man only by striking him. Yet La Fontaine's transposition of Aesop's story into seventeenth-century Christian France provides it with additional nuance, nuance that the fabulist further develops through his careful choice of words and voice. It would, for example, have been impossible for a seventeenth-century reader to encounter this fable without thinking of the episodes of violent iconoclasm that had marked Europe for over a century. By demonstrating that the destruction of the statue does nothing to alter the man's belief in its divinity – on the contrary, his anger at the statue shows it to be stronger than ever – La Fontaine seems to be echoing Luther's conviction, expressed in the Invocavit Sermons delivered in 1522 in Wittenburg, that iconoclasm is counter-productive insofar as it accords the image, properly viewed as *adiaphora*, or indifferent to worship, more power than it actually possesses, thereby paradoxically and counter-productively magnifying the original idolatry.

That said, the fable also appears to distance itself from the man's beliefs. In beginning the fable by identifying the man as "Certain Païen" (A certain pagan), La Fontaine demarcates the man and his strange practice of identifying the statue as a God from the reader who is easily able to identify the biblical source of the description of the god as one of "ces dieux qui sont sourds, bien qu'ayant des oreilles" (these gods who are deaf, though they have ears). Moreover, the word "Idole," which appears, capitalized, twice in the fable, is placed in contexts that make clear that this label, like that of Pagan, is that of the reader, and is not shared by the fable's subject, who continues to consider the statue a god, urging it, even after its destruction, to seek out other altars. The separation that La Fontaine establishes between the reader and the fable's main character, combined with the man's faulty logic and the lack of an explicit *morale*, renders its ultimate purpose perplexing. Indeed, one of La Fontaine's early commentators, the eighteenth-century writer and moralist Sébastien-Roch-Nicolas Chamfort, professed his confusion as to what lesson this fable could possibly convey:

> Qu'y a-t-il d'étonnant qu'une idole de bois ne réponde pas à nos voeux, et que, renfermant de l'or, l'or paraisse quand vous brisez la statue? Que conclure de tout cela? Qu'il faut battre ceux qui sont d'un naturel stupide? Cela

n'est pas vrai, et cette méthode ne produit rien de bon.⁴

Why is it shocking that a wooden idol does not respond to our prayers, and, containing gold, the gold appears when you break the statue? What should we conclude from this? That we should beat those who are naturally stupid? That is not true, and this method can lead to nothing good.

Yet the resemblance of Chamfort's frustrated reaction to this seemingly useless fable to the man's own exasperation with the impassive and unhelpful god is itself an indication of the fable's deeper significance. How, La Fontaine seems to ask, is the reader begging a poem for meaning and morality different from a Pagan imploring a wooden statue for help? The persistent search for what we narrowly define as wisdom, and our rejection of a fable that seemingly fails to deliver it, can lead us, like the man in the fable who cannot see that his God is in reality a piece of wood, to overlook the poem's materiality, its poetic prowess and subtle plays of language, which may or may not carry their own message.⁵

La Fontaine's intimation that the reading and writing of fables, whose beauty and verbal cleverness pull against the utilitarian morality that the reader expects and demands, are deeply connected to the logic of idolatry, wherein the materiality of the object must always be placed in service to, and eventually efface itself before, a higher truth, is also on display in his second idolatry fable, *L'Ane portant des reliques* (The Donkey Carrying Relics) (V, 14). In this short and charming fable, again adapted from Aesop, a donkey carrying relics believes that the incense and song with which he is greeted are intended for him, and begins prancing accordingly. Someone (quelqu'un) notices, and informs him: "Maître Baudet, ôtez-vous de l'esprit/ Une vanité si folle./ Ce n'est pas vous, c'est l'idole/ A qui cet honneur se rend,/ Et que la gloire en est due" (lines 6–10) (Master Donkey, take out of your head such a crazy vanity. It is not you, it is the idol to whom this honor is paid and to

---

⁴ *Les Trois Fabulistes, Esope, Phèdre, et La Fontaine*, Delance, 1796, II, 237, cited in La Fontaine, *OC*, p. 1116.

⁵ Other critics have noted the ways in which La Fontaine's fables work, explicitly and implicitly, against the *morales* that they purport to teach. As John D. Lyons notes in his 'Author and Reader in the *Fables*' (*French Review* 49.1 (October 1975), pp. 59–67), La Fontaine's frequent invocations of his own presence in the *Fables* serve to point out their literariness: "He reminds us that the fable is not a reality but the *image* of a reality, a generalization which *fits* a particular situation" (p. 65). Jean-Charles Darmon has done much to point out the philosophically complex and ultimately subversive role of the *Fables*, noting that "lorsque La Fontaine figure une doctrine, c'est généralement de façon indirecte, oblique et assez lointaine." (when La Fontaine uses a doctrine, it is generally in an indirect, oblique, and fairly far-off manner). See *Philosophies de la fable*, p. 192.

whom the glory is due). The *morale* follows, in the narrator's voice: "D'un magistrat ignorant/ C'est la robe qu'on salue" (lines 11–12) (In the case of an ignorant magistrate, it is the robe that one salutes).

Here, once again, the voice of reason points out the ridiculousness of mistaking the vehicle for that which it carries, or, in Augustinian terms, of substituting *frui* – particularly evident in the donkey's prancing – for *uti*. If the first fable drew an implicit parallel between the man and the reader, this fable invites a comparison between the donkey and La Fontaine himself, whose delightful presentation of messages that, after all, have already been articulated by Aesop seems designed to attract the admiration of the reader, potentially distracting him from the fable's ostensible lesson. This is all the more the case here, where the rather flat *morale* – "D'un magistrat ignorant/ C'est la robe qu'on salue" – stands, in its judicial aridity, in stark contrast to the lively picture of donkeys, relics, incense, and song that precedes it.

Yet the fable also explicitly constitutes a development of La Fontaine's reflections on idols and idolatry. The reader is subtly invited to make the connection between this fable and *L'Homme et l'Idole de bois* by the fable that immediately precedes *L'Ane portant des reliques*, *La Poule aux oeufs d'or* (The Chicken with Golden Eggs) (V, 13). In the context of a lesson about avarice, "qui perd tout en voulant tout gagner" (line 1) (who loses everything through wanting to win everything), La Fontaine presents the reader with the counterpart of the man with the idol. This man, fascinated by a hen who lays a golden egg once a day, decides to kill her and open her up, expecting to find her filled with gold but instead discovering that she is identical to other birds. While the explicit lesson of the fable is unrelated to that of the man with the idol, and, indeed, the expectation and outcome of the action depicted in the fable are completely opposite, the man, the breaking, and the gold serve to remind the attentive reader of the earlier fable, and to prepare him for the tale of the relic-bearing donkey.

For here, once again, La Fontaine's word choice points to the thicket of issues and judgments surrounding religious images in seventeenth-century France. While the first fable distanced the reader from its eponymous hero by designating him simply as "certain Païen," here the donkey is unironically depicted as charged with "reliques"; the existence of relics and their power is not called into question, either by the narrator or by those who greet the donkey with incense and chanting. This surprisingly credulous opening prepares the rather sly phrase that introduces the spectator's direct discourse: "quelqu'un vit l'erreur" (line 5) (someone saw the error). At this point, the reader could well expect that the error in question might not be the donkey's appropriation of the worship for himself, but rather the attribution of religious significance to the relics he carries, which is arguably no less misguided. The anonymous spectator's explanation maintains this ambiguity, since his admonition to the donkey to abandon his "vanité si folle" is closely linked, in proximity and rhyme, to his characterization of the relic as an "idole" in the next line. The irruption of the polemical word "idole" into the fable, in the context of the spectator's explicit criticism of the donkey's conduct, undercuts the very ground upon which the criticism is offered, delegitimizing with one fell swoop the worship of relics in which the incense-bearing chanters are engaged. La Fontaine implicitly invites the reader to extend this critical mechanism to the *morale*, whose obvious message concerns our respect for the trappings of authority regardless of the merits of their wearer. Yet if we extend the logic of the spectator's criticism to the *morale*, we are led to reflect upon the foundations of the legal system itself. The magistrate's ignorance is the obvious target, but it only incompletely masks the possibility that the law he represents and enforces might be based upon something other than justice. In short, what we regard as "relics," quasi-transparent signifiers, as Counter-Reformation Catholics would have it, of divine transcendence, might well be "idols," mute, ignorant, and empty symbols that still, inexplicably, demand respect.

For all of that, however, it would be a mistake to conclude that the spectator's voice is that of La Fontaine. For while the donkey's error consists in inflating his own role by attributing the praise destined for the relics he carries to himself, the spectator's spoken intervention moves too far in the opposite direction. All subjectivity is effaced. Not only is he himself anonymous, identified merely as "quelqu'un" ("someone"; it should be noted that the spectator could just as easily be a woman, or another animal); the wisdom he dispenses is entirely cast in the passive voice. This curious quality of his speech is underscored by the curious syntax – "Ce n'est pas vous, c'est l'idole" (It is not you, it is the idol) – which holds out the promise of agency only to retract it in the two following lines – "A qui cet honneur se rend,/ Et que la gloire en est due" (To whom this honor is paid, and to whom the glory is due). This faceless transparency, this agentless authority, are precisely what John D. Lyons argues that La Fontaine's many interventions and digressions – one might say, his prancing – are meant to call into question and even subvert. In this context, La Fontaine's adoption of Gabriele Faerno's sixteenth-century introduction of the figure of the magistrate into Aesop's original fable takes on a deeper, more portentous meaning. It opposes the faceless, anonymous authority of the law to the dizzying variety of beasts, words, and situations that La Fontaine presents to his reader, a variety that, as many critics have noted, precludes any stable, univocal notion of Truth.[6] As La Fontaine himself

---

[6] As Anne Birberick notes in her excellent *Reading Undercover: Authority and Audience in Jean de La Fontaine* (Lewisburg: Bucknell University Press, 1998), "While reason is crucial to the interpretative process, LF offers no formal set of procedures – 'un

notes, in *Le Cierge* (The Candle) (IX, 12), "Tout en tout est divers: ôtez-vous de l'esprit/ Qu'aucun être ait été composé sur le vôtre" (lines 17–18) (Everything in everything is diverse: take it out of your mind that any being has been composed according to yours).

L'Homme et l'Idole de bois and *L'Ane portant des reliques*, both published in 1668, in the first volume of fables, reveal La Fontaine's acute sensitivity to the logic of idolatry. The fabulist deftly exploits the history and emotions surrounding the subject – here evoking Luther's opposition to iconoclasm, there recalling John of Damascus's well-known truism that "the honor paid to the image passes to the prototype" – to highlight the complexity of negotiating materiality, representation, and belief in seventeenth-century France.

Yet in the second volume of *Fables*, published in 1679, eleven years after the first, La Fontaine's increasingly philosophical bent led him back to the subject of idolatry, which thereby acquired an even greater importance and centrality in his work. *Le Statuaire et la Statue de Jupiter* (The Sculptor and the Statue of Jupiter) (IX, 6) in many ways completes and deepens what could be called La Fontaine's idolatry cycle. As I have previously noted, Exodus 20: 4 addresses three aspects of idolatry all while leaving the relationship between them unclear. By singling out images for condemnation, the biblical text seems to mark statues and paintings as more dangerous than the written word; this particular danger of the visible is underscored by the anti-idolatrous passages in the Book of Wisdom, which identify the father's statue of his dead son as the root of idolatrous practices. Exodus 20: 4 also forbids the worship of such images, leaving open the possibility, which post-Reformation Catholics would exploit, that images could be acceptable as long as they themselves were not worshipped. It is notable that La Fontaine's first two idolatry fables line up rather well with these two aspects of Exodus 20: 4. *L'Homme et l'Idole de bois*, as the title indicates, focuses on the object worshipped as much as on the worshipper. It is hard to imagine that the man would have attributed personhood with such vehemence to a painting or even a relic. In *L'Ane portant des reliques*, the incense and chants cause the act of worship to emerge as the central aspect of the fable, rather than the object of worship, which fluctuates interestingly between relic and idol.

Le Statuaire et la Statue de Jupiter, the third and last fable in what could be thought of as La Fontaine's idolatry series, takes on the most contentious, and arguably most philosophically rich, aspect of the biblical injunction against idolatry: that of making. The fable relates the story of a sculptor who decides to carve a block of marble into the form of Jupiter. Upon completing his work,

---

art de penser' – on how to reason. Instead, reasoning processes must be inferred from the actions of his characters, characters who often draw poor conclusions because they fail to consider the ambiguities and complexities inherent in a particular situation" (p. 50).

he is frightened by the statue's resemblance to the god, and this development leads La Fontaine into several verses in which he compares the sculptor to the poet, and both artists to children with their dolls, invoking along the way the "erreur païenne" (pagan error) of idolatry before offering a conclusion that speaks to the universal human preference of lies to truth.

La Fontaine's depiction of the sculptor's demiurgic powers, along with his comparison of the sculptor's art to that of the poet, have led many critics to accord this fable a central place in the elaboration of the fabulist's own theory and practice of artistic creation. Patrick Dandrey has been particularly forceful in this reading of the fable, calling it a place where "La Fontaine a fait la métaphore de son propre travail en figurant celui d'un autre" (La Fontaine has made the metaphor of his own work by figuring that of another).[7] For Dandrey, the sculptor's opening negotiation with the beautiful block of marble exemplifies his humility before the raw material to be transformed, while his artistic mastery in turn invites comparison with the god whose likeness he so stunningly recreates: "L'affirmation implicite d'une maîtrise artistique conduit à entreprendre la figure concrète d'une maîtrise divine"[8] (The implicit affirmation of artistic mastery leads to the undertaking of the concrete figure of divine mastery). La Fontaine's uncanny ability to convey this delicate combination of humility and mastery that characterizes the essence of neoclassicism marks the fabulist as himself one of the great artists of his time. Dandrey sums up the author's technique in a sentence that is itself quite poetic:

> Plus encore que celle des théoriciens, la poétique de La Fontaine, poétique d'un "practicien", procède effectivement par glissements, contiguïtés et nuances, depuis l'ouvrage imité jusqu'à l'achèvement d'une oeuvre originale de tout autre facture: l'invention se délite en matière, la matière s'offre en projet, le projet se cristallise en sujet, le sujet commande la conduite et appelle la forme, qui choisit les ornements et les traits qui provoquent l'air agréable.[9]

> Even more than that of theoreticians, the poetics of La Fontaine, poetics of a practitioner, proceeds through slidings, contiguities, and nuances, from the imitated work all the way through to the achievement of an original work of a completely different making: the invention translates itself to the material, the material offers itself as a project, the project crystallizes itself in a sub-

---

[7] Patrick Dandrey, *La Fabrique des* Fables: *Essai sur la poétique de La Fontaine* (Paris: Klincksieck, 1992), p. 99.
[8] Dandrey, *La Fabrique*, p. 101.
[9] Dandrey, *La Fabrique*, p. 99.

ject, the subject orders itself to be led and calls for the form, which chooses the ornaments and aspects which provoke its pleasantness.

While Dandrey's effort to recuperate this fable for a somewhat idealized view of French classical literature and authorship overlooks the terror that the thunderbolt-wielding divinity inspires in its artist, Olivier Leplatre's reading of *Le Statuaire* emphasizes the terrible moment when the statue liberates itself from the sculptor's control. For Leplatre, the fable demonstrates La Fontaine's well-documented misgivings about the violence inherent in political power:

> Le statuaire croit, comme Pygmalion, à la réalité de sa créature. En dépit de l'acte de volonté qui semble inspirer l'oeuvre, il est prisonnier d'un travail réglé et imposé, et, plus que par la forme du matériau, par l'effet que le pouvoir impose au réel.[10]

> The sculptor believes, like Pygmalion, in the truth of his creature. Despite the act of will that seems to inspire the work, he is a the prisoner of regulated and imposed work, and even more of the form of the material, through the effect that power imposes on the real.

Despite the radically different emphasis, Leplatre, like Dandrey, views the sculptor, portrayed here as victimized and imprisoned by the exigencies of power, as a stand-in for La Fontaine himself.[11] Leplatre and Dandrey's readings of La Fontaine illustrate their vastly different conceptions of what has come to be called France's classical age. For Dandrey, it is the pinnacle of worldliness and civility, where differences are held in delicate and productive tension; for Leplatre, it is the century of exile and imprisonment, dominated by the capricious expression of the violent tyranny of political power. Yet insofar as both critics view art as unequivocally benevolent, they are able to advance interpretations that make the sculptor (and, by extension, the poet) the hero of the fable.

This benevolent view of artistic creation, however, is a product of our own, post-Romantic, secular times. As I hope to have shown in the preceding

---

[10] Olivier Leplatre, *Le Pouvoir et la parole dans les* Fables *de La Fontaine* (Lyon: Presses Universitaires de Lyon, 2002), p. 219.

[11] The great La Fontaine critic Jean-Pierre Collinet also views the sculptor as a figure for the fabulist himself, noting of the latter that "Devant les matériaux sur lesquels il allait travailler, l'écrivain connut la perplexité qu'il prêtera plus tard devant le 'bloc de marbre' à son 'statuaire': 'Sera-t-il dieu, table, ou cuvette?'" (In front of the materials upon which he is going to work, the writer knows the perplexity that he will later give his "sculptor" in front of his "block of marble": "Will it be god, table, or basin?") *Le Monde littéraire de La Fontaine* (Paris: Presses Universitaires de France, 1970), p. 244.

chapters, in a seventeenth-century France growing increasingly uncertain of the proper relation between the terrestrial and the transcendent, between creature and Creator, art – especially sculpture, with its three-dimensionality and evocation of God's creation of man – occupied a position of uncertain legitimacy.[12] The discourse of idolatry provided the language in which this uncertainty was expressed, and La Fontaine's clever deployment of its various aspects and echoes demonstrates his acute awareness of the complex issues surrounding the problem of human making. Reading *Le Statuaire et la Statue de Jupiter* in the context of La Fontaine's two other idolatry fables reveals that the sculptor's story may be read not as an ode to artistic practice, but as a deeply rooted critique of the elevation of creation, both divine and human, itself.

A close reading of the first stanza reveals a striking lack of agency on the part of the sculptor as his project gets underway. He is motivated to acquire the marble not by his own intention or decision, but rather by the stone's striking beauty. In the following lines, "Qu'en fera, dit-il, mon ciseau?/ Sera-t-il dieu, table, ou cuvette?" (lines 3–4) (What will my scalpel make of it? Will it be a god, a table, or a basin?), the sculptor evacuates himself from the decision as to what the marble should become, assigning it instead to his *ciseau*, the instrument of his craft.[13] The choices that he suggests – god, table, or basin – are certainly amusing in their incongruity, but they also demonstrate, once again, La Fontaine's sly awareness of the controversies surrounding theological representation. For if the sculptor decides to make a table or basin out of the marble, he will, in fact, have an actual table or basin. By including a god in this logic, La Fontaine indicates his awareness of the highly problematic juncture of the transcendent and the material, of heaven and earth. To what extent can we say of a statue that it *is* a god, in the same way that it is a table or a basin? To assert the identity of the work of art and the deity it represents is, quite plainly, idolatrous. Yet to assert the contrary, to maintain, along with the Church Fathers and seventeenth-century Counter-Reformation Catholics, that the work of art merely points to the divinity that it (imperfectly) represents is to posit the existence of a transcendent God who possesses, in some sense, more reality than the universe that he created

---

[12] For an overview of the tensions surrounding sculpture in early modern France, see Anne Betty Weinshenker, 'Idolatry and Sculpture in Ancien Régime France', *Eighteenth-Century French Studies* 38.3 (Spring 2005), pp. 485–507.

[13] Louis Marin notes the strange agency accorded to the sculptor's instrument in his *Des Pouvoirs de l'image* (Paris: Seuil, 1993): the sculptor seeks to "s'effacer derrière son instrument, supprimer son désir dans l'activité toute mécanique, quasi autonome du ciseau ... Comme si l'instrument guidait la main, et la main ouvrière, la pensée de l'oeuvre" (efface himself before his instrument, suppress his desire in the entirely mechanical, quasi-autonomous activity of his chisel ... As if the instrument guided his hand, and the fabricating hand, the thought of the work).

and that reflects his power and glory. It is my contention that La Fontaine's skepticism regarding the existence of such a figure is manifest not only in *Le Statuaire et la Statue de Jupiter*, but in the rest of the fables as well as in other of his works, and that it lies at the source of La Fontaine's own deep reluctance to assert himself as an author.

For the restraint exhibited by the sculptor in the fable's first stanza evaporates almost immediately. If the fable's opening is characterized by the artist's self-effacement, even humility, the second stanza, which continues the query he began in the first, has a sharply different tone. Here, the sculptor's initial hesitancy regarding what the marble should become is replaced with a pronouncement not unlike the *fiat lux* of the Christian God: "Il sera dieu" (line 5) (it will be god). The stanza continues: "même je veux/ Qu'il ait en sa main un tonnerre./ Tremblez humains. Faites des voeux;/ Voilà le maître de la terre" (lines 5–8) (I also want him to carry in his hand a bolt of lightning. Tremble, humans. Make your last wishes: Here is the master of the earth). Here, with the "je veux," the artist's will forcefully asserts itself, indulging in a fantasy of mastery – the phrase "maître de la terre" could be applied equally accurately to the god and to the sculptor whose raw materials come, after all, from the earth – that extracts him and his singularity from the anonymous community of human spectators who are ordered to tremble and pray. Indeed, the "même" that joins, along with the colon, the words "dieu" and "je" can itself be read as indicative of the equivalency that the sculptor wishes to establish between himself and the awesome power of the thunderbolt-wielding deity, just as the "voeux" that the public is exhorted to make are closely linked to the artist's voluntarism, which is expressed in the "veux" of the stanza's first line. All that separates the two words is the vowel "o," itself evocative of the nothingness with which Jupiter's destructive thunder threatens the world.

The verses that follow mark yet another sharp change in tone, as we leave the direct speech of the sculptor for, on the one hand, the silence of the statue – after all, "on trouva qu'il ne manquait rien/ A Jupiter que la parole" (lines 11–12) (one found that the only thing lacking in Jupiter was speech) – and, on the other hand, the voice of the anonymous "on" of a public that refuses to tremble in fear, but instead comments upon and witnesses the sculptor's own undoing at the hands of his creation: "Même l'on dit que l'ouvrier/ Eut à peine achevé l'image,/ Qu'on le vit frémir le premier,/ Et redouter son propre ouvrage" (lines 12–16) (One even says that the worker had scarcely finished his image when he was seen shuddering before everyone else and fearing his own work). From here, La Fontaine moves on to the comparison of the sculptor with the poet that has caused so many critics to view the fable as a thinly veiled allusion to La Fontaine's own poetic practice. Yet several aspects of this stanza should give us pause, not least the capitalization of the word "poète" that is unfortunately omitted from most recent editions of the

Fables. Conveying both singularity and self-importance, the capital "p" in "Poète" stands in stark opposition to the chattering anonymity of the "on" of the previous two stanzas, and renders the comparison with the sculptor of the fable's opening graphically explicit. Like the Statuaire, the Poète creates divinities that he then views with fear; but La Fontaine's emphasis on the artists' shared weakness ("A la faiblesse du sculpteur/ Le poète autrefois n'en dut guère" (lines 17–18) (To the weakness of the sculptor the poet of long ago owed nothing) suggests that the very desire to create gods, rather than the more useful tables and basins, is linked to their desire to attain godlike status themselves.

While it could well be objected that the desire for self-deification, for mastery and control, is a universal human quality (and La Fontaine seems to hint at this universality in the fable's closing lines), La Fontaine's poetic practice in this fable suggests that there might be other models that artists who wish to critique the fear-inducing desire for domination could follow. Unlike the sculptor, who sets out to create a thunderbolt-wielding deity, a "maître de la terre," and even unlike the "Poète autrefois" who invents his own terrible gods, La Fontaine emphasizes the instability of his material, which is never allowed to coalesce into a coherent, not to mention authoritative, whole. The actors of the fable are first the marble itself, then the sculptor, then the god, then the anonymous "on," then the Poète, then children, then pagans, then Pygmalion, before finally resting, in the final stanza, on "l'homme," an entity that has lost much of its cohesiveness as a result of the rather dizzying display of humanity's variety. Likewise, the fable refuses to stay in place temporally. We move from the intemporal passé simple of the sculptor's story to the "autrefois" inhabited by the poet, yet this distance from the reader is abruptly collapsed in the stanza that likens the poet to a child. Here, we encounter a truism that would seem to apply to every child in the world, past and present: "Les enfants n'ont l'âme occupée/ Que du continuel souci/ Qu'on ne fâche point leur poupée" (lines 22–24) (Children's souls are only occupied with the continuous worry that one might make their doll angry).

Yet this truth about children and dolls, distilled in the first verse of the following stanza – "Le coeur suit aisément l'esprit" (line 25) (the heart easily follows the mind) – slides into an observation that this tendency of the heart to follow the mind explains the rise of "l'erreur païenne, qui se vit/ Chez tant de peuples répandue" (lines 27–28) (the pagan error which saw itself spread among so many peoples). As in the other idolatry fables, the language of paganism is used to establish a distance between the subject of the reader and the presumably Christian, or at least non-pagan, reader. Indeed, Ralph Dekoninck sees the establishment of this distance, and the close association between idolatry and childlike behavior, as the fable's main purpose, noting that

En qualifiant d'enfantine "cette erreur païenne", le fabuliste renvoie l'idolâtre à un état pré-rationnel, sinon irrationnel, de l'humanité, laquelle s'ingénie à prendre la fiction pour la réalité, le mensonge pour la vérité.[14]

By qualifying this "pagan error" as childlike, the fabulist sends idolatry back to a pre-rational, if not irrational, stage of humanity, one that manages to mistake fiction for reality, lies for truth.

This would certainly be the case if the fable stopped here, or even after the following stanza that explains that those who had fallen victim to the "erreur païenne" "embrassaient violemment/ Les intérêts de leur chimère" (lines 29–30) (violently embraced the interests of their phantom) before finally mentioning the story of Pygmalion and Venus. However, the fable continues beyond this, and the closing stanza further blurs the lines between past and present, pagan and Christian, child and adult: "Chacun tourne en réalités,/ Autant qu'il peut, ses propres songes:/ L'homme est de glace aux vérités;/ Il est de feu pour les mensonges" (lines 33–36) (Everyone turns, as much as he can, his own dreams into reality. Man is ice-cold to truth; he is set afire by lies). In other words, we are all potential idolaters; human nature is such that we all seek to transform our fantasies, our inventions, into realities. Moreover, as La Fontaine's sly use of the conjugated form of the verb "pouvoir" in "autant qu'il peut" indicates, this tendency is rooted in a desire for domination – the desire expressed in the fable's second stanza by the sculptor's decision to stand apart from humanity by crafting a thunderbolt-wielding god that would reduce the populace to fearful trembling.

La Fontaine's frequent deployment of the figure of Jupiter in the *Fables* seems, at first glance, to place the god in the company of other figures of sovereign mastery, such as the lion, king of the beasts, or Louis XIV himself. La Fontaine's view of the arbitrary authority and casual use of violence and fear by such figures is exceptionally dim; one need only think of the horrible story told in the fable *L'Oeil du maître* (The Eye of the Master) (IV, 21), where an innocent deer, hidden by some cows in their stable, escapes notice by the estate's servants and valets, but is discovered by the master and beaten to death: "Ses larmes ne sauraient la sauver du trépas" (line 34) (Her tears were unable to save her from death). La Fontaine's concluding lines make his disapproval of such conduct explicit even as he reminds the reader of the existence of another way of looking: "Phèdre sur ce sujet dit fort élégamment:/ Il n'est, pour voir, que l'oeil du maître./ Quant à moi, j'y

---

[14] Ralph Dekoninck, 'Des idoles de bois aux idoles de l'esprit: Les métamorphoses de l'idolâtrie dans l'imaginaire moderne', *Revue théologique de Louvain* 35 (2004), pp. 203–16, here p. 211.

mettrais encor l'oeil de l'amant" (lines 37–39) (Phaedra says on this subject, quite elegantly: To see, there is nothing other than the eye of the master; As for myself, I would also include the eye of the lover). Elsewhere, we see the king of beasts manipulate his subjects, as in *Les Animaux malades de la peste* (The Animals Sick from the Plague) (VII, 1) or in *La Cour du lion* (The Lion's Court) (VII, 6). In both fables, the fear that the king inspires in the courtiers is such that they engage in dissimulation and flattery in order to survive.[15] In this context, the thunderbolt translates the arbitrary violence of the *coup d'état*, a sort of secular miracle of royal sovereignty first theorized by Gabriel Naudé in 1639. The link between Jupiter and the actual king of France is, indeed, made explicit in the second fable of the eleventh book, *Les Dieux voulant instruire un fils de Jupiter* (The Gods Wishing to Instruct a Son of Jupiter), which is dedicated to one of Louis XIV's sons with Madame de Montespan, the duc de Maine, and where the god is referred to as "le maître du tonnerre" (line 29) (the master of thunder). La Fontaine himself seems to identify with this figure occasionally, dreaming, in his *Discours à Monsieur le duc de La Rochefoucauld* (X, 14) of climbing a tree at the edge of a forest at dawn: "Et, nouveau Jupiter, du haut de cet Olympe,/ Je foudroie, à discrétion,/ Un lapin qui n'y pensait guère" (lines 15–17) (And, new Jupiter, from the height of this Olympus, I strike with lightning, at my discretion, an unsuspecting rabbit). Here, the violent suddenness of the lightning's destruction, as well as the vertical distance between the narrator and the rabbits, serves to establish a distance and distinction that the indeterminate setting "au bord de quelque bois" (line 14) (at the edge of some forest) at the hour where "n'étant plus nuit, il n'est pas encor jour" (line 13) (no longer being night, it was not yet day) initially denies. Of course, the satisfaction of violence and separation is short lived, not just because the rabbits, having fled the thunder, come back to the field, but because their behavior is revealed to be similar to that of humans, who also return to the scene of past dangers thinking that something will have changed: "Vrais lapins, on les revoit/ Sous les mains de la Fortune" (lines 33–34) (Real rabbits, we see them again under the hands of fortune).

As in the tale of the sculptor, La Fontaine's framing of the thunderbolt underscores its role as a forceful intrusion upon the plural commonality of existence, where blocks of marble and chisels play just as much of a role in a sculpture's outcome as the sculptor himself, and where day and night are indistinguishable from each other. The mastery associated with the thunder

---

[15] Louis Marin's classic studies of the *Fables* examine the violence lurking behind the animals' stories, as well as the effort to survive. See *La Parole mangée et autres essais théologico-politiques* (Paris: Méridiens Klincksieck, 1986), pp. 50–88 as well as the essay on the fable of the crow and the fox in *Le Portrait du roi* (Paris: Editions de minuit, 1981), pp. 117–29.

is expressed by the emergence of the first-person pronoun "je," which in the case of the *Discours à Monsieur le duc de La Rochefoucauld* fades back into a "Joignons" (line 35) (Let us join) that cleverly replaces the violent "bruit du coup" (noise of the shot) with a communal joining together. And Jupiter himself disappears; the humans that venture back into danger are described not as the playthings of a deity endowed with intention, but rather as under the hands of an indiscriminate "Fortune." In other words, like the author to whom this fable is dedicated, La Fontaine works to unsettle our notion of human agency, suggesting that while our "amour-propre" would like to cast us as the lightning bolt-wielding master of Olympus, in truth our actions are the confused, almost accidental, outcome of the interplay of a multitude of factors. In reality, the Jupiter to whom we attribute our fate is, as La Fontaine notes in *L'Horoscope*, "un corps sans connaissance" (line 68) (a body without consciousness).

Yet the characters in the *Fables*, human and animal alike, persist in invoking his name, whether as a simple *juron* – "Jupiter confonde les chats!" (II, 5, line 28) (Jupiter damn these cats!) – or as the addressee of wishes or prayers. As *L'Ane et ses maîtres* (The Donkey and His Masters) (VI, 11) recognizes, "Nous fatiguons le Ciel à force de placets./ Qu'à chacun Jupiter accorde sa requête,/ Nous lui romprons encor la tête" (lines 28–30) (We fatigue the heavens with all of our pleas; even if Jupiter granted everyone their requests, we would still give him a headache). In a passage reminiscent of the divine institution of monarchy in the biblical Book of Samuel, frogs implore him to grant them a king (*Les Grenouilles qui demandent un roi* (The Frogs Who Ask for a King) (III, 4); in another fable, a sharecropper obtains a farm from Jupiter after making an ill-advised promise to the god (*Jupiter et le métayer*; Jupiter and the Harvester) (VI, 4). At times solicitous – he deliberately averts his lightning to spare his son in *Jupiter et les tonnerres* (Jupiter and the Lightning Bolts) (VIII, 20) – and at times, as in *La Besace* (The Beggar's Bag) (I, 7), imperious, the god's malleability speaks less to the tyrannical capriciousness characteristic of a master, a lion, or a king than to humanity's need to fashion a deity not just to make sense of the world, but to create a prototype of the "Fabricateur souverain" (*La Besace*, line 31) on whom human creation can in turn be modeled.

La Fontaine, Prometheus, Aesop, and the Problem of Authorship

We return, then, to the Prometheus of the *Préface*, who stands as an example of making without mastery, fabrication without sovereignty, and whose work figures forth the continuity between humans and animals rather than their sharp division. By reading *Le Statuaire et la Statue de Jupiter* not as a model for La Fontaine's own creative process, but rather as an example of the excesses that result from human fantasies of creation and domination – fantasies that survive the transition from paganism to Christianity intact, or perhaps even stronger – we become aware of the manifold ways in which La Fontaine problematizes authorship throughout the two volumes of the *Fables*. Already in the *Préface*, he aligns himself with Prometheus, demonstrating a self-effacing humility that goes beyond the *honnêteté* required of a seventeenth-century author, relinquishing any claim on having the last word in a passage that is worth quoting at length:

> Il arrivera possible que mon travail fera naître à d'autres personnes l'envie de porter la chose plus loin. Tant s'en faut que cette matière soit épuisée, qu'il reste encore plus de fables à mettre en vers que je n'en ai mis. J'ai choisi véritablement les meilleures, c'est-à-dire celles qui m'ont semblé telles. Mais outre que je puis m'être trompé dans mon choix, il ne sera pas difficile de donner un autre tour à celles-là même que j'ai choisies, et si ce tour est moins long, il sera sans doute plus approuvé. Quoi qu'il en arrive, on m'aura toujours obligation; soit que ma témérité ait été heureuse, et que je ne me sois point trop écarté du chemin qu'il fallait tenir, soit que j'aie seulement excité les autres à mieux faire.[16]

> It may happen that my work will give rise to the desire of others to carry this thing further. Far from this matter being exhausted, there are still more fables to put in verse than those that I have done. I have truly chosen the best ones, which is to say those that appeared to me to be the best. But other than the fact that I may have been mistaken in my choice, it would not be difficult to give another turn to those that I have chosen, and if this turn is less lengthy, it will doubtless be approved of even more. Whatever happens, one will always be indebted to me; either my temerity has been fortunate, and I have not strayed too far from the path that I needed to follow, or I have merely excited in others the desire to do better.

Here, each move towards self-assertion is matched by a pull in the opposite direction; as in the *Fables*, this back-and-forth serves to acknowledge simultaneously the human desire for distinction and its ultimate vanity. The fables chosen are the best, or at least the ones that appeared so to La Fontaine; his contribution will be recognized, or at least only insofar as his failures will incite others to do better.

La Fontaine is also well aware that his chosen genre, the fable, is particularly well suited to the sustained questioning of authorship. After all, the truths that

---

[16] La Fontaine, *OC*, p. 6.

the fables convey appear to be timeless and universal; it is difficult to ascribe a single point of origin to them, although many have tried.[17] As La Fontaine – who, we should remember, would subject both comedy and tragedy to sustained critique in his *Amours de Psyché et de Cupidon*, a poetic novel, and therefore hybrid work, published in the interval separating the two volumes of *Fables* – notes in his *Préface*, the pagans of antiquity went so far as to attribute authorship of the fables to Socrates, "celui des mortels qui avait le plus de communication avec les dieux"[18] (he who, among the mortals, communicated the most with the gods). La Fontaine continues: "Je ne sais comme ils n'ont point fait descendre du ciel ces même fables, et comme ils ne leur ont point assigné un dieu qui en eût la direction, ainsi qu'à la poésie et à l'éloquence"[19] (I do not know how they did not have these very same fables descend from heaven, and how they did not assign them a god to direct them, as they did for poetry and eloquence) before moving on to the comparison, cited above, between the pagan fable and the Christian parable. Yet La Fontaine's professed puzzlement at the lack of a Muse devoted to the fable should be read in the same vein as his praise of conquering princes or bewitching royal mistresses. And indeed, the language of the *Préface* is almost completely reproduced in the dedicatory verses addressed to Madame de Montespan that open the second volume of *Fables* published in 1678. Here, once again, he notes the divine origin of the *apologue*, before, of course, casting doubt on that origin by suggesting that if they were invented by humans, that human should be deified: "Nous devons tous tant que nous sommes/ Eriger en divinité/ Le Sage par qui fut ce bel art inventé"[20] (We should all promote to divinity the sage who invented this beautiful art), before concluding that, similarly, a temple should be built for the woman who inspires his art. Referring to the fable, he tells Montespan that "Vous savez quel crédit ce mensonge a sur nous;/ S'il procure à mes vers le bonheur de vous plaire,/ Je croirai lui devoir un temple pour salaire;/ Mais je ne veux bâtir des temples que pour vous"[21] (You know how much credit this lie has among us; if it accords my verses the good fortune of pleasing you, I should owe it a temple as a salary; but I only wish to build temples for you).

However, as the tale of *Le Statuaire et la Statue de Jupiter* suggests, this matter of erecting statues, temples, and monuments to gods is highly

---

[17] For a discussion of the subversive and contentious authorship of Aesop in his own context, see Leslie Kurke's *Aesopic Conversations: Popular Tradition, Cultural Dialogue, and the Invention of Greek Prose* (Princeton: Princeton University Press, 2010).
[18] La Fontaine, *OC*, p. 7.
[19] La Fontaine, *OC*, p. 7.
[20] La Fontaine, *OC*, p. 247.
[21] La Fontaine, *OC*, p. 248.

problematic, and antithetical to the freedom and humility that La Fontaine espouses throughout his work.[22] It is, indeed, quite possible that La Fontaine chose to work on the genre of fables precisely *because* they were bereft of a divine origin, and thereby shaped by a conception of authorship, like that of Prometheus, that fails to adhere to the model supplied by that of a creative (and thereby destructive) God. La Fontaine's decision to follow his *Préface* with an account of the life of Aesop is therefore significant. On the surface, this *Vie d'Esope le Phrygien* would appear to be an attempt to supply and fortify the creation myth of the fables by elevating their purported author. Yet what La Fontaine offers the reader instead is a figure whose authorship escapes identification with mastery. Unlike Socrates, Aesop is a humble slave whose brilliance hinges not on absolute truth but on quick-witted responses to ever-changing context and circumstance. While, despite his outward appearance and condition, "son âme se maintint toujours libre et indépendante de la fortune"[23] (his soul maintained itself free and independent from fortune), this same Fortune (now capitalized) appears to him in a dream and grants him access to his voice, and significantly, to "cet art dont on peut dire qu'il est l'auteur"[24] (this art of which one could say he is the author). In this manner, the authorship of the fables cannot be reified, locked down, or attributed to one source, divine or human. La Fontaine recounts Aesop's passage from situation to situation, master to master, until his triumphant return to Babylon after having outwitted Necténabo, the king of Egypt. At this point, La Fontaine quietly notes, the king Lycérus "lui fit ériger une statue"[25] (erected a statue to him). This monumentalization of Aesop's talent changes everything. Although Aesop initially reacts to the honors conferred upon him by Lycérus by leaving Babylon, the statue has left its mark. Upon arriving in Delphi, the usually humble Aesop is outraged by the failure of its inhabitants to honor him appropriately, and this outrage leads him to make the remark that will prove his undoing. The rest of the story differs strikingly from the account that precedes

---

[22] This reading goes against that of Marie-Odile Sweetser, who takes the épîtres at face value, noting that "le poète sans doute sait manier le compliment galant lorsqu'il s'adresse à des femmes, élevées au rang de divinités, l'éloge des qualités viriles lorsqu'il s'adresse à des hommes élevés au rang de héros, mais il n'oublie jamais d'y infuser une voix et des sentiments personnel, de laisser parler son coeur." (the poet doubtless knows how to handle gallant compliments when he addresses himself to women raised to the status of divinity, the praise of virile qualities when he addresses himself to men raised to the level of heros, but he never forgets to infuse into these his personal voice and feelings, to let his own heart speak). 'Les Epîtres dédicatoires des *Fables* ou La Fontaine et l'art de plaire', *Littératures classiques* 18 (1993), 267–85, here p. 285.
[23] La Fontaine, *OC*, p. 12.
[24] La Fontaine, *OC*, p. 13.
[25] La Fontaine, *OC*, p. 25.

Aesop's arrival in Delphi; we are now in an economy governed by statues and temples, where efforts to appease the gods – in this case, Apollo, in whose temple Aesop attempts to seek refuge – indicate a society dominated by fear. Indeed, the Delphians' violation of the sanctity of Apollo's temple, and their subsequent murder of Aesop, is punished by a plague whose relentlessness leads them to consult the famous oracle. In response to the oracle's demand that they avenge Aesop's soul, they build another structure: "Aussitôt une pyramide fut élevée"[26] (They immediately erected a pyramid).

The *Vie d'Esope le Phrygien* is therefore much more than the "tissu de conjectures" to which La Fontaine makes reference in the *Préface*. La Fontaine uses Aesop's life both to adumbrate a model of authorship that manages to eschew mastery and to point to this model's ultimate fragility. Aesop's consistent embrace of liberty is eventually, and perhaps, inevitably, compromised by the cold immobility first, of the statue that Lycérus wants to erect in his honor, then, of the pyramid constructed by the Delphians to appease the angry gods. Significantly, these monuments represent a shift in how Aesop himself considers his authorship, which evolves from a random gift of Fortune to something belonging to him and demanding the respect of others. It is as if Aesop is transformed from the playful and tricky poet-narrator of *Le Statuaire et la Statue de Jupiter* into the vainglorious sculptor, whose attempt to attribute the statue's beauty to his own talent entails the invention, and involvement, of the figure of a vengeful divinity.

While the echoes between the life of Aesop and the tale of the sculptor and his statue are particularly resonant, La Fontaine periodically returns to the question of creation throughout the *Fables*. From the "Fabricateur souverain" of *La Besace* (I, 7) to the "Créateur" who makes an appearance in *L'Enfant et le maître d'école* (I, 19), concluding with the opening line of *Les Frelons et les mouches à miel* (The Wasps and the Honeybees) (I, 21), which declares "A l'oeuvre on connaît l'artisan" (one knows the artist from the work), the first book of *Fables* plays with the reader's notions of authorship, whether Jupiter, God, or a flying insect. The groundwork is thereby laid for the first fable of the second book, *Contre ceux qui ont le goût difficile* (Against Those Who Have Difficult Taste), where the fabulist seems to explain and justify both his choice of genre and his talent.

In this tricky, slippery fable, La Fontaine demonstrates his undeniable authorial virtuosity. After invoking the muses, specifically Calliope, only to deny that he is important enough to receive their favors, La Fontaine does note that he has been able to make wolves speak and lambs respond; he has also succeeded in giving speech to trees and plants: "Qui ne prendrait ceci pour un

---

[26] La Fontaine, *OC*, p. 26.

enchantement?" (line 13) (Who would not take this for an enchantment?). At this point, he imagines being beset by critics who maintain that such modest, childish imaginings constitute a far from noteworthy accomplishment, and he responds with a story about the Trojan Horse before imagining a critic telling him that such long-winded stories are even more improbable than those of foxes and crows. In the final story La Fontaine describes the shepherdess Amarylle who, thinking herself alone, confides her thoughts about Alcippe to the wind, yet she is overheard by Tircis. La Fontaine cuts this story off in the middle, anticipating that his censors will object to the rhyme he makes between "priant" and "Amant"; the fable concludes with La Fontaine's observation that "délicats" are impossible to please.

Cycling effortlessly through the language and tone appropriate to fables, epic, and pastoral, La Fontaine displays a stylistic malleability that undercuts the imagined responses of his various critics, and it would be tempting to read this fable as a clever illustration of technique. Yet it also cleverly continues and develops La Fontaine's ongoing undermining of dominant tropes of authorship and creation, and not merely because invoking the muses in the first lines reminds the reader that his chosen genre does not have one. By responding to his critics with a story of the Trojan Horse, La Fontaine chooses an episode of ancient history that not only highlights the relationship between gods and humans, but casts this relationship in terms of authorship. As La Fontaine states, the Trojans had spent ten years blocked in their city by the Greeks "Quand un cheval de bois par Minerve inventé/ D'un rare et nouvel artifice" (lines 23–24) (When a wooden horse invented by Minerva through a rare and new trick) finally breached its walls. After noting that Ulysses and Ajax hid themselves inside the Horse, La Fontaine returns to the theme of its novelty and its creators: "Stratagème inouï, qui des fabricateurs/ Paya la constance et la peine" (lines 30–31) (Unheard of strategy, which repaid the constancy and effort of the makers). The inventiveness of the goddess combines with the efforts of the builders to reduce, finally, Troy to rubble, "Livrant à leur fureur ses Dieux mêmes en proie" (line 29) (Giving it over as prey to the furor of the gods).

Here, once again, La Fontaine presents a highly ambiguous portrait of fabrication, authorship, creation, and invention. Indeed, the introduction of these concepts – pointedly absent from the beginning of the fable, where a humble La Fontaine objects that he can attempt only to add a bit of ornament to what others have created – summons into being divinity, furor, and, ultimately, destruction. By following this tale with the sheep, dog, and gentle breeze of the pastoral, where the soft consonants and admittedly lower tone stand in stark contrast to the harshness of the Trojan tale, La Fontaine is not merely showing off his stylistic prowess. Rather, he is offering an alternative world that is both more human and humane, whose open-endedness (after all, Amarylle entrusts her thoughts to the wind without knowing if there will be a response) could not be more different than the interior of the fabricated, monstrous machine of destruction that is the Trojan Horse.

And yet the fable itself is a kind of Trojan Horse. As Jean-Pierre Collinet notes, neither Homer nor Virgil names Ulysses and Ajax among the warriors who climb inside of the Horse to enter Troy.[27] Similarly, while the pastoral names invoked in the final story directly reference Honoré d'Urfé's *L'Astrée*, their coexistence in the same scene is impossible: Amaryllis and Alcippe are Celadon's parents, and as such are never in the same landscape with Tircis, the lovelorn shepherd who belongs to the younger generation and who joins the group of friends surrounding Astrée. The fact that these two "mistakes" occur in a fable that so directly engages with the question of invention suggests that here, as elsewhere, the contrast between what La Fontaine does and what he says creates a tension that complicates the fable's message all while preventing it from hardening into a monolithic entity that evokes the statues and temples that arise, problematically, from time to time in his work. La Fontaine's liberties with his source material are not directly acknowledged, and as such, they set forth a model of artistic creation that eschews authorial mastery and its attendant (and divinely underwritten) glory. Like Prometheus, who cobbled together humans by combining the dominant parts of different animals instead of fashioning an image of himself, La Fontaine moves around elements of literary history in a sort of *bricolage* that manages, somehow, to create without creating and thereby obviates the need for Muses or Minerva.

La Fontaine's authorial theory and practice thereby stands in sharp contrast to the dominant tropes of the time, such as that expressed by his good friend Paul Pellisson, who, in his *Préface* to the works of Sarasin, praises poetry as "estimée Divine, à l'égard de son sujet qu'elle produit d'elle-même ... faisant de rien quelque chose, comme par une espece de création qui semble surpasser la puissance humaine"[28] (esteemed as divine, with regard to the subject that it produces by itself ... making something out of nothing, as through a kind of creation that seems to surpass human powers). La Fontaine's ambition to take aim at this model of poetic creation is, as we have seen in *Le Statuaire et la Statue de Jupiter* and also throughout the *Fables*, grounded in his conviction that it feeds humanity's appetite for a certain kind of divinity, one that creates *ex nihilo* but thereby also is capable of great destruction. The alternative authorial stance adopted by La Fontaine seeks instead to promote humility and collaboration, but it also provoked puzzlement among the fabulist's contemporaries. In his magnificent work *Les Hommes Illustres qui ont paru*

---

[27] La Fontaine, *OC*, p. 1079.
[28] Paul Pellisson, *Préface* des *Œuvres de M. Sarasin* (Paris: Cramoisy, 1696 [1656]), pp. 27–8.

en France pendant ce siecle: Avec leurs Portraits au naturel (The Famous Men Who Appeared in France during this Century: With Their Portraits Painted from Life), which was published in 1696, Charles Perrault describes La Fontaine, who had died the year before, thus:

> Jamais Personne n'a mieux merité d'estre regardé comme Original & comme le Premier en son Espece. Non seulement il a inventé le genre de Poësie, où il s'est appliqué, mais il l'a porté à sa dernière perfection; de sorte qu'il est le premier, & pour l'avoir inventé, & pour y avoir tellement excellé que personne ne pourrai jamais avoir que la seconde Place dans ce genre d'écrire. Les bonnes choses qu'il faisoit luy coustoient peu, parce qu'elles couloient de source, & qu'il ne faisoit presque autre chose que d'exprimer naturellement ses propres pensées, & se peindre luy-mesme.

> Never had anyone better deserved to be regarded as original and as the first of his kind. Not only did he invent the genre of poetry where he applied himself, he took it to its last perfection; thus he is the first to have invented it and to have so exceeded at it that no one will ever be able to take better than second place at this kind of writing. The good things he did cost him little, since they flowed from their source, and he did almost nothing other than express his own thoughts naturally, and paint himself.

After taking several lines to explain the personal and financial difficulties that had led La Fontaine to live with Madame de la Sablière for twenty years, Perrault returns to the subject of literature:

> Il a composé de petits Poëmes épiques, où les beautez de la plus grande Poësie se rencontrent & qui auroient pû suffire à le rendre celebre, mais il doit son principal merite & sa grande reputation à ses Poësies simples & naturelles. Son plus bel Ouvrage & qui vivra éternellement, c'est son recueil des Fables d'Esope qu'il a traduites ou paraphrasées. Il a joint au bon sens d'Esope des ornemens de son Invention si convenables, si judicieux & si réjoüissans en mesme-temps, qu'il est mal-aisé de faire une Lecture plus utile & plus agreable tout ensemble. Il n'inventoit pas les fables, mais il les choisissoit bien, & les rendoit presque tousjours meilleures qu'elles n'estoient.[29]

> He composed small epic poems, where the beauties of the greatest poetry encountered each other, and this would have been enough to ensure his

---

[29] Charles Perrault, *Les Hommes Illustres qui ont paru en France pendant ce siecle: Avec leurs Portraits au naturel*. Paris: Antoine Dezallier, 1696, pp. 83–4.

fame, but he owes his chief merit and his great reputation to these simple and natural poems. His most beautiful work, which will live eternally, is his collection of Aesop's Fables which he has translated or paraphrased. He joined to Aesop's good sense ornaments of his own invention that were so appropriate, so judicious, and so delightful at the same time, that it is difficult to find reading that is more useful and more pleasant all together. He did not invent the fables, but he chose them well, and rendered them almost always better than they were.

Even accounting for the evolution of the meaning of "invention," which only gradually took on the sense of demiurgic creation to which Pellisson refers, Perrault's language reveals his difficulty in characterizing La Fontaine's artistic activity. Original and "premier" (a word that, in all fairness, connotes quality as much as temporality), La Fontaine invented the genre in which he excelled. Yet this highly inventive genius, who wrote from his own inimitable experience and who therefore can never be surpassed, was also nothing more than a paraphraser or translator of the work of others, including Aesop. Having invented "le genre de Poësie, où il s'est appliqué," when it comes to the *Fables*, it is important for Perrault to note that he did not invent them, but chose them well and improved them. This curious juxtaposition of incommensurable models of authorship constitutes an eloquent demonstration of La Fontaine's success in complicating the ideal of the demiurgic poet by engaging, instead, in the re-telling (and, it should be noted, often the original composition) of fables whose orphaned hybridity resists the monumentalization that killed Aesop and that La Fontaine decried.

Beyond Mastery: Conversation, Companionship, and the *Discours à Madame de la Sablière*

And indeed, it is in one of his indisputably original works, the *Discours à Madame de la Sablière* which closes the ninth book of fables without being labeled as such, that the various strands of La Fontaine's humble poetics come together. The *Discours* is well-known chiefly for its sustained questioning of Descartes' view that animals, since they are bereft of reason, do not possess souls. Yet La Fontaine's gentle suggestions that animals may in fact be capable of reasoning are placed within a framework that has received much less critical attention.[30] La Fontaine addresses his salonnière as *Iris*, a mythological name

---

[30] An important exception to this relative neglect is Russ Ganim's 'Scientific Verses: Subversion of Cartesian Theory and Practice in the *Discours à Madame de La Sablière*', in *Refiguring La Fontaine: Tercentenary Essays*, ed. Anne Birberick (Charlottesville: Rookwood Press, 1996), pp. 101–25. Ganim notes how La Fontaine's critique of Descartes

whose provocative resonances with rainbows and vision have been deftly explored by Russ Ganim.[31] Yet Iris's principal virtue, La Fontaine remarks, is her refusal of praise: "Iris, je vous louerais, il n'est que trop aisé;/ Mais vous avez cent fois notre encens refusé,/ En cela peu semblable au reste des mortelles,/ Qui veulent tous les jours des louanges nouvelles" (lines 1–4) (Iris, I would praise you, it is only too easy, but you have refused our incense a hundred times; in that you are unlike the rest of mortals who want new praises every day). La Fontaine moves on to include himself in the overwhelming number of humans who are vulnerable to flattery before noting that this trait is common "aux Dieux, aux Monarques, aux Belles" (to gods, monarchs, and beauties), a trio that deftly unites the thunderbolt-wielding Jupiter, the warmongering Louis XIV, and the imperious Madame de Montespan. The flattery elicited by such figures is due less to their inherent qualities than to the fear instilled in the flatterer by their power to destroy; as La Fontaine notes a few lines later, praise is "Le Nectar que l'on sert au Maître du Tonnerre" (line 9) (Nectar which is served to the Master of Thunder). Iris's distaste for flattery and praise thereby signifies more than a natural humility or an *honnêteté* befitting a noblewoman and salonnière. It goes hand in hand with her deliberate rejection of mastery and one might even say authorship; in a passage that recalls the opening lines of *Le Statuaire*, La Fontaine notes that the subjects for conversation in her salon are not imposed, but rather gently suggested by chance. The result is an alternate sociability that is conducted in freedom, far from the dominating gaze or threatening thunderbolts of gods, monarchs, and, frankly, egos:

> D'autres propos chez vous récompensent ce point,
> Propos, agréables commerces,
> Où le hasard fournit cent matières diverses:
> Jusque-là qu'en votre entretien
> La bagatelle a part: le monde n'en croit rien.
> Laissons le monde, et sa croyance:
> La bagatelle, la science,
> Les chimères, le rien tout est bon. Je soutiens
> Qu'il faut de tout aux entretiens:
> C'est un parterre, où Flore épand ses biens;

---

extends far beyond the content of the latter's philosophy: "Specifically, his refutation of Descartes involves style, method, and structure, as much as theme. In effect, the *Discours à Madame de La Sablière* can be read as a refutation to the *Discours à la méthode* in which La Fontaine purposely employs Cartesian procedure, language, and narrative point of view to undercut concepts fundamental to the geometer's argument" (p. 102).

[31] See 'Scientific Verses', pp. 104–5.

Sur différentes fleurs l'Abeille s'y repose,
Et fait du miel de toute chose.[32] (lines 12–23)

Other topics with you repay this point,
Propositions, pleasant encounters,
Where chance provides a hundred different topics.
Even in your conversation, bagatelles have their role,
although the world doesn't believe it.
Leave aside the world and what it believes:
Bagatelles, science, chimeras, nothing, everything is good.
I maintain that one needs a little bit of everything in conversations:
It's a garden where Flora spreads her gifts;
The bee rests on different flowers,
And makes honey out of everything.

Having, in his own words, laid this foundation, La Fontaine then moves on to consider the "new philosophy" of Descartes in the portion of the *discours* that has received the most attention. In the well-known passages that follow, La Fontaine subjects the Cartesian assertion that animals are bereft of souls to a sustained and often amusing critique. Yet, as I have already mentioned, the overwhelming scholarly focus on the animal-machine question has, I believe, served to obscure the true target of La Fontaine's critique, one that he hints at through the use of the word "fondement" (line 24). While it is true that La Fontaine disagrees with the idea that animals are fundamentally similar to watches and thereby devoid of independent thought or what we would call emotion, he is chiefly concerned with how this philosophy of domination, separation, and division grows out of a different foundation than that of Sablière's *salon*. Put simply, Descartes appears here as the anti-La Fontaine not merely for his ideas, although La Fontaine clearly finds them objectionable, but for the ideal of will and mastery that undergirds them.

It is in this light that we should pay close attention to La Fontaine's sly reference to Descartes as "ce mortel dont on eût fait un dieu/ Chez les païens" (lines 54–55) (this mortal whom the pagans would have deified). When placed against the life of Aesop or the encomiums to princes and mistresses (precisely those figures whom La Fontaine takes care to oppose to La Sablière in his introduction) this ostensible praise of the philosopher becomes something very different. Rather than an acknowledgment of Descartes' philosophical

---

[32] This ideal of the salon as a considered alternative to a society dominated by mastery and fear was widespread in the seventeenth century but, as Faith Beasley indicates, has received scant scholarly attention. See Beasley's *Mastering Memory: Salons, History, and the Creation of Seventeenth-Century France* (Burlington, VT: Ashgate Publishing, 2006).

prowess, it is a pointed mockery both of his pretention to greatness and to the "pagans" – who, we now know, are never quite as far from Christians as we would like to imagine – who are eager to elevate mortals to godly status and thereby subject themselves to their authority. We are, indeed, far from the flitting, gentle bees of La Sablière's salon.

The next lines follow the pattern that La Fontaine has established elsewhere, where the idolatrous elevation practiced by "païens" slides imperceptibly into a Christian worldview whose support of the doctrine of creation is, despite or perhaps because of its displacement onto the divinity, just as great, if not greater: "Voici, dis-je, comment raisonne cet auteur./ Sur tous les animaux, enfants du Créateur,/ J'ai le don de penser; et je sais que je pense (lines 58–60) (Here is how this author reasons. Over all animals, children of the Creator, I have the gift of thought, and I know what I think). La Fontaine's rhyme of "auteur" and "Créateur" serve to underscore the similarity that Descartes was often, and not without reason, seen as seeking to establish between humanity and God – the logical consequence of a philosophy that proclaimed, as we may recall, that "Il n'y a que la seule volonté, que j'expérimente en moi être si grande, que je ne conçois point l'idée d'aucune autre plus ample et plus étendue: en sorte que c'est elle principalement qui me fait connaître que je porte l'image et la ressemblance de Dieu"[33] (There is only the will, which I feel in myself to be so large that I cannot conceive any other idea more amply or more fully: in this manner it is chiefly the will that makes me realize that I carry the image and likeness of God). As I discuss elsewhere, this independence of will can be (and was) read as eliminating any relationship of dependence between humanity and the divine and replaces it instead with an assertion that humanity, somehow, is fundamentally – and potentially heretically – god*like*. The singularity of the creator God thus becomes a model for emulation for the philosopher or the artist who is seeking to assert a selfhood that La Fontaine mocks through his repetition of the "je" in this passage's last line.

La Fontaine then provides numerous examples of animals acting with an intelligence and emotion that rival that of humans, from the partridge who pretends to be wounded to save her young to dam-building beavers. He then attempts to explain such behavior with Cartesian philosophy, providing a tongue-in-cheek contrast between animals, whose prodigious memories and actions are held to be merely corporeal, and humans, who are endowed with free will: "Nous agissons tout autrement,/ La volonté nous détermine,/ Non l'objet, ni l'instinct" (lines 152–154) (We act otherwise, the will – not objects or instincts – determines us). Yet as La Fontaine, echoing Gassendi's objections to the *Meditations*, suggests, if this wonderful attribute of humanity is, as

---

[33] Descartes, *Méditations*, p. 141.

Descartes asserts, completely independent from the body – "Il est distinct du corps, se conçoit nettement,/ Se conçoit mieux que le corps même:/ De tous nos mouvements c'est l'arbitre suprême" (lines 158–160) (It is distinct from the body, can be conceived clearly, can even be conceived better than the body; of all of our movements it is the supreme arbiter) – how can it communicate with the body? Or, as La Fontaine states, "Mais comment le corps l'entend-il?/ C'est là le point: je vois l'outil/ Obéir à la main; mais la main, qui la guide?" (lines 161–163) (But how does the body understand it? That's the point: I see the tool obey the hand, but who guides the hand?). Here, La Fontaine's poetics allow him to point to the way in which the mind/body division implies a similar division and distinction between the "arbitre suprême" of the universe and the world he has created and governed. His use of the example of the tool that obeys the hand directly recalls *Le Statuaire*, but it also points to the way in which the system that Descartes constructs – based, as it is, on obedience – replicates authority and separation until we arrive at a certain idea of God. The tool obeys the hand, but this leaves open the question of whom the hand is obeying, which leads in turn to the question of who is guiding "les cieux et leur course rapide?" (line 164) (the heavens and their rapid course?). La Fontaine's suggestion that the heavens may be guided by angels is less a theological speculation than a demonstration of how gods are constructed through a mise-en-abyme of domination. Against this tyranny of the clear and distinct, La Fontaine proposes a more humble and muddled tableau in which the line between humans and animals is ultimately unclear and where even plants cannot safely be accorded a separate status: "Cependant la plante respire" (line 177) (However, plants breathe).

Appropriately, this alternate worldview is not expressed in declarative or authoritative terms, but in one last fable, which La Fontaine introduces with an open-ended invitation to conversation: "Mais que répondra-t-on à ce que je vais dire?" (line 178) (But how will one respond to what I will say?). What follows is the tale of *Les Deux rats, le renard et l'oeuf* (The Two Rats, the Fox, and the Egg) wherein the rats, having found an egg, are surprised by a fox. Faced with the dilemma of how to save the egg, the rats consider several possibilities before hitting on a solution: one of the rats lies down, holding the egg, while the other drags him by the tail. La Fontaine sums up the lesson of this story with "Qu'on m'aille soutenir après un tel récit,/ Que les bêtes n'ont point d'esprit" (lines 197–198) (Go ahead and maintain after such a story that animals have no soul), but it should be noted that the story of the rats differs from the stories told by La Fontaine in the *Discours* proper. While the examples of the partridge and the beavers are grounded in observed fact, the tale of the rats is obviously fictional, and thereby raises, once again, the place and the status of human invention and artistry. Once again, La Fontaine is quietly proposing a model of authorship that sharply diverges from that of his sculptor and, by extension, all humans who wish to be elevated to the status of gods. La Fontaine gives us not an immobile and imposing lifelike image of a thunderbolt-wielding deity, but rather a story dominated by movement and collaboration and from which both gods and humans are absent. The remainder of the fable only underscores La Fontaine's problematization of agency, as he uses it to imagine what he would do "si j'en étais le maître" (line 199) (if I were the master). He states that he would accord mind to animals as well as children all while rendering animals "capable de sentir, juger, rien davantage/ Et juger imparfaitement,/ Sans qu'un singe jamais fît le moindre argument" (lines 215–217) (capable of feeling and judging, nothing more, and judging imperfectly without a monkey ever making the least argument), a choice that reveals his embrace of imperfection and his suspicion of the alliance between reason and domination that he perceives in Descartes' philosophy. He goes on to note that he would treat humans differently, endowing them with "un double trésor" (line 220) (a double treasure): an animal soul "pareille en tout – tant que nous sommmes,/ Sages, fous, enfants, idiots./ Hôtes de l'univers sous le nom d'animaux" (lines 221–223) (similar in everything, insofar as we are, wise, crazy, children, idiots, the hosts of the universe under the name of animals) and a soul that would be shared with angels, signaling a shared affinity with the divine. This soul's light would be dim during childhood, but as humans grow older, it would grow stronger: "L'organe étant plus fort, la raison percerait/ Les ténèbres de la matière,/ Qui toujours envelopperait/ L'autre âme imparfaite et grossière" (lines 234–237) (The organ being stronger, reason would pierce the darkness of matter which would always envelop the other soul, imperfect and inexact).

La Fontaine's portrait of humanity undercuts Cartesian philosophy as well as the assumptions underpinning the social and political order of absolutist France. The emphasis on singularity that, since Bodin, had been used to establish the ideal of an indivisible and unshareable sovereignty that would reach its fullest expression in the person of the individual monarch is replaced with the idea of two souls, each of which is a hybrid. In fact, La Fontaine's souls are best described not as things in themselves, but rather as bridges between things – on the one hand the animal and the human, and on the other the human and the angelic. The angelic, and not the divine: La Fontaine replaces the fantasy of a singular, thunderbolt-wielding, creative deity with the gentler image of a host of angels. The angelic soul is, indeed, a "trésor à part créé" (line 226) (a treasure created apart), but we do not know, or even care to know, the identity of the creator or the moment of creation. The ostensible creator of this double-souled, hybrid humanity is, of course, La Fontaine himself, who is, after all, describing his ideal "ouvrage." But it is worth noting that in the last eighteen lines of the discourse, there is no "je", a paucity worth contrasting with La Fontaine's mischievous summary of Cartesian philosophy. Instead, we have a gentle plurality with blurred edges – a world where the clear and distinct is replaced with the imperceptible transition from childhood to the age of reason, which itself can never completely replace the materiality of our animal selves. Accordingly, the next-to-last word in the poem is "imparfaite," a word first evoked in reference to animals' judgment, but also a tender rebuke to those, like Descartes or the sculptor or even the king, who would run after perfection in a vain attempt at self-distinction and, by inevitable extension, domination.

4

Idolatry and the Love of the Creature in Sévigné's Letters

La jolie païenne

In a letter written to her daughter from Livry on Wednesday, April 29, 1671, the marquise de Sévigné recounts a visit to Pomponne to see Arnauld d'Andilly, the eldest member of the noted Jansenist family and a longtime family friend. She tells her daughter:

> Je le trouvai dans une augmentation de sainteté qui m'étonna: plus il approche de la mort, et plus il s'épure. Il me gronda très-sérieusement; et transporté de zèle et d'amitié pour moi, il me dit que j'étois folle de ne point songer à me convertir; que j'étois une jolie païenne; que je faisois de vous une idole dans mon cœur; que cette sorte d'idolâtrie étoit aussi dangereuse qu'une autre, quoiqu'elle me parût moins criminelle; qu'enfin je songeasse à moi. Il me dit tout cela si fortement que je n'avois pas le mot à dire. Enfin, après six heures de conversation très-agréable, quoique très sérieuse, je le quittai, et vins ici, où je trouvai tout le triomphe du mois de mai.[1]

> I found him in an increased sainthood which astonished me: the closer he comes to death, the more he is purified. He scolded me very seriously, and transported by zeal and friendship for me, he told me that I was crazy to not think of converting myself; that I was a pretty pagan; that I made of you an idol in my heart; that this kind of idolatry was as dangerous as any other, even though it might seem to me to be less criminal; finally, that I should think of myself. He told me all of this so strongly that I had nothing to say. Finally, after six hours of very pleasant, although very serious, conversation, I left him, and came here, where I found the entire triumph of the month of May.

---

[1] Madame de Sévigné, *Correspondance*, vol. 1 (mars 1646–juillet 1671), ed. Roger Duchêne (Paris: Gallimard, 1972), p. 238.

This account, written just a few weeks after Mme de Grignan's departure for Provence, distills the six-hour conversation during which the noted Jansenist laid out the stark opposition between earthly love and religious devotion in just a few skillfully written lines. The symmetry of this passage is striking; the two clauses that contain the verb "songer" open and close a series of observations in the middle of which are found the fateful words "idole" and "idolâtrie," which the Jansenist uses to characterize Sévigné's obsession with her daughter. Arnauld d'Andilly's words are granted even more weight by the "astonishing" air of sainthood that is conferred upon him by his proximity to death. Sévigné's use of semicolons to convey the salient points of a message delivered not out of anger, but out of friendly concern and love, simultaneously transmits both the force of his judgments and the one-sidedness of the conversation, a one-sidedness that conveys Sévigné's resistance, however silent, to what he is telling her. His opening statement, that she must be crazy to not think at all of converting, of turning her life towards God, takes note of her possibly incorrigible worldliness, a quality further underscored by the phrase "jolie païenne". Arnauld d'Andilly's location of the source of Sévigné's reluctance and indeed refusal to turn towards God in her love for her daughter is perceptive, and allows him to point towards the vast difference between the human perspective, in which this love cannot possibly be criminal or dangerous, and the divine perspective, in which it is, very much like the decision of the Book of Wisdom's woodworker to carve something to commemorate his dead son, the gateway to the most dangerous of sins. The brevity of Sévigné's letter, especially in comparison to the length of her conversation with her friend, conveys her understanding of the choice laid out to her by the aging Jansenist. Either she can continue to remain turned towards the world and her daugher, or she can convert. Arnauld d'Andilly's strong wording makes it clear that, at bottom, this choice isn't really one at all – any reasonable person would choose God.

Although Sévigné depicts herself as listening respectfully and enjoying the subsequent conversation, her closing sentence makes her ultimate decision clear: "je le quittai, et vins ici, où je trouvai tout le triomphe du mois de mai" (I left him, and came here, where I found the entire triumph of the month of May). Her use of the passé simple translates the decisiveness of her leaving *there* and coming *here*, not just physically but spiritually. While Arnauld d'Andilly is near death, she herself, in 1671, is full of life. The absence that concerns her is not that of a God to whom she rarely prays, but rather that of her daughter – an absence that she will continue to try to fill, through letters, for the next twenty-five years. Against the humility of religious devotion, a humility often brought about through the awareness of the immanence of death, Sévigné juxtaposes the gloriously pagan triumph of the month of May. Arnauld d'Andilly and his somber warnings, it might seem, are decisively left behind.

For the most part, Sévigné scholarship has also chosen to turn away from the religious themes in the correspondence; Roger Duchêne's invitation, issued in his 1968 analysis of the relationship between the marquise and God, to consider the role of religious faith in the *Lettres*, has gone largely unheeded. At a conference held in 1996 to commemorate the tricentenary of Sévigné's death, only one contribution focused on religious themes.[2] Recent work on Sévigné has focused on what the style and content of her extensive correspondence can tell us about seventeenth-century conceptions of female roles, noble sociability, the importance of conversation, and even the workings of the nascent French postal system.[3] On the relatively rare occasions when religion has re-entered the conversation about Sévigné, it has been placed in service to something else; John D. Lyons' excellent piece in the 2011 MLA volume on teaching early modern women writers, for example, is entitled 'The Marquise de Sévigné: Philosophe', and views aspects of the correspondence such as her increasing faith in Providence as part of her commentary on the philosophical movements of her time.[4] Similarly, Larry Wolff's article 'Religious Devotion and Maternal Sentiment in Early Modern Lent: From the Letters of Madame de Sévigné to the Sermons of Père Bourdaloue' provides a nuanced close reading of Sévigné's letters, including the letter cited above that recounts the visit with Arnauld d'Andilly, that amply demonstrates the predominance of religious concerns in the correspondence.[5] Wolff, like Duchêne before him, notes Sévigné's

---

[2] See Roger Duchêne, *Les Ecrivains devant Dieu: Madame de Sévigné* (Bruges: Desclée de Brouwer, 1968). The paper at the conference held in Grignan was Jean-Pierre Landry's 'Madame de Sévigné et les prédicateurs', which traced the influence of various clerics and preachers on Sévigné. See *Madame de Sévigné (1626–1696): Provence, spectacles, 'lanternes'*, ed. Roger Duchêne (Grignan: AACCDD, 1998), pp. 319–34.

[3] Here, I am referring to the excellent work done not only by Roger Duchêne, but also by Michèle Longino, Elizabeth Goldsmith, Katherine Jensen, and Roland Racevskis.

[4] John D. Lyons, 'The Marquise de Sévigné: Philosophe', in *Options for Teaching Seventeenth- and Eighteenth-Century French Women Writers*, ed. Faith Beasley (New York: Modern Language Association, 2011), pp. 178–87.

[5] Larry Wolff, 'Religious Devotion and Maternal Sentiment in Early Modern Lent: From the Letters of Madame de Sévigné to the Sermons of Père Bourdaloue', *French Historical Studies* 18.2 (Fall 1993), pp. 359–95. See also the article by Cécile Lignereux, 'Les Mots de l'idolâtrie dans les lettres de Mme de Sévigné', in *Amour divin, amour mondain dans les écrits du for privé de la fin du Moyen-Age à 1914*, ed. M. Daumas (Pau: Cairn, 2011), pp. 203–19. Lignereux concludes from her exhaustive survey of the vocabulary surrounding idolatry in Sévigné's letters that "le concept d'idolâtrie, décliné au gré des experiences intimes de l'épistolière, apparaît comme resultant moins d'une allegiance intellectuelle à une doctrine théologique que d'un imaginaire s'emparant d'un theme choisi autant pour son adéquation à un vécu que pour son acclimatation à la rhétorique de la lettre d'amour" (p. 219) (the concept of idolatry, derived from the intimate experiences of the letter writer, appears less as the result of an intellectual allegiance to a

frequent blurring of the line between divine worship and motherly love, between letters and prayers. Yet Wolff ultimately reads Sévigné's frequent deployment of religious language and themes as an often playful attempt to find the means to articulate the force of her love of her daughter. According to Wolff, religion provides Sévigné with a framework and language to express maternal feelings that would only be considered natural and valuable in and of themselves in the eighteenth century.[6]

Yet if we return to Roger Duchêne's provocative statement that "C'est vraiment Mme de Sévigné devant Dieu que montrent les *Lettres*, dans son être autant que dans sa pensée"[7] (It is truly Mme de Sévigné in front of God that her *Letters* show, in her being as well as her thought), and consider Sévigné's deployment of religious language and themes not as means to a philosophical or maternal end, but rather in their own right, the correspondence takes shape as a prolonged and complicated meditation on the complex dynamic between heaven and earth. Reading Sévigné's letters through the logic of idolatry, moreover, enables a reading in which style and religious sensibility are closely aligned, and even embedded in each other, rather than working at cross-purposes. In many ways, Sévigné's correspondence with her friends and daughter can be read as a continuation of the dilemma set out (and ultimately unresolved) by d'Urfé in his *Astrée*: can human and divine love ever be reconciled, or are they mutually exclusive?

Imagination

Sévigné's vulnerability to the charge of idolatry is centered upon her arguably unseemly love for her daughter, but it also consists in her unabashed embrace of the comings and goings and doings of the society that surrounds her, which she relates to her daughter with particular eloquence and enthusiasm. This descriptive care can of course be attributed to a natural desire to keep her daughter abreast of events in Paris, Bretagne, Livry, and the court, but it is also the result of her respect for the human imagination, understood in its early modern sense of thinking through images.[8] John D. Lyons' elegant

---

theological doctrine than as an imagination taking hold of a chosen theme as much for its description of lived reality as for its acclimatization to the rhetoric of love letters).

[6] In discussing the variations in Bourdaloue's sermon 'L'Amour de Dieu', Wolff concludes that "Bourdaloue, like Mme de Sévigné, articulated his ideas at a delicate transitional moment in the history of childhood and parental sentiment. Religious forms and values still shaped evolving conceptions of the family, while the forces of sentiment waited on the threshold of an eighteenth-century cultural revolution that would give them a certain independence by recognizing them as 'natural'" ('Religious Devotion', p. 380).

[7] Duchêne, *Ecrivains*, pp. 33–4.

[8] For an account of how early modern French writers and thinkers thought of

effort to read the correspondence through this kind of imagination, however, leads him to overstate the extent to which, for Sévigné, "imagination, as sensory thought, was a precious and highly developed faculty."[9] Such a reading is possible only if one discounts Sévigné's acute and sincere sense of religious anguish, which is brought on not, as Lyons asserts, by the lack of control implicit in human mortality, but instead by her consciousness that, under the régime of idolatry, the faculty that she takes such pride in is also spiritually criminal.

Unlike Descartes, for whom the imagination was a regrettably flawed consequence of human embodiment that could (and should) be overcome by a well-disciplined reason, Sévigné was only too aware of its sometimes delicious, sometimes dangerous, but nearly always unavoidable seductive force. Early in the correspondence, Sévigné regrets that her own imagination is ultimately incapable of overcoming the obstacles that separate her from her daughter. In a letter dated July 3, 1675, written before she herself has visited her daughter in Grignan, she notes "Je trouve de la commodité de connaître les lieux où sont les gens à qui on pense toujours; ne savoir où les prendre fait une obscurité qui blesse l'imagination"[10] (I enjoy knowing where the people of whom one thinks always are; not to know where to find them creates an obscurity that wounds the imagination). Likewise, Sévigné later deplores the failings of her imagination when exhorting her daughter's husband to look out for his wife's failing health. The idea of her daughter's ill health, she states, "me blesse toujours; je n'ai pas l'imagination assez forte pour la voir, ni comme elle est ni comme elle a été"[11] (still wounds me; I don't have a strong enough imagination to see her, either how she is or how she was).

Yet although Sévigné repeatedly expresses her desire to have a more powerful imagination, one that could eliminate the distance between herself and her daughter, she was also keenly conscious of the ways in which an ungoverned imagination could slip out of control, leading to ungrounded assumptions prone to disturb the imaginer's peace of mind. While Sévigné often reproaches her daughter for letting her imagination get away from her by asking her to "rectify" or "redress" it, she herself is not immune to its disorders.[12] In a letter dated July 10, 1680, the thought of the summer heat

---

imagination, and its differences with what we understand by the term, see John D. Lyons, *Before Imagination: Embodied Thought from Montaigne to Rousseau* (Stanford: Stanford University Press, 2005).

[9] Lyons, *Before Imagination*, p. 126.

[10] Madame de Sévigné, *Correspondance,* vol. 1, p. 750.

[11] Madame de Sévigné, *Correspondance*, vol. 2 (juillet 1685–septembre 1680), ed. Roger Duchêne (Paris: Gallimard, 1974), p. 508.

[12] Sévigné tries to convince her daughter that her own health is not as bad as she imagines in a letter dated February 4, 1685, "Rectifiez votre imagination sur tout cela"

and the possibility of fever in Grignan's Provence leads her to exclaim, "on a beaucoup de peine à gouverner son imagination, et le moyen de se mettre au-dessus de cette sorte de peine?"[13] (one governs one's imagination only with great difficulty, and how should one exempt oneself from that sort of pain?). For indeed, the imagination is unavoidable, even as it threatens the willing "je" of the rational subject, which is as notable in its absence here as in Sévigné's later exclamation: "mais est-on maîtresse de son imagination?"[14] (but is one the mistress of one's imagination?). Ungovernable and capricious, the imagination, which is, as Sévigné tells her daughter, "la plus cruelle et la plus dévorante compagnie que vous puissiez avoir"[15] (the most cruel and most devouring company that you can have), has a tendency to slip the constraints of reason and run about unchecked. Yet for all its unpredictability, and for all the chaos it causes, Sévigné is ultimately unwilling to live without it. As she ages, imagination becomes a delicious comfort rather than something to watch and train. Her letter to her daugher dated June 19, 1689 opens with the following eloquent description and defense of imagination:

> J'aime passionnément vos lettres d'Avignon, ma chère bonne. Je les lis et les relis. Elles réjouissent mon imagination et le silence de nos bois. Il me semble que j'y suis; je prends part à votre triomphe, je cause, j'entretiens votre compagnie, que je trouve d'un mérite et d'une noblesse que j'honore; je me fais refuser de tout ce qu'on demande à M. de Caderousse comme les autres, enfin je jouis de votre beau soleil, des rivages charmants de votre beau Rhône, de la douceur de votre air, mais je ne joue point à la bassette, parce que j'ai peur de perdre.[16]

> I passionately love your letters from Avignon, my dear. I read them and reread them. They delight my imagination and the silence of our forests. It seems to me that I'm there; I take part in your triumph, I converse, I entertain your company which I find of honorable merit and nobility; I refuse everything that is asked of M. de Caderousse as of others, finally I enjoy your beautiful sunshine, the charming banks of your beautiful Rhone, the

---

(Madame de Sévigné, Correspondance, vol. 3 (septembre 1680–avril 1696), ed. Roger Duchêne (Paris: Gallimard, 1968), p. 177). Soon afterwards, in a letter dated three days later, she similarly asks her daughter to stop imagining her in ill health: "Redressez donc votre imagination, ma chère Comtesse, et tirez les rideaux qui vous empêchent de me voir" (Correct your imagination, my dear countess, and pull the curtains that keep you from seeing me) (Correspondance, vol. 3, p. 180).

[13] Correspondance, vol. 2, p. 1006.
[14] Correspondance, vol. 3, p. 370.
[15] Correspondance, vol. 3, p. 381.
[16] Correspondance, vol. 3, p. 620.

gentleness of your air, but I don't play "bassette," because I'm afraid of losing.

Similarly, just a few months later, Sévigné praises her daughter's descriptive talents at the close of a letter dated November 2, 1689: "La peinture que vous me faites de vos orages est tellement belle et poétique que mon imagination en a été réjouie"[17] (The painting that you make of your storms is so beautiful and poetic that my imagination rejoices in them).

As these passages indicate, Sévigné reconciles herself to the powers and possibilities of imagination as she comes to recognize it not as the source of false hopes and disorder, but rather as a potent link between herself and her absent daughter.[18] This embrace of imagination, as Sévigné herself remarks, flies in the face of recent philosophical trends, most notably the philosophy inflected with Stoicism of Descartes, who, as I have already shown, had his own reasons for purging images from serious thought: "Je me trouve toujours avec vous, en quelque lieu que je sois, mais comme je ne suis pas philosophe comme M. Descartes, je ne laisse pas de sentir que tout se passe dans mon imagination, et que vous êtes absente"[19] (I always find myself with you, wherever I am, but since I am not a philosopher like M. Descartes, I always feel that everything is happening in my imagination, and that you are absent). As we will see, Sévigné's interaction with, and resistance to, Cartesian philosophy is both longstanding and complex. In this instance, she is referring to her daughter's suggestion, influenced by the philosophy of Descartes and Malebranche, that given the uncertain nature of the physical world and the compelling nature of the world of the mind, the thought of a person or object ultimately possesses as much, or even more, reality than the absence or presence of that physical person or object. Whether this idea, which for obvious reasons was anathema to the marquise, was an accurate reflection of Cartesian philosophy is somewhat beside the point. Sévigné's objection to it is at least partially grounded in her reservations concerning her daughter's espousal of Cartesian philosophy, whose rigor and hostility to imagination translate into a gendered challenge to her own place in her

---

[17] *Correspondance*, vol. 3, p. 745.

[18] As John D. Lyons notes, "In Sévigné's correspondence with her daughter each letter becomes a chance to invite – or compel – Mme de Grignan (always addressed, with aristocratic formality, as *vous*) to picture in vivid and sometimes grotesque physical detail the most recent events in her mother's life, and at the same time for the author to exhibit her own ability to make her daughter's distant life in Provence concretely present in her mind. These two scenes – typically one in Paris or in Brittany and the other in Provence – are part of almost every letter and show that for Sévigné imagination, as sensory thought, was a precious and highly developed faculty." *Before Imagination*, p. 126.

[19] *Correspondance*, vol. 3, pp. 396–7.

daughter's heart. Sévigné's playful practice of referring to Descartes in letters to her daughter as "votre père" (your father) underscores the stark opposition she draws between her own espousal of the gentle comforts of imagined rivers, forests, and storms and the starkness of the stripped-down reason wielded by a solitary, autonomous, thinking self.[20]

Letter as Prayer, Letter as Relic

While Sévigné's recognition and occasional espousal of the power of imagination demonstrate a certain vulnerability to the seductions of idolatry, her insistence in the letter above that she is capable of distinguishing between her imagination's representation of her daughter and the actual presence of her daughter both engages with and complicates the logic of idolatry which I have laid out in the preceding chapters. One of the main anxieties at play in the charge of idolatry turns on the possible confusion of the signifier and the signified. Such confusion happens when a statue of a divinity is worshipped as if it possessed divine attributes in its own right, a charge regularly leveled at Catholics by Protestants who did not limit their criticism to images, but rather extended it to relics, saints, and the Virgin Mary. As we have seen, Catholics responded by emphasizing that the esteem accorded to representations of the divine moved *through* them to ultimately, and appropriately, be accorded to a God rightly viewed as the first cause, not only of the created world, but also of the representations meant to glorify it, and Him. Confronted with this doctrine of the quasi-transparency and instrumentality of divine representations, Protestants rather gleefully pointed out that such a rigorous view of the instrumentality of the signifier undercut the idea, so very central to confessional differences in the early modern period, of the real presence of Christ in the Eucharist, and even, by extension, the divinity of Christ himself. In other words, Protestants used the Catholic insistence on the real presence in the Eucharist to call the Catholics' representational bluff. If the simple substances of bread and wine could be imbued with the actual presence of the divine and worshipped as such, what would prevent such interpenetration of heaven and earth in paintings, sculptures, or the saints themselves?[21]

---

[20] For letters where Sévigné speaks of Descartes as her daughter's "père", see vol. 2, pp. 307, 339, and 853, and vol. 3, p. 504. As Emma Gilby notes, Descartes was not only a remarkable rhetorician, but was deeply implicated in the poetic debates of his time, including debates around authorship and originality. See *Descartes's Fictions: Reading Philosophy with Poetics* (New York: Oxford University Press, 2019).

[21] Mia M. Mochizuki beautifully evokes the way in which "the degree of figural representation allowed in Reformed Church imagery was the direct result of the degree of Christ's presence believed to be in the Eucharist" in her nuanced study of Protestant iconoclasm in the Netherlands, *The Netherlandish Image after Iconoclasm 1566–1672:*

Despite, or perhaps because of, Arnauld d'Andilly's warnings against idolatry, Sévigné invites direct comparisons between her love for her daughter and religious devotion throughout the correspondence. As Larry Wolff demonstrates, Sévigné's struggle to imagine her daughter in the months immediately following their separation, including her effort to *place* her daughter in a specific landscape, is indebted to the language and methods of Loyola's *Spiritual Exercises*.[22] The letters are filled with instances where Sévigné encourages and exploits the blurring of love for God and love for her daughter. Wolff points out quite accurately that letters and prayers possess undeniable generic similarities; in his article, he also beautifully analyzes the ambiguity of Sévigné's exclamation at Livry, expressed in her letter of March 24, 1671, "Mon Dieu! où ne vous ai-je point vue ici?" (My God, where have I not seen you here?), where the pronoun could refer, with almost equal plausibility, to Mme de Grignan or God.[23] Likewise, Roger Duchêne makes note of the stubborn persistence of Sévigné's ongoing and admitted inability to subordinate the love for her daughter to that of God, even after the "conversion" of 1680 occasioned by her illness and by prominent deaths. Duchêne notes that after this point "Il y a pourtant, quoique rarement, quelques dissonances qui montrent que 'l'idolâtrie' condamnée par Arnauld restait vivace, par exemple, dans cette application à Mme de Grignan du vocabulaire de la prière" (there are however, albeit rarely, some dissonances which show that the "idolatry" condemned by Arnaud remains lively, for example, in the application of the language of prayer to Mme de Grignan), going on to cite a letter written on January 5, 1680, in which Sévigné closes with the following: "Je ne puis jamais rien aimer tant que je vous aime, ni rien à l'égal ni rien après. N'ai-je pas vu une oraison qui ressemble à ce que je dis? J'en demande pardon à Dieu, mais il veut que ce soit une vérité et j'ignore pourquoi."[24] (I cannot love anything as much as I love you, nor anything equal nor anything after. Have I not seen a prayer that resembles what I am saying? I beg pardon to God, but he wants this to be a truth, and I do not know why).

Sévigné's tone here suggests that she is not, as Larry Wolff would have it, playfully deploying religious imagery as a model for a maternal devotion that has not yet acquired the independent vocabulary and legitimacy that it will enjoy in the eighteenth century. Rather, she remains unsettled by her

---

Material Religion in the Dutch Golden Age (Burlington, VT: Ashgate, 2008), here p. 196.

[22] Wolff, 'Religious Devotion', p. 383–5; in these pages, he also notes her debt to the more overtly mystical, enthusiastic devotional practices of Teresa of Avila.

[23] Wolff's discussion of the March 24, 1671 letter is on pp. 367–9; his discussion of the similarities between the letters and prayer is on p. 363.

[24] See Duchêne, *Ecrivains*, p. 99; for the letter, see Sévigné, *Correspondance*, vol. 2, pp. 788–9.

persistent inability to subordinate the earthly – her daughter – to the heavenly – the divine. While I will return to Sévigné's frustration and her attempts to surmount it later in this chapter, for now it is enough to document that despite such misgivings, Sévigné continues to draw provocative and even heretical parallels between Mme de Grignan and God, telling her daughter, in a letter dated October 22, 1688 that closely echoes a prayer in the Catholic mass, "Nous sommes toujours dans une grande amitié, le Chevalier et moi. Ne soyez point jalouse, ma chère enfant; nous nous aimons en vous, et pour vous, et par vous"[25] (We are still great friends, the Chevalier and myself. Do not be jealous, my dear child; we love ourselves in you, and for you, and by you).

In the context of this problematic and persistent conflation of the human and the divine, the creature and the Creator, Sévigné's sustained attention to the materiality of the means through which she communicates with her daughter – the pens, the papers, the postal service – represents a curious extension and application of the discourse of idolatry. Indeed, while it is true that, as Wolff notes, the letters often come to resemble prayers, it is no less true that Sévigné's obsession with their arrival or absence, with their length and appearance, risks according them the much more problematic status of relics.[26] In fact, Wolff's point that Sévigné's "Mon Dieu! où ne vous ai-je point vue ici?" could refer either to God or to Mme de Grignan is true only if the letter is delivered orally rather than read; he elides the materiality of the means of communication in a way that Sévigné does not. In a letter written on December 13, 1671, Sévigné describes at length her emotional relationship to the actual letters that her daughter sends. Seeing the long-awaited postman arrive, "cet honnête homme, cet homme si obligeant, crotté jusqu'au cul, qui m'apportait votre lettre, je pensai l'embrasser"[27] (this good man, this obliging man, covered in mud, who brought me your letter, I wanted to kiss him). Not unlike La Fontaine's donkey transporting relics, the mud-spattered postman is transformed by what he carries. Sévigné goes on to relate her panic when she realized that her daughter was writing to her not just once a week, but twice; this meant that she was missing several letters: "j'ai eu des regrets et des douleurs de cette perte qui me faisaient perdre l'esprit"[28] (I had regrets and pains from this loss which made me lose my mind). Finally, the actual process of receiving and opening the package from her daughter is related in sonorous detail:

---

[25] *Correspondance*, vol. 3, p. 375.
[26] For a fascinating exploration of the idea of a textual relic, see Hall Bjørnstad, 'Twice Written, Never Read: Pascal's *Mémorial* between Superstition and *Superbia*', in *Representations* 124.1 (Fall 2013), pp. 69–95.
[27] *Correspondance*, vol. 1, p. 391.
[28] *Correspondance*, vol. 1, p. 391.

> Je reviens à la joie que j'eus de recevoir vos deux lettres dans un même paquet, de la main crottée de ce postillon. Je vis défaire la petite malle devant moi. Et en même temps, *frast, frast*, je démêle le mien, et je trouve enfin, ma bonne, que vous vous portez bien.[29]

> I return to the joy that I had to receive two of your letters in the same package from the muddy hand of this postman. I saw him undo the little case in front of me. At the same time, *frast, frast*, I unwrap mine, and I finally find, my love, that you are doing well.

Here, the letter is revered in and of itself, independently of its content. Its delicious materiality, so carefully described, renders it a talisman signifying the continued existence of its sender and thereby a suitable object of worship in and of itself.

Yet Sévigné's delight at receiving this tangible proof of her daughter's good health, this metonymical representation of her daughter's presence and care for her mother, is immediately complicated by the fear that the writing of the letter in some way diminishes her daughter's life force: "Ma bonne, rien n'est pareil à la joie sensible que me donna cette assurance de votre santé; je vous conjure de n'en point abuser. Ne m'écrivez point de grandes lettres; restaurez-vous, et ne commencez pas si tôt à vous épuiser"[30] (My love, nothing resembles the palpable joy that this assurance of your health gave me; I beg you to not abuse of it. Do not write me long letters; restore yourself, and don't fatigue yourself again so soon). Sévigné's worry can, of course, be explained by Mme de Grignan's recent bout of ill health. And indeed, these worries will be repeated even more intensely nearly ten years later following another, more serious illness. Here, Sévigné's anxieties become focused on an *écritoire*, or writing desk, that she had sent her daughter in October 1679, before Mme de Grignan became ill. Initially, Sévigné is delighted to have furnished yet another tangible link between herself and her daughter: "Ce sera donc *l'écritoire de ma mère*; elle est assez jolie pour me donner l'ambition que vous la nommiez ainsi, et d'autant plus que vous m'assurez que vous n'en faites point un poignard"[31] (This will thus be *the writing desk of my mother*; it is pretty enough to make me think that you'll call it that, and so much more so that you assure me that you will not make of it a sword). Yet as Sévigné becomes increasingly concerned for her daughter's health, she orders her to write letters of no more than one page each, and the *écritoire* gradually becomes more sinister. In a letter dated December 29, Sévigné tells

---

[29] *Correspondance*, vol. 1, pp. 391–2.
[30] *Correspondance*, vol. 1, p. 392.
[31] *Correspondance*, vol. 2, p. 754 (1 décembre 1679).

her daugher, "fermez votre écritoire; c'est le vrai temple de Janus. Et songez que vous ne sauriez faire un plus solide et sensible plaisir à ceux qui vous aiment le plus que de vous conserver pour eux, et non pas vous tuer pour leur écrire"[32] (close your desk; it's a true temple to Janus. And reflect that you could not make those who love you the most happier than by conserving yourself for them, and not killing yourself to write to them). A few weeks later, in a letter dated January 12, 1680, Sévigné begins her letter to her daughter, rather paradoxically, by once again exhorting her to refrain from writing:

> Je vous conjure, ma chère fille, de ne point vous raccommoder avec cette écritoire ennemie, qui suffit pour vous épuiser. Persuadez-moi bien que vous songez à vous conserver, et que ce n'est point par l'excès de la nécessité que vous retranchez cette terrible écriture, mais par un dessein ferme et constant d'être appliquée à éviter ce qui vous est mauvais.[33]

> I ask you, my dear daughter, to not reconcile yourself with that enemy desk which does so much to exhaust you. Persuade me that you will think of your health, and that it is not by excess of necessity that you cut that horrible writing short, but rather by a firm and constant intention to apply yourself to avoiding what causes you harm.

A week later, Sévigné intensifies her language, and her warnings: "N'écrivez guère, ma bonne. Ne vous poignardez plus comme vous avez fait ce 16e, que vous avouez vous-même; ne rendez point cette jolie écritoire un poignard que je vous aie donné!"[34] (Do not write, my love. Do not pierce yourself as you did on the 16th, which you yourself admit; do not make of this lovely desk a sword that I gave you!).

During this period of heightened anxiety surrounding her daughter's failing health, Sévigné regards the correspondence, symbolized by the *écritoire*, as an instrument of death for which she herself is responsible. Having given her daughter life, she fears that she is now, however indirectly, the agent for Mme de Grignan's progressive weakening, as the length of her daughter's letters becomes inversely proportional to her living presence. In other words, the written signifier, the vehicle of representation, comes to threaten the very existence of the signified, Mme de Grignan's physical body – her lungs, heart, stomach – of which Sévigné is painfully conscious and from which she is separated. It is as if Sévigné, having accorded a reliquary status upon the letters, then remembers that relics, quite like the statue that the father in

---

[32] *Correspondance*, vol. 2, p. 781.
[33] *Correspondance*, vol. 2, p. 792.
[34] *Correspondance*, vol. 2, p. 803.

the Book of Wisdom makes of his dead son, are signifiers of physical death. Yet for all the attention accorded their physicality, not just by Sévigné, but also by d'Urfé in *L'Astrée* and by Sévigné's friend Madame de Lafayette in the *Princesse de Clèves*, letters are not only relics. Insofar as they contain signs that are themselves vehicles of meaning and they respond to events and thoughts conveyed by the person to whom they are addressed, they represent the continued *aliveness* of the person writing them, who may be physically absent but who continues to answer the call of her correspondent. In some sense, therefore, letters straddle and reconcile the confessional divide between Catholics and Protestants insofar as they are *both* relic and Scripture. Yet insofar as both relics and Scripture attest, rather melancholically, to the unbridgeable distance between their source and their recipient, letters represent, tantalizingly and even dangerously, both the continued life of their author and the impossibility of actual physical contact between the sender and the recipient, at least for the time being.

Sévigné's fascination with the physicality of the letter stands in stark contrast to her attitude towards portraits of her daughter, which, as images, would seem to invite idolatrous worship more naturally. Sévigné of course enjoys looking at visual representations of her daughter; as Sévigné tells her in a letter dated April 29, 1671, "Votre portrait triomphe sur ma cheminée; vous êtes adorée présentement en Provence et à Paris, et à la cour et à Livry"[35] (Your portrait triumphs on my mantel; you are presently adored in Provence and in Paris, and at the court and at Livry). Here, as in other cases, Sévigné's language is playfully provocative; the image of Mme de Grignan, like the images used in Catholic churches, allows her to be *adored*, and adored *presently*. Unlike letters, portraits hold forth the promise of the elimination of physical and temporal distance. Yet here, once again, Sévigné is keenly aware of the yawning gap between the inert representation of her daughter and her living presence. Sévigné's heartbreak upon seeing the portrait in Livry in May 1675, soon after her daughter leaves for Provence – "Quelle différence! Quelle solitude! Quelle tristesse! Votre chambre, votre cabinet, votre portrait! Ne plus trouver cette aimable personne!"[36] (What a difference! What solitude! What sadness! Your room, your office, your portrait! To not find this lovable person!) – is unchanged thirteen years later, this time in Paris at the hôtel Carnavalet, but again after one of her daughter's departures: "Je suis dans la chambre de Monsieur le Chevalier. Plût à Dieu que vous y fussiez au lieu de votre portrait!"[37] (I am in the room of Monsieur le Chevalier. I wish to God that you were here rather than your portrait!). And even when Sévigné slips

---

[35] *Correspondance*, vol. 1, p. 240.
[36] *Correspondance*, vol. 1, p. 717.
[37] *Correspondance*, vol. 3, p. 444.

back into praising the portrait, noting that "votre portrait est aimable; on a envie de l'embrasser, tant il sort bien de la toile"[38] (your portrait is lovely; it emerges from the canvas such that one wants to kiss it) or that "votre portrait fait est toujours aimable et fait battre le coeur"[39] (your portrait is always lovely and makes one's heart beat), as the rather tepid adjective "aimable" indicates, she never loses sight of the distance between the portrait and its subject, and thereby of the very real distance between herself and her daughter. As she coyly notes in a letter dated May 1, 1676, "Ce monsieur qui m'a apporté cette robe de chambre (sent by M. de Grignan) a pensé tomber d'étonnement de la beauté et de la ressemblance de votre portrait. Il est certain qu'il est encore embelli. La toile s'est imbibée; il est dans la perfection. Si vous en doutez, ma bonne, venez-y voir."[40] (This man who brought me this dressing gown almost fainted from astonishment at the beauty and likeness of your portrait. It is certain that it is even more beautiful than before. The canvas has drunk it in; it is in perfection. If you doubt this, my dear, come see it).

Given Sévigné's all-too-painful awareness that portraits and letters are *not* substitutes for her daughter, she would seem to be immune from the charge of idolatry; indeed, her constant awareness of both the necessity and insufficiency of these means of representation is, in many ways, an exemplification of the ideal Catholic articulation of the proper use of material supports in worship. Letters, in particular, seem to be naturally inoculated against the possibility of elevation into an autonomous object of adoration. Rather, they are always incomplete, dependent on the context of an ongoing conversation that is itself a manifestation of the continued physical existence of the writer and sender. And indeed, Sévigné alludes repeatedly to this existence, to the living person who writes and receives letters but cannot be contained by them. In a letter dated March 4, 1689, Sévigné laments the late hour at which Mme de Grignan receives her letters: "Il nous prend une inquiétude à Monsieur le Chevalier et à moi depuis que nous savons l'heure que vous recevez nos lettres: c'est de comprendre, ma chère bonne, que, les lisant avant votre coucher, nous vous empêchons de dormir, tendrement, justement trois fois la semaine"[41] (Monsieur le Chevalier and I are worried ever since we knew the hour at which you receive our letters, since we understand, my dear, that, reading them before bed, we keep you from sleeping, tenderly, exactly three times a week). Here,

---

[38] *Correspondance*, vol. 1, p. 737.
[39] *Correspondance*, vol. 2, p. 9.
[40] *Correspondance*, vol. 2, p. 280. Roger Duchêne notes the ambiguity of the role of portraits in the correspondence, but in a section of his classic study of Sévigné's letters that links them to the discourse of romantic love rather than prayer or religion devotion. See *Madame de Sévigné et la lettre d'amour* (Paris: Klincksieck, 1992), pp. 257–8.
[41] *Correspondance*, vol. 3, p. 529.

as in the passages concerning the *écritoire/poignard*, Sévigné underscores the tension between the letter and its recipient in a way that devalues the actual content of the missive. As is so often the case in this correspondence, what is said is far less important than the act of sending and receiving. The words on the page function less as signifiers to their referents than as handwritten signs of continued care and, hopefully, health.

This aspect of the correspondence comes to the fore during Sévigné's prolonged bout with rheumatism, which not only sends her to the baths at Vichy, but forces her to employ secretaries, such as her son, to write down her dictated letters. During this time, the letters lose their metonymic relationship to their sender; they are not, and cannot be, written in her own hand. Yet this illness serves to underscore the *madeness* of the letters, which do not magically appear in the post but are written by physical, suffering hands. In other words, if idolatry consists in the adoration of the created object in and of itself, an adoration that entails the forgetting of the object's creator, Sévigné takes steps – either by referring to her own physicality or by imagining the conditions under which her daughter receives, reads, and writes letters – to ensure that her missives are read, first and foremost, as expression of a life and thought that exceeds them. And indeed, this emphasis on her own physical condition during her bouts with rheumatism sets in motion a recognition of her own fragility and dependence on something larger than herself, a state of mind that we can imagine that Arnauld d'Andilly would applaud. In a letter to her daughter dated March 18, 1676, speaking of the pain in her hands that makes writing difficult, she notes, "Mais il faut bien se soumettre quand Dieu le veut. C'est bien employé, j'étais insolente; je reconnais de bonne foi que je ne suis pas la plus forte. Excusez, ma fille, si je parle toujours de moi et de ma maladie"[42] (But one must submit when God wills it. It's well deserved, I was insolent, I recognize in good faith that I am not the strongest. Excuse me, my daughter, if I keep speaking about myself and my sickness).

The Problem of Style

Yet Sévigné's emphasis on the incompleteness of the letter, its dependence on both a living sender and a living receiver, as well as her periodic, somewhat contrite recognition that she herself is incomplete and dependent upon divine will, is offset by her undeniable desire to make her letters beautiful through an exemplary deployment of literary style. The question of style has long been central to Sévigné scholarship. On the one hand, critics like Bernard

---

[42] *Correspondance*, vol. 2, p. 255. For a useful overview of the relationship of the physical hand to questions of authorship and agency, see Katherine Rowe, *Dead Hands: Fictions of Agency, Renaissance to Modern* (Stanford: Stanford University Press, 1999).

Bray view Sévigné as the literary heir of such illustrious practitioners of the epistolary genre as Balzac, Chapelain, and Voiture; this is the Sévigné whose selected letters appear in literature anthologies meant to introduce students to the delights of the French language.[43] On the other hand, scholars like Michèle Longino read Sévigné's style as an attempt to convey the ineffable experience of motherhood through the masculinity of the symbolic order; in other words, the style established by her well-known male predecessors creates a necessary gap between what she is trying to express and how she expresses it.[44] Like Wolff, who carefully tracks Sévigné's attempt to capture motherhood in the more familiar (to her) language of religious devotion, Longino views Sévigné's language as an ill-fitting compromise that fails to describe accurately her relationship to her daughter. Roger Duchêne, in his magisterial *Mme de Sévigné et la lettre d'amour*, flatly counters the attempt of Bray and others to elevate the letters as self-consciously autonomous stylistic artifacts, arguing that such readings neglect the relational quality of the correspondence: "Tous ceux qui veulent donner aux *Lettres* une fonction qu'elles n'ont jamais eue s'égarent parce qu'ils refusent de placer en leur centre celle qui l'occupe si fortement, Françoise-Marguerite de Grignan"[45] (All of those who wish to give the *Lettres* a function that they never had become mistaken because they refuse to place at their center she who occupies them so strongly, Françoise-Marguerite de Grignan). Yet Duchêne also stops short of placing the mother–daughter relationship beyond language, instead viewing it, in all its messy complexity, as the motor driving the letters. As he beautifully notes, "Quand Mme de Sévigné déclare qu'elle aime écrire, cela n'a de sens que dans le contexte vécu d'une correspondance dans laquelle l'interlocutrice est le centre de son intérêt; l'amour va au destinataire de la lettre, non à l'écriture"[46] (When Mme de Sévigné declares that she loves to write, this only has meaning in the lived context of a correspondence in which her interlocutor is the center of her interest; her love goes to the person to whom the letter is sent, not to the writing). While Duchêne is, as I have already noted, one of the few critics to take Sévigné's religious concerns and doubts seriously, for the most part he views them as separate from the unfolding relationship between mother and daughter, asserting that

> A sa fille, qui partage l'essentiel de ses convictions, la marquise n'a pas besoin de transmettre cette certitude-là; elle lui confie seulement comment elle

---

[43] See Bernard Bray, 'Quelques aspects du système épistolaire de Mme de Sévigné', *R.H.L.F.* 69 (1969), pp. 491–505.
[44] Michele Longino Farrell, *Performing Motherhood: The Sévigné Correspondence* (Hanover: University Press of New England, 1991).
[45] Duchêne, *Mme de Sévigné et la lettre d'amour*, p. 327.
[46] Duchêne, *Mme de Sévigné et la lettre d'amour*, p. 326.

> vit, toujours intensément, parfois douloureusement, voire dramatiquement, sa religion et ses mystères ... Dans ses lettres, ce n'est pas elle que Mme de Sévigné veut découvrir, mais l'absente.[47]

> To her daughter, who shares the essential part of her convictions, the marquise does not need to transmit this certitude; she confides only how she lives, always intensely, sometimes painfully, even dramatically, her religion and its mysteries. In her letters, it is not religion that Sévigné wishes to discover, but her absent daughter.

Yet as we have seen, and as I will further demonstrate later in this chapter, Sévigné's own language encourages us to view her religion and her love for her daughter as inextricably intertwined, and the discourse that best allows and gives expression to this entanglement is that of idolatry. Insofar as idolatry consists, at least in part, in the elevation of the material of expression over that which is expressed – of losing the subordination of form to content – it can allow us to shed new light on the possible motivations behind Sévigné's alternation between the deployment of stylistic fireworks and the profession of negligence and humility. Longino cites as evidence of the latter a letter dated September 27, 1671, where Sévigné asks her daughter to read a letter she has written to the bishop of Marseille and decide whether it should be sent or burned: "Vous savez que je n'ai qu'un trait de plume; ainsi mes lettres sont fort négligées, mais c'est mon style, et peut-être qu'il fera autant d'effet qu'un autre plus ajusté."[48] (You know that I only have one way of writing; therefore my letters are very casual, but it's my style, and maybe this has as much effect as ones that would be more formal). Yet despite Sévigné's own protestations of epistolary humility, missives such as her letter to Coulanges describing the engagement of Lauzun and the Grande Mademoiselle or her letter to her daughter describing an upcoming trip to Sainte-Baume – "Il est bien difficile que je revoie ce lieu, ce jardin, ces allées, ce petit pont, cette avenue, cette prairie, ce moulin, cette petite vue, cette forêt, sans penser à ma très chère enfant"[49] (It is so difficult for me to see this place, this garden, these alleys, this little bridge, this avenue, this prairie, this windmill, this little vista, this forest, again without thinking of my dearest child) – provide ample demonstration of not just her stylistic talent, but of her evident, unapologetic joy in the sounds and rhythms of language.

Anyone as familiar as Sévigné with the Augustinian-inflected thought and writings of Port-Royal would have been keenly aware that such delight

---

[47] Duchêne, *Mme de Sévigné et la lettre d'amour*, p. 321.
[48] *Correspondance*, vol. 1, p. 355.
[49] *Correspondance*, vol. 1, p. 487.

in the instrument of representation risked becoming a theft of attention and homage away from that which it was meant to serve. In this regard, it is useful to place Sévigné's correspondence against the emerging hand of the artist in post-Reformation painting. For as scholars like Hans Belting and Joseph Leo Koerner have demonstrated in their seminal studies, Reformation iconoclasm did not put an end to religious works of art.[50] Rather, as Mia M. Mochizuki notes, iconoclasm should not be read as merely destructive, but rather as part of a cycle in which certain images are questioned or destroyed in order to make way for a new conceptualization of the relation between the material and the divine.[51] Both Koerner and Mochizuki describe the ways in which Reformation art worked to place Scripture front and center in paintings, sculpture, and architecture that articulated what Mochizuki terms "the aesthetic rejection of a figural devotional art that was equated with transsubstantiation."[52] This foregrounding of the letter, along with its concomitant conviction that absence cannot be transformed into presence through ritual, symbol, or figure, would have resonated with Sévigné, who would have nonetheless found the Protestant "solution" to the image question deeply unsatisfying, and not just because she finds "heretics" incomprehensible.[53] Indeed, her own experience would have led her to be

---

[50] See Hans Belting, *Likeness and Presence* and Joseph Leo Koerner, *The Reformation of the Image*.

[51] "Netherlandish iconoclasm is only one example within the many iconoclasms that precede, coincide, and postdate it. Conceptualizing it this way underscores the destructive/protective ambiguity of the decisive moment of attack and what it means to destroy a unique image in a repeated act. It also helps restore the full cycle to iconoclasm, something that has gained attention recently, so that instead of seeing destruction alone, we see more clearly the movement from object to negation of object to new object, void leading to creation yet again ... Locating the supernatural in terms of the truly mundane offers a more complex understanding of the variations of absence and presence to inform what happens when these ideas are given tangible form, because iconoclasm was always foremost a problem of objecthood confronting objectivity." Mochizuki, *The Netherlandish Image*, p. 116.

[52] Mochizuki, *Netherlandish Image*, p. 139.

[53] Despite her enduring friendship with the Princesse de Tarente, the notable Protestant whose castle at Vitré was near her own Rochers in Brittany, Sévigné, like many of her compatriots, heartily approved of the 1685 Revocation of the Edict of Nantes as well as the measures taken to forcibly convert Protestants in the countryside. As she writes to Moulceau in a letter dated November 24 1685, "En un mot, tout est missionnaire présentement. Chacun croit avoir une mission, et surtout les magistrats et les gouverneurs de province, soutenus de quelques dragons. C'est la plus grande et la plus belle chose qui ait jamais été imaginée et exécutée" (In a word, everything is presently missionary. Everyone believes they have a mission, and especially the magistrates and provincial governors, supported by several dragoons. It is the greatest and most beautiful thing ever imagined and executed.) *Correspondance*, vol. 3, p. 242.

quite sympathetic to the Catholic argument that the Reformers' foregrounding of Scripture was itself a form of idolatry, especially when conjoined with the impossibility of any material contact between the divine and the human. For Sévigné, such a configuration of belief would have been akin to asking her to content herself with her daughter's missives *as such*, rather than viewing them as signifiers of her daughter's continued life and health and promises of her eventual physical presence.

However, the refusal to view the substitution of the Word for the image as a satisfying resolution of the materiality of worship leads Sévigné directly to the conundrum faced by Catholic artists in the wake of the Reformation. How can an image that does not explicitly point to the materiality of text manage to escape the risks of idolatry? As François Lecercle states,

> En attirant l'attention sur l'œuvre, le peintre arrête l'esprit du spectateur, au lieu de le renvoyer directement au modèle immatériel. Sa visée, si elle ne coïncide pas exactement avec le crime majeur que les iconomaques imputent à l'image, n'en perturbe pas moins le mécanisme que les théologiens iconophiles ont imaginé pour conjurer l'idolâtrie. Certes, ce n'est pas dans la matière que le tableau cherche à engluer le spectateur, mais la sidération devant une œuvre qui défie l'entendement ne vaut guère mieux que la fascination abrutie qui met sa foi dans un bout de bois inerte.[54]

> By drawing attention to the work, the painter stops the mind of the viewer, instead of sending it directly to the immaterial world. His goal, although it does not coincide exactly with the major crime of which icon destroyers accused the image, disturbs the mechanism that iconophilic theologians invented to keep idolatry at bay just as much. Certainly, it is not in the way that the painting tries to entrap the viewer, but the astonishment in front of a work that defies understanding is not much of an improvement over the stupid fascination that places its faith in an inert piece of wood.

Avoiding this danger of astonishment without having recourse to the Protestant technique of pointing beyond the image to the text became a challenge to Jansenist artists who also wanted to avoid the unapologetic opulence of the Jesuits. In his masterful study of Philippe de Champaigne, Louis Marin indicates how the Jansenist artist managed to transcend the seduction of representation and establish the painted image as a *sign*, thereby operating the conversion of the viewing subject and, in no small part, the effacement of the

---

[54] François Lecercle, "'Des yeux pour ne point voir': Avatars de l'idolâtrie chez les théologiens catholiques au XVIe siècle', in *Rencontres de l'Ecole du Louvre: L'Idolâtrie* (Paris: La Documentation Française, 1990), pp. 35–51, here, p. 45.

artist, whose style disappears in service not merely to the sign, but to what the sign itself conveys.[55]

Champaigne's effort to transcend the material through the material demonstrates the unique richness of the discourses surrounding idolatry in seventeenth-century France, in part in response to the Jesuit initiative of Richeome, which changed and enlarged the terms (and stakes) of the debate. Champaigne's work, by deliberately uncoupling the close association of the religious image with idolatry, implicitly raises the possibility that idolatry could be found outside of the image, in words. In other words, idolatry becomes a risk inherent in any signifying system where the vehicle of meaning is capable of acquiring an opacity that obscures its referent. As Josiane Rieu notes, sixteenth-century French poets were already acutely aware of this risk and directly addressed it in their work.[56] Yet as I hope to have shown, the larger questions raised by the concept of idolatry did not fade away with the Edict of Nantes; rather, arguments over the proper relationship between signifier and signified, author and work, heaven and earth, instead moved into a polemical discourse facilitated and nourished by the sustained, royally sanctioned

---

[55] See, for example, his reading of Champaigne's famous portrait of Mère Angélique: "Le portrait fonctionne dès lors moins comme une représentation que comme un signe; il est traversé, sans être aperçu pour lui-même dans son appauvrissement sensible, vers celui dont il est le signe: le saint, le juste en qui Jésus-Christ se révèle particulièrement pour la communauté. Comme nous avons cru le discerner dans le portrait de la mère Angélique, le 'moi' du spectateur s'y anéantit par conversion vers l'être véritable, Jésus, conversion qu'opère le 'dispositif' de portraiture" (The portrait beings to function less as a representation than as a sign; it is traversed, without being perceived for itself in its manifest impoverishment, towards that of which it is the sign: the holy, the just in whom Jesus Christ revealed himself particularly for the community. As we saw in the portrait of Mother Angélique, the "moi" of the viewer disappears through conversion towards the true being, Jesus, a conversion operated through the vehicle of portraiture). Louis Marin, *Philippe de Champaigne ou la présence cachée (*Paris: Editions Hazan, 2005), p. 108.

[56] See Josiane Rieu, 'Esthétique de l'idolâtrie dans la poésie française du XVIe siècle', in *Rencontres de l'Ecole du Louvre: L'Idolâtrie* (Paris: La Documentation Française, 1990), pp. 133–57. Rieu states that "les poètes de ce temps avaient en effet une conscience aiguë des conséquences spirituelles de leur création esthétique, et les domaines poétique et théologique n'étaient pas séparés. Car la question de savoir si le mot, et l'image, cache ou révèle le sens, est aussi celle de l'appréhension de l'Etre derrière les signes, ou plus originellement, de Dieu derrière sa Création. De même que la création divine peut dire le Créateur aussi bien que s'interposer entre lui et l'homme, de même, l'idole de mots se fait transparente ou opaque à la lecture humaine" (the poets of this time were in fact sharply conscious of the spiritual consequences of their aesthetic creation, and the poetic and theological domains were not separate. For the question of whether the word and the image hides or reveals meaning is also that of the apprehension of Being behind signs, or more originally, God behind the Creation. In the same way that the creation can express the Creature all while interposing itself between itself and man, the idol of words can make itself transparent or opaque to human reading.) (p. 147).

cohabitation, unique in Europe, of French Catholics and Protestants in the same kingdom.[57]

Perhaps no work was more dedicated to uprooting the risk of linguistic idolatry than the *Logique* produced by the prominent Jansenists Pierre Nicole and Antoine Arnauld. From the outset of their work, they announce their intention, avowedly imbued with Cartesianism, to undo the confusion caused by the inappropriate introduction of materiality and imagination into human thought:

> Car, comme saint Augustin remarque souvent, l'homme, depuis le péché, s'est tellement accoutumé à ne considérer que les choses corporelles dont les images entrent par les sens dans notre cerveau, que la plupart croient ne pouvoir concevoir une chose quand ils ne se la peuvent imaginer, c'est-à-dire se la représenter sous une image corporelle, comme s'il n'y avait en nous que cette seule manière de penser et de concevoir.[58]

> For, as Saint Augustine often noted, fallen man has accustomed himself so much to only consider bodily things whose images enter our mind through the senses that most of them cannot conceive of something that they cannot imagine, that is to say, represent under a bodily image, as if there were in us only this way of thinking and conceiving.

Yet as their reference to Augustine and original sin indicates, the question of logic and reason – which is, in the end, a question of signs and their proper definition and arrangement – is tightly tied to a framework in which all referents have their sole legitimate *telos* in the divine Creator. The examples that Arnauld and Nicole use to illustrate their *Logique* are therefore telling. Already in the introduction, they offer the following definition of the verb *raisonner*:

> On appelle *raisonner*, l'action de notre esprit par laquelle il forme un jugement de plusieurs autres; comme lorsqu'ayant jugé que la véritable vertu doit être rapportée à Dieu, et que la vertu des païens ne lui était pas rapportée, il en conclut que la vertu des païens n'était pas une véritable vertu.[59]

> We call "reasoning" the action of our mind through which it forms a judgment of several other things; as when having judged that true virtue needs

---

[57] See also Dalia Judovitz's recent study *Georges de la Tour and the Enigma of the Visible*.

[58] Antoine Arnauld and Pierre Nicole, *La Logique ou l'art de penser* (Paris: Gallimard, 1992), pp. 33–4.

[59] Arnauld and Nicole, *La Logique*, p. 30.

to be referred to God, and that the virtue of pagans does not refer to God, it concludes that the virtue of pagans is not true virtue.

The language used here echoes that used by Arnauld's eldest brother while speaking to Sévigné: the only reasonable way to think and to live is to refer all emotions, creatures, virtues, to God; any virtue that presents itself as representing something else is, in a religious sense, but also according to strict logic, simply false. Elsewhere, the examples continue to push against the autonomy of the signifier in order to configure the linguistic referent as perpetually pointing beyond itself to the ultimate reality of the divine. Thus, to illustrate the principle by which an adjective can be used to restrict the meaning of a general noun, the authors add "comme si je dis *les corps transparents*"[60] (as if I said *the transparent bodies*). Likewise, their insistence on the falsity of Protestantism serves to warn the reader that the written language held in such high esteem by the Reformers is not in and of itself unproblematic.[61] As in his study of Philippe de Champaigne, Louis Marin has admirably documented the logicians' attempt to recognize the specificity of the sign while protecting against the danger of the sign's autonomization, an attempt which seeks to replace the logic of idolatry with the logic inherent in transsubstantiation:

> En ce point apparaît cette idée impensable que le langage semble réaliser par un "oubli" de sa réalité phonique, mais que va effectuer l'Eucharistie: à savoir que le signe "idéal" serait celui d'une matérialité dématérialisée, d'une "chose spirituelle" qui présenterait visiblement l'invisible dans la représentation; que le parfait signifiant serait simultanément visible et matériel pour véhiculer le signifié, et invisible et immatériel pour n'y point faire obstacle.[62]

---

[60] Arnauld and Nicole, *La Logique*, p. 59.
[61] So, for example: "Le mot de *sens de l'Ecriture* étant appliqué par un hérétique à une erreur contraire à l'Ecriture, signifiera dans sa bouche cette erreur qu'il aura crue être le sens de l'Ecriture, et qu'il aura, dans cette pensée, appelée le sens de l'Ecriture. C'est pourquoi les calvinistes n'en sont pas plus catholiques, pour protester qu'ils ne suivent que la parole de Dieu, car ces mots de *parole de Dieu* signifient dans leur bouche toutes les erreurs qu'ils prennent faussement pour la parole de Dieu" (The expression "the meaning of Scripture" applied by a heretic to an error contrary to Scripture would signify in his mouth the error that he thought was the meaning of Scripture and that he, in this thought, would have called the meaning of Scripture. This is why Calvinists are no longer Catholics, to protest that they only follow the word of God, for these words 'word of God' signify in their mouths all the errors that they falsely take to be the word of God.) (*La Logique*, p. 63). Elsewhere, the authors offer the following example of flawed logic: "Nous devons croire l'Ecriture: La tradition n'est point l'Ecriture: Donc nous ne devons point croire la tradition" (We should believe Scripture: Tradition is not Scripture: Therefore we should not believe tradition). (p. 193).
[62] Louis Marin, *La Critique du discours: sur la "Logique" de Port-Royal et les*

On this point appears the unthinkable idea that language seems to attain through a "forgetting" of its phonic reality, but that the Eucharist will achieve: that the "ideal" sign is one of a dematerialized materiality, of a "spiritual thing" that would visibly present the invisible in representation; that the perfect signifier would be simultaneously visible and material to carry the signified, and invisible and immaterial in order not to obstruct it.

Sévigné's sympathy for Augustine, her ongoing admiration for Nicole's *Essais de Morale* – which she finds "délicieuse"[63] – and her longstanding relationship with the Arnauld family would have led her to be deeply familiar with the ways in which the question of artistic style intersects with the issue of idolatry – the elevation, in Augustinian terms, of the creature over the creator. The rhythm of Sévigné's letters, which alternate between austerity and rhetorical flourish, mirrors the back-and-forth of her attention to worldly affairs and her awareness, at times rather unapologetic, of the peril in which such concerns place her soul. As Sévigné laments in a letter written in June 1671,

> Une de mes grandes envies, c'est d'être dévote; j'en tourmente tous les jours La Mousse. Je ne suis ni à Dieu, ni au diable; cet état m'ennuie, quoiqu'entre nous je le trouve le plus naturel du monde. On n'est point au diable, parce qu'on craint Dieu et qu'au fond on a un principe de religion; on n'est point à Dieu aussi, parce que sa loi est dure et qu'on n'aime point à se détruire soi-même. Cela compose les tièdes, dont le grand nombre ne m'inquiète point du tout; j'entre dans leurs raisons.[64]

> One of my greatest wishes is to be religious; I torment La Mousse every day about this. I don't belong to God, nor to the devil; this state of things bothers me, even though between us I find it the most natural in the world. One does not belong to the devil, because one fears God and deep down one has a principle of religion; one does not belong to god either, because his law is harsh and one does not like to destroy oneself. This constitutes the lukewarm, of whom the great number does not worry me at all; I understand them perfectly.

At once bothersome and entirely natural, the spiritual tepidness in which Sévigné finds herself is neither worrisome nor mysterious. Yet placed against Arnauld's warnings against idolatry as well as Sévigné's ongoing

---

"Pensées" de Pascal (Paris: Editions de Minuit, 1975), p. 96.

[63] *Correspondance*, vol. 1, p. 351.

[64] *Correspondance*, vol. 1, p. 271.

recommendation of books by Augustine and Nicole, this lack of anxiety is, paradoxically, concerning; it represents an embrace of this-worldliness (that "triomphe du mois de mai") that haunts the text through Sévigné's repeated admissions that she manages to forget God. For as Sévigné notes with her typical perceptiveness, "on n'aime point à se détruire soi-même." The self-abnegation that devotion to God seems to require (and that was amply, if problematically, demonstrated by her sainted grandmother Jeanne-Françoise de Chantal, friend of François de Sales and founder of the Congregation of the Visitation) appears to Sévigné not just impossible, but distasteful. In this context, the correspondence with her daugher offers Sévigné a forum where she is able to express herself without taking herself as the object of her attention all while using her style not to show off her rhetorical skills but rather to solicit a prompt response. In other words, while it is true that, as Duchêne notes, the relationship between Sévigné and her daughter is paramount, it is also true that the letters offer Sévigné a sort of alibi for her self and for its expression.

Providence and the Love of Creation

And yet. Although Sévigné's love is directed not at herself, but rather at her daughter, this love remains problematic insofar as it continues to detract from, and even, as we have seen by Sévigné's own admission, replace the love that is due to God. As I hope to have shown, the unfolding of the rival claims on Sévigné's devotion lends the correspondence its energy and momentum even as it takes its toll on Sévigné's conscience. However, as the correspondence progresses, Sévigné's efforts to reconfigure her understanding of the relationship between heaven and earth – a reconfiguration that would ideally result in the legitimization of her love for her daughter – become more apparent.

The devotional practices surrounding the Virgin Mary, which increased in fervor and frequency in Counter-Reformation France, would seem to provide Sévigné with a religiously sanctioned model of motherhood, and indeed, the Virgin makes periodic, if infrequent, appearances in the correspondence. In an early letter, dated September 30, 1671, Sévigné recounts to her daughter the amusing story of La Mousse's efforts to teach local children their catechism: "après plusieurs questions, ils confondirent tout ensemble, de sorte que, venant à leur demander qui était la Vierge, ils répondirent tous l'un après l'autre que c'était le créateur du ciel et de la terre"[65] (after several questions, they mixed everything together, so that when asked who was the Virgin, they replied one after the other that she was the creator of heaven

---

[65] *Correspondance*, vol. 1, p. 357.

and earth). Sévigné goes on to note that everyone else, "hommes, femmes, et même des vieillards" maintained the same opinion, such that La Mousse himself ended up completely confused. Sévigné herself arrives on the scene to straighten things out, but notes rather mischievously that "Cette nouvelle opinion eût bien fait un autre désordre que le mouvement des petites parties"[66] (This new opinion would have created a whole other disorder than the movement of small parts). On one level, this encounter with small-town heresy recalls the creative theology espoused by the sixteenth-century miller described in Carlo Ginzburg's *The Cheese and the Worms*, or even the tales of Jesuit missionaries recounting Chinese eagerness to attribute divinity to the woman holding a child. Yet the villagers' precise error of identifying the Virgin, rather than God the Father, as the "creator of heaven and earth" is telling, insofar as it seems (as the eager adhesion of everyone in the village, from women to old men, demonstrates) quite logical and natural. Why wouldn't the mother of Jesus also be the creator of the world? Sévigné's decision to recount this incident, along with her own intervention in it, to her daughter can be read as conveying a similar questioning all while exhibiting her awareness that there is, in fact, very little place for female, maternal creation in Catholic orthodoxy.

A similarly ambivalent attitude towards the Virgin can be found much later in the correspondence, when Sévigné writes to her daughter on the day of the Feast of the Annunciation, March 25, 1689. Sévigné opens her letter by acknowledging the holiday, noting that "Cette fête est grande et me paraît le fondement de celle de Pâques et, en un mot, la fête du christianisme et le jour de l'incarnation de Notre-Seigneur; la sainte Vierge y fait un grand rôle, mais ce n'est pas le premier"[67] (This feast is large and seems to be the foundation of that of Easter, and, in a word, the feast of Christianity and the day that Our Lord was incarnated; the Holy Virgin plays a large role in it, but not the preeminent one). Here, once again, the central role of the Virgin is noted only to be minimized at the end. Both Michèle Longino and Roger Duchêne have noted the ambiguous relation that Sévigné entertains with the Virgin Mary, who would, as Wolff notes, seem to be an ideal model for emulation. For Longino, who cites the passage quoted above, Sévigné's refusal to consider the Virgin as a viable model for her own motherhood lies chiefly in the Holy Mother's self-effacement in favor of the Son.[68] Such self-eclipsing is antithetical to the power and self-identification that Longino argues that Sévigné sought through her own motherhood. For Duchêne, Sévigné's resistance to the Virgin as a model either of adoration or of

---

[66] *Correspondance*, vol. 1, p. 358.
[67] *Correspondance*, vol. 3, p. 556.
[68] See Longino Farrell, *Performing Motherhood,* pp. 185–6.

motherhood lies principally in her adhesion to Jansensim, which held that devotion to the Virgin resulted in a kind of idolatry, insofar as it distracted from the adoration due to her Son.[69]

Yet Sévigné did not, for all that, give up trying to find the means to legitimize her love for her daughter and bring it in line with her faith. It is a sign of both her ingenuity and her progressive desperation at what she (and others) perceived as her failure to love God properly that she ultimately found the solution to this difficult problem in the very discourse that marked out the danger of earthly loves: the language of idolatry. If idolatry was the word used to threaten those who would place the love of the creature above that of the creator, Sévigné's response to this threat was, in part, to turn her attention to the problem of creativity itself. In a letter to her daughter dated April 20, 1672, during a playful discussion of the hair color of Grignan's children, Sévigné asks how her daughter's son could possibly have brown hair, before noting that "Il y a toujours à tous vos enfants la marque de l'ouvrier"[70] (all of your children bear the mark of their maker). This casual reference to the evidence of the children's paternity is echoed less than a month later, in a letter that this time references the evidence of her daughter's authorship in her correspondence: "Je reçois avec plaisir toutes vos petites lettres; il y a toujours la marque de l'ouvrière, qui ne peut jamais ne me pas plaire"[71] (I receive with pleasure all of your small letters; they always bear the mark of their maker, which cannot but please me). Sévigné's clear affection for this turn of phrase resonates beyond a clever way to characterize that most sticky of questions – the proper way to conceptualize the relationship between a maker and that which is made. In fact, Sévigné adopts this phrase directly from Descartes, who, as we have seen, uses it in the *Méditations métaphysiques* to characterize the relationship between the divine and the human in a way that minimizes the visuality to which the description of humans as "the image of God on earth" almost inevitably led. Sévigné's eager adoption of this phrase, and her application of it to such varying circumstances as the paternity of a child or the writing of letters, demonstrates that her attention to the thorny issues surrounding making and authorship – and the relation of human fabrication to divine creation – is no less keen than that of the celebrated philosopher.

Yet if Sévigné's adoption of Descartes' phrasing would seem to be an endorsement of the headway that he seemed to have made in imagining a relationship between the human and the divine without images and therefore

---

[69] "Voulant placer le Christ au centre de la piété catholique, les jansénistes avaient seulement invité à donner à sa mère une place en quelque sorte dépendante, pour éviter certains abus." Duchêne, *Ecrivains*, p. 65.
[70] *Correspondance*, vol. 1, p. 485.
[71] *Correspondance*, vol. 1, p. 511.

without idolatry, elsewhere Descartes serves as a foil, someone for Sévigné to write against. Sévigné's hostility to Cartesianism is partially grounded in her daughter's affection for the new philosophy; as I have already noted, Sévigné's frequent allusion to Descartes as the comtesse's *père*, or father, demonstrates her perception of Descartes as her primary rival. As we have seen, Sévigné strongly objects to Descartes' conflation – real or imagined – of the idea of a thing with the thing itself; Grignan's persistent presence in her mother's thoughts is keenly felt to be no substitute for physical proximity. Yet an even more significant distance from Descartes' thought manifests itself as the correspondence continues: Sévigné simply cannot fathom how Cartesian voluntarism can be reconciled with the Jansenist submission to divine design that she favors.

Sévigné was not the first to remark upon the potentially devastating effects that Descartes' radical reimagining of the relation between the divine and the human could have on the human understanding of the workings of the world. One of Descartes' sharpest, most incisive interlocutors, Princess Elizabeth of Bohemia, immediately seized upon the implications of Descartes' assertion that humans, applying mechanistic laws, can comprehend even the vast universe: "The knowledge of the great extent of the universe, which you have shown in the third book of your *Principles*, serves to detach our affections from that which we see in it, but it also separates the particular providence, which is the foundation of theology, from the idea we have of God."[72] In other words, an impersonal universe becomes a universe devoid of signs and messages that both facilitate and express the link between heaven and earth. For if, as Lorraine Daston contends, Descartes' philosophy takes direct aim at the concept of fortune by asserting that unexpected accidents are merely events that we are not yet capable of explaining according to scientific law, it similarly rules out the interpretation of such events as privileged communication from a divinity who takes an interest in the wellbeing of the world's inhabitants.[73] Moreover, if direct divine intervention in the world is endangered by the status of matter as ultimately comprehensible (and predictable) *substance étendue*, it is further, and perhaps fatally, imperiled by Descartes' unprecedented assertion of the power and independence of the human will. Elizabeth is therefore correct to note that, despite the philosopher's assurance of God's unrivaled status as creator, God's role in the Cartesian universe – and the theological implications of that role – remain unclear.

---

[72] *The Correspondence between Princess Elisabeth of Bohemia and René Descartes*, ed. and trans. Lisa Shapiro (Chicago: University of Chicago Press, 2007), pp. 114–15.

[73] See Lorraine Daston, 'Fortuna and the Passions', in *Chance, Culture, and the Literary Text*, ed. Thomas Kavanagh (Ann Arbor: University of Michigan Press, 1994), pp. 25–47.

Confronted with Elizabeth's questions, Descartes first offers an explanation that largely skirts the issue, telling her that "the independence that we experience and feel in us and that suffices for rendering our actions praiseworthy or blameworthy is not incompatible with a dependence that is of another nature, according to which all things are subject to God."[74] For Descartes, the freedom that humans feel is real, but on a social, interhuman level, where it leads to our actions being judged as worthy of praise or blame. Such distinctions are inapplicable to the human relationship with a God whose radical transcendence, Jean-Luc Marion reminds us, entails its no less radical unimaginability. Just as the mind remains completely different to, and therefore ungraspable by, categories that apply to matter and *substance étendue*, so does the Cartesian God, creator of all that existed, exists, and has yet to exist, including the eternal truths themselves, remain ultimately free from human categorization.

Descartes himself was conscious of the similarity between his theory of mind–body interaction – which, as we saw, formed the primary stumbling block to readers of the *Meditations* such as Hobbes and Gassendi – and his conviction that God could act directly upon a universe at once created by It and completely incommensurable with It. In an oft-quoted passage from a letter he wrote to Henry More, he notes "Of course I do not think that any mode of action belongs univocally to both God and his creatures, but I must confess that the only idea I can find in my mind to represent the way in which God or an angel can move matter is the one which shows me that way in which I am conscious I can move my own body by my own thought."[75] Just as we are certain that we control our bodily actions with our mind, even though we might not understand exactly how this interaction occurs, we can also be certain that God's providence governs the world in a way that does not impinge upon human freedom.[76] Yet in the correspondence with Elizabeth, Descartes does try to represent the relationship between God and humanity with an analogy: that of a king and his dueling subjects. In this example, Descartes evokes a monarch who has prohibited duels in his kingdom but who nonetheless arranges for two noble enemies to find themselves in the same place at the same time, knowing that if the two meet, it is very likely that they will engage in a duel. As Descartes notes, if the

---

[74] *Correspondence*, p. 126.
[75] Descartes, *Philosophical Writings*, vol. 3, p. 375.
[76] As C. P. Ragland puts it in his excellent article devoted to the question of Descartes, providence, and freedom, "Since providence and freedom are both clear and distinct, we must believe them despite their apparent incompatibility." 'Descartes on Divine Providence and Human Freedom', *Archiv für Geschichte der Philosophie* 87.2 (2005), pp. 159–88, here p. 181.

noblemen do indeed break the law and engage in a duel, they do so by their own volition, and can therefore be punished for their actions, even though the king created the conditions favorable to such an outcome. After comparing the king's actions to those of a God who has given humanity both a free will and the dispositions that will cause that will to exert itself in a certain way, Descartes concludes "As one can distinguish in this king two different degrees of will, the one by which he willed these gentlement to fight one another, since he made it so they would meet, and the other by which he did not will it, since he prohibited duels, so do the theologians distinguish in God an absolute and independent will by which he wills that all things happen such as they happen, and another which is relative, and which is related to the merit or demerit of men, according to which he wills that they obey his laws."[77] As Ragland points out, this example – which is Descartes' last word on the subject with Elizabeth – is not particularly original; in many ways it illustrates the Molinist (which is to say Jesuit) doctrine of non-causal providentialism, which found a way to safeguard human freedom without endangering the absolute liberty of the divine.

Yet for all that, Descartes' efforts to reconcile human freedom and divine providence are, however, unsatisfying and unconvincing both to Elizabeth and to contemporary readers.[78] Kathryn Tanner notes that the increase in debates over "divine sovereignty and the power and freedom of the creature" that occurred in the years following the Council of Trent served to disrupt the fragile if elegant equilibrium that scholasticism had managed to achieve around this topic.[79] In this sense, Descartes' philosophy, with its simultaneous emphasis on human independence and the divine creation of the world in which that independence unfolds, merely served to topple an already shaky theological edifice, even if Descartes himself viewed his efforts as safeguarding both. As Tanner puts it, "The more human freedom is defined as freedom from outside interference, the more a theological consideration of human powers and self-initiated action in themselves will suggest their real independence of God."[80] For readers like Elizabeth, this meant that even if Descartes' original formulation of the relation between divine providence and human freedom served to solve certain philosophical difficulties (not least Descartes' need to assert divine creation of the eternal truths), it nonetheless weakened the

---

[77] *Correspondence*, p. 131.

[78] C. P. Ragland notes bluntly, "To be clear, I do not think that Descartes' attempt to reconcile particular providence and human freedom is successful" ('Descartes on Divine Providence', p. 183).

[79] Kathryn Tanner, *God and Creation in Christian Theology: Tyranny or Empowerment?* (New York: Basil Blackwell, 1988), p. 142.

[80] Tanner, *God and Creation*, pp. 152–3.

direct and emotional relation between God and humanity; it is significant that the two duelists in Descartes' example remain completely unaware of the king's efforts to bring them together. A world in which providence becomes impersonal, incomprehensible, and almost imperceptible is in many ways a world bereft of the meaning and comfort that *providence particulière* confers.

And this, in short, is a world that Mme de Sévigné, as she reminds us through her frequent disparaging references to Descartes, refuses to inhabit. For Sévigné, providence, which she invokes with increasing frequency in her letters, designates the overarching plan and will of God to which she must submit in order to find peace.[81] Already in 1671, the marquise looks to providence for comfort, telling her daughter in a letter dated July 22, 1661 that "Tout est rangé selon l'ordre de la Providence; cette pensée doit fixer toutes nos inquiétudes"[82] (Everything is arranged according to the order of Providence; this thought should calm all of our worries). This recourse to divine design appears, at least in the 1670s, to be shared by her daughter; as Sévigné exclaims in a letter dated October 25, 1679, "Je suis bien de votre avis sur le besoin qu'on a, à tout moment, d'un peu de philosophie, de resignation, de regards vers la Providence, comme il vous plaira, mais enfin il faut quelque chose qui adoucisse un peu les troubles du coeur et les contretemps continuels de la vie"[83] (I share your opinion on the need that one has, always, of a little bit of philosophy, of resignation, of looking towards Providence, as you wish, but finally we all need something that softens a bit the troubles of the heart and the continual inconveniences of life).

These "contretemps continuels de la vie" consist, of course, in the physical separation from her beloved daughter and the various events that prevent Sévigné and Grignan from seeing each other more often. Yet Sévigné also refers to providence to explain or at least to assuage the effects of unforeseen and even shocking events, such as the disgrace of Pomponne ("Enfin il en faut revenir à la Providence, dont M. de Pomponne est adorateur et disciple. Et le moyen de vivre sans cette divine doctrine?"[84] (Finally, we must come back to the Providence which M. de Pomponne adored and followed. And how can one live without this divine doctrine?)) or the death of Turenne, which she cites, repeatedly, as incontrovertible proof that Providence exists. In the letter

---

[81] As Gérard Ferreyrolles notes, there are 25 allusions to providence in the letters that span the twenty months of Sévigné's physical separation from her daughter in 1675–6, 20 allusions during the five months of absence in 1677, and 100 between September 1679 and November 1680. 'Histoire et finalité: Sur les origines du discours providentialiste au XVIIe siècle', *Seventeenth-Century French Studies* 23 (2001), pp. 1–14, here p. 7.

[82] *Correspondance*, vol. 1, p. 302.
[83] *Correspondance*, vol. 2, pp. 717–18.
[84] *Correspondance*, vol. 2, p. 748.

she writes to her daughter on July 31, 1675, Sévigné asks "Peut-on douter de la Providence et que le canon qui a choisi de loin M. de Turenne, entre dix hommes qui étaient autour de lui, ne fût chargé depuis une éternité?"[85] (Can one doubt Providence, and that the cannon that chose M. de Turenne from afar, among ten men who were around him, had not been loaded since eternity?). The marquise elaborates upon these sentiments in a letter to her cousin Bussy-Rabutin written on August 6, 1675:

> Vous avez prévu en homme du métier tout ce qui est arrivé du coté de l'Allemagne, mais vous n'avez pas vu la mort de M. de Turenne, ni ce coup de canon tiré au hasard, qui le prend seul entre dix ou douze. Pour moi, qui vois en tout la Providence, je vois ce canon chargé de toute éternité; je vois que tout y conduit M. de Turenne, et je n'y trouve rien de funeste pour lui, en supposant sa conscience en bon état. Que lui faut-il ? Il meurt au milieu de sa gloire. Sa réputation ne pouvait plus augmenter.[86]

> You predicted, as someone in the business, everything that happened in Germany, but you did not see the death of M. de Turenne, neither the cannonball fired by chance, which took him alone among ten or twelve. For me, who sees in everything the hand of Providence, I see this cannon loaded since eternity; I see that everything leads M. de Turenne to it, and I find nothing sad about it, assuming that his conscience was clear. What more does he need? He dies in the middle of his glory. His reputation cannot go any higher.

Bussy-Rabutin's response, however, reveals his own doubts about the reality of Sévigné's personalized Providence: "il n'y a que deux sortes de gens à qui la mort imprévue soit la meilleure: les saints et les athées" (there are only two kinds of people for whom unexpected death is the best: saints and atheists). After noting that Turenne was certainly not an atheist, but was no less certainly not a saint, Bussy-Rabutin continues: "Je doute fort que la gloire du monde, pour qui il avait une si violente passion, soit un sentiment qui sauve les chrétiens"[87] (I doubt very much that the glory of this world, which he was so violently passionate about, is a sentiment that can save Christians). Bussy must have known that such language would unsettle his cousin, insofar as it formulates, once again, and in painfully stark terms, the extent to which love for the world, and those in it, pulls one away from divine design. If Sévigné thought that she could find, through belief in Providence, relief from her

---

[85] *Correspondance*, vol. 2, p. 25.
[86] *Correspondance*, vol. 2, p. 33.
[87] *Correspondance*, vol. 2, p. 49.

consciousness of her own idolatry and this-worldly passions, Bussy-Rabutin is letting her know that escape will not be as easy as she might wish.

Sévigné herself is quite conscious of the forces that pull against complete submission to God's plan. As Roger Duchêne notes in his study of the religious aspects of the letters,

> dans la douleur de la séparation, Mme de Sévigné a affronté une volonté divine qu'elle nomme Providence par tradition, mais dont elle a découvert surtout l'hostilité. Comment consentir à la volonté de Dieu sur ce qui lui est le plus sensible, l'absence de sa fille? Et voici que la séparation lui a de plus révélé la violence de sa passion et son caractère exclusif, ce qui entraîne un conflit entre le mouvement naturel de son coeur et les exigences de sa foi: comment donner à Dieu la première place qui lui revient de droit?[88]

> In the pain of separation, Mme de Sévigné affronted a divine will that she names Providence by tradition, but of which she mainly discovers the hostility. How to consent to the will of God regarding what touches her the most, the absence of her daughter? And here the separation has revealed to her the violence and exclusive nature of her passion, which leads to a conflict between the natural movement of her heart and the demands of her faith: how to give God the privileged place which is his by right?

In other words, Sévigné's consciousness of her own resistance to Providence, the cruel workings of which almost seem to intentionally thwart her dearest wishes, tracks closely with her unapologetic idolatry of her daughter, her reluctance to subordinate the love for her daughter to the love of God. As Sévigné declares in a particularly poignant letter dated December 28, 1673, speaking of her wish to be close to her daughter,

> il faut donner tout cela à Dieu, et je le ferai avec sa grâce, et j'admirerai la Providence, qui permet qu'avec tant de grandeurs et de choses agréables dans votre établissement, il s'y trouve des abîmes qui ôtent tous les plaisirs de la vie, et une séparation qui me blesse le cœur à toutes les heures du jour, et bien plus que je ne voudrais à celle de la nuit.[89]

> One must give all of this to God, and I will do this through his grace, and I will admire Providence, which allows that with so much grandeur and so many pleasant things where you are, there are also depths which take away all of the pleasures of life, and a separation which wounds my heart at all hours of the day, and much more than I would like during the night.

---

[88] Duchêne, *Ecrivains*, p. 28.
[89] *Correspondance*, vol. 1, p. 649.

In this context, Sévigné's professed belief, devotion, and even submission to providence can easily be read as an almost ironic act of desperation which entails the immolation not only of her pleasure, but of her will. In a letter dated October 30, 1675, Sévigné acknowledges her daughter's argument that their separation from each other is necessary in order for providence to unfold. Sévigné notes that such reasoning might be fine for her daughter, but that for her,

> quand je pense à notre éloignement, et combine je serais digne de jouir du plaisir d'être avec vous, et comme vous êtes pour moi, précisément dans le temps que nous sommes aux deux bouts de la terre, ne me demandez point de rêver gaiement à cet endroit-là de notre destinée; le bon sens s'y oppose, et ma tendresse encore plus. Il faut se jeter promptement dans la soumission que nous devons à la Providence.[90]

> when I think of the distance between us, and how I could be worthy of the pleasure of being with you, and how you are with me, precisely when we are at two different ends of the earth, do not ask me to happily dream about that point in our destiny; good sense opposes it, and my tenderness opposes it even more. We must throw ourselves promptly into the submission that we owe to Providence.

Yet as Roger Duchêne points out, Sévigné's attitude toward providence becomes much more reverent and serious (and, as Gérard Ferreyrolles notes, more frequent) as the letters progress. Duchêne locates this shift in the period from December 1676 until June of 1677, when Mme de Grignan was afflicted with a mysterious chest disease that left her mother so deeply worried that friends of the women deemed it best that they be separated. Grignan's illness and subsequent recovery seem to have left their mark; as Duchêne notes, "la volonté divine n'est plus, comme lors des premières séparations, une justification abstraite dont Mme de Sévigné usait assez souvent pour de grands événements ou de grands sacrifices, mais une idée familière, associée à des gestes quotidiens et à des circonstances banales" (divine will is no longer, as in the first separations, an abstract justification that Mme de Sévigé used fairly often for important events or sacrifices, but a familiar idea, associated with daily movements and banal circumstances).[91] It is around this time that

---

[90] *Correspondance*, vol. 2, p. 136.

[91] Duchêne, *Ecrivains*, p. 47. Duchêne's reading accurately notes a change in Sévigné's attitude towards providence, which John Lyons seems to miss, stating at the end of his otherwise excellent analysis of Sévigné's philosophy that "Sévigné accepted the real, as she experienced it, because she identified the real with divine providence. God was, for her,

Sévigné parts philosophical ways with her Cartesian daughter, precisely around the question of providence and divine design. Gently mocking references to Descartes as Mme de Grignan's "father" begin to dot the letters, and in a letter dated May 31, 1680, Sévigné lays things out directly:

> Je ne vous obligerai plus de répondre sur cette divine Providence, que j'adore et que je crois qui fait et ordonne tout. Je suis assurée que vous n'oseriez traiter de mystère inconcevable cette opinion, avec votre *père* Descartes; ce serait croire que Dieu eût fait le monde sans y régler tout ce qui s'y fait qui serait une chose inconcevable.[92]

> I will not oblige you to respond anymore to this divine Providence, which I adore and which I believe accomplishes and orders everything. I am assured that you would not dare treat this opinion as an inconceivable mystery, along with your father Descartes: that would imply believing that God made the world without ruling everything in it, which would be an inconceivable thing.

Sévigné's enthusiastic embrace of providence and concomitant rejection of Cartesianism could certainly be read as a consequence of her advancing years and her increased resignation to events over which she had very little control. It is undeniable that she found a real peace in such resignation. After hearing a particularly pointed sermon by Bourdaloue on the inefficacy and misguidedness of human prudence, Sévigné tells her cousin Bussy-Rabutin, in a letter dated April 3, 1681 (Holy Thursday), that such thoughts make resignation to divine providence much easier: "Cela console et fait qu'on se soumet plus doucement à sa mauvaise fortune. La vie est courte; c'est bientôt fait. Le fleuve est si rapide qu'à peine pouvons-nous y paraître"[93] (This consoles and helps one submit more gently to one's bad luck. Life is short; it is nearly over. The river is so rapid that we barely manage to appear in it). Yet it is also very possible that something besides a growing awareness of the inevitability of death is at play here. The profound peace that Sévigné finds in her determination to submit herself to a divine will that she had regarded warily in the first years of her separation from her daughter suggests that the question of providence bears directly upon the issue that had tormented her from the very beginning: her potentially idolatrous love for her daughter.

To understand the link between providence and idolatry, it is useful, as Ferreyrolles suggests, to "parler comme les dictionnaires" and consult its

---

what happened." 'The Marquise de Sévigné: Philosophe', p. 186.
[92] *Correspondance*, vol. 2, p. 952.
[93] *Correspondance*, vol. 3, p. 63.

definition as "ce sage gouvernement de Dieu sur la création."⁹⁴ (speak like the dictionaries/ God's wise government of his creation). While Ferreyrolles does not cite the source of this definition, it aligns with that given by Furetière, who notes in his *Dictionnaire* that it is a "terme de théologie" "qui ne se dit que de Dieu et de sa conduite sur toutes les choses créées" (which is only said about God and his management of all created things). Studies of providence have largely focused on the "government" aspect of this definition; indeed, the library search term one should use to avoid receiving results related to the capital of Rhode Island is "providence and the government of God." Yet both of these definitions, along with Sévigné's mention of Descartes cited above, also refer pointedly to the *madeness* of the world. God governs the world, quite simply, because he made it. Moreover, having made it, he loves it, which is why he cares for it. As Bourdaloue intones in his Sermon sur la Providence, the *mondain* who refuses to believe in the existence of providence is guilty of imagining a "Dieu monstrueux, c'est-à-dire un Dieu qui n'a nul soin de ses créatures"⁹⁵ (a monstrous God, that is to say, a God who takes no care of his creatures). Viewing providence through the lens of creation allows Bourdaloue to accuse those who deny it of idolatry:

> Car de n'avoir plus d'autre principe de sa conduite que la fortune, & d'en vouloir suivre le cours, n'est-ce pas tomber dans l'idolatrie des Païens, qui, comme l'observe saint Augustin, au lieu d'adorer les conseils de Dieu dans les événemens du monde, aimerent mieux se faire une divinité bizarre, qu'ils appellerent fortune ...?⁹⁶

> For to have no other principle for one's conduct than chance, and to want to follow its course, is that not to fall into the idolatry of the pagans, who, as Saint Augustine observes, instead of adoring the advice of God in the events of this world, preferred to fabricate a bizarre divinity that they named fortune?

As we know, Sévigné was an admirer of both Bourdaloue and Saint Augustine; this message would have resonated deeply with her, and she would have understood immediately the correlation between idolatry and a failure to recognize the workings of divine providence. Sévigné's repeated, and increasingly sincere, professions of faith in providence can therefore easily be read as an effort to relieve herself of the guilt of idolatry by acknowledging herself as a powerless participant in an overarching, ultimately benevolent

---

94 Ferreyrolles, 'Histoire et finalité', p. 1.
95 In *Sermons du père Bourdaloue pour le caresme* (Paris: Rigaud, 1713), vol. 2, p. 308.
96 Bourdaloue, *Sermons*, vol. 2, p. 317.

plan. Yet if Sévigné largely succeeds in subordinating her own rebellious will and interpretation of events to the larger narrative supplied by providence, this resolves only part of her dilemma, insofar as she continues to love her daughter. Here, I would like to argue that in fact Sévigné is using her faith in providence to achieve the seemingly impossible goal of aligning her love for her daughter with love of God.

To begin to understand how this is possible, we should examine the language that Sévigné uses to describe her daughter. More precisely, we should turn our attention to her tendency to refer to Mme de Grignan as a "créature." From April 24, 1676, when she asks, "Peut-on jamais trop aimer une créature comme vous, dont on est aimée?"[97] (Can one ever love a creature like you, by whom one is loved, too much?) to her repeated complaints, in the fall of 1679, that distance takes away from her "une créature dont la présence et la moindre amitié fait ma vie et mon unique plaisir"[98] (a creature whose presence and slightest friendship constitute my life and my only pleasure), Sévigné uses the word affectionately, often as a demonstration of tenderness. Yet a look at the constellation of "créatures" that populates the correspondence also reveals that Sévigné is acutely (and increasingly, as the correspondence progresses) conscious of the religious overtones of the word, overtones that are evident in Furetière's definition of the word as "estre qui a été créé, qui ne s'est point fait luy-même" (being which has been made, and which did not make itself) supplemented with the example "Toutes les *créatures* annoncent la gloire du Créateur" (all the creatures announce the glory of their Creator). Sévigné therefore uses the word when referring to her granddaughter Louise-Catherine, who had just announced her religious vocation in August 1680: "Je la regarde comme un vase d'élection, comme une créature choisie et distinguée, comme une âme remplie de la grâce de Jésus-Christ ... Et la pensée que tous ces dons viennent de Dieu fait en moi tout l'effet que je vous dis"[99] (I view her like an elected vase, like a creature chosen and distinguished, like a soul full of the grace of Jesus Christ). Here, the word "creature" allows Sévigné to capture the close and dependent relationship between Louise-Catherine and God that is so different than Sévigné's own experience of the divine. Yet only a few months earlier, in May of 1680, Sévigné offered an articulation of the relationship between providence and creatures that clearly lays out her understanding of the link between the two. As she tells her stubbornly Cartesian daughter,

> Je ne comprends point bien ce grand mystère que vous faites de la Providence de Dieu; je ne trouve rien au monde de si aisé à comprendre dès qu'on

[97] *Correspondance*, vol. 2, p. 277.
[98] *Correspondance*, vol. 2, p. 669.
[99] *Correspondance*, vol. 2, p. 1048.

> veut bien le regarder comme le créateur de toutes choses et le maître absolu de toutes ses créatures et de son univers.[100]

> I do not understand the great mystery that you make of divine Providence; I find nothing in the world as easy to comprehend once one decides to consider God as the creator of all things and the absolute master of all of his creatures and his universe.

What Sévigné says afterwards is significant, insofar as it marks a philosophical, theological, and affective shift that will lend a strikingly different tone to the final ten years of the correspondence. She continues: "Il fait agir nos volontés selon les fins qu'il a réglées. Par exemple, sans aller plus loin, *il veut que je vous aime* d'une inclination et d'une tendresse extraordinaires"[101] (We must adjust our will according to the ends that he has decreed. For example, without going farther, *he wants me to love you* with an extraordinary inclination and tenderness) [my italics].

It is difficult to understate the importance of what is happening here. Sévigné understands that by framing her love for her daughter in terms of providence and divine creation, by honoring her daughter not as her own, but as God's, she has finally found a way to transform her love for her daughter from idolatry to worship. God *wants* her to love her daughter; in a reasoning not dissimilar to that of Lycidas or Hylas in *L'Astrée*, this is why God has made her daughter so beautiful and charming. From this point forward, Sévigné becomes much less apologetic and much less guilty as she has convinced herself that by loving her daughter she is enduring and enacting God's plan. Perhaps nowhere is this newfound peace of mind more beautifully expressed than in a letter dated May 21, 1690, where maternal pride blends seamlessly with religious devotion:

> Je suis persuadée que la Providence vous récompensera de la confiance que vous avez en elle; il y a longtemps, ma bonne, que je vous observe et que je vous admire. Je vous vois la femme forte, toute sacrifiée à tous vos devoirs en faisant un usage admirable de la bonté et de l'étendue de votre esprit ... Remerciez-en Dieu, car assurément ce n'est pas de vous que viennent tous ces dons. Quand une belle et aimable femme les a reçus du Ciel, comme vous, c'est une merveille.[102]

> I am persuaded that Providence will repay you for the confidence that you have in her; my dear, I have been observing and admiring you for a long

---

[100] *Correspondance*, vol. 2, p. 938.
[101] *Correspondance*, vol. 2, p. 938.
[102] *Correspondance*, vol. 3, p. 877.

time. I see in you a strong woman, completely devoted to your duty while making admirable use of the goodness and breadth of your mind ... Thank God for this, for assuredly all of these gifts did not come from you. When a beautiful and lovely woman has received them from heaven, like you, that is a marvel.

Here, Sévigné as mother, as willing, wanting subject, disappears entirely. Instead, she is an admiring spectator, content to contemplate her daughter and, through her daughter's gifts, God. Sévigné has managed to cleanse herself of any taint of idolatry by aligning the heavenly and the terrestrial through her daughter, but the price of such innocence is her own identity as an author, either maternal or literary. Indeed, towards the end of her correspondence, and five years before the end of her life, she writes to her good friend Coulanges, who is horrified by what he's witnessing in Rome during the conclave that would result in the election of Innocent XII. In a letter dated July 26, 1691, she exhorts him to believe that

> quelque manège qu'il y ait dans le conclave, c'est toujours le Saint-Esprit qui fait le pape. Dieu fait tout; il est le maître de tout. Et voici comme nous devrions penser (j'ai lu ceci en bon lieu): "Quel trouble peut-il arriver à une personne qui sait que Dieu fait tout, et qui aime tout ce que Dieu fait?"[103]

> whatever politics are going on in the conclave, it is always the Holy Spirit which elects the Pope. God does everything; he is the master of everything. And this is how we should think (I read this somewhere good): "What trouble can happen to a person who knows that God does everything, and who loves everything that God does?"

---

[103] *Correspondance*, vol. 3, pp. 973–4.

5

Theatrical Idolatry in Molière and Racine

> Mais en cette leçon, si pompeuse & si vaine,
> Le profit est douteux, & perte certaine,
> Le remede y plaist moins que ne fait le poison;
> *Elle peut reformer un esprit idolâtre,*
> Mais pour changer leurs moeurs, & regler leur raison,
> Les Chrestiens ont l'Eglise, & non pas le theatre.[1]

> But in this lesson, so pompous and vain,
> The gain is doubtful, and the loss certain.
> The remedy pleases less than the poison;
> *It can reform an idolatrous mind,*
> But to change their morals and regulate their reason,
> Christians have the Church, and not the theater. [my italics]

These catchy lines, penned by Antoine Godeau, bishop of Grasse and onetime *salonnier*, concluded his *Sonnet sur la comédie*, published for the first time in the 1654 edition of his *Poésies chrétiennes*. As Laurent Thirouin notes, the sonnet was hugely successful, ushering in a series of polemical texts condemning the theater and cited by almost all of them.[2] The irresistible last line drew a firm distinction between religion and theater, asserting categorically that morality, reason, and, implicitly, utility, was the domain of the former and was dangerously absent from the latter.

Yet as my added emphasis shows, Godeau's condemnation of theater was incomplete, and the admission that theater is able to "reform an idolatrous mind" is both telling and intriguing. It points to the long, intimate, and uncomfortable relationship between theater and idolatry. Already in the third century, Tertullian argued that the two were closely associated, declaring that

---

[1] Antoine Godeau, *Poésies chrestiennes* (1660), cited by Julia Prest in *Controversy in French Drama: Molière's* Tartuffe *and the Struggle for Influence* (New York: Palgrave Macmillan, 2014), p. 31.

[2] See Thirouin's critical edition of Pierre Nicole, *Traité de la comédie et autres pièces d'un procès du théâtre* (Paris: Honoré Champion, 1998), here p. 122.

So, if it shall be established that the whole equipment of the public shows is idolatry pure and simple, we have an indubitable decision laid down in advance, that this profession of renunciation made in baptism touches the public shows too, since they, being idolatry, belong to the devil, his pomp and his angels.[3]

The anti-theatrical polemics that proliferated in France in the 1660s elaborated upon Tertullian's equation of plays and idolatry. If, for the Church Father, all public spectacles carried the danger of inappropriately distracting the audience from worship of the divine, seventeenth-century writers singled out the theater both for its content and for its unapologetic deployment of human embodiment, in actors and spectators alike. The prince de Conti, onetime protector and employer of Molière, turned against theater after his religious conversion in 1655, writing a *Traité de la comédie et des spectacles* meant to be read as a very public repudiation of his worldly past. There, Conti fulminates against the secular content of plays, noting that even if a play does not unleash uncontrollable emotions in the spectator, "n'est-ce pas un terrible mal que cette idolâtrie que commet le Coeur humain dans une violente passion, n'est-ce pas en quelque sens le plus grand péché qu'on puisse commettre?" (is it not a horrible ill, this idolatry committed by the human heart in a violent passion, is it not in some sense the greatest sin one can commit?) He continues, in terms that underscore the violation of the hierarchy between Creator and creature that so troubled the seventeenth century:

> La creature y chasse Dieu du Coeur de l'homme, pour y dominer à sa place, y recevoir des sacrifices et des adorations, y régler ses mouvements, ses conduits et ses intérêts, et y faire toutes les fonctions de souverain qui n'appartiennent qu'à Dieu, qui veut y régner par la charité, qui est la fin et l'accomplissment de toute la loi chrétienne.[4]

> The creature chases God from the human heart to dominate in his place, to receive sacrifices and adorations, rule his movements, his conduct, and his interests, and accomplish all of the sovereign functions which belong only to God, who wishes to reign there through charity, which is the end and accomplishment of the entire Christian law.

Writing after Conti, the Jansenist moralist Pierre Nicole emphasized many of the same points while also pointing to the mortal danger faced by actors

---

[3] Tertullian, *De Spectaculis*, trans. T. R. Glover (Cambridge, MA: Harvard University Press, 1977), p. 243.

[4] Armand de Bourbon, Prince de Conti, 'Traité de la comédie et des spectacles', in Thirouin, p. 202.

tainted by the emotions that they represent, and therefore feel, on stage. In his treatise *De la comédie*, first published in 1668 and then revised and republished in 1675, Nicole also condemns the effect on the spectator enchanted by the secular, passionate love he sees enacted. In a passage heavily inflected by the Augustinianism central to the Jansenist worldview, he notes:

> Un Chrétien qui sait ce qu'il doit à Dieu ne doit point souffrir dans son Coeur aucun mouvement, ni aucune attache de cette sorte sans la condamner, sans en gémir, et sans demander à Dieu d'en être délivré; et il doit avoir une extreme horreur d'être lui-même l'objet de l'attache et de la passion de quelque autre personne, et d'être ainsi en quelque façon son idole, puisque l'amour est un culte qui n'est dû qu'à Dieu, comme Dieu ne peut être honoré que par l'amour.[5]

> A Christian who knows what he owes God should not suffer in his heart any movement or attachment of this kind without condemning it, without deploring it, and without asking God to be delivered from it; and he should be extremely afraid of being that object of attachment for another person, and to be in some way their idol, since love is owed only to God, just as God can be honored only through love.

As Nicole goes on to explain, this is because the theater glorifies the passions that men feel for women, described in the 1668 version of the text as "une sacrilège idolâtrie."[6] This objection to the decidedly, and necessarily, secular content of plays – as Nicole points out later, a play that represented someone quietly worshipping God would hardly attract spectators – leads him to include novels in his condemnation, yet it is clear that theater presents a special danger. On the one hand, it excites passions in the actors and spectators that are imprinted – that is, impossible to unsee or unfeel. On the other hand, following Tertullian's neo-Platonist argument, the theater represents as lasting and real what is ephemeral and illusory, substituting temporal delights for the lasting love and glory of God. As Nicole notes near the end of the treatise,

> Car si toutes les choses temporelles ne sont que des figures et des ombres, en quel rang doit-on mettre les Comédies, qui ne sont que les ombres des ombres, puisque ce ne sont que de vaines images des choses temporelles, et souvent de choses fausses?[7]

---

[5] Pierre Nicole, *Traité de la comédie* (texte de 1668), in Thirouin, p. 56.
[6] *De la comédie*, p. 56.
[7] *De la comédie*, p. 109.

> For if all temporal things are only figures and shadows, how should we rank theatrical plays, which are only the shadows of shadows, since they are vain images of temporal things, and often of false things?

Similar to the sixteenth-century iconoclasts' arguments and violence against images and statues, Nicole's fervent opposition to theater constitutes an apparently paradoxical testimony to its power; as Laurent Thirouin notes, "Les ennemis du théâtre sont ceux qui croient le plus en son pouvoir; ils prennent le genre très au sérieux et soulignent sa puissance, son efficace."[8] (The enemies of theater are those who believe the most in its power; they take the genre very seriously and underscore its strength and efficacy.) The intensity of antitheatrical sentiment, tagged with the strong language of "sacrilège idolâtrie," is symptomatic of a deep unease with theater's apparent appropriation of modes of representation that lie at the contested heart of religious practice. Chief among these is the Incarnation, the manifestation of the divine in human form, which, as we have seen, can be used either as a defense or a condemnation of the use of images in worship. The physicality inherent in theatrical representation provides an uncomfortable reminder of the issues at the heart of idolatry polemics; as Michael O'Connell argues in his study of antitheatricality in early modern England, "theater makes present 'the truth of the god' on stage; the stage does not merely *refer* to a reality beyond itself, nor should we take this 'truth' in some vacant and abstract sense. Theatrical presence is not mere sign but a use of corporeality to 'body forth' the fiction it portrays."[9]

Moreover, for theater to "work," it needs to solve the very problem that bedeviled early modern religious communities and leaders by achieving a balance between the embodied vehicle of representation and that which it represents. A spectator who grows fixated on a certain actor or actress is unable to enjoy, or even understand, the play; on the other hand, a spectator who expects to experience the unmediated presence of the character portrayed will inevitably be distracted or disappointed by the flourishes that the actor brings to the role. Ideally, the theater charts a course between these two extremes through a productive tension between the skill of the individual actors – what one might call the materiality of their signifying bodies – and their ability to convey the roles that they have set out to play, to disappear, as it were, into their part. A successful play, then, is more than just another humanly fabricated distraction from the worship of God. It represents the tantalizing possibility

---

[8] Laurent Thirouin, L'Aveuglement salutaire. Le réquisitoire contre le théâtre dans la France classique. (Paris: Honoré Champion, 2007), p. 20.

[9] Michael O'Connell, *The Idolatrous Eye: Iconoclasm and Theater in Early-Modern England* (New York: Oxford University Press, 2000), p. 20.

that the problem of idolatry might not be quite as intractable as all that, a possibility that could well account, at least in part, for the central role that the Jesuits, with their unabashed celebration of the role of art in the always-open, bidirectional communication between heaven and earth, accorded theater in their schools.

It is in this context, then, that Godeau's admission that theater might actually be able to solve the problem of idolatry takes on its full significance as an implicit threat to the religious frameworks that theater might well outdo or displace. Godeau's line about idolatry might be eclipsed by the closing confidence that theater and church are incompatible, but it speaks to Godeau's own longstanding effort to reconcile literature and religion, evident in the preface to the first, 1641, edition of his poems, then entitled *Œuvres chrétiennes*, which Godeau opens with the astute recognition that poetry "est ou extremement utile, ou extremement dangereuse"[10] (is either extremely useful or extremely dangerous). In the extraordinary text that follows, the reader can see Godeau work through the intricate braiding of literature, religion, and idolatry, seeking to attain a stable, tenable equilibrium between the three. Tellingly, the effort to reconcile literature and religion necessarily entails the question of human authorship. As Godeau justifies the publication of his own religious poetry, he disavows any suspect attempt to win praise for himself. Speaking of his readers, he states:

> Je cherche leur conversion, & non pas leur applaudissemens ... Je ne mets pas non plus beaucoup en peine du jugement de ces Critiques, qui faisant leurs Idoles des ouvrages de leurs mains, disent aisément que les choses sont mal-faites, quand ils ne les ont pas faites ...[11]

> I seek their conversion, and not their applause ... I am not concerned with the judgment of those Critics, who make idols out of the work of their own hands and easily say that things are badly made when they were made by someone other than themselves ...

Framing authorship in terms of idolatry offers Godeau the opportunity to articulate his own humility, the subordination of style to substance and pleasure to salvation. This model of authorship is opposed to that of the "critiques," who not only elevate their own literary production as an end in itself but cannot abide the authorship of others (including, one can infer, God).

Later in the preface, however, Godeau offers as evidence of the happy coexistence of religion and literature a poem he has composed about the

---

[10] Antoine Godeau, *Œuvres chrestiennes* (Paris: Jean Camusat, 1641), 12.
[11] *Œuvres chrestiennes*, p. 13.

Virgin Mary. Defending this poem against "ceux qui se sont separez de nostre Communion, & qui semblent estre particulierement ennemis de l'honneur qu'on rend à la Mere de Dieu"[12] (those who have separated themselves from our Faith, & who seem particularly opposed to the honor that we pay to the Virgin Mary), Godeau begins by acknowledging that overzealous or simple writers may have implied that worship is due to the Virgin herself, but that "les pensées des particuliers ne sont pas des maximes Orthodoxes"[13] (the thoughts of individuals are not Orthodox maxims). Godeau then moves on to assert the incommensurable distance between "l'Estre eternel" (the eternal Being) and "l'estre crée" (the created Being), agreeing that misattributing the honor due to the "ouvrier" (maker) to the "ouvrage" (made) is not just a "simple aveuglement" (mere blindness) but rather "un espouventable impieté"[14] (a horrible impiety). What follows, then, is a theological mini-treatise, where Godeau explains that the Virgin's status, to which honor is paid, is solely due to her role in bringing the Son into the world; indeed, only Jesus can properly serve as a bridge between the Creator and the human creature, conferring unity and reflected holiness to the community of the faithful. As Godeau is well aware, there is nothing theologically unorthodox or original here; what is interesting is the way in which the monopoly of creation by the divine threatens to foreclose any possibility of human authorship. As Godeau himself notes,

> Nous sommes au temps de la lumiere, & nous devons servir Dieu en esprit & en verité. A plus forte raison doit-on lâcher toutes les foudres de l'Eglise, contre ceux qui seraient assez detestables, pour inventer des faux miracles, pour establir de leur propre authorité des devotions nouvelles, ou pour abuser de ceux qui sont des-ja establies, & les convertir en un instrument de gain deshonneste, d'empire sur les esprits foibles, & de trouble de l'ordre estably par le Saint Esprit dans l'Eglise.[15]

> We are in a time of light, & we must serve God in mind & in truth. All the more reason to release the thunderbolts of the Church against those who would be so detestable as to invent false miracles to establish their own authority on new devotions or to abuse those which are already established and convert them into an instrument of dishonest profit, of empire over weak minds, & of trouble in the order established by the Holy Spirit in the Church.

---

[12] *Œuvres chrestiennes*, p. 16.
[13] *Œuvres chrestiennes*, p. 18.
[14] *Œuvres chrestiennes*, p. 18.
[15] *Œuvres chrestiennes*, pp. 19–20.

While it may well be objected that Godeau's target here is religious, not literary, invention, his earlier invocation of the idolatrous "critiques" who elevate and jealously promote their own creations reveals that the line between the religious and the "merely" literary is blurry indeed. The puzzle, then, becomes how to situate literary production so that it is an augmentation of the honor due to the divine rather than a distraction from it. This, after all, is the project of the *Œuvres* (and then the *Poésies*) *chrestiennes*, yet Godeau's lengthy foray into the theological controversy surrounding the worship of Mary illustrates his consciousness that he is operating on ground that, under the pressure of the Protestants, has become quite shaky. Indeed, following a triumphant list of all of the honor rightfully, since grounded in recognition of the importance of the Incarnation, accorded to Mary, especially in the kingdom of France, Godeau's defense of his own hymn to the Virgin is quite tentative:

> J'espere aussi de la bonté [de Dieu] qu'il aura agreable le dessein que j'ay eu de conserver la memoire de cette grande action, dans l'Hymne à qui elle sert de subjet, & que les Lecteurs raisonnables n'y trouveront point de loüanges, apres les raisons que j'apporte dans ce discours, pour expliquer les sentimens de l'Eglise, ausquels les miens n'ont rien ce me semble de contraire.[16]

> I hope that God, in his goodness, will be pleased by my intent to conserve the memory of this great action in the Hymn of which it is the subject, & that reasonable readers will not find enough praise, after the reasons that I bring to the subject, to explain the sentiments of the Church, in relation to which my own sentiments do not seem to me to be contrary.

Although this preface survived, with some changes, in each of the editions of the *Œuvres*, then *Poésies*, Godeau's strong assertion that the theater was incapable of replacing or even complementing the Church in his 1654 sonnet indicates that the fragile equilibrium that he sought to attain between literary production and religious orthodoxy could not, in fact, hold. Yet unlike the polemicists who followed him, Godeau stopped short of an outright equation of theater and idolatry, holding out the hope, perhaps, that someone other than himself could reconcile divine worship with the danger of literature.

Molière, or the Ridiculousness of Idolatry

That person would not be Molière. Perhaps no *homme de théâtre* inhabited, reveled in, and exploited, the uncomfortably close proximity between theater and religion more than Molière. As I have already mentioned, his

[16] *Œuvres chrestiennes*, p. 33.

former protector, the prince de Conti, became one of the more notable (and vehement) opponents of theater after his religious conversion in 1655. While his *Traité de la comédie et des spectacles* singles out Corneille as a particularly scandalous author (even, or especially, because of his ostensibly Christian play *Polyeucte*), in the *Sentiment des pères de l'Eglise sur la comédie et les spectacles* that accompanies the treatise, he condemns *L'Ecole des femmes* and the *Festin de Pierre*, without mentioning Molière by name. Interestingly, Conti specifies that both of these plays are, like the rest of modern theater, exempt from idolatry and suspicion; the charge that he levels at them instead is impiety.[17]

Conti was on to something, but Molière's gleeful exploration (and mockery) of religious themes was, as the talking statue in *Dom Juan, ou le Festin de Pierre* rather directly suggests, intricately engaged with the problematics of idolatry. Moreover, this exploration began well before the first performance of *L'Ecole des femmes* in 1662, with one of Molière's earliest plays, the little-known one-act farce *Sganarelle ou le cocu imaginaire*. First performed in 1660, the play depicts the series of *malentendus* that result when Sganarelle's wife picks up the portrait of Lélie that was dropped by his lover Célie when she faints following the suggestion that Lélie's unfaithfulness is the reason for his prolonged absence. As Christopher Braider has noted, Sganarelle's wife's reaction to the portrait is not only comical, but also pointedly idolatrous; she falls in love not with the person that the portrait represents but with the materiality of the object.[18] As she gushes before she even opens the case, "L'émail en est fort beau, la gravure charmante"[19] (line 142) (The enamel is beautiful, the engraving charming), and Sganarelle's mistaken, yet altogether reasonable, conviction that she is in love with the person portrayed there stems from her decision to smell it – "Le travail plus que l'or s'en doit encor priser./

---

[17] Conti in Thirouin, p. 212: "Or il faut avouer de bonne foi que la Comédie moderne est exempte d'idolâtrie et de superstition. Mais il faut qu'on convienne aussi qu'elle n'est pas exempte d'impureté ... il n'y a rien par exemple de plus scandaleux que la cinquième scène du second acte de l'*Ecole des Femmes*, qui est une des plus nouvelles Comédies." Conti continues: "Il faut qu'on convienne encore que, si l'idolâtrie et la superstition en sont bannies, l'impiété leur a succédé. Y a-t-il une école d'athéisme plus ouverte que le *Festin de Pierre* ...?"/ "Or one must admit in good faith that modern theater is exempt from idolatry and superstition. But one must also admit that it is not exempt from impurity ... there is nothing, for example, more scandalous than the fifth scene of the second act of *L'Ecole des femmes*, which is one of the newest plays ... One must also admit that if idolatry and superstition are, in fact, banned from our plays, impiety has replaced them. Is there a more open school of atheism than the *Festin de Pierre*?"

[18] See Christopher Braider, 'Image and Imaginaire in Molière's *Cocu imaginaire*', *PMLA* 117.5 (October 2002), pp. 1142–57.

[19] *Sganarelle ou le cocu imaginaire*, in Molière, *Oeuvres complètes*, ed. Georges Forestier (Paris: Gallimard, 2010), vol. 1, pp. 33–81. Line numbers will refer to this edition.

Hon que cela sent bon" (lines 151–152) (The work is more valuable than the gold/ Oh, it smells so good) – which he interprets as a kiss.[20] For Braider, this direct evocation of idolatry serves to highlight the impossibility of achieving the clear separation of body and mind that is held forth by Descartes as not only a desirable ideal, but the foundation of scientific reason, and it is certainly true that Cartesian philosophy was one of Molière's favorite and enduring targets.[21]

Here, however, I would like to take Molière's unmistakable evocation of idolatry in another direction, one inspired by the patently farcical nature of Sganarelle's wife's infatuation with the material portrait. For indeed, this is less a portrayal of the threat of idolatry than a parodic literalization of its performance. At no point in the copious literature dealing with idolatry in the sixteenth or seventeenth century is a Catholic, or even a "pagan," depicted as extolling the smell of the paint on an image or the knifework on a statue. Rather, a common aspect of the crime of idolatry in the early modern period is the forgetting of the *madness* of the object, an erasure of its artistry, in order to portray the object not as a temporary, provisional, flawed extension of human imagination but rather as an emanation of the gods or, as in La Fontaine's portrayal of the sculptor of Jupiter, an active subject in its own right. The essential role played by the obscuring of the human work involved in fashioning the idol mirrors and intensifies the key crime of idolaters: that of forgetting the divine origins of the created world. And indeed, the Bible emphasizes the similarities in these forgettings, whether in the example of the Golden Calf or the statue forged by the grieving father to honor his dead son. As Augustine, then Calvin, reminded their readers, this elevation of created objects to subjects in their own right serves to obscure their flawed nature, their essential dependence on something or someone from which they came. As a result, in deifying human creations, humans are merely passing along their own forgetting of their own madness and origin in the divine. The Bible seeks to remind humanity of this origin while warning against the improper elevation of human creations: "No man can form a god which is like himself. He is mortal, and what he makes with lawless hands is dead, for he is better than the objects he worships, since he has life, but they never have" (Wisdom of Solomon 15: 16–17).

Molière would seem, therefore, to be joining the critics of idolatry by emphasizing the fabricated nature of the object of Sganarelle's wife's

---

[20] The decision of Sganarelle's wife to smell the portrait might seem odd to a contemporary spectator or reader, but this decision, accompanied by her exclamation upon how good the portrait smells, serves to accentuate the connection to idolatry insofar as it evokes Reformation associations of earthly beauty and its idolatrous worship to pestilence and filth since Calvin.

[21] See Olivier Bloch, *Molière/philosophie* (Paris: Albin Michel, 2000).

devotion, yet his depiction of her behavior is careful to indicate that she loves the object not *despite* its obviously human artistry, but rather *because* of it – so much so that the actual person represented, Lélie, is so incidental that she fails to recognize him when he appears in person. By stubbornly stopping her attention at the material signifier, she is doing precisely what Protestants accused Catholics of: preferring the representation (in the form of an image or statue) to what is represented. And yet her literality is absurd, if not nonsensical; by taking idolatry *à la lettre*, she – and by extension, Molière – incisively demonstrates its inherent ridiculousness.

This reading of Sganarelle's wife's behavior begs the question, however, of what Molière is really up to, and why he would take such direct aim at what was commonly characterized as the root of all sin in this manner. I believe that we can begin to reach a conclusion if we examine the way that the actions surrounding the portrait resonate with the treatment of God and religion in the rest of the play.[22] The opening scene presents us with a tyrannical paternal figure in the form of Gorgibus, who is insisting that his daughter, Célie, marry the rich suitor he has chosen instead of her lover Lélie, exclaiming, in the play's opening lines,

> Vous prétendez choquer ce que j'ai résolu?
> Je n'aurai pas sur vous un pouvoir absolu?
> Et par sottes raisons votre jeune cervelle
> Voudrait régler ici la raison paternelle?
> Qui de nous deux à l'autre a droit de faire loi? (lines 3–7)

> You claim to reject what I have resolved?
> I do not have absolute power over you?
> And through idiotic reasons your young brain
> Would like to impose itself on paternal reason?
> Who, of the two of us, has the right to make law over the other?

Such bluster immediately identifies Gorgibus as a stock character, the tyrannical father that will reappear periodically in Molière's theater and who cannot bear to see the actions of others, especially his children, escape his

---

[22] Roger Duchêne, in his authoritative *Molière* (Paris: Fayard, 1998), notes the religious discourse in the *Cocu imaginaire*, but sees it as an incidental forerunner of the themes that would be more fully developed in *L'Ecole des femmes*: "Au passage et sans y insister, dans une pièce dont le sujet n'était pourtant pas de mettre en cause l'autorité paternelle, Molière suggérait que la morale et la religion traditionnelles s'accommodaient mal des nouvelles formes de la sociabilité mondaine" (p. 316). (As an aside, and without insisting, in a play whose purpose is not to place paternal authority in doubt, Molière suggested that traditional morality and religion were ill-suited to the new forms of worldly sociability.)

control. Yet as the play continues, Gorgibus' language and behavior (a bit like those of Arnolphe in the not-yet-written *Ecole des femmes*) are increasingly associated with religion. Just a few lines later, he reproaches his daughter for filling her head with love-related nonsense, noting that "vous parlez de Dieu, bien moins que de Clélie" (line 30) (you speak much less of God than you do of Clélie). As a solution, he recommends that she read, instead, a variety of old-fashioned moralistic texts as well as "La Guide des pécheurs" (The Guide for Sinners), a work by the Spanish Dominican Louis de Grenade published in 1556.[23] Indeed, the God that Gorgibus has in mind, and whose presence he views as lamentably rare in his family and society at large, is not the God of grace and love, but rather the Old Testament divinity of law and obedience upon whom he styles his own authority; in the next-to-the-last scene of the play, as Célie declares her intention to marry Lélie, he sputters, significantly, "Est-ce répondre en fille à mes commandements?" (line 632) (is that how a daughter responds to my commandments?).

The language of religion is not confined, however, to Gorgibus's bluster. In the second scene, Célie's servant tries to explain the necessity of marriage by using her own life as an example of the truism that woman is like the ivy to the man's tree: "Et je l'éprouve en moi chétive pécheresse./ Le bon Dieu fasse paix à mon pauvre Martin,/ Mais j'avais, lui vivant, le teint d'un Chérubin" (lines 78–80) (And I feel in myself, humble sinner, may God accord peace to my poor Martin, that when he was living, I had the complexion of a Cherubim) before concluding that, if nothing else, a husband comes in handy to bless you when you sneeze: "Un mari sert beaucoup la nuit auprès de soi,/ Ne fût-ce que pour l'heur d'avoir qui vous salue/ D'un Dieu vous soit en aide alors qu'on éternue" (lines 88–90) (A husband is very useful at night, if only to have him ask that God help you when you sneeze). Coming on the heels of Gorgibus' exhortations to daughterly obedience, the *suivante*'s words demonstrate the extent to which love and religion have become closely, if clumsily and comically, intertwined.

The stage, as it were, is therefore set for the appearance of Lélie's portrait. We first see it in the hands of Célie, who contemplates it with what can only be described as reverence. Showing the portrait to her *suivante*, she refutes the *suivante*'s suspicion that Lélie's long absence is due to infidelity: "Vois attentivement les traits de ce visage,/ Ils jurent à mon coeur d'éternelles ardeurs,/ Je veux croire après tout qu'ils ne sont pas menteurs,/ Et comme c'est celui que l'art y représente/ Il conserve à mes feux une amitié constante" (lines 98–102) (Look closely at these features/ They swear eternal ardor to

---

[23] The full title is *La Guide des pécheurs, où est enseigné tout ce que le chrestien doit faire depuis le commencement de sa conversion jusques à la fin de la perfection.*

my heart/ I want to believe despite everything that they do not lie/ And that since he's the one represented by art here/ He conserves a constant loyalty to my passion). Célie's attitude towards the painted representation of her love is quite Catholic: for her, the portrait serves to render Lélie both present and timeless ("éternel"), thereby transforming her love for him into a sort of religion. As she herself states, "Je veux croire." The recent Pléiade edition of Molière's works notes that Célie's comment that "Et comme c'est celui que l'art y représente" has remained obscure to commentators and must surely be a mistaken transcription of the words that were used on stage. Yet in the context of representation, idolatry, and faith, her words make a certain amount of sense, especially insofar as they evoke the correspondence between signifier and signified that would soon find its most famous formulation in the *Logique* of Port-Royal and wherein someone viewing the portrait of the king exclaims, "C'est le roi" (It's the king).[24] Célie's rather comical "comme" associates the faithfulness of the representation with Lélie's actual fidelity – "Il conserve à mes feux une amitié constante." The ridiculousness of her logic has, perhaps, confounded centuries of commentators, yet it is, in fact, not so far removed from the actual economy of belief espoused by Counter-Reformation Catholics. In other words, Célie's reverent attitude towards Lélie's portrait is no less a ludicrous send-up of religious orthodoxy, based on an overly literal reading of actual doctrine, than the idolatry performed by Sganarelle's wife.

For as Lélie's choice of language indicates, the subject of this play is less the question of Cartesian models of representation as laid out by Braider than the question, central to both religion *and* love, of faith. Upon discovering that his portrait is no longer in the possession of Célie, Lélie immediately invokes the heavens: "Dieux! Qu'aperçois-je ici?/ Et si c'est mon portrait, que dois-je croire aussi?" (lines 255–256) (Gods! What do I see here? And if it is my portrait, what should I believe?). And just in case the spectator has not made the connection between the opening "Dieux" and the fairly anodyne and versatile verb "croire," Lélie's next statement directly invokes faith and its fragility: "Ce gage ne peut sans alarmer ma foi,/ Etre sorti des mains qui le tenaient de moi" (lines 259–260) (this pledge cannot, without alarming my faith, have left the hands to which I had given it). Once again, religion and love share the same language, a similarity brought to the forefront by the puzzle of the portrait. Indeed, when Célie, exposed to Sganarelle's conviction that Lélie and his wife are involved, comes to believe in Lélie's unfaithfulness, she expresses her indignation in the strongest language she knows: that of

---

[24] See, of course, Louis Marin's exploration of this formulation in his *Le Portrait du roi* (Paris: Editions de Minuit, 1981).

religion. Her exclamations – "O Ciel! ... Ah! Traître, scélérat, âme double et sans foi ... l'Enfer n'a point de gêne/ Qui ne soit pour ton crime une trop douce peine" (lines 391–394) (O Heavens! Oh! Traitor, scoundrel, double soul without faith ... Hell has nothing that would not be too gentle for your crime) – invoke damnation, and are greeted with head-shaking incredulity by her interlocutor, Sganarelle, whose interventions – "Que voilà bien parler!" (line 395) (Well spoken!) – serve to draw attention to her speech.

The circulating portrait at the center of Molière's play serves, much like the religious icons that it so obviously recalls, to pose the fundamental question of how belief is constructed and maintained. As the portrait finds its way into the hands of Sganarelle's wife, Sganarelle, Lélie, and Célie are confronted with seemingly incontrovertible, sense-based evidence of betrayal. The question facing them therefore becomes whether, faced with this evidence, they can or should maintain a faith that is maddeningly abstract and ultimately unprovable. This faith refers, of course, to that which underlies the amorous relationships between Lélie and Célie and even between Sganarelle and his wife, but, as the characters' language demonstrates, it is disturbingly similar to the faith that underlies religious devotion. A refusal to believe unless belief is supported by physical evidence would prove disastrous not only to marital relations but also to the connection between humanity and the divine; Sganarelle's pronouncement, uttered in reference to his wife's apparent infidelity, that "il faut toucher au doigt la chose" (line 317) (it must be touched with a finger) provides not only, as the Pléiade footnote points out, the opportunity for a winking nod to the physical aspects of love, but also a fairly explicit reference to the apostle Thomas probing the wound of the resurrected Christ.[25]

And yet, of course, as we have seen, recourse to literality, sense perceptions, and the material world does not inoculate society against misprision. After all, it is precisely Sganarelle's wife's inability to see the portrait as anything other than a beautifully fabricated object that leads to the unraveling of faith that follows. Likewise, Sganarelle's conviction that his wife is involved with Lélie is based upon what he has seen with his very own eyes. Such unreliability in the realm of the senses would seem to lead to the conclusion that one must maintain one's faith blindly, clinging to it in spite of what appears in the world, but this blindness, as Molière would demonstrate four years later in *Tartuffe*, would be just as ridiculous and destructive as the literality of

---

[25] The footnote states only, in reference to "toucher au doigt," "Expression courante, qui signifie être convaincu de manière absolue et définitive" (*cf. Le Festin de Pierre*, t. II, acte III, n. 32). "C'est l'occasion, dans le contexte de la vérification du cocuage, d'un jeu de mots grivois" (Molière, *Oeuvres complètes*, vol. 1, p. 1244). "Common expression which means to be convinced in an absolute and definitive manner. This is an opportunity, in the context of verification of cuckoldry, to introduce a double entendre."

Sganarelle's wife. Moreover, the construction of a faith that would remain firm independently of any knowledge conveyed by the senses flies in the face both of theatrical practice, with its embodied and envisioned incarnation of text, and, significantly, of romantic love. We are left at something of an impasse, forced to choose, in a way, between embodiment and belief. The last words of the play, voiced by a Sganarelle acted by Molière himself, offer an idea of what the play's author would choose: "Vous voyez qu'en ce fait la plus forte apparence/ Peut jeter dans l'esprit une fausse créance:/ De cet exemple-ci, ressouvenez-vous bien,/ Et quand vous verriez tout, ne croyez jamais rien." (lines 656–657) (You see that in this fact the strongest appearance can mislead the mind: From this example, remember well that when you see everything, believe nothing).

And yet, such an abandonment of belief would mean the end of religion, love, and, most significantly for Molière, theater itself. While Sganarelle's rather bleak conclusion follows fairly logically from the events portrayed by the play, it is also fundamentally untenable. Faced with this dead end, it is worth asking if the problem lies less with the conclusion than with the premises upon which it is based, and here, once again, Molière's rather gleeful mixture of religious and amorous language offers us a clue, as does the title of the play. For it is not impossible to see in Sganarelle the *Cocu imaginaire* who fears being betrayed by an image, a reference to the Christian God, author of the now-infamous second commandment: "Thou shalt not make unto thee any graven image, or any likeness of any thing that is in heaven above, or that is in the earth beneath, or that is in the water under the earth: thou shalt not bow down thyself to them, nor serve them: for I the Lord thy God am a jealous God, visiting the iniquity of the fathers upon the children unto the third and fourth generation of them that hate me; and showing mercy to the thousands of them that love me and keep my commandments" (Exodus 20: 4–6).

Read out of context, the God of this commandment sounds like a fearsomely ridiculous combination of both Sganarelle and Gorgibus; at once jealous of images and threatening paternal vengeance on those who fail to obey. Might Molière be asking, through his invocation of adultery and his perceptive indication of how the languages of love and religion contaminate each other, whether the problem with love lies not as much with the lovers, or with love itself, as with a deeply flawed conception of a jealous, tyrannical divinity?

Phèdre, or the Dangers of Idolatry

If the mischievous Molière deploys the logic of idolatry to point out the ridiculousness of the habit of referring to romantic love in religious terms (and of judging love by religious rules and standards), the great tragedian Jean Racine invokes idolatry for the almost completely opposite purpose of heightening the stakes of romantic love and pointing to its cosmic implications. Racine's deep familiarity with idolatry is amply on display, unsurprisingly, in the biblical plays with which he ended his career and where it plays a central role. In both *Esther* and *Athalie*, the purity of the Jewish faith is juxtaposed with the impotent religion of the pagan persecutors. As one of the young Israelites exclaims in *Esther*, "Moi! Je pourrais trahir le Dieu que j'aime?/ J'adorerais un Dieu sans force, et sans vertu,/ Reste d'un tronc par les vents abattu,/ Qui ne peut se sauver lui-même?"[26] (lines 763–766) (Me! I could betray the God I love? I would adore a God without power or virtue, The remainder of a trunk felled by wind, Who cannot save himself?)

The chorus responds: "Dieux impuissants, Dieux sourds, tous ceux qui vous implorent/ Ne seront jamais entendus./ Que les Démons, et ceux qui les adorent/ Soient à jamais détruits et confondus" (lines 767–770) (Impotent gods, deaf gods, all of those who implore you/ Will never be heard./ May the demons and those who adore them/ Be forever destroyed and confounded).

In *Athalie*, idolatry is invoked directly and repeatedly. Joad, speaking to Josabet, deplores that Athalie's faith risks polluting the temple: "Que dis-je?/ Le succès animant leur fureur,/ Jusque sur notre Autel votre injuste Marâtre/ Veut offrir à Baal un encens idolâtre" (lines 170–173) (What am I saying? Their furor augmented by their success, your unjust stepmother wants to offer Baal idolatrous incense upon our altar), while Mathan demonstrates that he is keenly aware of the fundamental difference between true and false divinities, and therefore incapable of idol worship: "Ami, peux-tu penser que d'un zèle frivole/ Je me laisse aveugler pour une vaine idole,/ Pour un fragile bois, que malgré mon secours,/ Les vers sur son autel consument tous les jours ?" (lines 919–922) (Friend, can you think that a frivolous zeal would lead me to be blinded by a vain idol, by a fragile piece of wood which worms, despite my efforts, consume each day on the altar?). Yet Racine's earlier plays, as his Jansenist critics were eager to point out, trafficked unapologetically in the pagan realm, with almost no discernable reference whatsoever to monotheism. If the frequent references to the gods in the earlier tragedies invite the spectator to reflect on the tangled relationship between heaven and earth, the unambiguous identification of those gods as mythological creatures ensures that such reflection remains more or less walled off from anything resembling Christian theology. With *Phèdre*, however, the neat division between pagan and Christian begins to dissolve. Like *L'Astrée*, but also like the Minotaur that haunts the title character's lineage, *Phèdre* is a hybrid, and as such, an ideal venue for the exploration of the vexed point of contact between pagan and

---

[26] Jean Racine, *Oeuvres complètes: Théâtre-Poésie*, ed. Georges Forestier (Paris: Gallimard, 1999). All line numbers are taken from this edition.

Christian, heaven and earth, represented by idolatry.

Readers, spectators, and students of Racine's masterpiece *Phèdre* have puzzled over the nature of the crime that is depicted as almost unspeakably monstrous in the play. Phèdre, after all, is not Hippolyte's biological mother, and therefore the characterization of her love for Thésée's son as incestuous can seem hyperbolic (especially given Oenone's quick conclusion that after Thésée's death, Phèdre's love immediately transforms into an "ordinary" passion).[27] Yet the panic that Phèdre's feelings instill in her becomes legible if we follow her lead in considering the profound religious implications of her attraction to Hippolyte:

> En vain sur les Autels ma main brûlait l'encens.
> Quand ma bouche implorait le nom de la Déesse,
> J'adorais Hippolyte, et le voyant sans cesse,
> Même au pied des Autels que je faisais fumer,
> J'offrais tout à ce Dieu, que je n'osais nommer.
> Je l'évitais partout. O comble de misère!
> Mes yeux le retrouvaient dans les traits de son Père.
> Contre moi-même enfin j'osai me révolter.
> J'excitai mon courage à le persécuter.
> *Pour bannir l'Ennemi dont j'étais idolâtre*,
> J'affectai les chagrins d'une injuste Marâtre,
> Je pressai son exil, et mes cris éternels
> L'arrachèrent du sein, et des bras paternels. (lines 284–296)
> [my italics]

---

[27] That said, Oenone's casuistry scandalizes the anonymous author of the treatise *Dissertation sur les tragédies de Phèdre et Hippolyte*, which appeared during the week before the publication of Pradon and Racine's rival plays in 1677: "Juste ciel! Peut-on avoir écrit ces Vers? ... Une flamme ordinaire. Quoi donc, brûler pour son beau-fils pendant la vie et après la mort de son mari, est un amour approuvé par les lois et reçu de tout le monde; en vérité cela fait horreur; et quand notre Auteur aurait prétendu que la coutume permettait à Phèdre d'épouser Hippolyte (ce qu'il ne peut nous faire voir); quand il dirait que c'est une vicieuse qui débite ses coupables maximes, il devait nous en prévenir par quelques Vers, et ne pas faire doucement glisser ces horreurs dans nos esprits sous le nom *d'une flamme ordinaire*... il est trop dangereux de débiter de méchantes maximes." (My God! Can these verses be possible? "An ordinary passion." So then burning for one's stepson during the life and after the death of one's husband is a love approved of by laws and custom? In truth, it is horrifying, and even if our Author claims that custom allowed Phèdre to marry Hippolyte (which he cannot do), or if he says that only vicious people speak such awful maxims, he should warn us by some lines and not slip these horrors into our minds under the guise of 'an ordinary passion' ... It is too dangerous to give voice to such awful maxims." Racine, *Théâtre et poésie*, p. 887.

> In vain did my hand burn incense on the altars
> While my mouth implored the name of the goddess,
> I adored Hippolyte, and seeing him ceaselessly,
> Even at the foot of the altars on which I sacrificed,
> I offered everything to this God which I dared not name.
> I avoided him everywhere. O utmost misery!
> My eyes found him in the features of his father.
> Against myself I finally dared to revolt.
> I used my courage to persecute him.
> *To banish the enemy of whom I was idolatrous,*
> I took on the role of an unjust stepmother,
> I urged his exile, and my eternal cries
> Tore him away from his father's breast and arms.

It might be tempting to dismiss Phèdre's confession, as it were, and interpret "idolâtre" in the figurative sense of "excessively attracted to" as a translation of the sentiment expressed, after all, by Hippolyte to Théramène regarding Aricie: "Je l'adore" (line 1125). Yet this similarity in sentiment points to the key difference between the two loves. While Hippolyte loves Aricie, he does so *despite* her family of origin, which consisted in political enemies eliminated from the state by his father. In other words, his attraction to Aricie is problematic precisely because her origin and family identity cannot be forgotten. Phèdre's problem is exactly the opposite, insofar as her love for Hippolyte obliterates and supplants all other objects of attention. Her efforts to render homage to Venus are hijacked; while her mouth praises the goddess, her heart worships Hippolyte. Likewise, her love for Hippolyte renders Thésée invisible; as she notes here and in her fatal confession to Hippolyte himself, she cannot look at Thésée without seeing Hippolyte. This is, of course, a complete reversal of the natural state of things, in which the features of the father are visible in the son, and looking at the son serves to remind one, ideally, of the absent father whom he resembles, and Phèdre's failings in this regard are only emphasized by Thésée's prolonged absence.[28] But as Racine and his audience (which included Madame de Sévigné) were well aware, this reversal – this mistaking of the father for the son, rather than the other way around – can be characterized precisely as the confusion of creator and creature that Augustine had identified as the essence of idolatry, and as what made idolatry such a terrifying crime. Phèdre understands this;

---

[28] Phèdre's reversal of father and son stands in stark contrast to Aricie's attraction to Hippolyte; as she tells Ismène, "J'aime, je prise en lui de plus nobles richesses,/Les vertus de son Père, et non point les faiblesses ..." (lines 441–2) (I love him, and I value in him more noble riches – the virtues of his father, and not his father's weaknesses).

her awareness that there is something terribly wrong with her inability to see Thésée in Hippolyte is reflected, and deepened, by her invocation of the theological implications of this reversal. Venus is also invisible to Phèdre, and Hippolyte himself has become a god ("J'offrais tout à ce Dieu, que je n'osais nommer").

Of course, Venus, along with the other gods invoked by Phèdre, differs sharply from the single Creator God of monotheistic Christianity. Yet the reversal of hierarchy between the father and son, alongside the elevation of Hippolyte's status to that of a god in his own right, would have resonated strongly with an audience sensitized to the problem of idolatry by over a century of sustained polemics. Indeed, Racine himself subtly invites the audience to consider Phèdre's dilemma in Christian terms, not just by his use of the adjective (ostensibly useless in a pagan context) "idolâtre," but in deliberately ambiguous passages such as the following, where Phèdre agrees to follow Oenone's advice and unite with Hippolyte to fight Aricie: "Hé bien ! A tes conseils je me laisse entraîner./ Vivons, si vers la vie on peut me ramener,/ Et si l'amour d'un Fils en ce moment funeste/ De mes faibles esprits peut ranimer le reste." (lines 363–366) (Well! I allow myself to be convinced by your counsel. We shall live, if I am able to be brought back to life, and if the love of a son in this fatal moment can reanimate what remains of my feeble mind.) Phèdre, as we learn later, has two sons. The use here of the singular, capitalized "Fils" serves to overlay Hippolyte with her own son; yet a Christian audience would have immediately, if unconsciously, heard in these lines a foreshadowing of the salvific power of the love of Christ. However, Phèdre remains trapped in the weightiness of materiality; the diaphanous veils meant to simultaneously hide and reveal have become heavy and opaque ("que ces voiles me pèsent!" [line 158] (these veils are so weighty!)). Unable, therefore, to serve as the instrument or vehicle of a higher authority, she recognizes herself as unfit to rule, opening the third act by imploring "Que l'on porte ailleurs les honneurs qu'on m'envoie" (line 737) (May the honors sent to me be brought elsewhere). Bereft of the legitimacy that a link to her ancestors – divine or human – would confer, she is likewise unable to transmit any sort of useful legacy to her own children, an impasse that, significantly, is once again described in terms of heaviness and weight:

> Pour mes tristes Enfants quel affreux héritage!
> Le sang de Jupiter doit enfler leur courage.
> Mais quelque juste orgueil qu'inspire un sang si beau,
> Le crime d'une Mère est un pesant fardeau ...
> Je tremble qu'opprimés de ce poids odieux
> L'un ni l'autre jamais n'ose lever les yeux. (lines 861–868)

> What a horrible inheritance for my sad children!
> The blood of Jupiter should inflate their courage.
> Yet however just the pride that such blood inspires,
> The crime of a mother is a heavy burden ...
> I tremble that oppressed by this odious weight,
> Neither of them will ever raise their eyes again.

Once again, the juxtaposition of the realm of the gods – here, Jupiter – and that of the terrestrial human serves only to emphasize the lack of contact between them. Whereas the legacy of Jupiter should inflate ("enfler") Phèdre's children, infusing them with the lightness of soul that could transport them beyond death through an enduring legacy of service and heroism, their mother's crime drags them ever further down into the depths of the sensual seduction of the resolutely mortal and material.

For all this, Phèdre does not give up trying to reestablish a link between herself and the divine. After Thésée's return, Phèdre learns of Oenone's attempt to spare her by shifting blame onto Hippolyte. Oenone tries to justify her decision by arguing, once again, that love cannot possibly be a crime. While Oenone based her first iteration of this argument on the supposed death of Thésée, after Thésée's return she bases it on the flawed nature of the gods:

> L'amour n'a-t-il encore triomphé que de vous?
> La faiblesse aux Humains n'est que trop naturelle.
> Mortelle subissez le sort d'une Mortelle.
> Vous vous plaignez d'un joug imposé dès longtemps.
> Les Dieux même, les Dieux de l'Olympe habitants,
> Qui d'un bruit si terrible épouvantent les crimes,
> Ont brûlé quelquefois de feux illégitimes. (lines 1300–1306)

> Has love triumphed only over you?
> For humans, weakness is only natural.
> Mortal, you are subject to the fate of a mortal.
> You complain of a burden imposed a long time ago.
> Even the gods, the gods residing on Olympus,
> Whose noise renders crime so fearful
> Even they have burned with illegitimate passion.

In other words, Phèdre's crime can be excused, but at the cost of bringing the gods down to earth and reducing any difference or distance between them and mortal humanity. Phèdre is shocked by this argument; in her response, she references both Oenone's "bouche impie" (line 1313) (impious mouth) and Thésée's subsequent "sacrilège voeu" (line 1316) (sacrilegious vow) to

Neptune. This wording reveals Phèdre's reluctance to buy her own innocence through atheism. Her crime is so terrible precisely because she refuses to forget divine transcendence. Unlike those who are puzzled to find their religious practices characterized as idolatrous, Phèdre's abiding faith in the gods places her in the unique position of committing the terrible sin of idolatry and watching herself commit it. Indeed, Phèdre's religiously freighted language in her rebuke to Oenone – which leads directly to Oenone's suicide – opens the question of whether Phèdre's fury can be attributed to Oenone's groundless accusation of the innocent Hippolyte, or, rather, to her suggestion that the flawed gods are unworthy of adoration. It is this push and pull of materiality and transcendence, the constant straining towards a divine realm that remains resolutely inaccessible, that accounts for much of the play's enduring magic and that is reflected, as Roland Barthes has famously noted, in the play's poetic language, wherein meaning struggles against the sonorous weight of the signifiers.

Phèdre's uniquely problematic relationship with the divine and human realms serves to shed light on the other, equally troubling, permutations of divine and human influence that populate the play. Hippolyte's reaction to Phèdre's confession, her "horrible secret," is one of extreme disgust; as he tells Théramène immediately following that scene, "Je ne puis sans horreur me regarder moi-même" (line 718) (I cannot look upon myself without horror). Once again, the idea that the innocent Hippolyte in some sense shares Phèdre's guilt is puzzling, although it has been attributed to Phèdre's skillful attempt to establish rhetorical intimacy with him, envisioning both of them lost in the labyrinth together. Yet if we frame Phèdre's transgression as the inability to see the father in the son, to see through Hippolyte to her husband, we begin to see that the roots of Hippolyte's guilty conscience may in fact lie in his professed wish to untie himself from his father's legacy, a desire that may well motivate, or at least enhance, his love for his father's enemy, Aricie. Hippolyte's efforts to disassociate himself from at least a part of his father could well be viewed as contributing to, or enabling, Phèdre's guilty passion. She cannot see Thésée in Hippolyte because he has willfully distanced himself from his father's example. Paradoxically, of course, the distance between father and son will become the greatest upon Thésée's physical return to Trézène. In the aftermath of Thésée's condemnation of his son and refusal to believe his innocence, the true incommensurability between them becomes apparent. If Thésée, a bit like Hylas, symbolizes "inconstance" by flitting between love objects, Hippolyte dreams of reconciling love with purity and stability – in essence, successfully combining the incompatible models set forth by his father and his Amazon mother. Of course, he is momentarily unsettled by his feelings for Aricie, but even his exclamation to Théramène on this subject at the outset of the play – "Et moi-même à mon tour je me verrais lié?" (line

95) (and I, in turn, would see myself bound?) – demonstrates his resistance to Thésée's character, insofar as Thésée is pointedly *not* "lié," or bound, but resolutely, frustratingly, disturbingly free.

Hippolyte's wish to combine love and legitimacy – to reconcile Thésée and Antiope in a coherent whole – is shared by Aricie, who insists upon a proper marriage before their flight. Yet this desire is literally utopic, unable to be realized within the confines of the city. Hippolyte famously proposes taking Aricie outside of Trézène, among the tombs of his ancestors where lying is punished by immediate death:

> Nous prendrons à témoin le Dieu qu'on y révère.
> Nous le prierons tous deux de nous servir de Père.
> Des Dieux les plus sacrés j'attesterai le nom.
> Et la chaste Diane, et l'auguste Junon,
> Et tous les Dieux enfin témoins de mes tendresses
> Garantiront la foi de mes saintes promesses. (lines 1401–1406)

> We will take as our witness the God worshipped there,
> We will ask him, both of us, to act as our father.
> I will invoke the name of the most sacred gods.
> And chaste Diana and august Juno,
> And all the gods, finally, witness to my tenderness
> Will ensure the truth of my holy promises.

Hippolyte's dream of a faith cleansed of lies, of a guaranteed faith underwritten by Diana's chastity, raises the Protestant question of whether unmediated access to the divine is possible. Yet throughout the play, Hippolyte views himself, and is viewed by others, as an image, the purified and idealized semblance of his inconstant, very physical father. Indeed, during his confrontation with Thésée, Hippolyte holds forth the possibility of his own transformation into a statue or monument, asking him to suffer "que d'un beau trépas la mémoire durable/ Eternisant des jours si noblement finis,/ Prouve à tout l'Avenir que j'étais votre Fils" (lines 950–952) (that through the enduring memory of a glorious death which renders the days so nobly ended eternal I will always be remembered as your son). However, bereft of this link to his father and endowed with an independence that he both wished for and feared, the worlds that the image bridges – Antiope and Thésée, the fearsome and foul materiality of the carnal represented by the stinking sea monster who emerges from the ocean to terrify Hippolyte's horses and the unbearable transcendence of the divine apparent in the god whom some eyewitnesses allege spurred the horses on – appear in their undiluted, unmediated forms. Hippolyte, caught between them, is destroyed, his body shredded and rendered iconoclastically unrecognizable. His life and identity as Thésée's son are not preserved for eternity by a statue or monument; rather, his gruesome death is available to posterity through the verbal *récit* offered by Théramène. Hippolyte's physical destruction, the dispersal of his body among the grass and bushes, ensure that unlike his ancestors, he will never become a "froide relique" (line 1555) (cold relic).[29]

Hippolyte's remarkable iconoclastic death serves to break apart and undermine the circuit of representation that underwrites the economy of legitimacy that structures the play (and, arguably, seventeenth-century French society at large). Divine ancestors are invoked and worshipped, but (as we have seen) never questioned; similarly, parents authorize and determine their children's identity and actions. Phèdre's love for Hippolyte is scandalous precisely because it violates this structure, but it does not call into question the structure itself. Hippolyte is something different. Both expelled from that structure through his father's condemnation and willfully rebellious to it ("Libres dans nos malheurs, puisque le Ciel l'ordonne,/ Le don de notre foi ne dépend de personne" (lines 1389–1390) (Free in our misfortune, since the heavens will it, the gift of our loyalty depends on no one), Hippolyte, in his unrecognizable innocence, introduces a crack in its increasing claustrophobia. This crack becomes visible in the impossibility of signification, the failure of language to name, that haunts the play's final scenes. First, of course, is Aricie's ominous message to Thésée that Hippolyte's death does not, in fact, represent closure: "Prenez garde, Seigneur. Vos invincibles mains/ Ont de Monstres sans nombre affranchi les humains./ Mais tout n'est pas détruit. Et vous en laissez vivre/ Un … Votre Fils, Seigneur, me défend de poursuivre" (lines 1443–1446) (watch out, my lord. Your invincible hands have freed humans from innumerable monsters, but all of them are not destroyed. You are allowing to live a ... Your son, sir, prevents me from continuing). In the following scene, Panope reports that Phèdre's behavior has become increasingly erratic: "Elle porte au hasard ses pas irrésolus./ Son œil tout égaré ne nous reconnaît plus./ Elle a trois fois écrit, et changeant de pensée/ Trois fois elle a rompu sa lettre commencée" (lines 1475–1478) (She walks indecisively and at random, and her distracted eyes no longer recognize us. She has written three times, and changing her thoughts, three times tore up the letter she had started). Another

---

[29] As Sylvaine Guyot points out, "De manière significative, alors qu'en 1677 la querelle du dessin et du coloris vient d'être relancée, Hipppolyte meurt 'sans forme et sans couleur' – ni Poussin ni Rubens: le trace des contours s'est évanoui en un corps qui dit à peine son identité et le pouvoir de seduction du héros s'est mué en un effet de repulsion." *Racine et le corps tragique* (Paris: Presses Universitaires de France, 2014), p. 194. Guyot's book, with its subtle attention to the status of the body in Racinian tragedy, treats many of the questions I address here, albeit from a slightly different angle.

interruption, another failure to name, but also, significantly, another instance of aimlessness. If Aricie cannot "pursue," admittedly in a figurative sense, Phèdre is literally directionless – her steps guided only by chance, her eye failing to assign an identity to the people who surround her. The destruction of Hippolyte, with its intimations of iconoclasm, has exploded a signifying system that the crime of idolatry (as Luther had noted over a century earlier) served only to reinforce. If the gods are replaced by chance, idolatry cannot be a crime.

The third instance of open-endedness occurs in Hippolyte's own dying words as reported by Théramène in his *récit*. His final wish is that Aricie be taken care of: "Cher ami, si mon père un jour désabusé/ Plaint le malheur d'un fils faussement accusé,/ Pour apaiser mon sang et mon ombre plaintive,/ Dis-lui qu'avec douceur il traite sa captive,/ Qu'il lui rende ..." (lines 1563–1567) (My dear friend, if my father, realizing the truth one day, deplores the misfortune of a falsely accused son, to appease my blood and my sorry ghost, tell him to treat his captive with kindness and give back her ...). This final sentence remains unfinished as Hippolyte, or the "triste objet" that remains of him, expires in Théramène's arms. Those listening to Théramène – the other characters in the play as well as its spectators – are left to wonder what Thésée could possibly give Aricie that could compensate her for the loss of Hippolyte and make her whole again. Once again, the economy of reciprocity, wherein wishes are granted and prayers are answered, is subverted in favor of an open-ended vastness that can never be overcome. The relationship between humanity and the gods is fundamentally altered into something which neither Thésée – whose wishes are granted all too quickly – nor Phèdre – whose chief frustration lies in her inability to access this economy in which she continued to believe – would, quite literally, recognize.

After the deaths of Phèdre and Hippolyte, Thésée is left to consider the damage. The final lines of the play call for the restitution that Hippolyte's unfinished speech, not to mention the events of the play, seems to undermine: "Allons de ce cher fils embrasser ce qui reste,/ Expier la fureur d'un voeu que je déteste./ Rendons-lui les honneurs qu'il a trop mérités;/ Et pour mieux apaiser ses manes irrités,/ Que, malgré les complots d'une injuste famille,/ Son amante aujourd'hui me tienne lieu de fille" (lines 1649–1654) (Let us go embrace what is left of my son and expiate the furor of a hated vow. Give him back the honors that he so deserved, and in order to appease his irritated ghost, may, in spite of the plotting of an unjust family, his lover today become a daughter to me). Not only will the honor due to (and unjustly taken from) Hippolyte be rendered, but Aricie will literally take his place. The troubling open-endedness, the unfinished sentences, letters, and speeches, is replaced by a strong rhyme that at least attempts to lock down the text's meaning and tie up loose ends, restoring, as much as possible, what has been lost. Yet the question of whether this ending represents a hopeful new start or, instead, a claustrophobic return of a closed economy of signification, obligation, and filial representation remains unresolved.[30] Thésée, after all, represents the frictionless ideal of the closed economy from which he benefits. Untroubled by the idolatrous fascination that plagues the immobile Phèdre, stuck and weighed down by her inability to transcend the seduction of the material, Thésée moves easily between lovers and geographical locations; even death, as we learn, cannot entrap him in its clutches. This easiness extends to his relationship with the gods, particularly Neptune; as Hippolyte notes to Théramène in tragically prophetic terms early in the play, "Le Ciel peut à nos pleurs accorder un retour/ Neptune le protège, et ce Dieu tutélaire/ Ne sera pas en vain implore par mon Père" (lines 620–622) (The heavens may respond to my tears by bringing him back; Neptune protects him, and this tutelary god will not be implored by my father in vain). For indeed, the communication between Thésée and Neptune is, tragically, *too* unmediated and smooth; Thésée's demand for vengeance is quickly and irrevocably satisfied.

Racine's play, not unlike *L'Astrée*, illustrates the impossibility of articulating a balanced relationship between gods and humans. Caught between Phèdre's idolatry and Thésée's Hylas-like easy immediacy, Hippolyte does not achieve a stable middle ground, but instead is torn apart, ushering in the troubling possibility of a *new* relationship of the gods characterized not by answered prayers and effective rituals, but by an indeterminacy that could very well undermine not just religious representation, but representation *tout court*. As Phèdre's three started and unfinished letters – as well as Thésée's fairly feeble attempt to close the gap left by Hippolyte's destruction by adopting Aricie – demonstrate, the disruption of the logic of idolatry does not open a space for the triumph of human authorship and creation, but rather leaves humans grasping for direction and meaning, unable to bring their sentences (and their literary creations) to a satisfying, convincing close.

Like d'Urfé, Racine augments the troubling implications of this indeterminacy by blurring the lines between paganism and Christianity, whether

---

[30] Lucien Goldmann, in his landmark study *Le Dieu caché: Etude sur la vision tragique dans les* Pensées *de Pascal et dans le théâtre de Racine* (Paris: Gallimard, 1959), views Thésée's final words as a jarring introduction of comedy and farce into everything that precedes: "Suivant de près et sans transition les vers tragiques de *Phèdre*, elle constitue un passage de comédie. Après la disparition du héros qui avait un instant ouvert nos yeux sur tout ce que la réalité a d'immensément riche, sur ses possibilités et sur ses dangers, le monde de la vie quotidienne paraîtra quelque temps – juste le temps qu'il faudra pour nous réhabituer à lui – un monde de farce et de comédie" (p. 428). "Following so closely and without transition upon the tragic verses spoken by Phèdre, they constitute a comedic passage. After the death of the heroes who had opened his eyes for a moment on all of the richness of reality, on its possibilites and dangers, the world of everyday life appears briefly – just the time needed to rehabituate ourselves to it – as a world of farce and comedy."

through the suggestive mention of the singular, capitalized "Fils," Phèdre's mention of idolatry, or the death of Hippolyte, so redolent of iconoclasm. Racine's contemporaries picked up on this layering, and were deeply troubled by it. The anonymous author of the *Dissertation sur les tragédies de Phèdre et Hippolyte*, published the week before the performance of the rival plays by Racine and Pradon in 1677, notes that while the incestuous love at the center of the play was certainly regarded as criminal by the pagan authors who first treated the subject, it is otherwise scandalous to a Christian audience:

> Je sais que les deux Auteurs Païens dont nous parlons, ont traité pourtant cette action comme criminelle; mais je suis persuadé qu'ils ne la regardaient pas aussi scrupuleusement que nous, qu'ils ne la voyaient pas dans toute l'étendue de son énormité; mille semblables crimes qu'ils imputaient à leurs Dieux, diminuaient l'horreur qu'ils en devaient concevoir; tous ces vices, soutenus et parés de ces vains et superbes fantômes de divinités, arrachaient de leurs cœurs plus de respect que de haine, et ces monstres de leur imagination forçaient avec tyrannie les maximes les plus justes de leur raison à se taire.[31]

> I know that the two pagan authors that we are talking about treated this action as criminal, but I am persuaded that they did not consider it as scrupulously as we do, that they did not fully grasp its enormity; thousands of similar crimes that they impute to their gods diminished the horror with which they should have considered it; all those vices, supported and decorated by those vain and superb phantoms of divinity, tore from their hearts more respect than hatred, and these monsters of their imagination tyrannically forced the more just maxims of their reason to be silent.

The author's characterization of the different reaction that the Ancients must have had to the subject of Phèdre and Hippolyte does not mention idolatry as such, but touches on almost each one of its elements. The "phantoms of divinity" adorning the worst vices are vain and superb, decorated with ostentatious and superfluous ornamentation. More important, however, these divinities do not possess an existence outside of humanity, but are rather monstrous products of the human imagination. As a result, their authority can never be legitimate but rather always tyrannical, an affront to human reason.

Elsewhere, the author objects to phrases that recall the Ancient Testament ("Devant ses yeux cruels une autre a trouvé grâce" (Before her cruel eyes another has found grace)) and to Racine's innovative divinization of Death

---

[31] Racine, *Théâtre et poésie*, p. 880.

("La mort est le seul Dieu que j'osais implorer" (Death is the only god to whom I dared pray)); as he points out, in the interest of consistency, if Racine is going to invent an ancient god, in keeping with the gender of the nous, it should actually be a goddess. The author goes on to express confusion at Racine's implication, again through Phèdre's words, that her incest is without example, citing many others of which, he asserts, Racine could hardly be unaware. One could continue to enumerate the author's problems with Racine's text, but it is significant that most of them turn on the question of the problematic and ambiguous theology at work in the play. Is this a Christian play or a reimagining of a classical text? Is Racine's goal to convince the audience that Phèdre and her crime are worthy of condemnation – relics of a pagan past happily transcended – or that the forces at work in the play continue their destructive work in and through the fissures in seventeenth-century Christianity?

For the beginning of a response, we may be tempted to turn to Racine's preface for clarification. As Lucien Goldmann has noted, the preface to *Phèdre* differs sharply, especially in its last lines, from the prefaces to Racine's previous plays.[32] Typically, Racine's prefaces serve as explanations for the poetic decisions he has made, and most often, these decisions are well grounded in the texts of antiquity. Aside from the famous "toute l'invention consiste à faire quelque chose de rien"[33] (the entirety of invention consists in making something from nothing) from the preface to *Bérénice*, Racine emphasizes his loyalty to his sources, even where it might seem as if he had departed from them. His remark in the preface to *Alexandre le Grand* that appeared in the 1675 edition of his works that "Les amours d'Alexandre et de Cléofile ne sont pas de mon invention"[34] (the loves of Alexandre and Cléofile were not invented by me) not only serves to bolster his opening claim that "Il n'y a guère de Tragédie, où l'Histoire soit plus fidèlement suivie que dans celle-ci"[35] (there are no tragedies where history is as faithfully followed as it is here); it also anticipates the slightly defensive "Cette Aricie n'est point un personnage de mon invention"[36] (this Aricie is not a person that I invented) in the preface to *Phèdre*. Occasionally, adjustments are made to seventeenth-century sensibilities – perhaps most famously, Andromaque is portrayed as having no other spouse than Hector and no other son than Astyanax – but even here, these poetic adjustments are depicted not as bold departures from the historical record but as efforts *not* to surprise or shock the public with

---

[32] Goldman, *Le Dieu caché*, pp. 416–20.
[33] Racine, *Théâtre et poésie*, p. 451.
[34] Racine, *Théâtre et poésie*, p. 192.
[35] Racine, *Théâtre et poésie*, p. 191.
[36] Racine, *Théâtre et poésie*, p. 818.

something new. As Racine states in his defense of his depiction of Andromaque, "J'ai cru en cela me conformer à l'idée que nous avons maintenant de cette Princesse"[37] (I thought that this would be consistent with the idea that we have now of this princess). The overall impression from these prefaces is one of a distinctly conservative playwright, one who proclaims in the first preface to Andromaque, "Ce n'est pas à moi de changer les règles du théâtre"[38] (It is not up to me to change the rules of theater). And while here, these rules refer to the nature of tragic heroes and their distance from the seventeenth-century ideal of the *honnête homme*, in the preface to Bérénice, Racine is categorical: the most important rule of theater "est de plaire et de toucher"[39] (to please and to touch).

The preface to *Phèdre* is similarly concerned with assuring the reader that the modifications that Racine has made to the well-known story are either grounded in the historical record (as in the already mentioned example of Aricie) or in seventeenth-century sensibilities. The latter are invoked to explain why Racine has not, like Euripides and Seneca, accused Hippolyte of actually raping Phèdre, and to explain why the accusations against Hippolyte are leveled by Oenone rather than her royal mistress. Yet the preface to Phèdre presents two significant departures from the earlier prefaces. Here, Racine's self-effacement as author and agent of the text is reinforced and overlaid by the centrality of the question of *volonté* to the events that the play depicts. Indeed, the first paragraph of the preface is devoted not to Racine's artistic choices, but instead to emphasizing that the situation in which Phèdre finds herself is the result of both "la destinée" and "la colère des Dieux" (fate and the anger of the gods). Moreover, her admission of her love for Hippolyte was not voluntary, but forced; all of this, Racine reminds us, demonstrates that "son crime est plutôt une punition des Dieux qu'un mouvement de sa volonté"[40] (her crime is more a punishment from the gods than a movement of her will). This foregrounding of the question of agency and constraint accentuates Racine's habitual playfulness around his authorial "Je," which is similarly asserted only to be almost immediately withdrawn or qualified: "Je rapporte ces autorités parce que je me suis très scrupuleusement attaché à suivre la Fable"[41] (I attached myself scrupulously to following the story). What had heretofore been a question of literary scruple takes on, through the lens of Phèdre's crime, moral and even theological implications.

And indeed, this brings us to the second major difference between the preface to *Phèdre* and the prefaces to the plays that precede it, the difference

---

[37] Racine, *Théâtre et poésie*, p. 297.
[38] Racine, *Théâtre et poésie*, p. 197.
[39] Racine, *Théâtre et poésie*, p. 452.
[40] Racine, *Théâtre et poésie*, p. 817.
[41] Racine, *Théâtre et poésie*, p. 818.

noted and remarked upon by Lucien Goldmann. Here, the purpose of theater is no longer to "plaire et toucher," but instead, as Racine explains in the concluding paragraph, to inspire horror of vice and love for virtue – in other words, to teach: "C'est là proprement le but que tout homme qui travaille pour le Public doit se proposer"[42] (this is properly the goal that everyone who works for the public should set himself). This extension of the playwright's audience beyond the theater, this replacement of spectators by the more diffuse "public," is, characteristically, legitimized through a reference to classical sources in the following sentence: "Et c'est ce que les premiers Poètes Tragiques avaient en vue sur toute chose"[43] (And that is what the first tragic poets aimed for more than anything), going on to add that virtue was taught in the School of Theater no less well than in the School of Philosophy. In what follows, for the first time, the word "utile" (useful) makes its appearance, before the final sentence in which the reference to Port-Royal is made explicit, and the reconciliation between theater and religion is held out as possible, precisely through this teaching function of spectacle:

> Ce serait peut-être un moyen de réconcilier la Tragédie avec quantité de Personnes célèbres par leur piété et par leur doctrine qui l'ont condamnée dans ces derniers temps, et qui en jugeraient sans doute plus favorablement, si les Auteurs songeaient autant à instruire leurs Spectateurs qu'à les diverter, et s'ils suivaient en cela la véritable intention de la Tragédie.[44]

> This would perhaps be a way of reconciling tragedy with many people well known by their piety and doctrine who have recently condemned it, and who would doubtless judge it more favorably if authors thought as much about instructing their spectators as entertaining them, and if they followed, in this, the true intention of tragedy.

Racine's "véritable," following closely on the heels of his earlier "proprement," can, even for non-Derrideans, be read as a symptom of his acute anxiety regarding the propensity of theater to stray from its purported goal, to deliver a pleasure that is only minimally related to the text's moral message (when it does not subvert that message entirely). That these issues should present themselves around *Phèdre* – a play that not only blurs the lines between paganism and Christianity but that also so beautifully foregrounds the sonorous weight of the signifier almost to the extent that what the characters say to each other is obscured by the how – is significant. Equally significant,

---

[42] Racine, *Théâtre et poésie*, p. 819.
[43] Racine, *Théâtre et poésie*, p. 819.
[44] Racine, *Théâtre et poésie*, p. 819.

of course, is Racine's subsequent theatrical production, in which the rich and delicious ambiguity, the monstrous hybridity, of *Phèdre* is forsaken in favor of the celebration and evocation of the purity of the Jewish faith and the solidity of a lineage that would eventually lead to Christ.

Conclusion:
The End(s) of Idolatry

On September 1, 1686, Louis XIV received three ambassadors sent from Phra Narai, the ruler of Siam, in the newly completed Hall of Mirrors at Versailles. This visit was a response to the diplomatic initiative taken by the French monarch, who had sent his own ambassador, the chevalier de Chaumont, to Siam a year earlier, accompanied not only by the colorful abbé de Choisy but by several Jesuit missionaries who had heard that the Siamese ruler was eager to convert to Christianity. Like the French visit to the Siamese court in Ayutthaya, the Siamese visit to France was well documented: in almanacs, in accounts written by the participants, and by Donneau de Visé's proto-newspaper, the *Mercure Galant*, which devoted four special issues to the event.

The French were particularly captivated by the letter carried by the Siamese delegation. This ornate document was written in gold and enclosed in a golden box, which was in turn placed in a silver box that was then placed in a box fashioned from Japanese wood. All of these boxes, the *Mercure* reports, were in turn covered in gold brocade and sealed with the seal of the first ambassador in white wax. The letter was treated with great care and reverence by the diplomats, since according to Siamese diplomatic protocol, it, not they, carried the representational character, the authority, of the king. Not only did the ambassadors place flowers on the box each day and bow when they approached it, they also needed to be lodged or located below the letter physically. The *Mercure* notes the alarm of the third ambassador when he is informed that his room in Vincennes is situated above the room of the first ambassador (and thus, above the king's letter). He informs his French hosts that even if they cannot find a suitable room for him, "il aima mieux estre incommodé & mal logé, que de ne pas satisfaire à un respect qu'il regardoit comme un devoir indispensable, & auquel il ne pouvoit manquer sans commettre un crime capital"[1] (he preferred being inconvenienced and badly lodged to not satisfying the respect that he viewed as an indispensable duty which he could not neglect without committing a capital crime).

---

[1] *Mercure Galant*, 'Voyage des Ambassadeurs de Siam en France' (1686), pp. 83–4.

This very real anguish would have been readily recognizable to the readers of the *Mercure* as evocative of the emotions surrounding idolatry, and this might explain what Rebecca Zorach describes as the "almost obsessive interest" that the French showed the letter during the visit; indeed, as she notes, the almanac print depicting the carrying of the letter to the palace of Versailles strongly evokes a Eucharistic procession.² The *Mercure Galant*, whose publisher Donneau de Visé was keenly aware of the power of almanacs, also printed images of the letter and its quasi-religious, chapel-like housing, explicitly inviting the reader to contemplate the practices of a country where the ruler's godlike status was directly invoked through diplomatic protocol.³ Like Ronald S. Love, another scholar of the Siamese embassy to France, Zorach concludes that the fascination, both official and popular, with the Siamese king's letter reflects a similar desire – again, both official and popular – to deify the French monarch, a process that had been underway throughout the seventeenth century, but that had reached its height during the 1680s, when, as Zorach notes, an unprecedented number of royal statues were erected in cities and towns across France.⁴ Zorach neglects, however, to specify *why* these statues were being erected; similarly, she expresses puzzlement at the absence of the Siamese king's letter from an elaborate almanac engraving depicting the official audience given by Louis XIV to the Siamese.⁵ Yet if we view this episode through the lens of the logic of idolatry operating in seventeenth-century France, not only does the fascination with the Siamese and their letter become clearer, we can also begin to see how the Siamese visit served to highlight the essential and significant *difference* between Louis XIV and his Siamese counterpart.

This difference begins with the means of diplomatic representation. The Siamese belief that the *caractère représentatif*, or the spirit of their king's authority, was present in their king's letter appeared to French observers both alien and familiar. Until the fifteenth century, European ambassadors had themselves been viewed, described, and honored as the sacrosanct vehicles

---

² Rebecca Zorach, 'An Idolatry of the Letter: Time, Devotion, and Siam in the Almanacs of the Sun King', in *Ut Pictura Meditatio: The Meditative Image in Northern Art 1500–1700*, ed. Walter S. Melion, Ralph Dekoninck, and Agnes Guiderdoni-Bruslé (Turnhout: Brepols Publishers, 2012), pp. 447–79, here p. 454.

³ Zorach, 'Idolatry', pp. 468–9.

⁴ Zorach, 'Idolatry', pp. 466–7. See also Ronald S. Love, 'Rituals of Majesty: France, Siam, and Court Spectacle in Royal Image-Building at Versailles in 1685 and 1686', *Canadian Journal of History* 31 (August 1996), pp. 171–98.

⁵ "Called upon to depict [the letter], perhaps the artist could not do so without obscuring the scene's important actors; or perhaps he could not bring himself to record an object that seemed idolatrous; or perhaps he simply Europeanized it, much as the classical idol substituted for the statue of the Buddha." Zorach, 'Idolatry', p. 472.

for messages from one prince to another – more as heralds than as diplomats. This began to change in the fifteenth century, when princes began employing resident ambassadors whose status was no longer tied to a definite and limited mission, but who were charged with living in and reporting on the country to which they were sent.[6] From the sixteenth century forward, Europeans struggled to describe what, exactly, an ambassador was, but all agreed that he needed both to represent his sovereign monarch and to possess a wide range of useful observational, reporting, and negotiating skills of his own. In other words, even as the unity of Christian Europe was permanently fractured into sovereign states, diplomacy became incarnational: only monarchs could send ambassadors (the representatives of non-monarchical states could send only envoys, who could not possess representational character since there was not one entity that they represented), and these diplomats were endowed with an independent will whose essential yet problematic relationship to the authority of their monarch mirrored the fraught relationship of humans to the God in whose image they were created.

Already, then, the mere presence of several ambassadors, rather than just one, marked the Siamese monarchy as inferior and flawed, incapable of dynamic authority and instead confined to the servile worship accorded its (dead) letter. As Simon de La Loubère, Louis XIV's ambassador to Siam who accompanied the Siamese diplomats back to their country in 1687, notes drily: "Un Ambassadeur par tout l'Orient n'est autre chose qu'un Messager de Roy: il ne represente point son Maistre. On l'honore peu à comparaison des respects, qu'on tend à la lettre de créance, dont il est porteur"[7] (an Ambassador in all of the Orient is just a Messenger of his King: he does not represent his Master. He is honored little by comparison to the respect that is given to the authorizing letter that he carries). The actual identity and skill of the diplomat therefore matter little, if at all; like the ancient herald, his job is merely to deliver a message and return.[8] This rather disdainful

---

[6] For a background of early modern diplomatic theory and its link to the evolution of divine right monarchy, see Ellen M. McClure, *Sunspots and the Sun King: Sovereignty and Mediation in Seventeenth-Century France* (Chicago: University of Illinois Press, 2006), pp. 103–51.

[7] Simon de La Loubère, *Description du royaume de Siam* (Amsterdam: Chez Henry & la Veuve de Theodore Boom, 1700), pp. 327–8.

[8] "Aussi les Orientaux ne mettent-ils nulle différence entre un Ambassadeur, & un Envoyé: & ils ne connoissent ni les Ambassadeurs, ny les Envoyez ordinaires, ny les Résidens; parce qu'ils n'envoyent personne pour résider en une Cour étrangere, mais pour y faire une affaire, & s'en retourner." (Thus the Orientals make no distinction between an Ambassador and an Envoy: & they do not know Ambassadors, Ordinary envoys, nor Residents, since they do not send anyone to reside at a foreign court, but to execute business there and then return.) La Loubère, *Description du royaume de Siam*, p. 328.

characterization of Siamese diplomatic practice is certainly meant to highlight La Loubère's own skills. But placed against the increasingly close association of diplomatic practice and divine-right monarchy in France – an association that set the tone and standards for diplomatic practice throughout Europe for years to come – it carries the implication that the respect accorded the Siamese king, and the ornate and impressive trappings that surround him and his letter, are, like his ambassadors, empty signifiers – pagan and idolatrous objects of worship rather than instruments of a living authority that flows through and animates them.[9] In other words, the surface similarities between Siamese and French diplomatic practice and royal protocol – the jewel-bedecked costumes, the elevation of the royal thrones – did not, as Love and Zorach argue, signify a secret penchant for idolatry among Louis XIV's courtesans (and in the monarch himself). Rather, they served to better highlight the crucial distinction between the two monarchs: one is the living embodiment of the authority conferred by the Christian God, and the other, as the presence of Jesuit missionaries in the diplomatic mission to Phra Narai led by Chaumont and sent by Louis XIV in 1685 demonstrates, is not. Therefore, the idolatrous letter is, indeed, absent from the almanac print depicting the official reception of the Siamese ambassadors at Versailles; in its place is the resplendent person of the king as well as his descendants, who figure forth the living, dynamic nature of the authority temporarily invested in his person.[10]

In other words, the Siamese visit offered Louis XIV a rare opportunity to accomplish the elusive, but much-desired goal pursued by theologians, writers, and artists throughout the early modern period of rendering legitimate, non-idolatrous authority visible. This goal was all the more important in 1686, the year following Louis XIV's much-criticized revocation of the Edict of Nantes, which had been promulgated by his grandfather Henri IV in 1598 to ensure the peaceful cohabitation of Protestants and Catholics in France.[11] Viewed from one angle, this decision demonstrated the French monarch's descent into an Asiatic tyranny that could arguably justify armed resistance.[12] Yet viewed

---

[9] The relationship between diplomacy and royal authority, including sovereignty, is the subject of my earlier book, *Sunspots and the Sun King*. See, especially, chapter 4, pp. 152–92.

[10] For Love, the presence of the king's natural (born out of wedlock) children at the reception was a scandal signifying "the unparalleled position of Asian despotism." (Love, 'Rituals', p. 195). I believe that, especially given the curious absence of the Siamese letter that Zorach highlights in this engraving, the signification is quite different.

[11] See Janine Garrison, *L'Edit de Nantes et sa révocation: Histoire d'une intolérance* (Paris: Editions du Seuil, 1985).

[12] This was the argument formulated by prominent members of the Protestant resistance, including Bayle and Jurieu, whose texts written against the Revocation were not shy about comparing Louis XIV to his Ottoman counterpart. This was also a theme in

from another, this was the effortless accomplishment of the alignment of divine and royal power that the king's given name, Dieudonné ("Given by God"), seemed to promise. According to this reading, encouraged by the king himself in the preamble to the edict, the Revocation was not a stunning *coup d'état*, but rather a recognition of the near-complete success of efforts to bring members of the Religion Prétendue Réformée (the "So-Called Reformed Religion," as Catholics called Huguenots) back to the true faith.[13]

And indeed, if we are to trust the *Mercure Galant*, this is precisely how Louis XIV's subjects viewed the Revocation and their king.[14] In a special issue that appeared in 1686, Donneau de Visé published poems, stories, and letters that his readership had submitted in response to the Revocation. These texts demonstrate the extent to which religion in France continued to be read through the lens of idolatry, well into the seventeenth century. They also shed light on how idolatry served to frame the king's political authority, as well as relations with non-Christian states such as Siam. Donneau de Visé's introduction to the special issue, which was part two of the February 1686 edition, testifies that the large number of texts submitted in response to the call to readers serves to transcend the limitations of history and thereby represent the extraordinary nature of the king's actions:

> En effet, l'Histoire est l'ouvrage d'un homme seul qui peut déguiser la verité, au lieu que ce que je vous envoye estant l'ouvrage de quantité d'Autheurs differens, est comme un Acte signé de tous les Sujets de SM, pour confirmer à ceux qui viendront aprés nous, des choses si éloignées de toute apparence de verité, que pour estre creuës elles ont besoin d'un nombre infiny de témoignages, & que ceux mesme qui en parlent ayent vécu du Regne du Roy, sans quoy la Posterité auroit peine à croire les étonnantes merveilles

---

anti-Louis XIV propaganda; see Peter Burke, *The Fabrication of Louis XIV* (New Haven: Yale University Press, 1992), pp. 135–49.

[13] For the early modern understanding of the *coup d'état*, see Gabriel Naudé's *Considérations politiques sur les coups d'Etat* (1639). The preamble to the Edit de Fontainebleau of 1685, more commonly known as the Revocation of the Edict of Nantes, reads in part: "Nous voyons présentement avec la juste reconnaissance que nous devons à Dieu, que nos soins ont eu la fin que nous nous sommes proposée, puisque la meilleure et la plus grande partie de nos sujets de la Religion Prétendue Réformée ont embrassé la Catholique." (We presently see, with the rightful recognition that we owe to God, that through our care, the goal that we had has been achieved, since most of our best subjects of the So-Called Reformed Religion have embraced Catholicism).

[14] As with any periodical purporting to represent the views of its readership, the *Mercure* both received these views and shaped them by its selection of the letters it printed. In any case, the *Mercure*'s approach to the Revocation demonstrates a keen awareness of its close association with the polemics surrounding idolatry.

qui font aujourd'huy l'entretien & l'admiration de tout l'Univers.[15]

> In fact, History is the work of one man alone, who can disguise the truth, and instead what I am sending you, as the work of many different authors, is like an Act signed by all of His Majesty's Subjects to confirm to those who come after us that things that seem completely unbelievable and far from truth therefore need an infinite number of witnesses having lived during the Reign of the King, without which Posterity will scarcely believe the astonishing marvels that constitute the conversation and admiration of the entire Universe.

De Visé's reference to the entire universe is noteworthy, and in some ways prepares the stage for the Siamese visit later that year. This expansive language reflected the sentiments of nearly all of the pieces included in the volume, which depicted the Revocation as a sign that Louis XIV was, truly and uniquely, the worthy instrument of God, and therefore compelled admiration not just in France, but throughout the known world. Take, for example, this excerpt from a panegyric of Louis XIV offered at the Convent of the Visitation in Rouen on the occasion of François de Sales' feast day:

> Le Roy donc, grand devant les hommes, grand devant Dieu; le Roy, le delice de ses Peuples, l'étonnement des Etrangers, & le spectacle de tout l'Univers, n'aura point à l'avenir de plus grande gloire que celle d'avoir fait regner dans toute l'étenduë de son Empire celuy par qui il regne luy-mesme si heureusement & si glorieusement.[16]

> The King then, great before men, great before God; the King, the delight of his Peoples, the astonishment of Foreigners, and the spectacle of the entire Universe, will not have any greater glory in the future than that of establishing throughout the Empire the reign of Him through whom he himself reigns so happily and gloriously.

The alignment of Louis XIV's authority with the reign of God himself stands in stark contrast to idolatrous practices and regimes which, as we have seen, are depicted as setting forth objects that are to be admired and worshipped in their own right, rather than as instruments of something greater than themselves. Language like this is meant to clear a space for the unprecedented number of statues erected to the glory of Louis XIV throughout France that Rebecca Zorach mentions. These statues are posited as, pointedly, *not*

---

[15] *Mercure Galant*, février 1686, 2e partie, pp. 2–3 (hereafter, MG).
[16] *MG*, février 1686, 2e partie, pp. 92–3.

idolatrous. In Marseille, a member of the town council argued for the erection of such a statue by noting that in "Siècles idolatres" (idolatrous centuries) the accomplishments of the king would have been commemorated through the building of altars and temples.[17]

The most extensive evocation of the polemics surrounding idolatry as they pertained to the thorny issue of how to heap praises upon and erect statues to the French monarch occurs in a submitted poem entitled *La Plainte de l'Eglise contre ses Enfans rebelles* (The complaint of the Church against its rebel children), which patiently lays out the distinction between idolatrous adoration and legitimate worship, fending off the age-old charges that Catholic use of relics and images is an illegitimate theft of the reverence due to God alone, but this time applying these arguments to the admiration due to the king:

> Quiconque aime du Roy la personne Sacrée
> Respecte son Portrait, son Sang & sa Livrée,
> Et ce Prince équitable au lieu d'estre jaloux
> Croit recevoir l'honneur qu'ils reçoivent de nous.
> Ainsi loin d'outrager le Monarque suprême,
> Nous servons sa grandeur en aimant ceux qu'il aime;
> Tout ce que je revere en Terre ou dans les Cieux
> Ce n'est que par rapport à son Nom glorieux,
> Et je proscris tout haut toute la déference,
> Qui va se terminer dans une autre puissance.[18]

> Whoever loves in the King his sacred person
> Respects his portrait, his blood, and his ornaments,
> And this equitable prince instead of being jealous,
> Sees that he receives the honor that we pay them.
> Thus, far from outraging the supreme Monarch,
> We serve his grandeur by loving that which he loves;
> Everything that I revere on Earth or in the Sky
> Is only because of its relation to his glorious Name,
> And I forbid loudly any deference
> Which takes as its end any other power.

The writer of this poem is clearly well versed in the subtleties of idolatry, arguing slyly that the monarch's benevolence and equanimity lead him to understand that the admiration accorded the trappings of monarchy are not paid to them, but rather to himself. This sets up a comparison with the Christian

---

[17] *MG*, février 1686, 2e partie, p. 51.
[18] *MG*, février 1686, pp. 117–18.

God, who must surely possess such magnanimous traits in abundance, and who is therefore flattered by the praise accorded to those whom he loves. The jealous God of the Old Testament, invoked so well by d'Urfé and Molière, is absent here, and this absence clears the way for elaborate celebrations of the king's (and by an extension as natural as it is necessary, God's) benevolence, whether through images, statues, jewels, ceremonies, or halls of mirrors. Indeed, the Revocation is celebrated as an event that makes manifest the status of the French monarch as the favored son of God, the apotheosis of divine-right monarchy wherein the distance between Louis XIV and the divine has collapsed in a commonality of intent and interest. As the Marseille town councilman evoked above exclaims, "il semble qu'il n'est pas sorty de cette longue suite de Rois celebres qui revivent en sa personne, mais que Dieu seul a pris plaisir à le former" (it seems that he did not emerge from the long series of famous kings who find new life in his person, but that God himself took pleasure in creating him).

The almost defiant luxuriating in royal statues and magnificence that characterized the 1680s and that was on display during the official reception of the Siamese ambassadors signified a widespread desire to be finished with the nuances and ambiguities inherent in the logic of idolatry. By declaring the French king to be the undisputed instrument of the Christian God, his subjects inherently exempted the admiration accorded him from idolatry, describing it instead as the logical consequence of the worship rightfully due to the divine. The visit of the Siamese was the answer to the exhortation voiced in one of the pieces near the end of the special issue of the *Mercure* devoted to the Revocation: "Monde, viens voir ce que je voy,/ Et ce que le Soleil admire,/ Rome dans un Palais,/ dans Paris un Empire/ Et tous les Cesars en un Roy"[19] (World, come see what I see,/ and what the Sun admires,/ Rome in a Palace,/ in Paris an Empire/ and all of the Caesars in a King). And, not unlike Astrée's wish to become a druidess once she meets and loves Alexis, the predictable Siamese response to the French king's glory, duly reported by the *Mercure*, was the desire to convert to Christianity. Upon the ambassadors' entrance into the cathedral of Tournay, which they toured after their official reception at Versailles, they informed the bishop that "ils prioient d'obtenir du vray Dieu qu'ils le pussent connoître, & qu'il luy plût de les tirer des Tenebres où ils pouvoient estre pour professer la veritable Religion"[20] (they prayed to obtain knowledge of the true God, and asked him to pull them from the Darkness where they were to profess the true Religion). The reader is left to assume that, had Louis XIV himself been able to visit the king of Siam, the latter's

---

[19] *MG*, février 1686, p. 316.
[20] *MG*, décembre 1686, 2e partie, p. 297.

conversion would have been both sincere and instantaneous. What is a bit more surprising is the Siamese ambassador's exclamation, a few days later while watching an exercise of the king's troops in Valenciennes, that "il voudroit n'estre pas Ambassadeur, ou du moins n'est pas le Premier, afin de faire une Campagne ou deux avec le Roy en cas qu'il y eût Guerre"[21] (he would have wanted not to be an Ambassador, or at least not the First ambassador, so that he could follow the King into a military campaign or two in case of War).

In short, with the Revocation of the Edict of Nantes and the propaganda surrounding it, the French public was offered the tantalizing prospect of solving the sticky problem of idolatry once and for all. To be French was to be exempt from idolatry, insofar as the special relationship posited between the monarch and the God of whom he was the instrument provided the much wished-for alignment of heaven and earth that had proved so elusive for so long. The Revocation has long provoked puzzlement in historians; from an economic and even political view, in many ways it makes no sense. But if we view it through the lens of over a century of struggle around the central, and potentially destabilizing, issue of idolatry, the excess that accompanied it – the statues, the praise, the gems, the patently false assertion that all of the Protestants in the kingdom had converted – it appears as the impatient, and perhaps understandable, desire to move beyond the messiness of representation, both artistic and political, that necessarily fell short of the Augustinian ideal of transparency.[22]

Of course, as Zorach and Love argue, and as the Protestant resistance saw clearly, this longed-for apotheosis of divine-right monarchy had a way of resembling that very thing that it purported to vanquish: a king elevated as an object of worship in his own right, rather than an instrument of a transcendent and benevolent divinity. The hyperbolic tone of the art, journalism, and images of the 1680s, whether in praise of the Revocation or in admiration of the Siamese visit, in many ways constitutes the last, best attempt to configure political power along the lines laid out by the logic of idolatry, which in fact provided the elements that would contribute to its own undoing. In her book *Craft and the Kingly Ideal: Art, Trade, and Power*, the anthropologist Mary W.

---

[21] *MG*, décembre 1686, p. 317.

[22] And, not unlike Descartes' optimistic attempt to "solve" idolatry fifty years earlier, this proclamation of success was premature. As Jean-Vincent Blanchard has shown, accusations of idolatry greeted Claude Menestrier's efforts to monumentalize the king in 1689. Blanchard implies, I think correctly, that the modernism of Menestrier, and of the statecraft of Louis XIV, with its eschewal of subordination to a transcendent authority, or even an overarching history, is linked to these criticisms – further evidence of the increasing energy surrounding idolatry as a symptom of the anguish surrounding the historical, philosophical, and political changes of the time. See 'Claude-François Ménestrier and the "Querelle des Monuments"', *PFSCL* vol. 36.71 (2009), pp. 507–14.

Helms argues that in most societies, artistic creation is endowed with quasi-divine power, an extension of the gods' "original acts of crafting and creation of and for man."[23] If crafting constitutes a means of connecting humans and the divine along a vertical axis, it also connects societies along the horizontal axis of geographical distance; often either artists are sent away from their home communities or crafted objects from abroad are seen as reinforcing and signifying the vertical relationship of the community to the divine. Although her attention is mainly directed to non-European societies, she recognizes that the special status accorded crafting and crafters characterized European monarchies at least until the Renaissance, and her description of the value that attached to the accumulation of exotic crafts and contacts encapsulates, in many ways, the importance accorded to the Siamese embassy:

> To the extent that the horizontal and vertical cosmological axes are but variations on a common theme, indeed compose a common cosmological realm, of outside contacts and connections, it is understandable that the exotic riches of geographically distant worlds should grace the temples of the vertically distant gods and enhance the palace and the person of the king who mediates between the gods above as well as with the foreigners without.[24]

For Helms, this view of crafting, crafters, and creation is eventually superseded, especially in Western Europe, by the development of a utilitarian or economic relationship towards created objects and by the emergence of art, that is, the crafted object seen not as a means of "moving or communicating between qualitatively different cosmological realms," but as an expression of individual uniqueness.[25]

While Helms does not mention idolatry explicitly, one cannot read her account of craft without being struck by the signal difference between the cosmological configurations and religions described in her book, in which creation is seen as a tribute to or a gift from divine creators, and the Judeo-Christian stricture contained in the second commandment not just against images or the worship of them but, as both sides of the Protestant–Catholic divide in early modern France pointed out, human making. Helms's framework, placed alongside the elaborate ceremony that welcomed the Siamese, suggests that idolatry emerged as a particularly fraught problem during the seventeenth century in part due to the pressures exerted on a fragile alliance between Church and state not only by the increased foregrounding of human

---

[23] Mary W. Helms, *Craft and the Kingly Ideal: Art, Trade, and Power* (Austin: University of Texas Press, 1993), p. 32.
[24] Helms, *Craft*, p. 81.
[25] Helms, *Craft*, p. 19.

knowledge and innovation, but also by unprecedented levels of exploration and trade.[26] Combined with a religious framework that viewed making as threatening to the status of the divine, these pressures contributed to a deep anxiety that permeated the century, wherein the question (and possibilities) of the legitimacy of human authorship assumed center stage.

In the Introduction, I cautioned against viewing the polemics surrounding idolatry merely as a symptom of other, non-religious historical forces, such as the advent of the printing press or longstanding political rivalries. Helms's framework is different, insofar as it takes quite seriously the mystical and religious aspects surrounding crafting and craftsmanship, forces that she argues are, or were, nearly universally felt. These were the forces that the French monarchy sought to tap into through the language and trappings of divine right, yet they were also the forces being undermined or thrown into question by the rapid rise of both the transactional and the artistic views of the object world. I hope to have shown that looking at the century through the lens of idolatry not only demonstrates the widespread awareness of this neglected means of configuring the complex relation between heaven and earth, but also leaves place for an appreciation of the deep-seated ambivalence that accompanied what we have come, rather simplistically, to call secularization.

Needless to say, the forces of individual expression and economic transaction have, at least in the West, drowned out almost any remnants of the cosmological role of crafted objects that Helms describes. As a result, idolatry, with its connotations of anxiety regarding the relationship between this world and the divine, has become, if not completely incomprehensible, then largely invisible. In the studies that comprise this book, I have tried to show how idolatry provided a shared logic and vocabulary for exploring the questions that surrounded the fraught emergence of human agency in early modern France. Some authors were deeply disturbed by the loss of transcendence; some gleefully greeted it as overdue; some treated it as a puzzle to be solved by imagining new ways of conceiving God and humanity. As we ourselves hurtle into a century that both promises and threatens unprecedented technological change, our failure to understand the powerful, longstanding logic of idolatry that is activated by the anxieties surrounding these changes has arguably led to another *dialogue de sourds*, where any possible middle ground seems even more impossible to discern than in the early modern period.[27] Voltaire's

---

[26] For an account of the shifting scientific terrain of this period and its relation to theology, see Stephen Gaukroger, *The Emergence of a Scientific Culture: Science and the Shaping of Modernity 1210–1685* (Oxford: Clarendon Press, 2006).

[27] For a considered examination of the relevance of religion in our technological times, see Jean-Pierre Dupuy, *The Mark of the Sacred*, trans. M. B. Debevoise (Stanford: Stanford University Press, 2013).

dismissal of idolatry as an empty insult may have been a symptom of the move towards secularism in which the Enlightenment played such an important role, but it was not motivated by atheism. Today, religion is often dismissed entirely as an atavistic and illogical relic which can teach us nothing of value. This view is helped along by the existence of the other extreme, which holds that protecting the divine – especially its role in creation – is *all* that matters, even at the expense of terrestrial wellbeing and life. Positions such as the absolute rejection of reproductive choice or the denial of any possible human role in climate change are often viewed as incomprehensible, yet once they are placed against the long and complicated history of idolatry, they can be seen to follow a certain kind of logic. A better understanding of this logic – which I have called "the logic of idolatry" – can lead to an appreciation of the depth of our current cultural divides and of the necessity of finding alternate discourses if we are to move forward together. Looking to the dexterity, inventiveness, and, indeed, beauty of seventeenth-century French writers' attempts to negotiate this divide can, perhaps, give us hope.

Acknowledgments

This book is itself a testimony to the limits of thinking of authorship as a solitary and autonomous activity; it could not possibly have been completed without the help and support of others. The first inklings of this project appeared in a graduate class at the University of Michigan that I took with Larry Kritzman; his words of encouragement and enthusiasm kept the pilot light burning for many years. A National Endowment for Humanities summer seminar in 2004 on "The Intersection of Philosophy, Science, and Religion in the Seventeenth Century" set in motion all sorts of ideas and encounters that eventually led to this project, and so much else. Throughout the research and writing of this book, I have enjoyed, and benefited from, the close proximity of the Newberry Library and especially its Center for Renaissance Studies, led by Carla Zecher and now Lia Markey. A fellowship at the University of Illinois at Chicago's Institute for the Humanities allowed me to get this project off the ground, and I would also like to thank the institutions who invited me to speak about this work, including the University of Kentucky, the University of Buffalo, the University of Chicago, the University of Minnesota, the University of Southern California, and Indiana University. I am also indebted to the many conference audiences who provided helpful feedback on early versions of these ideas, with a special nod to the North American Society for Seventeenth-Century French Literature and the Society for Interdisciplinary Seventeenth-Century French Studies.

I have the great good fortune to be a seventeenth-century French specialist in the twenty-first century, which means that I am surrounded by kind and brilliant scholars whose friendship I treasure. Hélène Bilis, Chris Braider, Juliette Cherbuliez, Didier Course, Indravati Félicité, Andrea Frisch, Richard Goodkin, Amy Graves-Monroe, David Harrison, George Hoffman, Katherine Ibbett, Larry Norman, Joy Palacios, Jeff Peters, Anne Régent-Susini, Anna Rosensweig, Jennie Row, Lewis Seifert, Chris Semk, Antonia Szabari, and Kathleen Wine have patiently listened to me talk about idolatry and occasionally other things over the last several years. At the University of Illinois at Chicago (UIC), where I have spent my career, I am surrounded by smart and committed colleagues, and would especially like to acknowledge the support and friendship of Mark Canuel, Laura Dingeldein, Stephen

Engelmann, Sam Fleischacker, Lisa Freeman, Sara Hall, Rachel Havrelock, Laura Hostetler, Imke Meyer, Amalia Pallares, Junaid Quadri, Yann Robert, Mary Beth Rose, and Margarita Saona. I am also indebted to my students, graduate and undergraduate, who have contributed indirectly and directly to the thinking that went into this book. Special thanks to Janée Allsman, Augustin Leroy, Richard Reinhardt, Sarah Schaefer, and Esther Van Dyke for keeping me on my toes and reminding me, over and over, why I love what I do. Peggy McCracken played a key role, first in bringing me to UIC over twenty years ago, and now, in bringing this project to the Gallica series at Boydell & Brewer, and I would also like to thank Caroline Palmer for her patient guidance as well the anonymous reader for their perfect blend of enthusiasm and constructive, insightful feedback. While working on this project, I was also often knee- (and neck-) deep in the snowdrifts of administration, and Hall Bjornstad was the persistent St. Bernard who repeatedly dug me out and set me back on my path. I can never thank him and his partner, Sonia Velázquez, enough for their kindness, hospitality, and friendship.

Behind and beneath it all are the members of the Spring Wind Sangha, especially Susim Bob Kessler. The peace and community that I have found at the Zen Buddhist Temple-Chicago have nourished and sustained me, always reminding me of the bigger (and smaller) pictures. I offer this book to the Venerable Samu Sunim as a small token of my boundless love and gratitude. My family has given me support and places to rest and recover. The friendship and food of Tony Giaquinto have literally nourished me over many years. I remain indebted to the hospitality and friendship of the Lagier family, especially Benoit and his late wife, Anne Sordello, who provided me a home away from home through thick and thin.

And finally, my husband, Dan Cherry, has lived with me and this project for the last ten years. His unflagging love, patience and encouragement were indispensable ingredients in the final product, such as it is. "Finish your book," he would kindly whisper. Well, sweetheart, here it is.

Bibliography

Primary Sources

Arnauld, Antoine, and Pierre Nicole. *La Logique ou l'art de penser*. Paris: Gallimard, 1992.
Augustine. *On Christian Doctrine*. Translated by D. W. Robertson, Jr. New York: Liberal Arts Press, 1958.
——. *The Trinity*. Translated by Stephen McKenna. Washington, DC: Catholic University Press, 1963.
Bansilion, Jean. *L'Idolatrie papistique opposée à l'idolatrie huguenote de Louys Richeome, Provincial des Jesuites*. Geneva, 1608.
Bourbon, Antoine de. 'Traité de la comédie et des spectacles.' In Thirouin, 1998.
Bourdaloue, Louis. *Sermons du père Bourdaloue pour le caresme*. Paris: Rigaud, 1713.
Calvin, Jean. *Institution de la religion chrestienne*. Paris: Vrin, 1957.
Correspondence between Princess Elisabeth of Bohemia and René Descartes. Edited and translated by Lisa Shapiro. Chicago: University of Chicago Press, 2007.
de Barthélemy, Edouard. *Mémoires de Charlotte-Amélie de la Trémoille 1652–1719, comtesse d'Altenbourg*. Geneva: J-G Fick, 1876.
Descartes, René. *Méditations métaphysiques*. Paris: Flammarion, 1993.
——. *Oeuvres de Descartes*, 11 vols. Edited by Charles Adam and Paul Tannery. Paris: Vrin, 1964.
——. *Philosophical Writings of Descartes*, vols 2–3. Edited and translated by John Cottingham, Robert Stoothoff, and Degald Murdoch. New York: Cambridge University Press, 1985.
Gassendi, Pierre. *Disquisitio metaphysica seu, Dubitationes et instantiae adversus Renati Cartesii Metaphysicam et responsa. Recherches métaphysiques; ou, Doutes et instances contre la Métaphysique de R. Descartes et ses réponses*. Edited and translated by Bernard Rochot. Paris: Vrin, 1962.
Godeau, Antoine. *Œuvres chrestiennes*. Paris: Jean Camusat, 1641.
Karlstadt, Andreas. *A Reformation Debate: Three Treatises in Translation*. Translated by Bryan D. Mangrum and Giuseppe Scavizzi. Ottawa: Dovehouse Editions, 1991.
La Fontaine, Jean de. *Oeuvres complètes: Fables et contes*. Edited by Jean-Pierre Collinet. Paris: Gallimard, 1991.

———. *Oeuvres complètes*, vol. 2. Edited by Pierre Clarac. Paris: Gallimard, 1958.
La Loubère, Simon de. *Description du royaume de Siam*. Amsterdam: Chez Henry & la Veuve de Theodore Boom, 1700.
Mercure Galant. Février 1686, deuxième partie.
Mercure Galant. Décembre 1686, deuxième partie.
Mercure Galant. 'Voyage des Ambassadeurs de Siam en France' (1686).
Molière. *Oeuvres complètes*. Edited by Georges Forestier. Paris: Gallimard, 2010.
Naudé, Gabriel. *Considérations politiques sur les coups d'Etat*, 1639.
New Oxford Annotated Bible. Edited by Herbert G. May and Bruce M. Metzger. New York: Oxford University Press, 1977.
Nicene and Post-Nicene Fathers. Edited by Philip Schaff and Henry Wace. Buffalo: Christian Literature Publishing Co., 1898.
Nicole, Pierre. 'Traité de la comédie'. In Thirouin, 1998.
Pellisson, Paul. *Préface* to the *Oeuvres de M. Sarasin*. Paris: Cramoisy, 1696 [1656].
Perrault, Charles. *Les Hommes Illustres qui ont paru en France pendant ce siecle: Avec leurs Portraits au naturel*. Paris: Antoine Dezallicr, 1696.
Racine, Jean. *Oeuvres complètes: Théâtre-Poésie*. Edited by Georges Forestier. Paris: Gallimard, 1999.
Richeome, Louis. *L'Idolatrie huguenote figurée au patron de la vieille payenne, Divisée en huit livres & dediée au Roy tres chrestien de France & de Navarre Henri III*. Lyon: Pierre Rigaud, 1608.
———. *Le Panthéon huguenot découvert et ruiné contre l'auteur de l'Idolatrie papistique ministre de Vauvert, cy devant d'Aigues Mortes*. Lyon: Pierre Rigaud, 1610.
Sévigné, Madame de. *Correspondance*. Edited by Roger Duchêne. 3 vols. Paris: Gallimard, 1972–1978.
Tertullian. *De Spectaculis*. Translated by T. R. Glover. Cambridge, MA: Harvard University Press, 1977.
Thirouin, Laurent, ed. *Traité de la comédie et autres pièces d'un procès du théâtre*. Paris: Honoré Champion, 1998.
Urfé, Honoré d'. *L'Astrée. Première partie*. Edited by Delphine Denis. Paris: Honoré Champion, 2011.
———. *L'Astrée. Deuxième partie*. Edited by Delphine Denis. Paris: Honoré Champion, 2016.
———. *L'Astrée*, vol. 3. Edited by Hugues Vagannay. Geneva: Slatkine Reprints, 1966.
———. *L'Astrée*, vol. 4. Edited by Hugues Vagannay. Geneva: Slatkine Reprints, 1966.
———. *Epistres morales*. Lyon: Jean Laudret, 1627.
Voltaire. *Dictionnaire philosophique*. Paris: Flammarion, 1964.

Secondary Sources

Adam, Antoine. 'La Théorie mystique de l'amour dans *L'Astrée* et ses sources italiennes'. *Revue d'histoire de la philosophie et d'histoire générale de la civilisation* 4 (1936), pp. 193–206.
Albanese, Ralph. *La Fontaine à l'école républicaine: du poète universel au classique scolaire*. Charlottesville: Rookwood Press, 2003.
Ariew, Roger, and Marjorie Green. *Descartes and His Contemporaries: Meditations, Objections, and Replies*. Chicago: University of Chicago Press, 1995.
Armogathe, Jean-Robert. *Theologia cartesiana: L'explication physique de l'Eucharistie chez Descartes et dom Desgabets*. La Haye: Nijhoff, 1977.
Asad, Talal. *Formations of the Secular*. Stanford: Stanford University Press, 2003.
Assmann, Jan. *Of God and Gods: Egypt, Israel, and the Rise of Monotheism*. Madison: University of Wisconsin Press, 2008.
Banderier, Gilles. 'La Bibliothèque d'Honoré d'Urfé: Notes complémentaires'. *Bibliothèque d'Humanisme et Renaissance* 68, no. 2 (2006), pp. 321–32.
Beasley, Faith. *Mastering Memory: Salons, History, and the Creation of Seventeenth-Century France*. Burlington: Ashgate Publishing, 2006.
Belting, Hans. *Likeness and Presence: A History of the Image Before the Era of Art*. Translated by Edmund Jephcott. Chicago: University of Chicago Press, 1994.
Bergin, Joseph. *The Politics of Religion in Early Modern France*. New Haven: Yale University Press, 2014.
Birberick, Anne. *Reading Undercover: Authority and Audience in Jean de La Fontaine*. Lewisburg: Bucknell University Press, 1998.
Bjørnstad, Hall. 'Twice Written, Never Read: Pascal's *Mémorial* between Superstition and *Superbia*'. *Representations* 124, no. 1 (Fall 2013), pp. 69–95.
Blanchard, Jean-Vincent. 'Claude-François Ménestrier and the "Querelle des Monuments"'. *PFSCL* 36, no. 71 (2009), pp. 507–14.
Bloch, Olivier. *Molière/philosophie*. Paris: Albin Michel, 2000.
Braider, Christopher. 'Image and Imaginaire in Molière's *Cocu imaginaire*'. *PMLA* 117, no. 5 (October 2002), pp. 1142–57.
———. *The Matter of Mind: Reason and Experience in the Age of Descartes*. Toronto: University of Toronto Press, 2012.
Bray, Bernard. 'Quelques aspects du système épistolaire de Mme de Sévigné'. *R.H.L.F* 69 (1969), pp. 491–505.
Brisville, Jean-Claude. *L'Entretien entre M. Descartes avec M. Pascal le jeune*. Paris: Actes Sud, 1992.
Brown, Deborah J. *Descartes and the Passionate Mind*. New York: Cambridge University Press, 2006.
———. 'The Sixth Meditation: Descartes and the Embodied Self'. In *The Cambridge Companion to Descartes' Meditations*, edited by David Cunning, pp. 240–57. New York: Cambridge University Press, 2014.
Burke, Peter. *The Fabrication of Louis XIV*. New Haven: Yale University Press, 1992.

Bynum, Caroline Walker. *Christian Materiality: An Essay on Religion in Late Medieval Europe*. New York: Zone Books, 2011.
Chakrabarty, Dipesh. *Provincializing Europe: Postcolonial Thought and Historical Difference*. Princeton: Princeton University Press, 2007.
Cherpack, Clifton. 'Form and Ideas in *L'Astrée*'. *Studies in Philology* 69, no. 3 (June 1972), pp. 320–33.
Christin, Olivier. *Une Révolution symbolique: l'iconoclasme huguenot et la reconstruction catholique*. Paris: Editions de minuit, 1991.
Clarke, Desmond M. *Descartes's Theory of Mind*. Oxford: Clarendon Press, 2002.
Cole, Michael W. and Rebecca Zorach, eds. *The Idol in the Age of Art: Objects, Devotions, and the Early Modern World*. New York: Routledge, 2009.
Collinet, Jean-Pierre. *Le Monde littéraire de La Fontaine*. Paris: Presses Universitaires de France, 1970.
Courtès, Huguette. 'Méditations métaphysiques et méditations chrétiennes.' In *La Méditation au XVIIe siècle*, ed. Christian Belin. Paris: Honoré Champion, 2006, pp. 103–35.
Cousinié, Frédéric. *Le Peintre chrétien: Théories de l'image religieuse dans la France au XVIIe siècle*. Paris: L'Harmattan, 2000.
Cunning, David, ed. *The Cambridge Companion to Descartes'* Meditations. New York: Cambridge University Press, 2014.
Dandrey, Patrick. *La Fabrique des* Fables*: Essai sur la poétique de La Fontaine*. Paris: Klincksieck, 1992.
Darmon, Jean-Charles. *Philosophies de la fable: Poésie et pensée dans l'oeuvre de La Fontaine*. Paris: Hermann, 2011.
Daston, Lorraine. 'Fortuna and the Passions'. In *Chance, Culture, and the Literary Text*, edited by Thomas Kavanagh, pp. 25–47. Ann Arbor: University of Michigan Press, 1994.
De Boer, Wietse, Karl A. E. Enenkel, and Walter Melion, eds. *Jesuit Image Theory*. Leiden: Brill, 2016.
Dekoninck, Ralph. *Ad Imaginem: Statuts, fonctions, et usages de l'image dans la littérature spirituelle jésuite du XVIIe siècle*. Geneva: Droz, 2005.
———. 'Des idoles de bois aux idoles de l'esprit: Les métamorphoses de l'idolâtrie dans l'imaginaire moderne', *Revue théologique de Louvain* 35 (2004), pp. 203–16.
Dekoninck, Ralph, and Myriam Watthee-Delmotte, eds. *L'Idole dans l'imaginaire occidental*. Paris: L'Harmattan, 2005.
Denis, Delphine, ed. *Lire* L'Astrée. Paris: Presses de l'Université Paris-Sorbonne, 2008.
Dennett, Daniel. 'Descartes's Argument from Design'. *The Journal of Philosophy* 105, no. 7 (July 2008), pp. 333–45.
Dompnier, Bernard. *Le Vénin de l'hérésie: image du protestantisme et combat catholique au XVIIe siècle*. Paris: Le Centurion, 1985.
Duchêne, Roger. *Les Ecrivains devant Dieu: Madame de Sévigné*. Bruges: Desclée de Brouwer, 1968.
———. *Madame de Sévigné et la lettre d'amour*. Paris: Klincksieck, 1992.

——. *Molière*. Paris: Fayard, 1998.
Dupuy, Jean-Pierre. *The Mark of the Sacred*. Translated by M. B. Debevoise. Stanford: Stanford University Press, 2013.
Ehrmann, Jacques. *Un Paradis désespéré: L'amour et l'illusion dans* L'Astrée. New Haven: Yale University Press, 1963.
Freinkel, Lisa. *Reading Shakespeare's Will: The Theology of Figure from Augustine to the Sonnets*. New York: Columbia University Press, 2002.
Frisch, Andrea. *Forgetting Differences: Tragedy, Historiography, and the French Wars of Religion*. Edinburgh: University of Edinburgh Press, 2015.
Ganim, Russ. 'Scientific Verses: Subversion of Cartesian Theory and Practice in the *Discours à Madame de La Sablière*'. In *Refiguring La Fontaine: Tercentenary Essays*, edited by Anne Birberick, pp. 101–25. Charlottesville: Rookwood Press, 1996.
Garber, Daniel. *Descartes Embodied: Reading Cartesian Philosophy through Cartesian Science*. New York: Cambridge University Press, 2001.
Garrison, Janine. *L'Edit de Nantes et sa révocation: Histoire d'une intolérance*. Paris: Editions du Seuil, 1985.
Gauchet, Marcel. *Le Désenchantement du monde: Une histoire politique de la religion*. Paris: Gallimard, 1985.
Gaukroger, Stephen, ed. *The Blackwell Guide to Descartes' Meditations*. Malden: Blackwell Publishing, 2006.
Gaukroger, Stephen. *The Emergence of a Scientific Culture: Science and the Shaping of Modernity 1210–1685*. New York: Oxford University Press, 2006.
Ghitt, Jean-Marc. 'Le Forez comme foyer poétique dans *L'Astrée*'. In *Audace et modernité d'Honoré d'Urfé: Actes du colloque international (10 et 11 juin 2011, Château de Goutelas)*. Paris: Honoré Champion, 2013, pp. 225–33.
Gilby, Emma. *Descartes's Fictions: Reading Philosophy with Poetics*. New York: Oxford University Press, 2019.
Ginzburg, Carlo. 'Our Words, and Theirs: A Reflection on the Historian's Craft, Today'. *Cromohs* 18 (2003), pp. 97–114.
Goldmann, Lucien. *Le Dieu caché: Etude sur la vision tragique dans les* Pensées *de Pascal et dans le théâtre de Racine*. Paris: Gallimard, 1959.
Gouhier, Henri. *Cartésianisme et augustinisme au XVIIe siècle*. Paris: Vrin, 1978.
Gregorio, Laurence A. 'Implications of the Love Debate in *L'Astrée*'. *French Review* 56, no. 1 (October 1982), pp. 31–9.
Gregory, Tobias. *From Many Gods to One: Divine Action in Renaissance Epic*. Chicago: University of Chicago Press, 2006.
Helms, Mary W. *Craft and the Kingly Ideal: Art, Trade, and Power*. Austin: University of Texas Press, 1993.
Henein, Eglal. *La Fontaine de la vérité d'amour*. Paris: Klincksieck, 1999.
——. *Protée romancier: Les déguisements dans* L'Astrée *d'Honoré d'Urfé*. Paris: Nizet, 1996.
Horowitz, Louise. *Honoré d'Urfé*. Boston: Twayne Publishers, 1984.
Jackson, Ken, and Arthur F. Marotti. 'The Turn to Religion in Early Modern English Studies.' *Criticism* 46, no. 1 (2004), pp. 167–90.

Javelet, Robert. *Image et ressemblance au douzième siècle (De saint Anselme à Alain de Lille)*, 2 vols. Paris: Editions Letouzey & Ainé, 1967.
Judovitz, Dalia. 'Emblematic Legacies: Hieroglyphs of Desire in *L'Astrée*'. *EMF* vol. 1: *Word and Image*, edited by David Lee Rubin, pp. 31–54. Charlottesville: Rookwood Press, 1994.
——. *Georges de la Tour and the Enigma of the Visible*. New York: Fordham University Press, 2018.
Kahn, Victoria. 'Allegory, Poetic Theology, and Enlightenment Aesthetics'. In *The Insistence of Art: Aesthetic Philosophy after Early Modernity*, edited by Paul A. Kottman, pp. 271–84. New York: Fordham University Press, 2017.
Koch, Erec R. *The Aesthetic Body: Passion, Sensibility and Corporeality in Seventeenth-Century France*. Newark: University of Delaware Press, 2008.
Koerner, Joseph Leo. *The Reformation of the Image*. Chicago: University of Chicago Press, 2004.
Koistinen, Olli. 'The Fifth Meditation: Externality and True and Immutable Natures'. In *The Cambridge Companion to Descartes'* Meditations, edited by David Cunning, pp. 223–39. New York: Cambridge University Press, 2014.
Kurke, Leslie. *Aesopic Conversations: Popular Tradition, Cultural Dialogue, and the Invention of Greek Prose*. Princeton: Princeton University Press, 2010.
Landry, Jean-Pierre. 'Madame de Sévigné et les prédicateurs'. In *Madame de Sévigné (1626–1696): Provence, spectacles, "lanternes"*, edited by Roger Duchêne, pp. 319–34. Grignan: AACCDD, 1998.
Larmore, Charles. 'Descartes and Skepticism'. In *The Blackwell Guide to Descartes'* Meditations, edited by David Cunning, pp. 17–29. New York: Cambridge University Press, 2014.
Latour, Bruno, ed. *Iconoclash: Beyond the Image Wars in Science, Religion, and Art*. Cambridge, MA: MIT Press, 2002.
Lecercle, François. '"Des yeux pour ne point voir": Avatars de l'idolâtrie chez les théologiens catholiques au XVIe siècle'. In *Rencontres de l'Ecole du Louvre: L'Idolâtrie*, pp. 35–51. Paris: La Documentation Française, 1990.
Leplatre, Olivier. *Le Pouvoir et la parole dans les* Fables *de La Fontaine*. Lyon: Presses Universitaires de Lyon, 2002.
Lestringant, Frank. *Une Sainte horreur ou le voyage en Eucharistie*. Paris: Presses Universitaires de France, 1996.
Lichtenstein, Jacqueline. *La Couleur éloquente: rhétorique et peinture à l'age classique*. Paris: Flammarion, 1989.
Lignereux, Cécile. 'Les Mots de l'idolâtrie dans les lettres de Mme de Sévigné'. In *Amour divin, amour mondain dans les écrits du for privé de la fin du Moyen-Age à 1914*, edited by M. Daumas, pp. 203–19. Pau: Cairn, 2011.
Lofton, Kathryn. *Consuming Religion*. Chicago: University of Chicago Press, 2017.
Longino, Michele. *Performing Motherhood: The Sévigné Correspondence*. Hanover: University Press of New England, 1991.
Love, Ronald S. 'Rituals of Majesty: France, Siam, and Court Spectacle in Royal Image-Building at Versailles in 1685 and 1686'. *Canadian Journal of History*

31 (August 1996), pp. 171–98.
Lyons, John D. 'Author and Reader in the *Fables*'. *French Review* 49, no. 1 (October 1975), pp. 59–67.
——. *Before Imagination: Embodied Thought from Montaigne to Rousseau*. Stanford: Stanford University Press, 2005.
——. 'The Marquise de Sévigné: Philosophe'. In *Options for Teaching Seventeenth- and Eighteenth-Century French Women Writers*, edited by Faith Beasley, pp. 178–87. New York: Modern Languages Association, 2011.
Macé, Stéphane. 'La Double italianité de *L'Astrée*: pour une approche des formes poétiques'. In *Lire* L'Astrée, edited by Delphine Denis, pp. 65–76. Paris: Presses de l'Université Paris-Sorbonne, 2008.
Marin, Louis. *La Critique du discours: sur la "Logique" de Port-Royal et les "Pensées" de Pascal*. Paris: Editions de Minuit, 1975.
——. *Des Pouvoirs de l'image*. Paris: Seuil, 1993.
——. *Détruire la peinture*. Paris: Galilée, 1977.
——. *La Parole mangée et autres essais theologico-politiques*. Paris: Méridiens Klincksieck, 1986
——. *Philippe de Champaigne ou la présence cachée*. Paris: Editions Hazan, 2005.
——. *Le Portrait du roi*. Paris: Editions de Minuit, 1981.
Marion, Jean-Luc. *Sur la théologie blanche de Descartes*. Paris: Presses Universitaires de France, 1981/2009.
McClure, Ellen M. *Sunspots and the Sun King: Sovereignty and Mediation in Seventeenth-Century France*. Chicago: University of Illinois Press, 2006.
Meding, Twyla. 'Pastoral Palimpsest: Writing the Laws of Love in *L'Astrée*'. *Renaissance Quarterly* 52, no. 4 (Winter 1993), pp. 1087–117.
Mercer, Christia. 'The Methodology of the *Meditations*: Tradition and Innovation'. In *The Cambridge Companion to Descartes' Meditations*, edited by David Cunning, pp. 23–47. New York: Cambridge University Press, 2014.
Merlin-Kajman, Hélène. *L'Animal ensorcellé: traumatismes, littérature, transitionnalité*. Paris: Ithaque, 2016.
Miernowski, Jan, ed. *Early Modern Humanism and Postmodern Antihumanism in Dialogue*. New York: Palgrave Macmillan, 2016.
Miller, Isaac. 'Idolatry and the Polemics of World-Formation from Philo to Augustine'. *The Journal of Religious History* 28, no. 2 (June 2004), pp. 126–45.
Minnis, A. J. *Medieval Theory of Authorship: Scholastic Literary Attitudes in the Later Middle Ages*. London: Scolar Press, 1984.
Mochizuki, Mia M. *The Netherlandish Image After Iconoclasm, 1566–1672: Material Religion in the Dutch Golden Age*. Burlington: Ashgate, 2008.
Mondzain, Marie-José. *Image, icône, économie: Les sources byzantines de l'imaginaire contemporain*. Paris: Seuil, 1996.
Moriarty, Michael. *Early Modern French Thought: The Age of Suspicion*. New York: Oxford University Press, 2003.
——. 'Image and Idol'. *Seventeenth-Century French Studies* 25 (2003), pp. 1–20.

Norman, Larry. *The Shock of the Ancient*. Chicago: University of Chicago Press, 2011.
O'Connell, Michael. *The Idolatrous Eye: Iconoclasm and Theater in Early-Modern England*. New York: Oxford University Press, 2000.
Ong-Van-Cung, Kim Sang. *Descartes et l'ambivalence de la création*. Paris: Vrin, 2000.
Osler, Margaret. *Divine Will and the Mechanical Philosophy: Gassendi and Descartes on Contingency and Necessity in the Created World*. New York: Cambridge University Press, 1994.
Quint, David. *Origin and Originality in Renaissance Literature: Versions of the Source*. New Haven: Yale University Press, 1983.
Ragland, C. P. 'Descartes on Divine Providence and Human Freedom'. *Archiv für Geschichte der Philosophie* 87, no. 2 (2005), pp. 159–88.
Ramachandran, Ayesha. *The Worldmakers: Global Imagining in Early Modern Europe*. Chicago: University of Chicago Press, 2015.
Rieu, Josiane. 'Esthétique de l'idolâtrie dans la poésie française du XVIe siècle'. In *Rencontres de l'Ecole du Louvre: L'Idolâtrie*, pp. 133–57. Paris: La Documentation Française, 1990
Rowe, Katherine. *Dead Hands: Fictions of Agency, Renaissance to Modern*. Stanford: Stanford University Press, 1999.
Schmaltz, Tad M. *Radical Cartesianism: The French Reception of Descartes*. New York: Cambridge University Press, 2002.
Schreiner, Susan E. *Are You Alone Wise? The Search for Certainty in the Early Modern Era*. New York: Oxford University Press, 2011.
Sheehan, Jonathan. 'Sacred and Profane: Idolatry, Antiquarianism and the Polemics of Distinction in the Seventeenth Century'. *Past & Present* 192 (August 2006), pp. 35–66.
Tanner, Kathryn. *God and Creation in Christian Theology: Tyranny or Empowerment?* New York: Basil Blackwell, 1988.
Taylor, Charles. *A Secular Age*. Cambridge, MA: Harvard University Press, 2007.
Thirouin, Laurent. *L'Aveuglement salutaire. Le réquisitoire contre le théâtre dans la France classique*. Paris: Honoré Champion, 2007.
Verbeek, Theo. *Descartes and the Dutch: Early Reactions to Cartesian Philosophy*. Carbondale: Southern Illinois University Press, 1994.
Weinshenker, Anne Betty. 'Idolatry and Sculpture in Ancien Régime France'. *Eighteenth-Century French Studies* 38, no. 3 (Spring 2005), pp. 485–507.
Wine, Kathleen. *Forgotten Virgo: Humanism and Absolutism in Honoré d'Urfé's L'Astrée*. Geneva: Librairie Droz, 2000.
Wolff, Larry. 'Religious Devotion and Maternal Sentiment in Early Modern Lent: From the Letters of Madame de Sévigné to the Sermons of Père Bourdaloue'. *French Historical Studies* 18, no. 2 (Fall 1993), pp. 359–95.
Zorach, Rebecca. 'An Idolatry of the Letter: Time, Devotion, and Siam in the Almanacs of the Sun King'. In *Ut Pictura Meditatio: The Meditative Image in Northern Art 1500–1700*, edited by Walter S. Melion, Ralph Dekoninck, and Agnes Guiderdoni-Bruslé, pp. 447–79. Turnhout: Brepols Publishers, 2012.

Index

Abraham (biblical) 20
acheiropoeton (image generated by incarnated Christ) 13
Adam, Antoine 28
adiaphora (indifferent to worship) 3, 117
Aesop 116, 117, 119, 132–3, 137
agency
  of animals 142
  divine 60, 69
  human 6, 26, 69, 109, 129, 208, 221
Alberti, Leon Battista 14
Alexandre le Grand (Racine) 207
allegory 7 n.15, 84, 90
Amours de Psyché et de Cupidon, Les (La Fontaine) 115, 131
Ancients and Moderns 116 n
angels 82 n.23, 86, 98, 141, 142
Animal ensorcellé, L' (Merlin-Kajman, 2016) 25 n.57
animals 42, 52, 86, 114
  continuity with humans 129, 140, 141
  reason and 137–9
  See also Fables (La Fontaine, 1668–1694)
Apelles 105–9, 112
Aquinas. *See* Thomas Aquinas
Arianism 61
Aristotelianism 27, 28, 30, 79
Aristotle 29, 84
Arnauld, Antoine 164–5
Arnauld d'Andilly, Robert 24, 144–5, 146, 152, 158
art 6, 37, 67, 123
  ancient, pre-Christian 109, 112
  art history 2, 22
  Christian art 13

querelle du coloris 23
Reformation's effect on visual sacralization of secular art 14
sculpture 124, 128, 151, 161
transcendence and 32
See also painting; representation; theater
Assmann, Jan 3 n.6
Astrée, L' (d'Urfé) 23–4, 135, 147, 156, 180
  ambiguity of religion 41–54
  commandment of Astrée 33–4
  disguise as theme in 65–6, 72
  gender identity and reality of the divine 63–73
  idolatry and the Temple de l'Amitié 54–63
  Meditations of Descartes compared with 75, 79
  Phèdre compared with 196–7, 205
  scholarly debates over 28
  sight versus sound in touching human soul 27–32
  sources of idolatry explored in 39–41
  threat of idolatry in 34–9
  volume one 27, 30, 39, 40 n.30, 42, 43, 48 n.52, 66, 69–70
  volume two 27–8, 41, 43 n.36, 45, 47–8, 50, 54, 68
  volume three 54, 65–8, 71
  volume four 68, 72–3
  volume five 72
Athalie (Racine) 196
atheism 51, 74, 78, 85, 90, 222;
  Christian anti-idolatry held responsible for 102;
  of Hobbes 100, 103;
  science/knowledge and 110

Augustine 15, 18, 83, 94, 164, 190
  on difference between Creator and creature 11–12, 39, 198
  discontinuity with Descartes 88 n.39
  on distinction of *dulia* and *latria* 9
  idolatry as central concern of 14
  on idolatry of the pagans 178
  Sévigné's sympathy for 166, 167
  On the Trinity 13
Augustinianism 2, 88, 160, 184, 219
authorship 23, 66, 94, 123, 141
  idolatry and 186
  La Fontaine's *Fables* and problem of 129–37
authorship, divine 18, 19, 20, 69, 72
  critics of Descartes and 97
  Descartes's emphasis on 87
authorship, human 97, 109, 110, 186, 187
  disrupted logic of idolatry and 205
  divine creation and 102
  human self and 88
  legitimacy of 221

Bacon, Francis 77
Bamyan (Afghanistan), Buddhist statues destroyed by Taliban (2001) 2
Bansilion, Jean 19–20, 21
Baro, Balthazar 72, 73
Barthes, Roland 201
Basil of Caesarea 9, 15
beauty 8, 16, 34, 35, 39, 70
  as abstract entity 28
  divine 38, 40, 46
  loss of 49–50
  Neoplatonic view of 28, 40
  seduction of worldly beauty 12, 72
  strangeness of 26
Belting, Hans 13, 14, 112, 112 n.92, 161

Bérénice (Racine) 207
Beza, Theodore 19
Bible 3, 19, 41, 107, 190
  Deuteronomy 7, 37
  Exodus 7, 8, 37, 121
  Genesis 90, 95n52
  New Testament 84
  Numbers 8
  Old Testament 84, 192, 218
  Samuel 129
  See also Book of Wisdom; Scripture
Blanchard, Jean-Vincent 219 n.22
blasphemy:
  in *L'Astrée* 57, 58, 69, 70
  Hobbes on idea of God as blasphemous 100, 101, 102
Bodin, Jean 142
Book of Wisdom (Wisdom of Solomon) 3, 39, 64
  father's statue of dead son as origin of idolatry 10, 37, 121, 145, 155–6
  warning against elevation of human creations 190
Bourdaloue, Père 146, 147 n.6, 177, 178
Bourdin, Pierre 111, 112
Braider, Christopher 93, 189, 190, 193
Bray, Bernard 158–9
Bremond, Henri 16
Brown, Deborah J. 76
Bynum, Caroline Walker 13

Calvin, John 9–10, 11, 14–15, 18, 190
  emphasis on Divine authorship 19, 20
  on separation of creator and creature 20–21, 39
  view of images as illegitimacy 62
Calvinism 2, 20, 96, 113 n.94, 165 n.61
Canada, native inhabitants of 97

canon, French cultural 6, 23, 25
Caravaggio 22–23
Castelvetro 29
Caterus 94, 95, 96
Catholicism 19, 60, 73, 90
 coexistence with Protestantism in France 2, 5, 164, 214
 "pagan" worship equated with 1
 post-Reformation 121
 transubstantiation doctrine 90 n.44, 161, 165
 See also Counter-Reformation
Catholic Ligue 23, 66
Censura philosophiae cartesianae (Huet, 1671) 94
Chamfort, Sébastien-Roch-Nicolas 117–8
Champaigne, Philippe de 22, 162–3, 165
chance 22, 42, 46, 47 n.50, 139, 174, 178. *See also* fortune
Chantal, Jeanne-Françoise de 167
Chaumont, chevalier de 211, 214
Cheese and the Worms, The (Ginzburg) 168
Cherpack, Clifton 29
Choisy, abbé de 211
Christianity 3, 38, 40, 59, 62, 67, 195–210
 blurred distinction from paganism 205–7, 209
 Cartesian philosophy and 76
 central truths inaccessible to reason 103
 single Creator God of 199
 transition from paganism to 130
 wisdom presented through fables 115
 See also Catholicism; Protestantism
Church Fathers 10, 17, 124, 183
Clarke, Desmond 76
Clymène (La Fontaine) 115
Collinet, Jean-Pierre 123 n.11, 135
Congregation of the Visitation 167
Conti, prince de 183, 189

Corneille, Pierre 189
Cornelius the centurion, story of 11
Council of Nicaea 9, 61, 62
Council of Trent 8, 15, 172
Counter-Reformation 8, 14–15, 40, 75, 193
 on art and divinity 124
 baroque masterworks of 83
 devotion to Virgin Mary and 167
 relics and 120
Cousinié, Frédéric 15
Craft and the Kingly Ideal (Helms) 219–20
craftsmanship 221
creation 18, 24, 57, 105, 111, 163 n.56
 artistic 6, 122, 123, 135, 220
 biblical creation story 114
 divine creation versus human invention 94, 99, 107–8, 112
 human capacity for 21, 87
 the Incarnation 90, 98
 in La Fontaine's *Fables* 133, 134
 maternal 168
 seductive materiality of 73
creationism 26, 87 n.33, 88
Creator–creature relation 17, 39, 54, 105–6, 108, 183
 Augustine's definition of idolatry and 11–14, 198
 Jesus as bridge between 187
Cunning, David 87 n.33
Curley, Edwin 100

Dandrey, Patrick 122, 123
Darmon, Jean-Charles 118 n.5
Daston, Lorraine 170
David, Jan 16 n.43
De Cive (Hobbes) 100
De Doctrine Christiana (Augustine) 12
Dekoninck, Ralph 126
De la comédie (Nicole, 1668) 184
Denis, Delphine 27–28
Descartes, René 5, 6 n.12, 24, 151, 177

on animals' lack of reason and souls   137, 139
on authorship, creation, and the divine   87–93
on ball of wax   81–2, 91
confessional divide of Europe and   75
on imagination   81–2, 148
La Fontaine's critique of   137–43
metaphysics of   75–6, 99
Principes de la philosophie (1647)   76, 170
on relationship of human and divine   169–70
reliability of the senses questioned by   78–9
response to critics   97–9, 102–3
Sévigné's hostility to   169–73
Stoicism and   150
See also God, Descartes on existence of; *Meditations on First Philosophy*
Descartes and the Passionate Mind (Brown, 2006)   76
Dinet, Jacques   112
Dissertation sur les tragédies de Phèdre et Hippolyte (anonymous, 1677)   197 n.27, 206
divine and human   14, 34, 69, 95 n.52, 124, 201
    difference between   102
    incommensurability of   90, 94
    similarity of   92
    special relationship   107
divine intervention   42, 66, 170
Dom Juan, ou le Festin de Pierre (Molière)   189
Donneau de Visé, Jean   211, 212, 215–16
dualism   105
Duchêne, Roger   146, 147, 152, 157 n.40
    on Molière   191 n.22
    on mother–daughter relationship in Sévigné letters   159, 167

on Sévigné and providence   175, 176
on Sévigné and Virgin Mary   168–9
dulia (worship reserved for God)   9, 10, 11

Ecole des femmes, L' (Molière)   189, 191 n.22, 192
Edict of Nantes (1598)   2, 5, 25
    idolatry concept and   163
    revocation of (1685)   5, 161 n.52, 214–6, 219
education system, secular and republican   6
Ehrmann, Jacques   28, 47 n.50
Elizabeth of Bohemia, Princess   76, 111, 170–2
English studies   6
Enlightenment   2, 222
Epistres morales (d'Urfé)   29
Essais de Morale (Nicole)   166
Esther (Racine)   196
Eucharist   5, 15, 151, 166, 212
Euripides   208

Fables (La Fontaine, 1668–1694)   114–6
    Against Those Who Have Difficult Taste   133–5
    The Beggar's Bag   129
    The Chicken with Golden Eggs   119
    Discours à Madame de la Sablière   137–43
    Discours à Monsieur le duc de la Rochefoucauld   128, 129
    The Donkey and His Masters   129
    The Donkey Carrying Relics   118–21, 153
    The Eye of the Master   128
    The Frogs Who Ask for a King   129
    The Gods Wishing to Instruct a Son of Jupiter   128

Jupiter and the Harvester 129
*Jupiter and the Lightning
    Bolts* 129
The Lion's Court 128
*The Man and the Wooden
    Idol* 116–8, 119, 121
Preface 114–5, 129–31
*The Sculptor and the Statue of
    Jupiter* 121–9, 131–2, 135,
    138, 141
*The Two Rats, the Fox, and the
    Egg* 141
Vie d'Esope le Phrygien (life of
    Aesop) 132–3
*The Wasps and the
    Honeybees* 133
Faerno, Gabriele 120
Fall, biblical 19
"Fashion and the Catholic
    Imagination" (Metropolitan
    Museum of Art exhibit, 2018) 2
Ferreyrolles, Gérard 173 n.81, 176,
    177–8
Ficino, Marsilio 40 n.30
Flaminio e Nobili 40 n.30
fortune 44, 47, 71, 132, 178
    Descartes's attack on concept
        of 170
    indifference of 22
    See also chance
France:
    anti-theatrical polemics of
        1660s 183
    Catholic-Protestant
        irreconcilability 62
    civil wars (16th century) 2
    coexistence of Catholics and
        Protestants 2, 5, 164, 214
    devotion to the Virgin in 167
    Siamese ambassadors' visit
        (1686) 25–26, 211–6, 218–9
François de Sales, St. 167, 216
Freinkel, Lisa 12 n.33
French studies, early modern 6, 23
Furetière, Antoine 178, 179

Galileo Galilei 90
Ganim, Russ 138
Gassendi, Pierre 102–9, 112, 140,
    171
Gaul, fifth-century 40
gender identity 63
Ginzburg, Carlo 168
God 3 n.8, 5, 10, 64, 124–5
    accessibility without images or
        revelation 75
    as author 18, 87, 111, 186
    in Cartesian philosophy 76
    as Creator 11–14, 41, 59, 60, 63,
        68, 140, 170, 199
    as extrapolation of human
        qualities 77, 78, 97
    French king and 66, 67
    idolatry punished by 7
    innate idea of 99
    invented versus discovered 95
    jealous God of Old Testament 218
    knowledge based on reality of 96
    profusion of names for 61
    visibility and 8
God, Descartes on existence of 74,
    77, 78, 85, 86, 88, 95
    creation and 98
    critics of Descartes and 100–1,
        103, 113
Godeau, Antoine 182, 186–8
golden calf, worship of 7, 15, 190
Goldmann, Lucien 207, 209
Gregorio, Laurence A. 32, 48 n.52,
    59 n.86
Gregory of Nazianzus 29
Gregory the Great (Pope Gregory
    I) 8, 8 n.20, 10, 15
    Grignan, comtesse de (Françoise-
        Marguerite de Sévigné) 24,
        145, 152, 153, 154, 159, 170
    Cartesianism of 177, 179
    image of 156–7
    separation from mother 173, 175
    weakening health of 155, 176
"Guide des pécheurs, La" [The Guide

for Sinners] (Louis de Grenade, 1556)   192
Guyot, Sylvaine   203 n.29

heaven and earth   1, 5, 9, 221
  in *L'Astrée*   24, 39, 51, 70, 93
  beauty as link between   70
  distance between   24, 39, 93
  impersonal universe and   170
  in *Phèdre*   196–7
  as problematic juncture of transcendent and material   124
  role of art in communication between   186
  in Sévigné's correspondence   147, 151
Helms, Mary W.   219–20
Henein, Eglal   31 n.13, 32, 43 n.35, 67, 72–3
Henri IV (Henri le Grand; Henri de Navarre)   16, 29, 32, 66
  conversion to Catholicism   29
  Edict of Nantes promulgated by   214
  as Protestant   23
heresy   10, 17, 58, 112, 168
  idolatry and   99
  Protestantism as   18
Hobbes, Thomas   100–2, 105, 171
*Hommes Illustres, Le*s [Famous Men] (Perrault, 1696)   135–7
homo faber, celebration of   6, 21
homoousios ("of one substance")   61
honnête homme   67, 208
honnêteté, ideal of   71, 130, 138
Horowitz, Louise   49 n.55
Huet, Pierre-Daniel   94
Huguenots   29–30, 215

iconoclasm   3, 117, 161, 204, 206
  Luther's opposition to   121
  of the Taliban   2
Idolatrie huguenote figurée au patron de la vieille payenne, L' (Richeome, 1608)   16

Idolatrie papistique, L' (Bansilion, 1608)   19
idolatry   69, 70, 71–2, 95, 163
  artistic representation and   23
  as atavistic concept   2
  biblical prohibition of   7, 34, 38, 41
  Catholicism charged with   3–4, 151
  as confusion of creator and creature   198
  confusion of signifier and signified   151
  Descartes's philosophy and   74–8, 98–9
  devotion to the Virgin as   169
  as empty insult   1, 222
  in France of 17th century   22–6
  glorification of the French monarch and   212, 216–8
  idolatry fables of La Fontaine   116–29
  as incorrect interpretation of signs   12
  invisibility in modern era   26
  linguistic   164–5
  overview of   7–10
  question of creation and   11–14, 21
  Reformers' emphasis on Scripture as   162
  as root of all crimes   3
  Sévigné's love for her daughter and   147, 151, 153, 173, 175, 177, 180–1
  sources/origin of   39–41, 64, 121, 145
  three aspects (images, worship, creation)   24
idolatry, logic of   2, 6, 26, 37, 151, 221
  accessibility of God and   75
  current cultural divides and   222
  indeterminacy following disruption of   205

INDEX 239

La Fontaine and 121
   persistent sway of 94
   replaced with logic of transubstantiation 165
   Siamese embassy to France (1686) and 212
idolatry, theater and 24–25, 182–8
   Molière 188–95
   Racine's *Phèdre* 195–210
Ignatius of Loyola, St. 83, 152
images 8, 17, 61, 185
   artist's creation of 106
   Catholicism's unapologetic use of 30
   celebration of 30, 84
   idolatry untethered from 2, 21
   image as idea 91, 104
   knowledge and 90
   man created in image of God 90–1, 107
   mortality and 10
   prohibition of graven images 7, 34, 41
   prototype and 9, 10, 121
   redefined to include word 32
   Richeome's new Catholic theory of 15
   of saints 3n8
   thought and 80
imagination, human 80–1, 86, 91, 104, 164
   discovery of truth and 5, 85
   floating fantasies of 96
   "phantoms of divinity" and 206
   as thinking through images 147–51
Incarnation, the 90, 98, 185
Innocent XII, Pope 181
Institution de la religion chrétienne (Calvin, 1561) 9–10
invention 45, 95 n.52, 122, 188
   allegory as human invention 7 n.15
   human invention versus divine creation 57, 89, 94, 99
   idolatry and 17
   in La Fontaine's *Fables* 133, 134, 135, 137, 141
   legitimacy of human invention 111
   as making of something from nothing 207

Jansenism 2, 22, 24, 144, 145
   art and 162
   Cartesian philosophy in conflict with 170
   Port-Royal stronghold of 160, 193, 209
   Sévigné's adhesion to 169
   theater viewed by 183–4, 196
Jerome, St. 9
Jesuits 2, 40, 75, 83, 168
   Descartes and 111, 112
   discourses surrounding idolatry and 163
   doctrine of non-causal providentialism 172
   French relations with Siamese court and 211, 214
   theater and 186
Jesus Christ 9, 163 n.55, 179, 199
   as bridge between Creator and creature 198
   divinity of 8, 151
   godhead of 98
   as Son of God 11
   Veronica (*vera icona*) image and 13
Jews and Judaism 10 n.25, 17, 196, 210
Job (biblical) 20
John of Damascus 10, 15, 121
Judovitz, Dalia 22
Jupiter (Greco-Roman god) 19, 89
   in *L'Astrée* 62
   in La Fontaine's *Fables* 116, 121, 124–5, 127–9, 133, 138, 190
   in *Phèdre* 200

240   INDEX

Kahn, Victoria   7 n.15
Karlstadt, Andreas   3
knowledge   16 n.42, 24, 43, 98, 109, 195, 221
   divine foundation for   90, 93, 110
   human intellect and   85
   imagination and   80–1, 82, 96
   language and   83
   mechanistic laws and   170
   romantic love and knowledge of the divine   34
   senses as foundation of   79
Koerner, Joseph Leo   22, 161
Koistinen, Olli   77 n.10

Lafayette, Madame de   156
La Fontaine, Jean de   6, 24, 102, 153
   Les Amours de Psyché et de Cupidon   115, 131
   bricolage method of   114, 135
   Descartes's view of animals critiqued by   137–43
   idolatry fables   116–29
   pagan myth and   115
   Perrault's description of   136–7
   problem of authorship and   129–37
   sculptor in fable as stand-in for   123
   See also *Fables*
La Loubère, Simon de   213–4
language   11, 31, 159, 165
   idolatry perpetrated through   37
   impossibility of signification and   203
Larmore, Charles   79
La Tour, Georges de   22
latria (respect afforded to "excellent creatures")   9, 10, 11
Lecercle, François   162
legitimacy   1, 66, 67, 68, 114, 199
   of human authorship   110, 221
   human invention as illegitimate   57
   loss of   21
   love and   202

   of maternal devotion   152
   religious legitimacy and romantic love   63
   of religious truth   111
   representation and   203
   uncertain legitimacy of art   124
Leiden crisis   104, 113 n.94
Lenain, Thierry   14
Leplatre, Olivier   123
Lestringant, Frank   5
Leviathan (Hobbes)   100
Lichtenstein, Jacqueline   23
literature   6, 25, 26, 136, 186–7, 188
Lives of the Artists (Vasari, 1550)   14
Logique (Nicole and Arnauld)   164–5, 193
Longino, Michèle   159, 160, 168
Louis de Grenade   192
Louis XIII   23–4, 66, 67, 70
Louis XIV   22, 128, 138
   Edict of Nantes revoked by   25, 214–16
   Siamese ambassadors' visit to   211–6, 218–9
   statues erected to glory of   216–7
love   23, 41, 62, 65
   as conduit to the divine   34, 52
   divine and human   34, 36, 40 n.30, 147
   foundationlessness accompanying   47
   of God   51, 55, 152, 167, 175
   language shared with religion   193, 195
   Neoplatonic view of   73
   reconciled with legitimacy   201, 202
   theology and   37, 59
   threat of idolatry and   34, 39, 58, 71–2
Love, Ronald S.   212, 214, 219
Lucretius   102
Luther, Martin   3, 117, 121, 204
Lyons, John D.   80, 118 n.5, 120, 146, 147–8

Mâle, Emile   15
Malebranche, Nicolas   150
Man Who Broke a Statue, The (Aesop)   116
Marin, Louis   22, 124 n.13, 162, 165
Marion, Jean-Luc   86 n.29, 87 n.33, 89–90, 93, 171
mastery   125, 126, 127, 128–9, 139
   artistic   122, 125
   authorial mastery eschewed   133, 135, 138
   divine   122
   monotheism and   22, 24
   self-mastery   45
materialism   50, 53, 103
materiality   1, 75, 199
   of the carnal   202
   celebration of   2
   of text   162
Meding, Twyla   56
Meditations on First Philosophy [*Méditations métaphysiques*] (Descartes, 1641)   24, 74, 75, 83, 90
   on freeing the mind from images   78–86
   objections of Descartes's contemporaries to   93–113, 140, 171
   on relationship of human and divine   169
   solution to problem of idolatry posited in   77–8
Menestrier, Claude   219 n.22
Mercer, Christia   83
Mercure Galant (literary gazette)   25, 211, 212, 215, 218
Merlin-Kajman, Hélène   25 n.57
Mersenne, Marin   79, 89–90, 97, 107
metaphysics, of Descartes   75–6, 99
mind–body interaction   76, 104, 171, 190
Minnis, A. J.   14
Mme de Sévigné et la lettre d'amour (Duchêne)   159

Mochizuki, Mia M.   22, 151 n.21, 161
modernity   11, 88, 102, 116 n
Molière   6, 25, 183, 188–95, 218
   Dom Juan, ou le Festin de Pierre   189
   L'Ecole des femmes   189, 191 n.22, 192
   Sgnarelle ou le cocu imaginaire   25, 189, 190–5
   Tartuffe   194
monotheism   3n6, 7, 22, 34, 62, 196, 198
   ideals of authority and mastery inherent in   24
   idolatry separated from   40
Montespan, Madame de   128, 131, 138
More, Henry   171
Moriarty, Michael   43 n.33
Morin, Jean-Baptiste   97
Moses (biblical)   7, 8, 57

Naudé, Gabriel   128
Nemours, duke of   29
neoclassicism   6, 22, 122
Neoplatonism   5, 23, 29, 59, 184
   earthly beauty as conduit to the divine   40
   romantic love in service to the divine   73
   Urfé's espousal of   28, 40, 45
   Urfé's turning away from   34
Nicole, Pierre   164–5, 166, 183–5
Norman, Larry   115 n.3

occasionalism   100
O'Connell, Michael   185
Ong-Van-Cung, Kim Sang   111
On the Trinity (Augustine)   11, 13

pagan gods   38, 40, 41, 58–9, 198–202, 205
   confirmed existence of   41–2
   druids and   60, 61

king of France and   128
reality and benevolence of   70
sculptor's representation of   127
See also Jupiter
paganism   40, 59, 115, 126
   blurred distinction from Christianity   205–7, 209
   modern "pagans"   1, 18, 90, 190
   transition to Christianity   130
painting   32, 67, 106–7, 161
Panthéon huguenot découvert (Richeome, 1608)   19–20
Pascal, Blaise   6 n.12
Pellisson, Paul   135, 137
Perrault, Charles   116 n, 136–7
Peter, Saint   11
Phèdre (Racine)   5–6, 25, 195–210
philosophy   6, 29, 49, 76, 90, 112
   Cartesian   76, 90 n.44, 140, 142–3, 150
   Scholastic   79
   Stoic   150
   theology supplanted by   93
Phra Narai   211, 214
Plainte de l'Eglise contre ses Enfans rebelles, La (The complaint of the Church against its rebel children)   217
Platonism   30
Poésies [Œuvres] chrétiennes (Godeau)   182, 186, 188
poetry   32, 57, 136–7
Polyeucte (Corneille)   189
polytheism   18, 61
Poussin, Nicolas   22
Pradon, Jacques   197 n.27, 206
Praxiteles   107, 109, 112
Princesse de Clèves, La (Madame de Lafayette)   156
Principes de la philosophie (Descartes, 1647)   76, 170
Prometheus (mythological)   114, 129–30, 135
Protestantism   15, 19, 73, 90, 151, 188

   coexistence with Catholicism in France   2, 5, 164, 214
   conversion to Catholicism from   3–5, 16, 29
   divinity approached through revelation and Scripture   85
   Protestants accused of idolatry   16, 18
   Revocation of the Edict of Nantes and   25, 161 n.53, 219
   unmediated access to the divine sought by   202
   See also Reformers
providence   24, 43 n.35, 45, 46, 53, 72
   human freedom and   172
   meaning conferred by   22
   in Sévigné's correspondence   173–81
   theology and   170
Pseudo-Dionysius   94
Pygmalion (mythological)   123, 126, 127

Questions cartésiennes (Marion)   89–90

Racine, Jean
   Alexandre le Grand   207
   Athalie   196
   Bérénice   207
   Esther   196
   Phèdre   5–6, 25, 195–210
Ragland, C. P.   171 n.76, 172
Ramachandran, Ayesha   6, 21, 95 n.52
reason   46, 58, 75 n.4, 164, 206
   Cartesian   104, 107
   Christian religion accessed through   74, 103
   existence of God proved through   93
   imagination versus   148
   love and   45, 52–53, 59
   mind–body separation and   190
   Neoplatonism and   28

Reformation 3, 5, 99, 162
  depictions of Catholic abuses 9
  second commandment and 7
  visual art and 22, 161
Reformers 14, 16–18, 62, 66, 75
  foregrounding of Scripture
    by 162
  written language held in high
    esteem by 165
  See also Protestantism
relics 9, 120, 217
  letters as 153–8
  mortality and 10
religion 6, 112
  coexistence with literature 186–7
  languages of love and religion
    entangled 25
  place of humanity in the world in
    relation to 23
  theater contrasted with 182
Renaissance 14, 28, 73, 220
representation 23, 50, 85, 93, 157,
    161
  Cartesian models of 193
  Diplomatic 212–3
  instability of 27
  mimetic 82, 91, 92
  signifier–signified relation 156,
    163
  theater and idolatry polemics 185
  undermining of 205
  visual versus verbal 32
revelation 7 n.15, 28, 74, 75, 85, 94
Revius 104
Richeome, Louis 2–3, 14–22, 32, 40,
    84, 104, 163
  See also *Tableaux sacrez*
Rieu, Josiane 163
Rolland, Jean-Brice 28–29

Sablière, Madame de la 136, 139,
    140
saints 3 n.8, 9, 151, 174
Santner, Eric 3 n.6
Sarasin, Jean-François 135

Schmaltz, Tad 113
Scholastics 17, 79, 113 n.94
science 85, 90, 109
Scripture 10, 18, 75 n.4, 85, 165
    n.61
  Protestant following of 19, 20–1
  Reformers' foregrounding of 162
  See also Bible
secularism 222
secularization 6, 221
self, modern 88
Seneca 208
Serenus, bishop of Marseille 8 n.20
Sévigné, marquise de 6, 24, 198
  hostility to Descartes 169–73
  on imagination 147–51
  letters as prayers and relics 151–8
  literary style and 158–67
  on providence 173–81
  religious themes in correspondence
    of 144–7
  scholarship on 146–7, 158–9
  Virgin Mary as model of
    motherhood 167–9
Sgnarelle ou le cocu imaginaire
    (Molière) 25, 189, 190–5
Siam, diplomatic mission to France
    (1686) 25–26, 211–6, 218–9
siècle de Louis le Grand 2, 6
sin 4, 19, 63, 65
  God as author of human
    sinfulness 18
  idolatry as 18, 21, 39, 59, 73, 201
  intent versus medium as location
    of 37
  original sin 164
skepticism
  in *L'Astrée* 51, 53, 55
  of Descartes 78, 80, 97, 105
  of La Fontaine 125
Socrates 131, 132
Sonnet sur la comédie (Godeau) 182
soul, human 17, 20, 23, 43
  children's souls 126
  death of 12 n.30

distinguished from body through reason 93
immateriality of 30, 74, 75, 86
immortality of 113
love and 49
natural liberty of 47
passivity of 84
sight versus sound in relation to 27, 30
sovereignty 128, 129, 142, 172
Spinoza, Baruch 100
Spiritual Exercises (Ignatius of Loyola) 152
Stoicism 150
Suarez, Francisco 90, 94
Sur la théologie blanche de Descartes (Marion) 89–90
Sweetser, Marie-Odile 132 n.22

Tableaux sacrez (Richeome, 1601) 15, 16, 17, 19, 30, 84
Taliban 2
Tanner, Kathryn 172
Tarente, Princesse de 161 n.52
Tartuffe (Molière) 194
Taylor, Charles 88 n.39
Ten Commandments 3, 34, 57
Teresa of Avila 152 n.22
Tertullian 3, 18, 24, 182–3, 184
theater 24–5
 danger of idolatry and 182–8
 pastoral 27
 sight versus sound in relation to 30
 See also idolatry, theater and
theology 38, 49, 69
 Augustinian 14
 Descartes's philosophy and 98, 99, 104
 poetic 7 n.15
 Protestant 18
 supplanted with philosophy 93
Thirouin, Laurent 182, 185
Thomas Aquinas 9, 15, 94
Traité de la comédie et des spectacles (Conti) 183, 189
Treatise on human love (Flaminio e Nobili) 40 n.30
Trémoille, Charlotte-Amélie de la 3–5
Trinitarian orthodoxy 29
Trinity 12
truth 80, 85, 111, 120, 152, 187
 absolute 132
 abstract 83
 allegory as revelation of 7 n.15
 a priori metaphysical 32
 awareness of God and 110
 confessional divide and 111
 confusion of truth and fiction 95
 divine 17, 18, 84
 existence of God and 98
 fables/parables and 115, 118
 history and 216
 human search for 5, 24
 images/imagination and 85
 Judeo-Christian 40
 lies preferred to or mistaken for 122, 127
 Protestant version of 4
 revealed 18, 47
 theater and 185, 202, 204
Turks (Muslims) 17

Urfé, Honoré d' 5, 6, 37, 63, 70, 75, 205
 aesthetic theories of 28
 Catholic Ligue and 23, 29, 66
 death of 72
 Descartes compared with 93
 Epistres morales 29
 marquise de Sévigné compared with 24
 Neoplatonism and 28, 34, 40, 45
 separation of monotheism and idolatry 41
 on sight versus sound 27, 30, 48
 See also Astrée, L'
use (*uti*)–enjoyment (*frui*) distinction 12

Vasari, Giorgio   14
Verbeek, Theo   96
Veridicus Christianus (David)   16 n.43
Veronica, Saint   13
Virgin Mary   9, 151, 167, 187
Voltaire   1–2, 3, 221–2

will, divine   55, 69, 71, 176

will, human   20, 92, 93, 172
Wine, Kathleen   56 n.76, 62 n.93, 64–5, 67
Wolff, Larry   146–7, 152, 153, 159, 168

Zorach, Rebecca   212, 214, 216, 219

Gallica

Already Published

1. *Postcolonial Fictions in the* Roman de Perceforest*: Cultural Identities and Hybridities*, Sylvia Huot
2. *A Discourse for the Holy Grail in Old French Romance*, Ben Ramm
3. *Fashion in Medieval France*, Sarah-Grace Heller
4. *Christine de Pizan's Changing Opinion: A Quest for Certainty in the Midst of Chaos*, Douglas Kelly
5. *Cultural Performances in Medieval France: Essays in Honor of Nancy Freeman Regalado*, eds Eglal Doss-Quinby, Roberta L. Krueger, E. Jane Burns
6. *The Medieval Warrior Aristocracy: Gifts, Violence, Performance, and the Sacred*, Andrew Cowell
7. *Logic and Humour in the Fabliaux: An Essay in Applied Narratology*, Roy J. Pearcy
8. *Miraculous Rhymes: The Writing of Gautier de Coinci*, Tony Hunt
9. *Philippe de Vigneulles and the Art of Prose Translation*, Catherine M. Jones
10. *Desire by Gender and Genre in Trouvère Song*, Helen Dell
11. *Chartier in Europe*, eds Emma Cayley, Ashby Kinch
12. *Medieval Saints' Lives: The Gift, Kinship and Community in Old French Hagiography*, Emma Campbell
13. *Poetry, Knowledge and Community in Late Medieval France*, eds Rebecca Dixon, Finn E. Sinclair with Adrian Armstrong, Sylvia Huot, Sarah Kay
14. *The Troubadour* Tensos *and* Partimens*: A Critical Edition*, Ruth Harvey, Linda Paterson
15. *Old French Narrative Cycles: Heroism between Ethics and Morality*, Luke Sunderland
16. *The Cultural and Political Legacy of Anne de Bretagne: Negotiating Convention in Books and Documents*, ed. Cynthia J. Brown
17. *Lettering the Self in Medieval and Early Modern France*, Katherine Kong
18. *The Old French Lays of* Ignaure, Oiselet *and* Amours, eds Glyn S. Burgess, Leslie C. Brook
19. *Thinking Through Chrétien de Troyes*, Zrinka Stahuljak, Virginie Greene, Sarah Kay, Sharon Kinoshita, Peggy McCracken
20. *Blindness and Therapy in Late Medieval French and Italian Poetry*, Julie Singer
21. Partonopeus de Blois: *Romance in the Making*, Penny Eley
22. *Illuminating the* Roman d'Alexandre*: Oxford, Bodleian Library, MS Bodley 264: The Manuscript as Monument*, Mark Cruse
23. *The* Conte du Graal *Cycle: Chrétien de Troyes'* Perceval*, the Continuations, and French Arthurian Romance*, Thomas Hinton
24. *Marie de France: A Critical Companion*, Sharon Kinoshita, Peggy McCracken

25. *Constantinople and the West in Medieval French Literature: Renewal and Utopia*, Rima Devereaux
26. *Authorship and First-Person Allegory in Late Medieval France and England*, Stephanie A. Viereck Gibbs Kamath
27. *Virgilian Identities in the French Renaissance*, eds Philip John Usher, Isabelle Fernbach
28. *Shaping Courtliness in Medieval France: Essays in Honor of Matilda Tomaryn Bruckner*, eds Daniel E. O'Sullivan, Laurie Shepard
29. *Violence and the Writing of History in the Medieval Francophone World*, eds Noah D. Guynn, Zrinka Stahuljak
30. *The Refrain and the Rise of the Vernacular in Medieval French Music and Poetry*, Jennifer Saltzstein
31. *Marco Polo's* Le Devisement du Monde: *Narrative Voice, Language and Diversity*, Simon Gaunt
32. *The* Pèlerinage *Allegories of Guillaume de Deguileville: Tradition, Authority and Influence*, eds Marco Nievergelt, Stephanie A. Viereck Gibbs Kamath
33. *Rewriting Arthurian Romance in Renaissance France: From Manuscript to Printed Book*, Jane H. M. Taylor
34. *Unsettling Montaigne: Poetics, Ethics and Affect in the* Essais *and Other Writings*, Elizabeth Guild
35. *Machaut and the Medieval Apprenticeship Tradition: Truth, Fiction and Poetic Craft*, Douglas Kelly
36. *Telling the Story in the Middle Ages: Essays in Honour of Evelyn Birge Vitz*, eds Kathryn A. Duys, Elizabeth Emery, Laurie Postlewate
37. *The Anglo-Norman Lay of* Haveloc: *Text and Translation*, eds Glyn S. Burgess, Leslie C. Brook
38 *Sacred Fictions of Medieval France: Narrative Theology in the Lives of Christ and the Virgin, 1150–1500*, Maureen Barry McCann Boulton
39. *Founding Feminisms in Medieval Studies: Essays in Honor of E. Jane Burns*, eds Laine E. Doggett and Daniel E. O'Sullivan
40. *Representing the Dead: Epitaph Fictions in Late-Medieval France*, Helen J. Swift
41. *The* Roman de Troie *by Benoît de Sainte-Maure: A Translation*, translated by Glyn S. Burgess and Douglas Kelly
42. *The Medieval Merlin Tradition in France and Italy: Prophecy, Paradox, and* Translatio, Laura Chuhan Campbell
43. *Representing Mental Illness in Late Medieval France: Machines, Madness, Metaphor*, Julie Singer

is enjoying something for which it is
idolatrous?

selective examples put deeply the
general notion of a shaken faith rather
than an assertive faith, to which various
forms of representation contribute.

problem of literalism — so's the criticism
                            boucher du doigt

    music
    popular culture
    [Romanesque?] Corneille

    relaxed attitude to "idolatry".

Was D. a christian despite himself?
    Arnauld.

        Burch Brown

            aesthetic
the necessity of aesthetic success of the
recognition of/success need not displace etc.
    a question of drawing attention to.